CHRISTIAN-MUSLIM DIALOGUE IN NORTHERN NIGERIA

George,

God bless you and family always.

Fr Thaddeus Umoru
05-06-16

CHRISTIAN-MUSLIM DIALOGUE IN NORTHERN NIGERIA

A SOCIO-POLITICAL AND THEOLOGICAL CONSIDERATION

THADDEUS BYIMUI UMARU

To order additional copies of this book, contact:
Xlibris LLC
0-800-056-3182
www.xlibrispublishing.co.uk
Orders@xlibrispublishing.co.uk
307087

CONTENTS

Dedication

To Dad and Mum, thanks for the gifts of faith, love, and peace in the family

Preface

Religion is a powerful impulse in human existence that has contributed significantly in shaping the socio-political, economic and spiritual life of millions of people in northern Nigeria and a source of conflict in the region. The aim here is to examine critically the incessant inter-religious conflicts in Northern Nigeria, to identify the true causes of such conflicts and to suggest theological and practical ways to sustain peace building endeavours. Conflicts as an inevitable part of human existence can be triggered and exacerbated by numerous factors. Religion has been used to fuel conflict in Northern Nigeria.

Radical religious strife, quest for more converts, colonisation, ethnicity, and perceived political domination have strengthened stereotypical views of the self and the other. Religion which is closely intertwined with culture and thus central in the understanding and establishment of peace in society; continue to play paradoxical role in the locality. Religion can be a cause of conflict and a way of conflict resolution. In Nigeria, religion has failed to establish the peace which it has claimed to promote, because deep historical feuds have found expression in religion, and religion is thus at the core of the strife as experienced in contemporary Northern Nigeria.

The theology of the Second Vatican Council, in which the Roman Catholic Church reflects on its self-understanding as a community and its role in the world, provides a first model for the encounter between Christianity and other religions in mutual understanding. In the pages of this book, I want to consider the theological potential of this interreligious encounter (or dialogue) between Islamic and Christian traditions in general and the possibilities and difficulties of dialogue between Muslims and Christians in Northern Nigeria in particular.

Moreover, this study delves into the need for engagement between theology and politics in addressing issues of conflict. It explores the theology of interreligious dialogue as a means for a promising peace-building process in Northern Nigeria. Religion as a significant part of the problem is equally essential in proffering solutions. However, taken on their own terms, neither religion nor politics have comprehensive answers. Hence, any peace building project in Northern Nigeria must be multifaceted. It could be modelled on a theological approach for encounter and dialogue which examines common grounds for collaboration within the two faith traditions, in an attempt to consider and strengthen peace-building endeavours within the region.

Tables and Figures

Table 1 A summary of major violent ethno-religious conflicts in Northern Nigeria from 1980 to 2011

Figure 1 Map of Nigeria illustrating the section above the river Niger (north) where interreligious violence is most prevalent.

Acknowledgement

Thus says the Lord, I will send Peace overflowing like a river over the nations (Is. 66: 12). All praise to God for the grace to undertake this study. My appreciation goes to my Bishop Martin I. Uzoukwu, Catholic Diocese of Minna Nigeria, and the Archbishop emeritus of Glasgow, Joseph Mario Conti for their encouraging support through my research years. Many special thanks to Fr. Pat Hogan in Ireland, Msgr. Peter Smith, Fr. Tom White, and the community of St. Mary's Parish Calton for their welcome and warm support during my studies in Glasgow, Scotland.

I am particularly appreciative of the School of Critical Studies, department of Theology and Religious Studies, College of Arts, University of Glasgow for a stimulating research experience. To my supervisors, Prof. Werner G. Jeanrond and Prof. David Jasper, words are inadequate to express my profound gratitude for your kind, encouraging, challenging but gentle academic, spiritual, moral, and motivating guidance through my work. You both inspired me to develop a critical and daring mind with confidence and humility, the hallmark of scholarship. Thanks a million for your patience with me, and I admire your courage and commitment to the making of a scholar.

I am indebted to the Interfaith Mediation Centre, Kaduna, Northern Nigeria (the Pastor and Imam), the Da'Wah Institute of Nigeria/Islamic Education Trust, Minna (Nuruddeen Lemu), Sheikh Musa Ibrahim, College of Arts and Islamic Studies (CAIS), Minna, Nigeria, Prof. Jesper Svartvik and the Swedish Theological Institute (STI), Jerusalem, for thought-provoking discussions and access to the use of their libraries. Special thanks to Fr. Joseph Burke, Sr. Gina Cardosi, and Anna Fisk for reading through my text.

Very many thanks to my family, the late Michael Dato Umaru (dad), Veronica Ladi, (mum). Willy, Dr Ben, Christopher, Helen, Godfery, Donatus, Julius, Comfort, Felicia, Joseph, and especially to Barnabas and Nkiru, John and Claudine, Paula, Nadia, Tony and Anna Gallagher, Margaret, Steve and Lizz, Micheal, Jacqui and Clare McMenemy and Caroline Peacock—I appreaciate all your care for me in Glasgow. Thanks also to Frs. J. D O'Connell (SPS), Billy Greene (SPS), Anthony Efeturi Ojakaminor (OMV), Joseph Walsh, Paul Brady, and Msgr. Hugh Bradley for your kind encouragent. Special thanks to Mrs Agnes Sholanke, Cecilia E Ajibade, Emmanuel B. Samari, Alex Bala, and Lorna Willison for your unflinching support. To all my friends Gopsie, Musa, Tonie, Adamu, Likoko, Chinve, Ifeoma, Tonia, and all others, I say *Salama Allaikum*!

Abbreviations/Definitions

ACMMRN   Association for Christian-Muslim Mutual Relations in Nigeria

ACF   Arewa Consultative Forum

ALMAJIRI   A corruption of the Arabic word *al-muhajir* which means the migrant child or children

CAN   Christian Association of Nigeria

CBCN   Catholic Bishops Conference of Nigeria

CWEENS   Christian Women for Excellence and Empowerment in Nigerian Society

CM   Christian Mothers

CPFN   Christian Pentecostal Fellowship of Nigeria

CSN   Catholic Secretariat of Nigeria

C.S.P.   Missionary Society of St. Paul (Catholic Religious Order)

CWO   Catholic Women Organisation/Christian Women Organisation

DFI   Dialogue with People of Living Faith

DIN   Da'wah Institute of Nigeria

ECWA   Evangelical Churches of West Africa

FBO   Faith Based Organisation

FOMWAN   Federation of Muslim Women Association of Nigeria

FR	Father (a Catholic Priest)
IAP	Islam in Africa Project
IFMC	Interfaith Mediation Centre
IPCR	Institute for Peace and Conflict Resolution
ISESCO	Islamic Economic Social and Cultural Organisation
JDPC	Justice Development and Peace Commission
JNI	Jamalat-ul-Nasril Islam
LCCN	Lutheran Church of Christ in Nigeria
MADRASA	Islamic Qur'anic School or Seminary
MCDF	Muslim-Christian Dialogue Forum
MSGR	Monsignor
MSS	Muslim Student Society
MZL	Middle Zone League
NGO	Non-Governmental Organisation
NIREC	Nigerian Interreligious Council
NEF	Northern Elders Forum
NSCIA	Nigerian Supreme Council for Islamic Affairs
OAIC	Organisation of African Instituted Churches
OFM	Friars Minor (Franciscans Catholic Religious Order)
OIC	Organisation of Islamic Conference
O.P.	Order of Preachers (Dominican Catholic Religious Order)
PCID	Pontifical Council for Interreligious Dialogue
PFN	Christian Fellowship of Nigeria
PROCMURA	Project of Christian Muslim Relations in Africa

RTC   Responding To Conflicts

SJ   Society of Jesus (Jesuit Catholic Religious Order)

SMA   Society of African Mission (Catholic Religious Order)

SURA   The Arabic-Hausa word for 'Chapter'

TEKAN   Denominations based in Northern Nigeria and other indigenous Christian Assemblies in Nigeria (or *Tarayyar Ekklesiyoyyin Kristi A Nigeria* meaning—Fellowship of the Churches of Christ in Nigeria)

UMBC   United Middle Belt Congress

UNESCO   United Nations Educational, Scientific and Cultural Organisation

USIP   United States Institute for Peace

WOLF   Women Opinion Leaders Forum

WRAPA   Women's Right Advancement and Protection Alternative

WCC   World Council of Churches

Religion: a system of beliefs and symbols which act to establish powerful, persuasive, and pervasive long-lasting moods and motivations in people, formulating conceptions of a general order of existence and giving such conceptions an aura of factuality that makes the moods and motivations uniquely realistic.[1]

Christianity: a monotheistic faith that believes in the existence of God, distinguished from other faiths by belief in salvation through the redemption accomplished by Jesus of Nazareth.[2] It is a system of beliefs and practices based on the Old Testament and the revelations and teachings of Jesus Christ in the New Testament of the Bible.[3]

Islam: a monotheistic religion started in the Arabian Peninsula by Prophet Muhammad in the AD sixth century. The word Islam is derived from Arabic *Salema* which means peace, purity, submission, and obedience. In the religious sense, Islam means submission to the will of God and obedience to his law. Islam affirms the oneness of God (Allah) and no other. Muhammad is his prophet. Islam enjoins good character as expressed in the Qur'an and Prophetic traditions.[4]

Community: oneness or togetherness with others that springs from shared vision, values, goals, memories, and shared interests that unite a people for the common good of all.[5] Humans participate in a number of communities: religious, clerical, local, regional, political, socio-economic, faith, academic, etc. Thus in this thesis the term 'community' will be used to refer to a religious or faith community and 'larger community' to refer to everyone in society.

Peace: tranquillity of order, a situation of justice, rightly ordered social relationships that are marked by respect for the rights of others which provide favourable conditions for integral human growth and harmonious coexistence.[6] It is

---

[1]   Cliffortd Geertz, *The Interpretations of Cultures: Selected Essays* (New York: Basic Books, 1973), 90. *Note*: The term 'Religion' in this work will be used to refer to an institutional framework within which specific theological doctrine and practices are advocated, pursued and lived-out usually within a community of like-minded believers. See Shadrack Gaya Best, 'Religion and Religious Conflict in Northern Nigeria,' *University of Jos Journal of Political Science* 2, no. 111 (2001), 66.

[2]   Jaroslav Pelikan, 'Christianity,' in Mircea Eliade (ed.) *The Encyclopaedia of Religion*, vol. 3 (New York: Macmillan Publishing, 2005), 348.

[3]   Joseph Keating, 'Christianity,' in *The Catholic Encyclopaedia,* vol. 3 (New York: The Encyclopedia Press, 1913), 712.

[4]   Tariq Ramadan, *Western Muslims and the Future of Islam* (New York: Oxford University Press, 2004), 11.

[5]   See Ernest Kurtz and Katherine Ketcham, *The Spirituality of Imperfection Story Telling and the Journey of Wholeness* (New York: Bantam Books, 1994), 82.

[6]   Francis Arinze, *A Call for Solidarity to the Religions of the World Religions for Peace* (New York: Doubleday, 2002), 1.

from the Hebrew word *Shalom,* which translates into English as peace, with a wide range of meaning. *Shalom* can refer to wholeness or well-being and can be used in both a secular and religious context. Within the Christian and Islamic traditions, peace is a gift from God and is eschatological.[7]

Peace building: any effort or intervention aimed to overcome the root causes of conflict. It is an attempt to deal with structural, relational, cultural, or socio-religious contradictions which lie at the root of conflict in order to support a peace making process.[8]

Peace culture: a process that fosters habitual interaction among people as they get on with their lives and work, negotiating differences rather than engaging in never-ending battles over how to solve each conflict issue as it occurs.[9]

Tolerance: the ability to endure, the practice and quality of accepting, recognising and respecting the fact that individuals and situations can be uniquely different from one's own experience and judgement.[10]

---

[7] John L. McKenzie, 'Peace,' *Dictionary of the Bible* (London: Geoffrey Chapman, 1968), 651-652; and Earle H. Waugh, 'Peace,' in Jane Dammen McAuliffe (ed.), *Encyclopaedia of the Qur'an,* vol. 4 (Boston: Martinus Nijhoff Publishers, 2004), 33-34.

[8] David J. Francis, 'Peace and Conflict Studies: An African Overview of Basic Concepts,' in Shedrack G. Best (ed.), *Introduction to Conflict Studies in West Africa* (Ibadan, Nigeria: Spectrum Books, 2005), 21.

[9] Elise Boulding, 'Peace Culture: The Problem of Managing Human Difference,' *Cross Currents* 48, no. 4 (1998). http://www.crosscurrents.org/boulding.htm

[10] Abdul Razaq O. Kilani, 'Issues and Trends on Religious Tolerance in Nigeria: The Contemporary Scene,' *Journal of Muslim Minority Affairs* 16, no. 2 (1996), 273.

General Introduction

The aim of this dissertation is to examine critically the incessant interreligious conflicts in Northern Nigeria, to identify the real causes of such conflicts, and to suggest theological and practical ways to sustain peace building endeavours.

In the last three decades, Northern Nigeria has experienced violent conflicts between its two largest religious groups, Christians and Muslims. Christianity and Islam are two major world religions that have lived with each other for over fourteen centuries. However, there have been many changes and fluctuations in culture and territorial boundaries during this long period of time marked by confrontation as well as fruitful cooperation on both sides. Sadly, the greater part of this relationship has been punctuated by hostilities, enmity, accusations, and counteraccusations over interpretations of history and experience, with prejudice and violence rather than friendliness and understanding.[11] In the name of religion, people have suffered acts of violence against eaach other. It can be argued that this is a failure of religion because it is often used to justify inhumane acts where there are deep-rooted historical conflicts of inequality, cultural divide, tribal disputes, and economic and social distinction. Hence religion is used to attack the other with devastating consequences. Despite that, a closer look at religion shows that while it can be used to promote violent conflict, it can equally be central to our understanding and establishment of peace within society.[12]

Generally, the story of the relationship between Islam and Christianity in Northern Nigeria is marred by conflicts, doubt, mutual mistrust, and violence. Many people have been killed in the name of religion. Scholars in the field of African history, philosophy, and religion, such as John Mbiti, Ikenga Metuh, Placid Tempels, and Jim Harries, have described the 'African' as deeply religious with religious

---

11   Alwi Shihab, 'Christian-Muslim Relations into the Twenty-first Century,' *Islam and Christian-Muslim Relations* 15, no. 1 (2004), 65.

12   Cf. Kathleen McGarvey, 'Gender, Peace and Religious Coexistence: Insight from Nigeria,' *Joras Journal of Religion and Society,* no. 1 (2011), 54-55.

practices permeating every aspect of life.[13] This religious sensibility has come into conflict between Christians and Muslims in Northern Nigeria. Even though Islam and Christianity both claim to be religions of peace, hardly a year goes by without religious violence in some part of the country, especially in the Northern region.[14] Religion has been manipulated to enforce issues of identity, ethnicity, and political differences, and this has fuelled disharmony between the two faith communities. The peace and harmony of Christianity and Islam is almost completely lost in the Northern Nigerian experience. The question remains today: is religion really the cause of such violence? Can people of different religious affiliations live in peace with one another? Is it part of religious experience that people want to kill each other in the name of religion? How can the evil of killing, bloodshed, maiming, and destruction of property in the name of religion be addressed and stopped responsibly?

Over the years, the Northern Nigerian states of Adamawa, Bauchi, Borno, Gombe, Jigawa, Kaduna, Kano, Katsina, Niger, Plateau, Sokoto, Yobe, and Zamfara have experienced recurring violent religious riots leading to the death of thousands of people and the destruction of property.[15] The adoption of Islam as state religion and the consequent introduction of Islamic sharia legal system by some Northern states, without cognisance of the religious diversity of the inhabitants, has further polarised Christians and Muslims.[16] This has resulted in heightened suspicion, distrust, and violent confrontation, for example in the city of Kaduna in the year 2000.[17]

However, this state of persistent crisis can be attributed to several other factors, such as the effect of colonial rule in Nigeria, ethnicity, political instability, underdevelopment, economic deprivation, poverty, corruption, ignorance, bad governance, violation of fundamental human rights, lack of the proper knowledge

---

[13] See Vincent Nankpak Fazing, 'Religiosity without Spirituality: The Bane of the Nigerian Society,' *Jos Studies,* vol. 12 (2003), 13.

[14] Cf. Demola Abimboye, 'The Damages Religious Crises Have Done To the North,' *Newswatch,* 28 October 2009. http://www.newswatchngr.com

[15] Eghosa E. Osaghae and Rotim T. Suberu, 'A History of Identities, Violence and Stability in Nigeria,' *CRISE: Centre for Research on Inequality, Human Security and Ethnicity,* no. 6 (2005). http://www.dfid.gov.uk/r4d/PDF/Outputs/Inequality/wp6.pdf

[16] The Twelve Nigerian Northern States that are Pro-Islamic sharia: Bauchi, Borno, Gombe, Jigawa, Kaduna, Kano, Katsina, Kebbi, Niger, Sokoto, Yobe and Zamfara states.

[17] Ignatius A. Kaigama, 'An Address Presented to the Prefect of the Congregation for the Evangelisation of Peoples, by the 2nd Group of the Catholic Bishops' Conference of Nigeria on the Occasion of the AD LIMINA VISIT to Rome 24th February 2009,' in Michael Ekpenyong (ed.), *The Threshold of the Apostles* (Abuja, Nigeria: Catholic Secretariat of Nigeria, 2009), 50.

about other faiths, and the manipulation of religion for political and social goals.[18] Today, the sensitive nature of religion in Northern Nigeria calls for greater attention. Where conflicts were once political, ethnic or land related, they have now assumed a religious dimension. An example is the 2008 crisis in Jos North Local Government Plateau. The conflict started as a political protest over local government elections. The Muslim community of Jos North Local Government had anticipated an unfavourable result, and the youths began an early morning protest by attacking places of worship.[19] Consequently, what began as a simple demonstration eventually became a religious conflict resulting in the destruction of churches, mosques, property, and the loss of human lives. Such crisis has continued to sharpen the religious divide among citizens. Despite this, millions of Muslims and Christians in Nigeria rub shoulders and engage with one another in their day-to-day activities. Nevertheless, it can be argued that such physical closeness is characterised by a socially distant relationship between the adherents of the two faiths.[20]

The important questions addressed in the following pages include the following: Why is it that Islam and Christianity have caused so much pain and disunity, especially in Northern Nigeria, when both profess to be religions of peace? Why is it that the adherents of these faiths cannot live in peace and face the challenges of development, security, and stability together? Is religion truly the cause of the death and destruction as is often alleged? Is there hope that religion can build peace and unity in Northern Nigeria? Can there be peace between Muslims and Christians in Northern Nigeria? Religion is used by some ambitious politicians, community, and even religious leaders to acquire political power in order to dominate, thus causing incessant conflict and crisis. Can theology and politics engage to offer solutions? How can religious-theological engagement provide a model for addressing failure in the social and economic structures of the Nigerian society?

THE POTENTIAL OF THEOLOGY IN THIS STUDY

The dawn of the new millennium sharpened the awareness of pluralism in the world and brought about a shift that challenged the old paradigm of exclusive attitudes and ushered in a new approach to life in general and to religion in particular. New and increasingly easy means of communication and travel have facilitated the meeting of people from different groups, culture, and backgrounds. Mass migration

---

[18] Cf. Ukoha Ukiwo, 'Politics, Ethno-Religious Conflict and Democratic Consolidation in Nigeria,' *Journal of Modern African Studies* 41, no. 1 (March 2003), 116-20.

[19] See Ignatius Ayau Kaigama, *Peace, Not War: A Decade of Interventions in the Plateau State Crises (2001-2011)* (Jos, Nigeria: Hamatul Press, 2012), 73-74.

[20] Akinbade Laide, 'Jos Crisis Unfortunate—FG,' *Vanguard* (Nigeria), 29 November 2008. http://www.vanguardngr.com/content/view/22933/42/

resulting from the two World Wars, the end of the Cold War, and the sharp level of inequality in the distribution of labour and world resources have led to a much greater level of encounter between people of different religions traditions.[21]

In the theology of the Second Vatican Council, the Catholic Church's 1965 *Declaration on the Relationship of the Church with Non-Christian Religions* (*Nostra Aetate*) began a new era in which the Catholic Church rejects nothing true and holy in other religious traditions.[22] This new self-understanding of the Roman Catholic Church presents an opportunity for theological and dialogical engagement with other religions. Furthermore, social multiplicity challenges every religious tradition to examine and clarify its assessment and understanding of other religions and evaluate the need to reconsider its own self-understanding in the light of increased and deepened knowledge of the other.[23] In our globalised world, where full awareness of religious diversity is one of its most striking features, the plurality of religions must be recognised in fostering dialogue.[24] Moreover, it is becoming increasingly clear that the relationship between people of different religions and the interaction of different communities are of fundamental importance to local, national, and international peace and security.[25]

Additionally, research in the field of theology as a resource for peace building and better understanding among religions (and religious adherents) is ever more dynamic. According to religious historian Scott Appleby, religion has an impressive power on people and society.[26] It is one of the world's greatest agents of healing, health care, education, and reconciliation. It inspires men and women to pursue justice, forgive their enemies, and seek reconciliation.[27] Luc Reychler affirms that although religion has the capacity to cause conflicts and massacres, it also possesses the potential for peace building and conflict resolution between communities and

---

[21]   Werner G. Jeanrond, 'Belonging or Identity? Christian Faith in a Multi-Religious World,' in Catherine Cornille (ed.), *Many Mansions? Multiple Religious Belonging and Christian Identity* (New York: Orbis Books, 2002), 111.

[22]   See 'Declaration on the Relationship of the Church to Non-Christian Religions,' in Walter M. Abbott (ed.), *The Documents of Vatican II*, trans. Joseph Gallagher (London: Geoffrey Chapman, 1966), 656.

[23]   Lloyd Ridgeon and Perry Schmidt-Leukel, 'Introduction,' in Lloyd Ridgeon and Perry Schmidt-Leukel (eds.), *Islam and Interfaith Relations: The Gerald Weisfeld Lectures 2006* (London: SMC Press, 2006), 1.

[24]   Cf. Ibid., 1-2.

[25]   Kevin McDonald, 'Christians in a Multi-Faith Society,' in *Pro Dialogo* (Vaticano: Pontificum Consilium Pro Dialogo Inter Religiones, 2004), 54.

[26]   Scott R. Appleby, 'Globalization, Religious Change and the Common Good,' *Journal of Religion, Conflict and Peace* 3, no. 1 (2009). http://www.religionconflictpeace.org

[27]   Ibid.

individuals.[28] In the religiously pluralistic world of today, where conflicts and violence are prevalent in places like Northern Nigeria, religion has the potential to be a rich source of peace building. Religion can be a powerful resource for social tolerance, a link between different religions and a means of constructive conflict management. Religion can empower the weak and influence the moral-political climate by developing cooperation among people and communities.[29] Thus interreligious dialogue is essential for better understanding between people.

In his Post-Synodal Apostolic Exhortation, *Christifideles Laici* of 1988, Pope John Paul II wrote, 'Dialogue among religions has a pre-eminent part, for it leads to love and mutual respect, and takes away, or at least diminishes, prejudices among the followers of various religions and promotes unity and friendship among peoples.'[30] Religious pluralism challenges faith communities to create the needed space for intra and interreligious dialogue that fosters friendship, understanding, and cooperation in society.

How can such dialogue be fostered? What are the resources within Islam, and Christianity in particular, that will enhance and sustain interreligious dialogue and peace building in both traditions? Why should one engage in dialogue and listen to another of a different religious tradition? There is also the challenge of what Catherine Cornille calls 'interreligious hermeneutics.'[31] This involves the use of hermeneutical techniques in the process of interreligious dialogue to cover a wide variety of critical issues in interreligious interpretation and understanding. This vital understanding and interpretation across religious traditions is multidimensional. Furthermore, there is the continual challenge of understanding the meaning of particular practices or teachings within their original religious context. This affects the dynamics and ethics of appropriating and reinterpreting elements from different religious traditions.[32] Furthermore, a shifting religious, political, social, economic, and cultural situation must challenge the most treasured hermeneutical assumptions and question the approach to interpretation and the need for a more dynamic

---

[28] Luc Reychler, 'Religion and Conflict,' *The International Journal of Peace Studies* 2, no. 1 (1997). http://www.gmu.edu/programs/icar/ijps/vol2_1/Reyschler.htm

[29] Cf. Ibid.

[30] Pope John Paul II, 'Christifideles Laici,' *Post-Synodal Apostolic Exhortation of His Holiness John Paul II on the Vocation and the Mission of the Lay Faithful in the Church and in the World* (Rome Vatican City: Libreria Editrice, 1998), no. 35. http://www.vatican.va/holy_father/john_paul_ii/apost_exhortations/documents/hf_jp-ii_exh_30121988_christifideles-laici_en.html

[31] Cf. Catherine Cornille, 'Introduction: On Hermeneutics in Dialogue,' in Catherine Cornille and Christopher Conway (eds.), *Interreligious Hermeneutics* (Eugene, OR: Cascade Books, 2010), ix.

[32] Ibid.

model.[33] Therefore, interreligious hermeneutics is faced not only with the task of understanding the religious other but also of evolving principles that will interpret both the religious self and the religious other in a fair and realistic way.[34]

METHOD

To achieve the aim of this study, qualitative data will be generated and collated from published literature (including books, articles from journals, magazines, and newspaper articles) to expound the topic of interreligious conflicts in Northern Nigeria. Given that the study is a theological contribution to the process of sustained peace building in the region, the theology of the Second Vatican Council (1962-65) provides a dialogue model that will be explored for both religious and political engagement in proffering solutions.

Furthermore, Islamic and Christian traditions are valuable resources for peaceful cooperation among people. The Bible, Qur'an, Hadith, Church documents and pronouncements are examples of such indispensable resources. I shall therefore analyse these resources to further and strengthen the ongoing grassroots peace building efforts of institutions such as the Interfaith Mediation Centre/ Muslim-Christian Dialogue Forum in Kaduna Northern Nigeria (IFMC/MCDF) and the Nigeria Interreligious Council (NIREC). The documentary film *The Imam and the Pastor* will be part of this analysis, offering a good insight into present attempts of peaceful negotiations in the region.

The approach of this study shall be from a Roman Catholic perspective as the theology of the Second Vatican Council has implications for a wider prospect that impacts even on the Northern Nigerian experience.

PLAN OF THE STUDY

Since this study is a theological reflection towards Christian-Muslim dialogue and peace-building in Northern Nigeria, its scope will be limited to Northern Nigeria, where violent interreligious conflict has been most prevalent. Consequently, the study will not deal in depth with the peace building process using interreligious dialogue in other parts of the country.

The study is divided into five chapters. Chapter 1 begins with a general contextual religious-political history of conflicts in Northern Nigeria. It examines the historical background of the spread of Islam and Christianity and the British colonial

---

[33] Werner G. Jeanrond, 'Towards an Interreligious Hermeneutics of Love,' in Catherine Cornille and Christopher Conway (eds.), *Interreligious Hermeneutics* (Eugene, OR: Cascade Books, 2010), 45-46.

[34] Ibid., 47.

rule from 1875 until 1960 when Nigeria gained political independence from Britain. Furthermore, it will focus on religion in Nigerian politics and the challenges resulting from the implementation of Islamic sharia law in the region.

Chapter 2 reviews three relevant resourses of this study: the Second Vatican Council's *Declaration on the Relationship of the Church to Non-Christian Religions (Nostra Aetate)* of 1965, the World Council of Churches 1979 document on *Guidelines on Dialogue with People of Living Faith and Ideologies*, and *A Common Word Between Us and You* issued in 2007 by leading Muslim scholars and intellectuals. The chapter offers a theological analysis of the relationship between Islam and Christianity since the Second Vatican Council. It further examines the field of interreligious dialogue between Islam and Christianity on the global scene and how such an encounter might impact on the Nigerian experience. It also considers the theological potential for peace building in Islam and Christianity.

Chapter 3 discusses the contributions of Islam and Christianity to peace building through constructive interreligious dialogue in Northern Nigeria. It explores the resources for peace building in the two faith traditions, the theology and praxes of love and its implications for Christians and Muslims.

Chapter 4 embarks on an assessment of ongoing Christian-Muslim dialogue efforts in Northern Nigeria by focusing on the activities of the Interfaith Mediation Centre/Muslim-Christian Dialogue Forum in Kaduna, Northern Nigeria (IFMC/ MCDF), the Nigeria Interreligious Council (NIREC) and the dialogue initiatives of Faith Based Organisations (FBOs) in the region. It examines the role of religious education in addressing stereotypes, conflicts, peace education, and the use of language and symbols to foster a better understanding for peaceful coexistence.

Chapter 5 considers the complexities of engaging in interreligious dialogue in Northern Nigeria. It analyses the complications, possibilities, challenges, and prospects for dialogue and suggests the way forward to attain this goal.

Finally, in our religiously diverse world of the twenty-first century, dialogue between religions can lead to better understanding in addressing complex conflict issues that may be religiously motivated. Moreover, religion has the potential to provide the needed space for dialogue. It is, however, vital to affirm the teaching of peace which religions hold in common, and the theology of Vatican II presents a first needed breakthrough for such interreligious interaction.

This work is therefore intended to serve as a guide to the numerous Christians and Muslims in Northern Nigeria (religious leaders/clerics, religious actors, academics, teachers, NGO/FBOs, and volunteers), influenced by the spirit of *Nostra Aetate*, who engage in the process of engendering and fostering grassroot dialogue encounter between faith communities, to provide an inventory of the available theological as well as local resources in the region to further enhance their peace building endeavours.

Chapter 1

A CONTEXTUAL RELIGIOUS-POLITICAL HISTORY OF CONFLICTS IN NORTHERN NIGERIA

INTRODUCTION

This chapter examines the religious-political history of Northern Nigeria. I argue that the historical dynamics of the spread of Islam and Christianity as well as the politics of the colonial administration in the region prepared the breeding ground for ongoing violent conflict.

Religion has made a significant contribution in shaping the spiritual, economic, and socio-political lives of people in Northern Nigeria. In the fifteenth century, Islam made inroads into the region and was established as the religion of the locality. However, centuries later, the advent of Christianity into the same territory challenged both Islamic and Christian self-understanding of community with social and political implications, leading to conflict and violence. Historical events in Nigeria—such as missionary activities, British colonial rule, the political independence of the Nigerian state in 1960, and the subsequent manipulation of religion for political reasons—have continued to influence the relationship of Christians and Muslims for decades.

Currently, the need to recognise and affirm the plurality of religions for peaceful coexistence cannot be over-emphasised. Moreover, a relationship between Islam and Christianity marked by hard, contradictory, and painful experiences dates back many centuries. Belief in God has separated Islam and Christianity far more than it has united them. According to Jacques P. Lanfry, past and recent events have left deep feelings of bitterness, doubt, mistrust, and even violence towards the other in certain regions of the world.[35] Dialogue between Muslims and Christians is thus essential if a theological understanding and the concept of community which excludes the religious other are to be addressed.

Nigeria is a nation that makes world news headlines about recurring religious tension and violence. A theological and political analysis of the situation will seek to understand the causes of such conflicts in the name of religion and be proactive in proffering solutions.

This chapter is divided into six sections. The first section examines the historical background of the spread of Islam and Christianity in Northern Nigeria and delineates the geographical area of study.

The second section explores the period of British colonial rule in Northern Nigeria and the consequential impact of Indirect Rule on the religious-political status quo, which sharpened the consciousness of identity and the feeling of domination and competition between the two main religious traditions.

The third section delves into the history of religious conflicts in Northern Nigeria. It centres on how the political preferences and policies of the British colonial administration, even after independence in 1960, continued to polarise the people in religion and politics. It further examines particular events and incidences that have resulted in violent clashes between Muslims and Christians in the region.

The fourth section discusses the use of religious sentiments in politics and how these impinge on deep-rooted historical feuds which lead to violence. In addition, it gives in tabular form a summary of major violent clashes between the two religious groups from 1980-2011, stating the cause and effect of such violence.

The fifth section expounds on the introduction of Islamic Shari'a law in Northern Nigeria. It focuses on the impact of Shari'a on the right and freedom of religion for non-Muslims and the consequent violence that resulted from the implementation of Islamic Shari'a in the locality.

The sixth section offers further insight on factors that continue to fuel conflicts in the locality by examining how the government's inconsistent policies have fermented crises, the ethnic and economic aspect of the conflict, the challenge of *Almajiri* and the threat of 'Boko Haram' Islamic sect in Northern Nigeria.

---

[35] Jacques P. Lanfry, 'Islamic-Christian Dialogue: Approaches to the Obstacles,' 1992. http://www.interfaithdialog.org/reading-room-main2menu-27/122-Islamic-Christian-dialogue-approaches-to-the-obstacles

1.1   HISTORICAL BACKGROUND TO THE SPREAD OF ISLAM AND CHRISTIANITY IN NIGERIA

In this section, I shall delineate the geographical area of study and examine briefly the history of the spread of Islam and Christianity and the dynamics of encounter between the two faith traditions.

Nigeria is located in Sub-Saharan West Africa, bordering Benin Republic in the west, Chad and Cameroon in the east, and Niger in the north. Its coast in the south lies on the Gulf of Guinea in the Atlantic Ocean. The land mass covers 923,768 sq km (356,669 sq miles), with three major ethnic groups: Hausa in the north, Yoruba in the south, and Igbo in the east. The population is about 140 million inhabitants, 300 tribes, and 200 languages.[36] Two religions, Islam and Christianity, are prevalent in the country with almost equal numbers of adherents, as well as a minority who profess the traditional African religion.[37] The history of Islam and Christianity in Northern Nigeria from the beginning to the present day testifies to massive manipulation of religion for political, economic, and social reasons, which can be traced back to the colonialists. Both Christians and Muslims have used religion for political advantage.

1.1.1   THE SPREAD OF ISLAM IN NORTHERN NIGERIA

Islam made inroads into West Africa in the middle of the fifteenth and sixteenth centuries through a slow process of migration, infiltration, conquest, and trade among the nomadic Fulani in Futa Toro in Senegal.[38] The Fulani are nomadic herdsmen who moved from one place to another in search of pasture. A few of the sedentary Fulani were religious fanatics who became ardent scholars and teachers of the basic principles of Islam. Some of them became militant and were ready to die for the cause of Islam. They contributed greatly to the spread of Islam in Chad, Sudan, and Cameroon and across Northern Nigeria into the Kanem Borno Empire north-east of Nigeria.[39]

According to Arabic Islamic historian Joseph Kenny, the demand for slaves and trade in gold and spices paved the way for the emergence of different empires

---

[36] Philip Maigamu Gaiya, *Religion and Justice: The Nigerian Predicament* (Kaduna, Nigeria: Espeep, 2004), 52.

[37] Abdullahi A. Arazeem and L. Saka, 'Ethno-Religious and Political Conflict: Threat to Nigeria Nascent Democracy,' *Journal of Sustainable Development in Africa* 9, no. 3 (2007), 21. *http://www.jsd-africa.com*

[38] Hans Küng, *Islam: Past, Present and Future*, trans. John Bowden (Oxford: Oneworld, 2007), 28.

[39] Toyin Falola and Biodun Adediran, *Islam in West Africa* (Ile-Ife, Nigeria: University of Ife Press, 1983), 52-53.

in the western Sahara.[40] Muslim Arabs fuelled trade while their lifestyle, culture, and religion affected the people. As a result, an African Muslim community soon developed as these Arab Muslim traders needed partners and associates for their business.[41] This trans-Saharan trade became a stimulus for state formation in sub-Saharan Africa as African kings welcomed the presence of Muslim traders in their midst for several reasons: the economic advantages the Muslims brought to various kingdoms in northern Africa were beneficial to the kings who accepted Islam as a religion and way of life.[42] It granted these kings citizenship in the Muslim *ummah* (community) with equality and brotherhood with their trading partners far away in Arabia.[43] The presence of Muslim scholars was of immense help to these kings because they served as palace administrators, interpreters, and teachers of the Arabic language and Islamic faith.[44]

The beginning of the eighteenth century saw Islam spread throughout Northern Nigeria as the recognised religion, a unifying cultural force with an established central political administrative system of government—'the Sokoto Caliphate'. Islam gave the northern region useful connections with the Islamic world through exchange of knowledge (Islamic education), commerce, and sustained political relationships. One very significant event was the movement of the Fulani from Futa Toro in Senegal after the fall of the Ghana Empire to the state of Gobir in the north-eastern part of Nigeria. They eventually conquered the seven Hausa states in the kingdom of Borno and established their political and religious influence.[45]

The Hausa-Fulani gained prominence, consolidated their presence in Northern Nigeria, and organised the nineteenth-century Jihad: a holy war organised and fought by Muslims against non-Muslims with the aim of conversion.[46] The Jihad led by Uthman dan Fodio, a Fulani man (1754-1817), was not aimed primarily at the conversion of pagans but at reforming lax Muslims. He challenged the Hausa kings to accept his proposals to live strictly according to the Islamic legal system of shari'a. When they refused, he overthrew them, setting up the Sokoto Caliphate,

---

40 See Joseph Kenny, 'The Spread of Islam in Nigeria: A Historical Survey,' 22-24 March 2001, A Paper Presented at a Conference on Sharia in Nigeria, Enugu, Nigeria. http://www.josephkenny.joyeurs.com/Sist.htm

41 Ibid.

42 Ibid.

43 Ibid.

44 Ibid.

45 Falola and Adediran, *Islam in West Africa,* 32-34.

46 Cf. Frederich M. Denny, 'Islam and Peace Building,' in Harold Coward and Gordon S. Smith (eds.), *Religion and Peacebuilding* (Albany: State University of New York Press, 2004), 134-35.

a federation of emirates covering most of what is now Northern Nigeria.[47] The Sokoto Caliphate became the seat of political administrative power established by the ruling Hausa-Fulani tribe after they had conquered the Hausa states. They expanded and dominated the whole of Northern Nigeria as the centre of Islamic faith. The Islamic *Ummah* developed with strong economic, social, and political administrative structures that supported the Fulani ruling class and the spread of the Hausa-Fulani domination over other ethnic groups (hegemony) in the region. This meant that traditional and religious leaders (emirs and local chiefs) became powerful defenders of the faith within the Islamic Empire, as well as political and state administrators.[48]

Islam was successful in Northern Nigeria partly because of the Jihad carried out by the Fulani during the years 1804-1815. This Jihad revived the spread of Islam with the primary aim of purifying the religion. The first generation of Fulani rulers introduced Islamic social, judicial, and political institutions that replaced a number of traditional customs and rituals of the local people. The Jihad contributed to the promotion of Islamic education, literary development, as well as a philosophical and theological framework for holy war. The Jihadists, who were eyewitnesses to these historical events, produced works that have shed light on the contemporary Hausa society, elaborating in varying degrees on the socio-political, economic, and religious situation of that time.[49]

Peace brought an end to the Jihad war, followed by security and state development within the Caliphate. These became the stimulus for economic, social, industrial, and commercial activities. Towns like Kano, Yola, Egga, and Kulfi became very important commercial centres. Native produce, such as dyed and woven cotton cloth, spices, and animal hides and skins, were common trade commodities that stocked the market as far as Mursuk, Ghat, Tripoli, and Timbuktu in North Africa and from there to the western world. Politically, the Jihad contributed to the collapse of the old empires of Oyo, Kanem Borno, and the Nupe Kingdom. It led to the formation of a large political entity which replaced the divided and disunited Hausa states. This established a political system over the whole of Northern Nigeria with its headquarters in Sokoto where the Caliph, the political and religious leader, reigned. He ensured the spread of Islam, proper administration, and maintenance of a good relationship between the capital and the emirates. The emirates were self-governing though not fully independent, choosing their emirs which were confirmed by the Caliph, who also oversaw the appointment of the emir's chiefs. Islamic administrative

---

[47]   Joseph Kenny, 'Sharia and Islamic Revival in Nigeria,' in E. Metuh (ed.), *The Gods in Retreat: Continuity and Change in African Religion* (Enugu, Nigeria: Forth Dimension Publishers, 1986), 245-56.

[48]   Matthew Hassan Kukah, *Religion, Politics and Power in Northern Nigeria* (Kaduna, Nigeria: Spectrum Books, 1993), 1-4.

[49]   Cf. Falola and Adediran, *Islam in West Africa,* 62.

policies were set down by the Caliph. There were regular tours of inspection by the officials from the capital. Each emirate was obliged to send two kinds of regular tribute to the capital. The first was produce of manufactured goods, farm products, livestock, and a certain percentage of war booty. The second type of regular tribute consisted of military levies and slaves. Non-payment of regular tribute was indicative of the desire to break away from the capital (Sokoto).[50]

Islamic education and the legal system received considerable attention from the Caliph. He encouraged the emirs to invest in Islamic education and training, with Arabic as the language of learning. Quar'anic schools were established as a tool for effective and efficient political organisation and as a means of converting more people to Islam. Emirs and local chiefs were obliged to promote Islamic education along with the training of teachers and jurists. The Sokoto Caliphate became popular as a centre of Islamic learning, education, and enlightenment. Impartial justice was emphasised and courts were established to promote the Islamic juridical system (shari'a). The Caliph could overrule a judgment which he viewed as unfair as he had total control over every section of the caliphate. This was the political and religious arrangement within the Caliphate for many decades until the advent of the British colonialists in 1875.

1.1.2 THE SPREAD OF CHRISTIANITY IN NORTHERN NIGERIA

According to African church historian Adrian Hasting, attempts were made by missionaries to evangelise in West Africa south of the Sahara as early as the fifteenth century when the first missionaries carrying the gospel arrived from Europe. These missionaries, both Catholic and Protestant, were not very successful, although there were occasional cases of momentary success. For example, the Island of Sao-Tome and Cape-Verde remained Christian even in the early seventeenth century when missionary activities went into decline in the rest of West Africa.[51] Furthermore, minor missionary successes were recorded in Gambia, Fetu, Elmina, Dahomey, Benin, and Warri in southern Nigeria.

According to historians Toyin Falola and Biodun Adediran, various factors were responsible for the failure of early missionary activities in West Africa. They suggest that the Europeans did not fully understand the nature of African society and were not sufficiently tolerant to make allowances for local African customs.[52] The missionaries misinterpreted the hospitality and generosity of Africans, especially the rulers, as a burning desire to become Christians, which was not so in most cases. By accepting Christian names, baptism, preaching, and building of churches, the African ruler

---

[50]   Ibid., 65.

[51]   Adrian Hasting, *The Church in Africa, 1450-1950* (Oxford: Clarendon Press, 1994), 71.

[52]   Falola and Adediran, *Islam in West Africa,* 87-91.

was only demonstrating the religious tolerance of most West African societies and not a desire to convert to Christianity.[53] Missionary activities were mostly limited to the palaces of the kings in the hope that once the king had accepted the new faith his subjects would follow suit. The kings accepted Christianity not out of religious conviction but because of the benefits they would derive from their association with the missionaries. Besides, missionaries encountered difficulties of travel, financial resources, and lack of trained African clergy as well as involvement in commercial activities. All these factors were instrumental in the failure of the initial attempt to evangelise in West Africa.[54]

However, fresh attempts were made by the Portuguese to explore the coast of West Africa in the eighteenth and nineteenth centuries with the aim of spreading Christianity and engaging in trade with the Africans.[55] Nevertheless, organised strategic missionary activities did not begin until the nineteenth century when English religious societies sent missionaries to evangelise in Africa. The abolition of the slave trade helped religious bodies, for example Anglicans, Methodists, Presbyterian, and Catholics, to take more interest in the missionary evangelisation of Africans.[56] This new phase of evangelisation was more systematic and thorough with missionary activities centred on the establishment of schools and the provision of formal western and religious education.[57] Thus by the late 1800s, missionary stations were established along the coast on the western and eastern side of the Niger, penetrating into the interior of the Igbo land in Nigeria.[58] The success of evangelisation in the southern part of Nigeria was due to the missionary policy of education of building schools in most villages. The outcome was an increase in the number of schools throughout the south-east of Nigeria, making education the most successful means of Christian evangelisation.[59]

According to a missionary priest in Northern Nigeria, Edward O'Connor (SMA), in 1710 two Franciscan priests set out to visit Borno from Tripoli because they heard of a Christian kingdom in the Kwararafa-Borno state in north-eastern Nigeria. In

---

[53] Ibid.

[54] Ibid.

[55] Lamin Sanneh, *West African Christianity: The Religious Impact* (New York: Orbis Books, 1983), 20.

[56] Ibid., 35-44.

[57] C.A. Imokhai, 'Evolution of the Catholic Church in Nigeria,' in O.A. Makozi and Afolabi G.J. Ojo (eds.), *The History of Catholic Church in Nigeria* (Lagos, Nigeria: Macmillan Nigerian Publishers, 1982), 1-4.

[58] V.A. Nwosu, 'The Growth of the Catholic Church in Onitsha Ecclesiastical Province,' in O.A Makozi and Afolabi G.J. Ojo (eds.), *The History of Catholic Church in Nigeria* (Lagos, Nigeria: Macmillan Nigeria Publishers, 1982), 5-44.

[59] Ibid.

1846, Fr. Philipo da Segni (OFM) was visiting Kukawa, the then-capital of Borno. By 1890, Christian missionaries had made significant contact with the middle-belt and the northern part of Nigeria. Contacts had been made in places like Baro, Bida, Lafiyagi, Lokoja, Minna, Zaria, Kaduna, Jigawa, Kebbi, Katsina, Sokoto, Kano, Nguru, Benue, Shandam, Damshin, Muri, Ibi, Dekina, Wase, Bauchi, Kukawa in Borno, and Zinder, about 150 miles into the Sahara desert.[60] Missionaries built schools to provide modern, western, and religious education and churches as places of worship for the growing Christian community in these northern towns and villages. These structures were symbolic of the fact that Christianity was beginning to take root in the north of Nigeria.[61] However, although Christianity was gradually making inroads in this vast area, there was stiff opposition from the already established Muslim community.

In the late eighteenth century (1886-1902), missionary activities in Ibi, Dekina and Wase, and many other places had to be suspended due to the hostility of some emirs, chiefs, and Islamic communities towards the missionaries. Consequently, attempts at evangelisation had to be abandoned.[62] O'Connor argues that the early attempts to preach the Christian faith in Northern Nigeria was not successful due to the vastness of the region, the difficulty of finding a more convenient route for travelling, and the existence of an already large and expanding number of practising Muslims who were hostile to the idea of a new religion (Christianity) in the region.[63] As a result, movement towards Christianity was watched closely by both local and colonial authorities. Buildings erected for worship were often destroyed, and community church leaders were frequently summoned to court. Such encounters forced missionary activities to be confined to the remote villages to avoid confrontation with the emirs, chiefs, and local authorities.[64]

1.1.3 RELIGIOUS GROUPS AND IDENTITIES IN NORTHERN NIGERIA

Nigeria is a multireligious country with a secular constitution since independence in 1960. Whether viewed from its past or contemporary period, religion continues to

---

[60] See Edward O'Connor, *From the Niger to the Sahara: The Story of the Archdiocese of Kaduna* (Ibadan, Nigeria: SMA Fathers, 2009), 9-25.

[61] Ibid., 9-25.

[62] Raymond Hickey, *The Growth of the Catholic Church in Northern Nigeria 1907-2007* (Jos, Nigeria: Augustinian Publications, 2006), 13-18 and 37.

[63] O'Connor, *From the Niger to the Sahara,* 97-98.

[64] Aisha Lemu, 'Religious Education in Nigeria: A Case Study,' in *Teaching for Tolerance and Freedom of Religion or Belief* (Oslo: The Oslo Coalition on Freedom of Religion or Belief, 2002). http://www.folk.uio.no/leirvik/OsloCoalition/AishaLemu.htm

impact on every aspect of life in Nigeria.[65] Northern Nigeria is host to a multiplicity of religious groups (sects) under the umbrella of Islam and Christianity.

Within Islamic religious identity, it is not easy to pin-point the dominant strand of Islam and its international influence. Indigenous Islamic sects have developed either in reaction to the mainstream ones or in response to the socio-political, cultural, religious, and economic experience in the locality. I am arguing that the kind of Islam practised in Northern Nigeria is unique to that locality due to the vastness of the area and factors characteristic of the region. In the same vein, within the Christian tradition, other sects have developed alongside the traditional Christian identities (Catholic, Anglican, Methodist, Presbyterian, and Lutheran Churches). These include the Pentecostal and neo-Pentecostal churches or ministries as well as the African indigenous churches. These have also evolved in reaction to the mainstream traditional Churches and in response to the prevailing challenges present in the environment.

Islamic Religious Identities: The key to understanding Islam is to recognise the central position of the Sokoto Caliphate which serves as the structure or model for exerting a strong Islamic cultural influence in northern Nigeria and the West African sub-region.[66]

During the nineteenth and twentieth centuries, Northern Nigeria and indeed most West African countries, witnessed the spread of two main Sufi Islamic brotherhoods, the Qadriyya and the Tijaniyya. The Qadriyya in West Africa was founded by Abd al-Qadir (AD1077-1166) in Baghdad. Uthman dan Fodio, who led the major reformist jihad in Northern Nigeria and founded the Sokoto Caliphate, belonged to the Qadriyya. Similarly, the Tijaniyya sect was founded by Ahmad al-Tijani (1737-1815) in Fez, Morocco, and reached Nigeria in the 1820s through the northern city of Kano.[67] According to a Nigerian scholar, Abiodun Alao, even at that early stage of the spread of these sects in the region, ethnicity and socio-political factors influenced the relationship of the two groups. The Quadriyya was firmly linked to the Fulani leadership of Sokoto Caliphate, with five legitimate independent sub-sects and several semi-independent groups, of which the Shaziliyya considered themselves an entirely separate brotherhood. Meanwhile, the Tijaniyya settled mainly in Kano and preached a doctrine that symbolised their independence from Sokoto, the seat of the Caliphate, where the Quadriyya was most dominant.[68] Like the Quadriyya, the

---

[65] Two religions, Islam and Christianity, are prevalent in the country with an almost equal number of adherents, as well as a minority who profess traditional African religion.

[66] John N. Paden, *Faith and Politics in Nigeria: Nigeria as a Pivotal State in the Muslim World* (Washington, DC: United States Institute for Peace Press, 2008), 27.

[67] Abiodun Alao, 'Islamic Radicalisation and Violence in Nigeria,' 2012. http://www. securityanddevelopment.org/pdf/ESRC%20Nigeria%20Overview.pdf

[68] Ibid., 7.

Tijaniyya too had various sub-sects. The Quadriyya and Tijaniyya had similarities and major differences in their doctrines, often becoming the cause of friction and tensions resulting in riots, for example in 1949 and 1956.[69] Immediately after Nigerian independence, riots broke out again between the two groups; ethnicity and politics played prominent roles in the violence.[70]

By the late nineteenth century, the practice of Quadriyya, originally associated with the Sokoto Caliphate, reached the city of Kano, led by Nasiru Kabara, whose home and school were located just opposite the central mosque and the emir's palace. This gave the impression that the tradition of Quadriyya was part of the emirate establishment. Nasiru's link with West African form of Quadriyya and his trips to Baghdad resulted in the birth of new ritual practices in the Hausa land which proved to be a source of tension between various Islamic sects.[71]

The Tijaniyya remained the dominant brotherhood in Kano with links to the Tukulor Fulani tribe from Senegal, who emphasised individual rather than group prayers. However, a reformed Tijaniyya developed; they introduced group prayers, community, modernisation of the means of communication, and the use of Hausa language. This appealed to common traders in the city. The reformed group spread to all parts of the emirate and other urban centres in Nigeria so much so that Sufi-Tijaniyya became a dominant brotherhood in Nigeria.[72]

Eventually, an anti-Sufi sect developed called *Jama'atu Izalatil Bid'a Wa'ikamatis Sunnah* (JIBWIS), meaning the Islamic organisation for eradicating innovation and establishing Sunnah, also known as Izala. This movement was founded in 1978 by Sheik Isma'ila Idris in Jos, Northern Nigeria, with the support of Sheik Abubakar Gumi, a former Grand Kadi of the Shari'a Court of Appeal of the Northern Region.[73]

According to socio-cultural anthropologist Roman Loimeier, the processes of change in Northern Nigeria are often expressed in religious terms; hence the Izala movement became the most influential and powerful movement of reform and the most outspoken opponent of the established Sufi order.[74] The Sufi orders were challenged by various means, such as the occupation of their mosques. Becoming a member of the Izala meant breaking with established society, including parents,

---

[69] Cf. Philip Ostien, *A Survey of the Muslims of Nigeria's North Central Geo-Political Zone* (London: Nigeria Research Network University of Oxford, 2012), 15. http://www3.qeh. ox.ac.uk/pdf/nrn/Wp1Ostien.pdf

[70] Alao, 'Islamic Radicalisation and Violence in Nigeria,' 8.

[71] See Paden, *Faith and Politics in Nigeria*, 28.

[72] Ibid., 28-29.

[73] Cf. Ostien, *A Survey of the Muslims*, 18.

[74] Roman Loimeier, 'Boko Haram: The Development of Militant Religious Movement in Nigeria,' *Africa Spectrum* 47, nos. 2-3 (2012), 141.

and rejecting all allegedly un-Islamic ways and social customs such as a bride price, extensive mourning and praying in some Sufi style ritual. The Izala sect not only fought against many features of northern Nigerian society but also advocated substantial reforms by establishing, for example, modern Islamic schools even in some rural areas and calling for the political and religious mobilisation of women. They offered Muslim women, youth, and usually urban Western-educated Muslims an alternative vision of Islam not mediated by established Sufi religious authorities who were accused of perpetrating major non-Islamic innovations.[75] Their radical preaching and ideology appealed to many Muslims and attracted a large followership, sometimes causing tension and violent conflicts with other Islamic sects as well as within the Izala movement. For some years now, the sect has been split into two factions, Izala 'A'and Izala 'B', based in Kaduna and Jos respectively.[76] It is, however, argued by some Nigerian religious and social analysts that the Izala sect is one of the largest Islamic movements in Northern Nigeria. The introduction of shari'a in northern Nigeria in the 2000s has given the sect plans for more activities in the region.

Another group of Muslims in Northern Nigeria is the Shia, who prefers to be called 'the Islamic Movement' or 'the Muslim Brothers Movement'.[77] This movement started in the early 1980s when many Nigerian Muslim students in northern Nigerian Universities were inspired by the ideological purity of the 1979 Iranian Revolution. It emphasises that Western imposition and culture must be rejected, pious Muslims must rule, and Islamic shari'a must be the law of the land.[78] As a result, Nigeria was flooded with ideological literature from Iran; some Muslim students visited Iran to study or gain experience by holding counsel with Iranian ruling mullahs. Among them was Ibraheem Yaqoub Zakzaky, now known as Sheikh Ibraheem El Zakzaky. He became the leader of the (Shia) Islamic Movement or the Muslim Brothers Movement in Northern Nigeria. This movement following the Iranian ideology believes that only pious Muslims must rule and shari'a must be the law of the land. Thus they reject the Nigerian constitution and laws because they are derived from illegitimate sources. They call for the establishment of an Islamic state in Nigeria, with a constitution based on the Qur'an and Hadith. They denounce democracy as it exists and is practised in Nigeria; they don't sing the national anthem or say the pledge and have no respect for the Nigerian national flag. Furthermore, they criticise the programme of shari'a as implemented by the twelve northern states, saying it is

---

[75] Cf. Ibid.

[76] Ostien, *A Survey of the Muslims*, 19.

[77] Ibid., 10.

[78] Ibid.

deceptive because it was introduced by non-Islamic government. Muslims groups who behave differently are seen as apostates and unbelievers (*kafir*).[79]

However, this sect, the Islamic Movement or the Muslim Brothers Movement (Nigerian Shia), and their doctrines are rejected by most Muslims in Nigeria, and because of their views, they are under the security radar even though they are allowed to preach. Sheikh El Zakzaky has been arrested many times, and today, after thirty years of proselytisation, the Shia remains a small minority group of Muslims in Northern Nigeria.

The Sunni sect is another group of Muslims in Northern Nigeria, operating simply as 'Sunni Muslims'. They are neither Sufi nor anti-Sufi. They live quietly, pray along with other Muslims in their mosques, and form their own networks for socialising, preaching, and charitable works. The people of this sect are neither attracted nor against Sufi Islam. The Sunnis welcome all people of Islamic background who do not believe violence or conflict with other groups.[80]

Other sects are the Ahmadis and Qur'aniyyun. The Ahmadis sect stems from India and has been present in Nigeria since the 1920s, mostly among the Yoruba ethnic group. They are mainly a minority group found in the north. This group has suffered persecution from other Muslim sects because they believe that the Ahmadis are a heretical sect and non-Muslims. The sect is known for its efforts to promote a modern system of education and like the vast majority of other Muslims upholds the Nigerian constitution and works within the ambiance of the law. The Qur'aniyyuns are Muslims who only accept the Qur'an as an authoritative guide to faith and practice excluding the Hadith.[81] They reject all reports about the Prophet because of the uncertain veracity of the Hadiths. They believe that with the exception of when the Prophet received the revelation of the divinely dictated Qur'an, the sayings and the doings of the Prophet were not divinely inspired since he was a mere human being like any other. Furthermore, they reject most Islamic laws taught in the various schools of *fiqh* (shari'a) which are largely based on the Hadith literature.[82]

There are two strands of Qur'aniyyun in Northern Nigeria, the 'Kala-Kato' or Yan-Tatsine (Maitastine),[83] and the Submitters. The Kala-Kato or Maitatsine was formed by Muhammadu Marwas, a Cameroonian, in 1980. He was a Qur'anic teacher, who gradually called together a local community of followers united in their ideology and doctrines. They rejected the Hadith and Sunnah and condemned

---

[79]   Ibid., 11.

[80]   See ibid., 14 and 21.

[81]   Ibid., 12.

[82]   Ibid., 12-13.

[83]   Elizabeth Isichei, 'The Maitatsine Rising in Nigeria 1980-85: A Revolt of the Disinherited,' *Journal of African Religion* 17, no. 3 (1987), 194. They are called 'Kala-Kato' for their use of the phrase to mean the Prophet is mere human.

the reading of any other book other than the Qur'an as paganism.[84] Marwa seemed to have rejected the prophethood of Prophet Muhammad and declared himself a prophet.[85] The sect stirred up many violent conflicts in Northern Nigeria between 1980 and 85, in which many people were killed and property destroyed. The group continues to be nurtured within and around the system of traditional Islamic education which focuses exclusively on learning to recite the Qur'an and write some parts of it. A lot of young people follow this sort of education even though some of them end up as orthodox Sunnis. However, only those who join Kala-Kato do not consider it necessary to be read other books than the Qur'an.[86] Accordingly, members of Kala-Kato remain largely uneducated in the modern sense and reject any form of western influence. They continue to exist quietly in many places in Northern Nigeria, not mixing much with other Muslims and living at the margins of society as *malams*, teaching the Qur'an.

The Qur'aniyyun, or the Submitters as they call themselves (Islam), are inspired by the ideology of Rashid Khalifa, an Egyptian biochemist. They are also known as Al-Quraniyyun, that is, those who accept the Qur'an only. Their creed is straightforward; they do not accept any Hadith of the Prophet but do accept him as a prophet of Allah. Adherents of this sect, in sharp contrast to Kala-Kato, are evidently well-educated, academics, and business people acquainted with modern ways of life.[87] They are present in Kaduna, Kano, and Katsina.

Occasionally, small unorthodox Muslim sects like 'Salaf' spring up and fade away, some quietly while others not without conflict and confrontations. Darul Islam is an example. The group was founded by a Hausa orthodox Sunni *malam* in 1993, to form a pious community isolated as much as possible from the rest of the 'sinful world'.[88] He gathered a group of followers of about four thousand people from within and outside of Nigeria, all—men, women, and children—living together. They built a settlement and applied a strict Maliki shari'a in all matters civil and criminal. They did not claim the right to execute any harsh punishment on anyone, as serious cases meant excommunication from the group. They had their own *qadi* (Islamic judge), an Islamiyya school, and hospital. They accepted modern western education as some of their children were receiving such learning. According to a Nigerian lawyer Philip Ostien, the Niger State government knew about them and even inspected them, and relations were friendly.[89] But with the rise and violent attacks of Boko Haram in

---

[84]   Niels Kastfelt, 'Rumours of Maitatsine: A Note on Political Culture in Northern Nigeria,' *African Affairs* 8, no. 350 (1989), 83.

[85]   Ibid.

[86]   Ostien, *A Survey of the Muslims*, 13.

[87]   Ibid., 14.

[88]   Ibid., 24.

[89]   Ibid.

2009, the government took the drastic step of arresting and repatriating all of them to the states and countries (Chad and Niger) they had come from. Today, the leader of the sect and some members are in Kano, Northern Nigeria.

Contemporary Northern Nigeria continues to experience the rise of more radical-violent religious sect like Boko Haram. The ideology of this sect is that western education and values are sinful and thus forbidden. They believe that Northern Nigerian politics have been taken over by a group of false Muslims. The sect is out to wage a war against them and the Nigerian state in order to create an Islamic republic ruled by Islamic shari'a law[90] (for the discourse on Boko Haram, see sub-section 1.6.4.).

Generally, to answer the question on the form of Islam most prevalent in Northern Nigeria and their international influence or affiliations is not easy. A critical analysis of the situation brings to fore complex factors as well as issues of scriptural (and traditional) interpretation which continue to shape and affect how Muslims (Christians) respond religiously. Consequently, Islam as practised in the region is unique to that locality characterised by various elements. However, Islam in the area tends to follow the Sunni custom within the Sufi tradition, with the Shi'a tradition in Sokoto and other parts of the north-west Nigeria. The Quadriyya and Tijaniyya are most prominent, alongside smaller sects: the Tariqa, the Malikiya, the Ahmadiya, and the Islamiyya. It can nevertheless be concluded that Muslims in Northern Nigeria do not form a homogeneous block but are divided into numerous large and small movements and groups that mirror the socio-political and religious divides and orientations present in the region.[91] While some of these sects/movements fight against the Nigerian state, others are deeply involved in the dynamics of political positioning that foster competition among religious traditions leading sometimes to bitter conflicts within and between faith groups.

Christian Religious Identities: Contemporary (northern) Nigeria has experienced an incredible upsurge and growth of African style independent churches, Pentecostal and neo-Pentecostal ministries since early twentieth century. According to a Nigerian scholar of religion Musa A. B. Gaiya, these African churches and Pentecostal movements are the Africans' way of domesticating the Christian faith.[92] Meanwhile, some Nigerian analysts of religion contend that the explosion and proliferation of these Charismatic-Pentecostal churches is the result of a growing dissatisfaction among some members of the mainstream churches. This is due to the inability of western missionaries (Catholic, Anglican, Methodist, Presbyterian, and

---

90   Cf. Andrew Walker, 'What is Boko Haram?' *Special Report* (Washington, DC: United State Institute of Peace, 2012), 1. http://www.usip.org
91   See Loimeier, 'Boko Haram,' 152.
92   Musa A.B. Gaiya, 'The Pentecostal Revolution in Nigeria,' *Occasional Paper* (2002), 3. http://www.teol.ku.dk/cas/research/publications/occ._papers/gaiya2002.pdf

Lutheran Churches) to establish and foster Christian principles that are culturally liberating, anthropologically enhancing, and religiously fulfilling within the African context.[93] Moreover, the aim was to outgrow the agony of religious colonisation and a reaction against political as well as social discrimination.[94] In addition, the political and religious scenario of the time, intensified by economic poverty, lack of development, and of course, the great influence of American Pentecostal spirituality, all fostered the growth of African indigenous/Pentecostal churches because the religious yearnings of the people were not met adequately by the liturgical ceremonies of the traditional Churches.[95]

Some of these African indigenous Pentecostal and neo-Pentecostal churches and ministries not only introduce an intensive practice of prayer, they also seek to liberate Christianity from western practices and indigenise the faith wihtin the religious parameters of Traditional African Religion.[96] These churches are characterised by their charismatic nature, with emphasis on scripture, prayer and the power of the Holy Spirit, fasting, holiness, miracles, and evangelism. They continue to overwhelm their congregations with the doctrine of material prosperity, healing, success, wealth, deliverance from sickness, and overcoming financial difficulties. They persist in organising crusades (service) and revivals aimed at solving the numerous problems afflicting people.[97] The Nigerian socio-political analyst Olusegun Fakoya has described these churches/ministries as the most flourishing business empires in Nigeria in an era of religious materialism.[98]

Alongside the mainstream missionary churches (Catholic, Anglican, Methodist, Presbyterian, and Lutheran Churches), indigenous African Independent Churches include United Native African Church, Christ African Church (Bethel), United African Methodist Church, and Kingdom of God and New Life Church. Others are the Eternal Sacred Order of the Cherubim and Seraphim (*Aladura*-praying people), Church of the Lord, Christ Army, Celestial Church of Christ, and Christ Holy Church.[99] Evangelical Churches include Christ Apostolic Church and the Evangelical Church of West Africa (ECWA). Pentecostal Churches include The Apostolic Church,

---

[93] Cf. Donatus Pius Ukpong, 'The Presence and Impact of Pentecostalism in Nigeria,' (2006), 7. http://www.glopen.net

[94] Ibid., 8.

[95] Ibid.

[96] Ibid., 9.

[97] See Olusegun Fakayo, 'The Gospel of Materialism—Nigerian Pentecostalism and Hypocrisy,' 2008. http://www.nigeriansinamerica.com

[98] Ibid.

[99] Gaiya, 'The Pentecostal Revolution in Nigeria,' 7; The Pew Forum on Religious and Public Life, 'Historical Overview of Pentecostalism in Nigeria,' 2006. http://www. pewforum.org

the Apostolic Faith, Faith Tabernacles, Congregation United Gospel, Assemblies of God, and the Foursquare Gospel Church. The neo-Pentecostal Churches include Deeper life Bible Church, Church of God Mission, Living Faith, Redeemed Church of God, Latter Rain Assembly, Harvesters Church of Christ, Christ Embassy, Living Faith, Winners Chapel, and Grace of God Ministries. Numerous other Charismatic ministries are present and thriving especially in towns and cities in (northern) Nigeria. Furthermore, these churches are increasingly Pentecostal in their theology, charismatic in liturgy, and competitive in practice.[100] There have been moments of mistrust, suspicion, and tension within and between these Churches; however, such conflicts have never degenerated to violence even though sometimes their extremist approach to scriptural interpretation has caused friction with the Islamic community.

1.2   A BRIEF HISTORY OF BRITISH COLONIAL RULE IN NORTHERN NIGERIA, 1875-1960

This section explores the history of British colonial rule in Northern Nigeria and the religious-political consequences of Indirect Rule as introduced by the imperial administration.

The end of the seventeenth century witnessed a very significant event that would change the future of Africa in general and Nigeria in particular: the rush to partition Africa into independent nation states by European colonisers.[101] By 1875, Nigeria had become a British colony, and colonial rule was established in Nigeria by 1901.[102] Meanwhile, the Jihad of Uthman dan Fodio was well underway. What had started as a movement to purify Islam developed and degenerated into a fully-fledged war of conquest against non-Muslims further south, causing major political and social upheaval in the middle belt of Nigeria. The arrival of the British colonial administrators under the leadership of Sir Fredrick Lord Lugard put an end to this war and consolidated the system of Indirect Rule.[103] This involved the use of local chiefs and traditional institutions to implement colonial policies in the Northern region.[104] Nigeria at the dawn of the British colonial rule had distinct ethno-linguistic groups, split between Muslims, Christians, and a significant number who professed traditional African religions.

---

[100]   The Pew Forum, 'Historical Overview of Pentecostalism.'

[101]   Cf. Ieuan Griffiths, 'The Scramble for Africa: Inherited Political Boundaries,' *The Geographical Journal* 152, no. 2 (1986), 204-205.

[102]   Walter Rodney, *How Europe Underdeveloped Africa* (London: Bogle-L'Ouventure Publications, 1973), 74.

[103]   John Onaiyekan, 'Muslims and Christians in Nigeria: The Imperatives of Dialogue,' 2001. http://www.sedosmission.org

[104]   Kukah, *Religion, Politics and Power in Northern Nigeria,* 2-3.

The colonial administrators governed Nigeria as two distinct colonies: the Northern and Southern Protectorates. There were three major ethnic groups: the Hausa-Fulani in the North, Yoruba in the south-west, and the Igbo in the south-east, as well as many other ethnic groups across the length and breadth of the country. In 1914, through a system of amalgamation, the North and Southern protectorates were merged to create one whole colony called Nigeria.[105]

The British colonial administration inherited existing social, economic, political, and judicial systems that operated in Northern Nigeria, with an organised Islamic community and Islam as the established religion of the region. However, Christian missionary activity was growing through formal western and Christian religious education. Consequently, the British administrators sought the cooperation of the ruling aristocrats of the Sokoto Caliphate and took on board the already established Islamic political structures, revised the conquered Islamic states, and introduced the Indirect Rule system of government. This meant that under British rule, emirs, district heads, and local chiefs acquired a great deal of political power, especially over unassimilated non-Muslims.[106] Consequently, communal identity was reinforced even where none had existed previously and deep-rooted historical conflicts of inequality, cultural divide, tribal dispute, and economic and social distinction were entrenched. As religious and political anthropologist Matthew Kukah argues, the introduction of Indirect Rule institutionalised the inferior status of non-Muslims in the Middle Belt.[107] Moreover, it increased the status and unchecked powers of the emirs, and disillusioned the common people who were hoping to be liberated from the dominance of Hausa-Fulani, who had been masters over them for centuries.[108] Thus Islamic faith enjoyed the support and preference of the British colonial authorities, while the Christian missionaries were ignored and refused permission to build more schools or churches to continue their work of evangelisation.[109]

Kenny maintains that the Colonial (British) rule favoured the Muslims. They were able to build mosques, interact with people, and proselytise freely throughout the country. Christian missionaries were not free to move around or build churches in Muslim-dominated areas, and priests were forbidden to evangelise in Muslims areas.[110] O'Connor argues that 'approaches by missionaries to the non-Muslims were frustrated not just by the local chiefs who were imposed on the people but by the

---

[105] John Lola Okunlola, 'Solidarity Step: Inter-Religious Unity in Nigeria,' *Journal of Stellar Peacemaking* 4, no. 1 (2009).

[106] Joseph Kenny, 'The Challenge of Islam in Nigeria,' *West African Journal of Ecclesial Studies,* no. 4 (1992), 46-58.

[107] Cf. Kukah, *Religion, Politics and Power in Northern Nigeria*, 3.

[108] Ibid.

[109] See O'Connor, *From the Niger to the Sahara*, 23.

[110] Kenny, 'The Challenge of Islam in Nigeria.'

colonial administrators who frequently used their own interpretation of Lugard's policy of Indirect Rule to thwart the advance of the Christian missions'.[111]

Indirect Rule as introduced by the colonial masters was a system of government which recognised, elevated, promoted, and empowered traditional rulers within the Sokoto caliphate. This made it possible for the Northern Region to be governed by the British colonisers through the emirs and local chiefs, using existing traditional institutions. Meanwhile, the rapid growth and success recorded by the Christian missionaries led the Northern traditional rulers to exert pressure on the colonialists to stop the advance of Christianity in the north-western and north-eastern parts of the country.[112] Thus the British formed a major compromise to discourage Christian missionary activity in Northern Nigeria. The North was strongly Islamic at the time of the British incursion, so the rulers and the common people had a great interest in keeping Christian missionaries out of their part of the colony.[113] By this arrangement, the colonial masters not only took sides but created an identity that was geographical and at the same time religious, creating division and strengthening stereotypes and bias. To this day, the general assumption in Nigeria is that those from the North are all Muslims and Hausa-speaking, and those from the South are Christians.[114]

Indirect Rule as introduced by the colonialists was successful in the north and south-west of Nigeria, because the Yoruba of the south-west, like the Hausa-Fulani in the North, had a centralised traditional system of government. This system of government did not succeed in the south-east because the Igbos had a decentralised traditional system of government. Consequently, the British colonialists handpicked loyalists as chiefs and imposed them on the Igbos and other ethnic groups in south-eastern Nigeria, just as numerous ethnic groups in the north were placed under the control of the Sokoto Caliphate

To further decentralise the south, which had embraced western education and begun to agitate for independence, the British split it into two regions, south-west and south-east, leaving the northern part of Nigeria intact as one whole entity. Thus at independence in 1960, under a parliamentary system of government, Northern Nigeria had the numerical advantage in ensuring its political dominance over the rest of the country. As a result, the Nigeria that became independent from British rule in 1960 was a time bomb waiting to explode.[115]

---

[111]   O'Connor, *From the Niger to the Sahara*, 48.

[112]   Hickey, *The Growth of the Catholic Church in Northern Nigeria*, 36-46.

[113]   Kukah, *Religion, Politics and Power in Northern Nigeria*, 2-5.

[114]   Cf. Joseph Kenny, *The Church and Islam in West Africa in the 20th Century: With Particular Reference to Nigeria* (Rome: Istituo per le Scienze Religiose and L'Ecole Francaise, 1998).

[115]   See Muhib O. Opeloye, 'Religious Factor in Nigerian Politics: Implications for Christian-Muslim Relations in Nigeria,' *Journal of Muslim Minority Affairs* 10, no. 2 (1989), 352.

By 1962, the Tiv of central Nigeria revolted against the perceived domination of the Northern regional government controlled by the Sokoto Caliphate. Violence erupted in western Nigeria following federal elections in 1964 and regional elections a year later. It was alleged that the Northern People's Congress, the political party in control of the central government, had rigged the elections for its preferred candidates. By January 1966, a group of military officers, mainly Igbos from the south-east, staged the first coup.[116] Their aim was to end the Hausa-Fulani dominance over the rest of the country. Although the coup failed, the government collapsed and the most senior army General, Thomas Aguiyi-Ironsi, an Igbo from the south-east, took power.[117]

Six months later, a group of mainly northern military officers launched what became known as the 'revenge coup'. Aguiyi-Ironsi was killed, and Gen Yakubu Gowon (then a colonel) took power. In most of Northern Nigeria, pogroms against Igbo from the South-East ensued, resulting in the massacre of more than 50,000 people. Colonel Emeka Odumegwu-Ojukwu, whom Ironsi had appointed governor of the South-Eastern region, refused to accept Gowon's authority, and after months of political impasse, declared an independent republic of Biafra in May 1967.[118] Biafra was defeated in 1970 at the end of a brutal civil war in which about a million people died. This was followed by years of military rule, punctuated by a four-year period of democracy from 1979-1983. Military rule in Nigeria ended in 1999.

1.2.1 THE EFFECTS OF BRITISH COLONIAL RULE ON RELIGION AND POLITICS OF NORTHERN NIGERIA

According to sociologists Arazeem and Saka, the recurring political, ethnic, and religious violence that has characterised the Nigerian state can be attributed to the state formation of the British colonial and postcolonial era. They maintain that present-day Nigeria is built upon the foundation laid by the colonial administrators, the choices they made, the policies they put in place, and the political, ethnic, and religious identities they created.[119] The colonialists succeeded in planting the seeds of division, tension, and conflict between the two major religious groups. The divide between Muslims and Christians in the north grew with political, social, economic, educational, and religious consequences for the future. For instance, the systematic educational discrimination ensured that only Christian children were admitted into school run by Christian missionaries; any Muslim child seeking western education

---

[116] Molefi Kate Asante, *The History of Africa: The Quest for Eternal Harmony* (New York: Routledge, 2007), 314-15.

[117] Ibid.

[118] Kukah, *Religion, Politics and Power in Northern Nigeria*, 36-42.

[119] Arazeem and Saka, 'Ethno-Religious and Political Conflict,' 28.

had to convert to Christianity first.[120] The deep political suspicion that resulted in periodic religious riots, prompted more by ethnic, historical, and political rivalries than religious differences, was exacerbated by the colonial system of government and preferential choice.[121] However, Kenny argues that Islamic resistance to the spread of Christianity did not dampen the missionaries' optimism but spurred them on to give more vigorous attention to the non-Muslim population bordering on Muslim-dominated areas.[122]

Consequently, as soon as British rule was established, mission-trained southern Nigerian civil servants began settling in major towns in Northern Nigeria and built private schools run mostly by the Christian missionaries. Simultaneously, government-owned schools were established to attract Muslim students who were very reluctant to attend because of the perception that any British school was a Christian school. Thus most Muslim children received only Qur'anic education in the Islamic tradition that had been institutionalised in the region.[123] As a result, tension grew in the north between the Muslims who, under the shadow of the British, controlled the political scene and the Christian southerners who had acquired western education and skills.[124] Today Northern Nigeria lags behind in terms of formal western education. Education in the North has largely remained within religious control and is very Islamic in character. Only recently some state governments in the north started considering integrating Qura'nic education with formal western education. The legacies of colonial educational and religious policies have had significant repercussions on the regional, political, economic, social, and religious development of Nigeria.

Contemporary Nigeria remains divided along political, religious, and ethnic lines. The north (Hausa-Fulani) tries to maintain political dominance over the rest of the country. Recently, a Nigerian political analyst, Chuks Okocha, observed that the 2011 presidential election had been zoned to the northern part of the country.[125] This meant that, geographically, the president would have to hail from Northern Nigeria. There is no doubt that northern Muslims have featured prominently in the political

---

[120]   See Rafiu Oriyomi, 'Nigerian Muslims in Focus: United We Stand Divide We Fall,' 2010. http://www.onIslam.net/english/politics/africa/432172.html

[121]   Ibid.

[122]   Kenny, *The Church and Islam in West Africa in the 20th Century.*

[123]   Cf. Moses T. Aluaigba, 'Circumventing or Superimposing Poverty on the African Child? The Almajiri Syndrome in Northern Nigeria,' *Childhood in Africa* 1, no. 1 (2009), 20. http://www.afrchild.ohio.edu/CAJ/articles/AluaigbaCAJ2009.pdf

[124]   Joseph Kenny, 'Christians and Muslims in Nigeria: A Case of Competitive Sharing,' *Nigerian Dialogue,* no. 4 (1982), 5-8.

[125]   Chuks Okocha, 'PDP Insist on Zoning Presidency to North,' *This Day,* Nigeria, 03 May 2010. http://www. allafrica.com/stories/201005030062.html

scene as the ruling elite. For example, Nigeria has had fifteen heads of state since independence, eight have been Muslims and close to two-thirds of the members of the Nigerian Parliament are Muslims from the core northern states of Katsina, Kano, and Sokoto. However, they were duly elected on the platform of their political parties and not on the platform of Islam (religion).[126]

1.3 A BRIEF HISTORY OF RELIGIOUS CONFLICTS IN NORTHERN NIGERIA

In this section, I shall focus on the history of religious conflicts in Northern Nigeria by analysing significant historical, religious, and political events.

Conflict, as an intrinsic and inevitable part of human existence, can be defined as disagreement, the clash of opinions or principles between peoples, or the pursuit of incomparable interest and goals by different groups or individuals.[127] In Northern Nigeria religious conflict is a common phenomenon. From independence until the present day, Nigeria has experienced much religious violence, especially in the north.[128] What has been the cause of these conflicts? Are these conflicts caused by religion, or is religion only used to express the deep-rooted ethnic-political divide?

British colonial rule in Nigeria lasted sixty years. On 1 October 1960, colonial rule ended in Nigeria, and political administrative power was handed over to a Muslim Northern Hausa-Fulani man, Sir Ahmadu Bello, who said, 'The imposition of British colonial domination was an expression of the grace of Allah.'[129] This was perceived by most non-Muslims as consolidating the Hausa-Fulani Islamic domination over the rest of the country and the North (Islam) having the upper hand in all political affairs. Although Muslims and Christians continued to live together, it was obvious that Muslims had more political, social, and economic opportunities than non-Muslims.[130] Hence, the legacy of the colonial masters continued in a subtle way. There was discrimination against non-Muslims, and various restrictions were imposed on Christian missionaries—denial of land to build places of worship, a ban on the circulation of Christian literature, lack of freedom to worship or associate, degrading treatment of traditional rulers who were not Muslims, and cultural domination.[131] Nigerian historian and ethicicist Abulrazaq Kilani observed

---

[126] Oriyomi, 'Nigerian Muslims in Focus.'

[127] Francis, 'Peace and Conflict Studies,' 204.

[128] Cf. Muhammad I. Ashafa and James P. Wuye, 'Warriors and Brothers,' in David Little (ed.), *Peace Makers in Action Profiles of Religion in Conflict resolution* (New York: Cambridge University Press, 2007), 247-48.

[129] Kukah, *Religion, Politics and Power in Northern Nigeria*, 2.

[130] Ibid., 6.

[131] Ibid., 2-8.

that Muslims in the Niger-Delta region, in the southern part of Nigeria, suffer discrimination and persecution because of their faith: they are not allocated land to build places of worship and have no access to state media.[132]

One would imagine that independence from British rule and a change of political power would have enabled Nigeria to unite in trying to find ways to respond to growing ethnic, social, economic, and security problems,[133] yet that has not been the case. Instead, religion and ethnicity have taken centre stage in polarising Nigerians, fostered by some politicians. Muhammad Haruna, a political commentator in Northern Nigeria, observed that different religious and ethnic groups lived in relative harmony until the late 1970s, when power-hungry politicians began to use tribal identity, religion, and ethnicity as primary weapons to seek political office.[134] The result is that Nigerians are divided along religious and ethnic lines, and some political leaders continue to manipulate religious sentiments for their personal interest.[135] Religion has become a very sensitive and opinionated issue. Whatever happens in terms of policy, decision-making as it affects public administration, is perceived and interpreted from a biased religious perspective by both Muslims and Christians. Each religious group feels unfairly treated and politically discriminated against, deepening the tension, mistrust, and stereotypes that already exist.[136]

One spectacular event, which generated much tension between Muslims and Christians, was the visit of Pope John Paul II to the city of Kaduna in Northern Nigeria. The Pope was invited by the president of the Federal Republic of Nigeria. On arrival in February 1982, the Pope said he was visiting in order to meet with people of various religious backgrounds, individuals and faith communities, hoping earnestly that his presence would express his love and esteem for the worthy religious values of the people of Nigeria. However, the political opponents of the president and other religious adversaries perceived the visit as an increase in the power and confidence of the Christian community in Nigeria, particularly in the north. Comments included questions as to how the president, a Muslim, could fraternise with the Pope in such a conspicuous way and claim to be a good Muslim. Meanwhile, some saw this as a sign that Islam was losing out to Christianity; others felt the president was losing

---

[132]   Abdul Razaq Kilani, 'Islam and Christian-Muslim Relations in Niger-Delta (Nigeria),' *Journal of Muslim Minority Affairs* 20, no. 1 (2000), 131-33.

[133]   David J. Francis, *Uniting Africa: Building Regional Peace and Security Systems* (Aldershort: Ashgate, 2007), 56.

[134]   Cf. Muhammad Haruna, 'People and Politics, Genocide on the Plateau: The Way Out,' *Gamji* (Nigeria), 2010. http://www.gamji.com/haruna/haruna312.htm

[135]   Ignatius A. Kaigama, *Dialogue of Life: An Urgent Necessity for Nigerian Muslims and Christians* (Jos, Nigeria: Fab Educational Books, 2006), 18-19.

[136]   Kilani, 'Islam and Christian-Muslim Relations,' 130.

a grip and failing to assert himself as an Islamic leader.[137] An unprecedented large crowd gathered to welcome the Pope to witness the ordination of ninety-four deacons to the priesthood from Catholic dioceses around Nigeria. This made Kukah comment that, 'If this event and the venue generated a sense of hubris among Catholics in particular and Christians in general, it may have had diverse effect on the meeting planned between the Pope and the Muslim leaders in Kaduna . . . '[138] This planned meeting with the Pope never took place. It was claimed that the Muslim community was unable to agree on who should represent them.[139] O'Connor confirms that it was a great disappointment that the planned meeting of the Pope with Muslim leaders did not take place.[140] The meeting would have been an important step in the Roman Catholic Church's quest for dialogue, but not a single representative of the Muslim leaders honoured the Pope's invitation.[141] While politicians were busy bickering over power, economic growth, and other material things, the Pope spoke about living in peace with each other, development, brotherhood, and the improvement of the human condition.[142]

Two months after the visit of the pontiff, Archbishop Robert Runcie (Archbishop of Canterbury 1980-1991) visited the city of Kano, where he laid the foundation stone for a new church building at Fagge in the Kano metropolis. Although there was no evidence of hostility shown during the Archbishop's visit, six months later the site of the new church was attacked. The Muslim rioters destroyed the church building, claiming it was too close to a mosque.[143] Assessing the situation, the church members alerted the police, whose immediate response averted the clash. The rioters turned to other churches in the city, set some ablaze, and severely damaged others. By the time the situation was brought under control, eight churches had been burnt and several people injured.[144]

Religion has been heavily politicised in Nigeria. Since independence, regional, ethnic, and religious tensions have marred progress in the country. Although adherents of Christianity and Islam form the majority in Nigeria, neither religion has been able to overcome the obstacles of the political class which continues to manipulate religious sentiments in setting one group against the other.[145] In 1986, the Federal Government of Nigeria's secret registration as a fully-fledged member of

---

[137] Kukah, *Religion, Politics and Power in Northern Nigeria,* 156.

[138] Ibid., 156-57.

[139] Ibid.

[140] See O'Connor, *From the Niger to the Sahara,* 177.

[141] Ibid.

[142] Cf. Kukah, *Religion, Politics and Power in Northern Nigeria,* 158.

[143] Ibid.

[144] Ibid., 158.

[145] Cf. Kaigama, *Dialogue of Life,* 19.

the Organisation of Islamic Conference (OIC), changed from an observer status, was perceived by Christians as a plot to finally turn Nigeria into an Islamic state.[146] The Catholic Bishops Conference of Nigeria (CBCN) reacted thus:

> The fact that secrecy and rumour eventually gave way to belated official admission that Nigeria has joined the OIC cannot but disappoint us. With the majority of Nigerians, we have come to expect openness and free debate to form this government. The lack of previous debate on such a sensitive matter, either in public or in government, is a blow to the trust and the hope that freedom loving Nigerians have been led to expect from the present administration.[147]

The sharia debate of 1978 is an example of the use of religion in politics. The Federal Government set up a committee to draft a constitution for the country. Some members of the committee sought vehemently to incorporate a clause establishing a Federal Sharia Court of Appeal. This generated heated arguments and fierce debate between Muslims and Christians, with both sides using religion as a tool for mobilisation.[148] However, the consequent introduction of the Islamic sharia legal system in most of the northern states in the 2000s, without considering the significant population of non-Muslims in these states, only strengthened the doubt, mistrust, and suspicion between the two faith communities.[149]

Generally, the relationship between Muslims and Christians, especially in the last three decades, has been marred by mistrust, tension, mutual suspicion, and physical violence which have left many people injured, some killed, and properties destroyed. The real causes of tension and violence may be deep-rooted social, political, ethnic, and economic distinctions which find expression in religion. The term religion as used here is broad with myriads of meanings that can be opinionated and bigoted with inclusive as well as exclusive predisposition. At the same time, religion understood as part and parcel of political life can have divisive and violent tendencies; for instance, the political adoption of religious language that promote religious ideologies, reinforces ethnic rivalries, prejudice, and discrimination, especially on religious grounds. This, however, highlights the paradoxical nature of religion as, on the one

---

[146] Nathaniel I. Ndiokwere, *The African Church Today and Tomorrow: Prospects and Challenges*, vol. 1 (Onitsha, Nigeria: Effective Key Publishers, 1994), 91-94.

[147] Ibid., 95.

[148] Kukah, 'Religion, and Politics and Power in Northern Nigeria,' 118; Peter Bauna Tanko, 'Sharia: Implications for Christians,' in Joseph Salihu (ed.), *Interreligious Dialogue and the Sharia Question* (Kano: Jaleyemi Group, 2005), 30.

[149] See Klaus Hock, 'Christian-Muslim Relationship in the African Context,' *The International Journal for the Study of Christian Church* 3, no. 2 (2003), 52.

hand, sentiments that can be expressed in the worship of the divine and on the other, can be adopted as a political means with various consequences.

The challenge, as theologian William T. Cavanaugh indicates, is the seeming distinction often made between the so-called religious violence and violence that are secular or political.[150] He asks, can religion independently cause violence? At what point is the distinguishing line drawn between that which is religious, secular and/ or political? Moreover, if religion builds community so does politics and ethnicity. Besides, given the fact that religion, politics, and secularism are closely intertwined, what are the criteria for separating these realities of human existence?[151] Cavanaugh maintains that religion is an inescapable universal human feature, and thus violence, as such, does not result from the fact that people are religious. The conditions that lead to conflict are matters of ideological, social, political or ethnic identities, to which sentiments of religion can add an eccentric, precarious, and violent twist.[152] For instance, the elevation of political or ethnic misunderstanding into a full-blown conflict, or the use of religious sentiments in the quest for political power by discrediting others based on their religious affiliation. Interestingly, the example of Northern Nigeria where some conflicts are ethnic or resource based, with the difference being that one ethnic group may be predominantly Muslim and the other Christian. Religion, however, by itself does not simply cause violence, even though there is no doubt that under certain circumstances particular religious action or interpretation contribute to violence which gives religion the unique propensity to exacerbate violence.[153]

The 2008 riot in Jos was apparently a political dispute about local government elections which eventually became a violent clash between Muslims and Christians.[154] This further brings to fore the complex nature of conflict and the obvious difficulty in categorising conflicts. The Catholic Archbishop of Jos, Ignatius Kaigama, observed that when a church or a mosque is attacked, it is because both are the most visible sign in the community that is targeted, not because they are places of worship.[155] But why is it that religion has continued to generate such controversy and violence? What are the hidden causes for such reactions? The next section examines the manipulation of religion in politics.

---

[150]   Cf. William T. Cavanaugh, *The Myth of Religious Violence: Secular Ideology and the Roots of Modern Conflict* (New York: Oxford University Press, 2009), 15.

[151]   Ibid., 28.

[152]   Ibid., 36.

[153]   Ibid., 36 and 55.

[154]   Akinbo Laide, 'Jos Crisis Unfortunate—FG.'

[155]   Ignatius A. Kaigama, 'Nigeria . . . Religion Is Not the Cause of the Clashes,' *Irish Missionary Union*, no. 2 (2010).

1.4 THE INSTRUMENTALISATION OF RELIGION IN NORTHERN NIGERIAN POLITICS

This section will highlight how religious sentiments have dominated the Northern Nigerian political scene and the resulting conflicts in a tabular illustration.

According to Philip Maigamu Gaiya, a religious anthropologist in Nigeria, at the root of religious manipulation for political reasons is fundamentalism, which leads to religious extremism, competition, antipathy between faith communities, intolerance, unjust treatment, and lack of respect for others and the rule of law.[156] In such a situation, political leaders implement policies that will interest and benefit a particular religious affiliation, for example, the case of OIC mentioned above and the introduction of Islamic sharia in the region.[157] Very often there are allegations of segregation, marginalisation, and political manipulation against others. In Christian circles, there are complaints that Muslims have dominated politics, controlled the government of the day, and segregated non-Muslims. Within Islamic circles, there are similar complaints about Christians dominating the political life of the nation and segregating Muslims.[158] This shows the depth of mutual suspicion and mistrust between people of different faith traditions.

In recent years, religious violence in Northern Nigeria has remained persistent. The role of religion in building peaceful coexistence has been challenged. Table 1 gives a summary of major violent ethno-religious conflicts in Northern Nigeria from 1980 to 2011:[159]

Date	Place	Cause of violence	Effects
December 1980	Kano	Maitastine: a fanatical Islamic sect who claimed their brand of Islam was superior to every other religious tradition, including Christianity.	An estimated 4,177 people were killed. Churches and mosques were destroyed. The violence spread to other places: Bauchi, Gombe, Maiduguri, and Yola.[159]

---

[156] Gaiya, *Religion and Justice,* 73.

[157] For the Discourse on Islamic Sharia, see Section 1.5 below.

[158] John O. Onaiyekan, *Thy Kingdom Come Democracy and Politics in Nigeria Today: A Catholic Perspective* (Abuja, Nigeria: Gaudium Et Spes Institute, 2003), 35.

[159] Anthony Akaeze, 'From Maitatsine to Boko Haram,' *Newawatch Magazine* (Nigeria), 28 October, 2009. http://www.newswatchngr.com

Date	Place	Cause of violence	Effects
Between 1980 and 1985	Bullumkutu, Dobeli, Jimeta, Maiduguri, Nasarawa, Pantami-Gombe, Rumde, Yelwa, and Zango.	The Maitastine sect collaborated with the Kala-kato sect to instigate violence at different times.	An estimated 223 people lost their lives, and property was destroyed.[160]
October 1982	Fagge-Kano.	The building of a new church was disrupted by Muslim rioters, who claimed the church was too close to their mosque.	Churches were burnt, severely damaged or desecrated.[161]
March 1987	Kafanchan/ Kaduna	Misunderstanding between Muslim and Christian students at the College of Education, Kafachan, over a weekend of Christian religious activities.	This violence spread rapidly around Kaduna state for a period of about two weeks. Properties and places of worship were destroyed, and people were killed.[162]
October 1990	Kano	The Federal Government allowed a Christian preacher to come to Nigeria and preach. Previously, a Muslim preacher was denied the same opportunity.	Violence broke out in opposition, leaving 500 people dead and properties destroyed.
April and May 1991	Katsina, Bauchi, and Tafawa-Balewa.	An Islamic religious sect masterminded a bloody protest in Katsina. Violence in Tafawa-Balewa	Following the situation in Katsina, violence errupted in Bauchi and environs; 764 people were killed. By November

160161162

---

[160]   Ibid.

[161]   Kukah, *Religion, Politics and Power in Northern Nigeria,* 158.

[162]   Ibid., 186.

Date	Place	Cause of violence	Effects
		between Muslims and Christians over the alleged selling of pork in the market.[163]	of the same year, the violence had spread to Kano. What was meant to be a peaceful demonstration by the Izala sect turned out to be a violent protest. People were killed and some wounded.[164]
October 1991	Taraba	Ethnic crisis between Tiv and Jukun ethnic groups over land ownership and political domination.	Over 500 people died, dozens of villages destroyed, and about 150,000 people were displaced.[165]
May 1992	Kaduna/ Zangon-Kataf	Deep-rooted community conflicts centred on ethnicity, domination, interrelations between the Hausa and the Kataf ethnic groups, as well as economic and political issues.	About 95 people were killed, 252 were injured, and there was a huge loss of property. In a second wave of attacks, 662 houses were burnt and more lives were lost.[166]
December 1994	Kano	A Christian was accused by Muslim fundamentalists of desecrating the Qur'an and inscribing blasphemous words against the Prophet.	The man was beheaded, and his head was paraded through the streets of Kano.[167]

163164165166167

[163]   Ibrahim R. Adebayo, 'Ethno-Religious Crises and the Challenges of Sustainable Development in Nigeria,' *Journal of Sustainable Development in Africa* 12, no. 4 (2010), 215-16.

[164]   Akaeze, 'From Maitatsine to Boko Haram.'

[165]   Adebayo, 'Ethno-Religious Crises,' 216.

[166]   Hajiya Bilkisu Yusuf, 'Managing Muslim-Christian Conflict in Northern Nigeria: A Case Study of Kaduna State,' *Islam and Christian-Muslim Relations* 18, no. 2 (2007), 242-45.

[167]   Akaeze, 'From Maitatsine to Boko Haram.'

Date	Place	Cause of violence	Effects
May 1995 and July 1999	Various northern towns	Small-scale religious violence	At times all it takes is for two people of different faiths, ethnic, or political groups to have minor quarrel that would be enough to trigger violence.[168]
February 2000	Kaduna	Following the adoption of the Islamic sharia legal system as state law in Kaduna, what was intended as a peaceful protest became violent.	About 609 people were killed, 1,295 were displaced, nearly 2000 houses, hotels, and other business centres were destroyed, and a total of 132 churches and 55 mosques were set ablaze.[169]
May 2000	Kaduna; Narayi and spread to Barnawa, Gwanin-Gora, Kakuri, and Makera.	Violent riots were ethnically motivated, as there was conflict between the Southern Kaduna youths and the Hausa-Fulani ethnic groups.	300 people were killed, and 1,000 houses and other properties were destroyed.[170]
2001	Jos	Political differences between the mainly Christian natives and the settler community made up mainly of the Hausa-Fulani.	Many lives were lost and property destroyed.[171]

168169170171

[168]   Ibid.

[169]   Yusuf, 'Managing Muslim-Christian Conflict in Northern Nigeria,' 246-47.

[170]   Ibid.

[171]   Akaeze, 'From Maitatsine to Boko Haram.'

Date	Place	Cause of violence	Effects
Between 2001 and 2004	Plateau state: Jos, Ndash, Shandam Wasse and Yelwa.	Political and ethnic conflicts became a religious clash between Muslims and Christians.	It is estimated that during these years, 4,000 lives were lost, property destroyed, places of worship were destroyed, and people were displaced. In 2004, the Federal government of Nigeria declared a state of emergency in the Plateau state.[172]
November 2002	Kaduna	A newspaper publication about the Miss World beauty contest held in Nigeria was alleged to be blasphemous towards Islam.	Christians were attacked, churches were burnt, religious leaders were killed, and properties destroyed. The riots spread to Abuja.[173]
February 2006	Kontagora, Maiduguri, and Minna	Publication of Danish newspaper cartoons which were considered insulting to the Prophet.	Churches were burnt, 50 people including Christian religious leaders were killed, 50 houses and 100 vehicles were either burnt or vandalised. This triggered further reprisal attacks in the eastern part of Nigeria and 30, mainly Hausa Muslims, were killed.[174]

172173174

---

[172] Ibid.

[173] Abimboye, 'The Damages Religious Crises Have Done to the North.'

[174] See Akaeze, 'From Maitatsine to Boko Haram.'

Date	Place	Cause of violence	Effects
February 2006	Kano	A school teacher was alleged to have made blasphemous remarks against Islam.	30 people were killed.
December 2007	Bauchi	Riots between Muslims and Christian over the construction of a mosque.	6 people were killed, dozens injured, and many houses were set ablaze.
February 2008	Kano and Bauchi	Violent clash between Muslim mob and the police over a woman accused of blaspheming against the Prophet.	1 person was killed and 5 were seriously injured.
November 2008	Jos	The results of Jos-north local government elections were announced.	About 700 people were killed, churches and mosques were either burnt or razed to the ground, and business centres were attacked. This also triggered reprisal attacks in the eastern part of Nigeria.[175]
April 2009	Gwada-Minna	Easter Monday procession was attacked by Muslim youths.	Violent clash between Christians and Muslims, 26 people were injured, churches, mosques, and properties were destroyed.[176]

175176

[175] Adebayo, 'Ethno-Religious Crises,' 217. Jude Owuamanam, 'Jos Crisis: CAN, AC Condemn Action . . . PDP Calls for Caution,' *Punch* (Nigeria), 30 November 2008.

[176] 'Religious Violence in Niger State,' *Punch* (Nigeria), 26 April 2009; and Israel Ayegba Ebije, 'Gwada Easter Mayhem—Muslim, Christian Trade Blame,' *Daily Trust* (Nigeria), 18 April 2009.

Date	Place	Cause of violence	Effects
July 2009	Bauchi, Kano, Maiduguri, and Yobe	'Boko Haram,' an Islamic sect claimed that western education and western values were forbidden. They refused to recognise any constituted government and condemned western education, technology, and all other cultures and traditions that are not based on Islam. They organised and caused mayhem across the north-eastern region of Nigeria.[177]	They attacked government/public facilities, security agents, churches, and businesses. This led to the death of many people and the destruction of property.[178]
January-July 2010	Jos: Plateau state and environs	Ethnic-political conflicts between the natives of the state and the Hausa-Fulani (which became a religious conflict).	It is estimated that more than 800 people were killed, properties and places of worship were burnt or destroyed, and many people were displaced.[179]
July 2010	Wukari-Taraba state	Violent conflict between Christian youths and Muslims as a result of siting a mosque at the divisional police headquarters in the local government headquarters complex.	4 people were killed and 40 injured. The mosque was destroyed, leading to riots with massive destruction of property. 5 other mosques and 3 churches were set on fire.[180]

177178179180

---

[177] 'Boko Haram Scare in Abuja,' *Vanguard* (Nigeria), 2 October 2010. http://www.vanguardngr.com/2010/10/boko-haram-scare-in-abuja/

[178] Adebayo, 'Ethno-Religious Crises,' 217.

[179] Ibid.

[180] Matthew Onah, 'Taraba: 8 Die, 40 Injured in Wukari Religious Riot,' *This Day* (Nigeria), 14 July 2010.

Date	Place	Cause of violence	Effects
August 2010	Ibadan Oyo state	Sectarian clash between two Islamic sects as a result of public preaching by the Tijaniyyah-Adriyyah sect which was considered offensive by the Izala sect.	13 people were injured in the clash, 3 mosques were vandalised, and 4 vehicles were destroyed.[181]
October-December 2010	Abuja, Jos Plateau State	Series of bomb blasts (political, ethno-religious)[182]	32 people killed, 74 injured, and property destroyed.[183]
January 2011	Plateau-Jos: (Bisichi, Bukuru, Fagawang, Nyarwai, Riyom, Wereng) and Bauchi: Tafawa Balewa.	Political, ethno-religious attacks and reprisal attacks.	Plateau-Jos and environs: 77 people are killed; 4 others are injured and property destroyed. Bauchi and environs: 24 people are killed, 4000 are displaced, property and places of worship destroyed.[184]

181182183184

---

[181] Bisi Oladele and Oshsre Okwuofu, '13 Injured in Ibadan Sectarian Clash,' *The Nation* (Nigeria), 23 August 2010.

[182] BBC News Africa, 'Jos Bombing: Politicians Fuel Nigeria Unrest,' 2010. http://www.bbc. co.uk/news/world-africa-12086630?asid=6cd0fcc1

[183] Taye Obateru and Daniel Idonor, 'Jos Xmas Eve Blast: 32 People Confirmed Dead, 74 Hospitalised,' *Vanguard* (Nigeria), 26 December 2010.

[184] Abarham James, 'Fresh Violence Erupts in Jos,' *Sunday Mirror* (Nigeria) 09 January 2011; Idegu A. Yusufu, 'Jos Boils Again, 10 Feared Dead,' *The Nation* (Nigeria), 09 January 2010; Isaac Shobayo and Chris Agbambu, 'Jos Crisis Spreads, 18 Killed in Riyom,' *Tribune* (Nigeria), 12 January 2011; Isaac Aimurie, Chizoba Ogbeche, Achor Abimaje, and Palang Gonji, 'Fresh Attacks: 18 Killed in Jos Children, Women Feared Dead,' *Leadership* (Nigeria), 12 January 2011.

Date	Place	Cause of violence	Effects
April 2011	Bauchi, Gombe, Kaduna, Katsina, Kano, Kogi, Niger, Sokoto, Taraba and Zamfara States.	Post-election political-religious violence[185]	About 151 people were killed, 130 injured, 84 churches and some mosques were destroyed. 4,500 people were displaced.[186]
August 2011	Jos metropolis and environs.	Reprisal attacks as a result of 2010 Christmas Day Boming. A bomb blast disrupted Christmas celebrations.[187]	20 people were killed, 20 injured and 50 vehicles were torched.[188]
November 2011	Damaturu Yobe State and Miduguri Borno State.	Attack by the Boko Haram sect on police headquarters, 3 police stations, 1 bank, and 6 churches.	An estimated 136 people were killed, 17 injured, several buildings and places of worship destroyed.[189]

185186187188189

Table 1 A summary of major violent ethno-religious conflicts in Northern Nigeria from 1980 to 2011

These attacks usually trigger reprisal attacks in other parts of the country. Akaeze Anthony, a journalist in Nigeria, observed that between 1980 and 2009, there have been copious cases of ethno-religious confrontations, resulting in more than ten thousand deaths, in addition to the destruction of property.[190] Many of these

---

[185] See Paul Orude, 'Presidential Poll Riots: 59 Killed, 84 Churches Burnt in Bauchi, Gombe, Kaduna,' *The Sun* (Nigeria), 21 April 2011. http://www.sunnewsonline.com;

[186] 'Breaking News: Fresh Post-Election Violence Claims Lives in Northern Nigeria,' *Punch* (Nigeria), 18 April 2011.

[187] Isaac Shobayo, 'Renewed Hostility: 20 Killed, 50 Vehicles Burnt in Jos,' *Tribune* (Nigeria), 30 August 2011. *http:www.tribune.com*

[188] Jude Owuamanam, '20 Killed in Renewed Jos Violence,' *Punch* (Nigeria), 30 August 2011. http://www.punchng.com

[189] Kunle Akogun and Michael Olugbode, 'Over 136 Dead in Yobe Boko Haram Attacks,' *This Day* (Nigeria), 06 November 2011. http://www.thisdaylive.com

[190] Akaeze, 'From Maitatsine to Boko Haram.'

attacks may not be religiously motivated but are a result of many ethnic nationalities asserting their identities in a forceful way. Since tension and rivalry already exist between the dominant religious groups, religion becomes the spark for unleashing horror.[191] Another cause of religious violence in Northern Nigeria is the absence of justice for the victims.[192] The structural weakness and the independent nature of the Nigerian judicial system do not allow the courts to bring the perpetrators of such heinous acts to face justice.[193] The Nigerian government's reaction has always been to set up a commission to investigate these crises, but no one has ever been held accountable for the crimes.[194]

However, the reaction of most Nigerians is that of total condemnation of such evil.[195] Religious leaders, religious organisations, traditional rulers, politicians, policy makers, and government institutions have always voiced their condemnation of the violence publicly and called for peace and tolerance among the various groups.[196] While some perceive these conflicts as ethno-political, others think they are purely attacks aimed at particular religious groups. For example, the Catholic Archbishop Ignatius Kaigama of Jos remarked thus:

> [W]e were taken aback by the turn of events in Jos. We thought it was political, but from all indications it is not so. We were surprised at the way some of our churches and property were attacked and some of our faithful and Clergy killed. The attacks were carefully planned and executed. The questions we are asking are why were churches and Clergy attacked and killed? Why were politicians, political party offices, National Assembly and government institutions not attacked if it was a political conflict? Why were the business premises and property of innocent civilians destroyed?

---

[191] Gaiya, *Religion and Justice*, 75.

[192] Cf. Isa Abdulsalami, 'Jos Crisis: Government Gives Shoot—On Sight Order,' *Guardian News* (Nigeria), 30 November 2008. http://www.ngrguardiannews.com/news/article02//indexn2_html?pdate=301108&ptitle=Jos%20Crisis:%20Govt%20Gives%20Shoot-on-sight%20Order

[193] Seriki Adinoyi, 'Plateau Raises Alarm over Fresh Plot to Attack Jos: Speakers want FG to Intervene in Recurring Crisis,' *This Day* (Nigeria), 14 June 2010.

[194] See 'Revenge in the Name of Religion: The Cycle of Violence in Plateau and Kano States,' *Human Rights Watch* 17, no. 8 (2005), 53.

[195] Ibrahim Muhammad, 'Religious, Traditional Rulers Urge Christians and Muslim Unity,' *Daily Trust* (Nigeria), 19 July 2010. http://www.dailytrust.com

[196] Ibid.

> We strongly feel that it was not political, but a pre-meditated act under the guise of elections.[197]

Others have observed that it is unfair that the Muslim faithful are relaxed during their Friday prayers in the mosque, while on Sundays Christians in the same areas pray in fear of threats to their lives.[198]

Table 1 further brings to fore the challenging security situation and the need for religious, community and government leaders to address the causes of conflict effectively in the region and chart the way forward for peaceful coexistence. It is difficult to assess and pinpoint a particular cause of the religious crisis in Nigeria, because opinion varies. Some hold that it is ethnic, tribal, social, economic, and political, while others opine that it is purely religious. In as much as I agree with the afore-mentioned reasons, in this work I argue that conflict, violence, and insecurity in Northern Nigeria is a result of all the reasons given above, plus ignorance and lack of education. Consequently, it is important that the process of theological analysis takes all the issues into consideration in making sustainable efforts in peace building.

1.5 THE INTRODUCTION OF ISLAMIC SHARIA IN NORTHERN NIGERIA

In this section, I shall examine the politics of Islamic sharia implementation and the conflict and controversy it has generated in the region.

The argument over the adoption of Islamic sharia in Northern Nigeria is an issue that has dominated the constitutional debate for decades and yet remains unresolved. The impasse continues to polarise the country along political, religious, and social divides, resulting in violent conflict. According to Islamic philosopher Nasr Hossein, Islamic sharia is divine law, rooted in the immutable sources of the Qur'an, Hadith, and the Sunna, which have remained unchanged through the ages.[199] He argues that sharia is the divine law that moulds Islamic society and Muslims wish to return to this law that was changed forcibly during the colonial periods.[200] Kenny affirms that Islamic sharia is as old as Islam in Northern Nigeria.[201] As discussed above, Islam

---

[197] Chuks Okocha, Buhari Ruben, and Seriki Adinoyi, 'Death Toll in Jos Rises to 350,' *This Day* (Nigeria), 30 November 2008. http://www.thisdayonline.com/nview.php?id=129535

[198] Cf. Andrew Agbese, Lalo Mahmud, and Bashiru Misbahu, 'Many Killed in Jos Violence,' *Daily Trust* (Nigeria), 18 January 2010; Abdulsalami, 'Jos Crisis: Government Gives Shoot—On Sight Order.'

[199] Nasr S. Hossein, 'Islamic-Christian Dialogue: Problems and Obstacles to be Pondered and Overcome,' *Islam and Christian-Muslim Relations* 11, no. 2 (2000), 216-17.

[200] Ibid.

[201] Kenny, 'Sharia and Islamic Revival in Nigeria,' 245.

came to Nigeria through trade, slave-raiding, and Jihad. Communities that embraced Islam had to live by the Islamic principles of sharia. For Muslims, Islam is not just a religion but a way of life, guided by the sharia law which shapes the world view of the Islamic *Ummah* (community), setting moral and religious values for their daily lives.[202]

Sharia was introduced to Northern Nigeria by Uthman Dan Fodio during his Jihad of 1804 in which he defeated the Hausa Kings of Northern Nigeria. Sokoto became the seat of the Caliphate and the headquarters of Islamic religious and political powers across Northern Nigeria. This Jihad aimed to establish an Islamic state based on the sharia legal system, under the administration of the Caliph as the supreme leader of the state and the chief custodian of Islam. In this administration, every king, emir, and local chief within the Caliphate had to maintain the supremacy of the shari'a legal system within their domain.[203] By 1902, the British colonialists imposed their authority over Northern Nigeria. Whilst they recognised traditional institutions and Islam as the religion of the region, the British did not endorse sharia as the law to guide their conquered territory.[204] Instead, under the Proclamation Act of 1906, native laws and customs of the people were adopted as the legal system. Consequently, native courts were set up to administer justice and were later confirmed in the Native Courts Act of 1956.[205] Nonetheless, Sir Frederick Lord Lugard, the British governor of Nigeria, promised the emirs that the British colonialists would not interfere with their religion in any way. The emirs pressed this promise to the limit by incorporating all the ramifications of Islamic law into the adopted system. When Lord Lugard realised that the fundamental law in the native law and custom of Northern Nigeria was basically Islamic sharia law, which covered all matters, sharia courts were allowed to operate. As a result, both sharia and customary courts became operational in Northern Nigeria. Penalties such as death by stoning, amputation, and crucifixion were not allowed because they were regarded by the British as repugnant to natural justice, equity, and good conscience. However, public flogging was allowed as a form of punishment.[206] The conflict of laws ensued, which persists to this day. The challenge is how to harmonise these laws to create a modern secular and democratic state in Nigeria.

The British tried to resolve the conflict by sending three delegations to Pakistan, Sudan, and Libya to study sharia law and how to apply it in Nigeria. In 1957, the British introduced the right to appeal when sentence is passed. According to Tanko,

---

[202] See Ndiokwere, *The African Church Today and Tomorrow,* 83-84.

[203] Kenny, 'Sharia and Islamic Revival in Nigeria,' 245-56.

[204] Tanko, 'Sharia: Implications for Christians', 29.

[205] Ibid.

[206] Kukah, *Religion, Politics and Power in Northern Nigeria*, 115-17; 'Political Sharia? Human Right and Islamic Law in Northern Nigeria,' *Human Right Watch* 16, no. 9 (2004), 9-10.

this challenged the authority and legitimacy of the emirs and the traditional ruling class. The right to appeal became an opportunity for ordinary people to escape from the power of the emirs.[207] An example of this was the case of a man who was accused and convicted of deliberate homicide. He was found guilty and sentenced to death according to sharia law. When the man appealed, his sentence was overturned because he was guilty of manslaughter and not murder, an offence which was not punishable by death. The outcome of this case caused conflict in the law and an attitude of suspicion. The impression was that a life or death sentence depends in some cases not on the crime but on the juridical area of the crime. The emirs were completely powerless as sharia was subservient to British justice. To pacify the emirs, in 1956 the British established an Islamic Court of Appeal. This move was welcomed by chiefs and Islamic jurists as it protected Islamic law from appeal to the British courts.[208]

When the British left Nigeria, it was necessary to harmonise the various laws. Under British rule, religion had become a cause of conflict. With the recommendation of the three delegates sent to Sudan, Libya, and Pakistan, on 1 October 1960, a sharia court of appeal was established in Kaduna, consisting of a Grand Khadi, a deputy, and two other judges learned in Islamic law. Kukah observed that by introducing the sharia appeal procedure, the British had pacified the emirs and thus guaranteed their short-term interest, but they had also planted the seed of conflict and discord because appeal was hitherto unknown in sharia law.[209]

The Islamic sharia legal system has continued to generate the most heated controversy and bitterness between Muslims and Christians in Nigeria. Since independence, the question about the status of sharia within the constitution has remained unanswered.[210] This controversy started in 1979, when a new constitution was being drafted. The Muslims demanded that the sharia legal system be recognised in the Nigerian constitution and a sharia court of appeal established in all the states of the federation. Christians vehemently opposed this demand and argued that the establishment of sharia was an attempt to Islamise the country, thus contradicting the secular status of the Nigerian state and was a subtle way of entrenching the old Hausa-Fulani Islamic hegemony.[211] The sharia issue was not resolved and sharia courts continued to exist.

The same debate resurfaced during the 1997 constitution review again with heated arguments and debates. Some politicians went ahead, took advantage of the

---

[207]   Tanko, 'Sharia: Implications for Christians,' 29-30.

[208]   Matthew Hassan Kukah, 'Religious Liberty in a Plural Society: The Nigerian Experience,' in *A Theme for Christian-Muslim Dialogue* (Vatican City: The Pontifical Council for Interreligious Dialogue the Commission for Religious Relations with Muslims, 2006), 106-08.

[209]   Kukah, *Religion, Politics and Power in Northern Nigeria,* 117-18.

[210]   Opeloye, 'Religious Factor in Nigerian Politics,' 355-56.

[211]   See Kukah, *Religion, Politics and Power in Northern Nigeria,* 118-30.

constitutional gap, and adopted Islam as the state religion and the Islamic sharia legal system as the state law.[212] By 2002, Islamic sharia was operational in twelve northern states of Nigeria.[213] This generated condemnation and caused tension and violence, especially in the city of Kaduna, where violence erupted between the Christians and Muslims, resulting in heavy casualties on both sides.[214] The mayhem in Kaduna generated retaliatory killings, especially of Muslims in the eastern part of the country. Many critics called for the partitioning of Nigeria rather than the adoption or abandonment of Islamic sharia.

The media analyst Jibrin Ibrahim observed that the conflict in Kaduna demonstrated the fundamental problem posed by the adoption of the sharia. It creates acute insecurity among Christians and other minority groups in the affected states who fear that the new legal regime will affect them adversely despite claims to the contrary by Muslim supporters of sharia.[215]

The CBCN also spoke against the implementation of sharia:

> The adoption of sharia by some states in Nigeria has continued to create a situation of unrest in which people are killed and maimed and thousands of others are displaced from their homes and places of work . . . many indigenes of the states concerned continue to suffer in silence because they cannot defend their rights and have nowhere to relocate. We have warned repeatedly that the adoption of sharia as a state law and extension of its scope are flagrant violations of the human rights of non-Muslims in a multi-religious society and a secular state like Nigeria.[216]

Today, Nigeria continues to grapple with the question of Islamic sharia amidst economic, social, political, and ethnic problems. Religion takes the centre stage because it is a form of identity and is highly significant in the lives of the people. These challenges increasingly call into question the theological understanding of community from both Islamic and Christian perspectives and how such

---

[212] Cf. ACCORD/UNHCR, *Nigeria, The Final Report of 8th European Country of Origin Seminar*, June 28-29 2002, Vienna, 161. http://www.unhcr.org/refworld/country, ACCORD, NGA, 402d06554, 0.html

[213] Pro-Islamic shari'a States in Northern Nigeria: Bauchi (2001), Borno (2000), Gombe (2001), Jigawa (2000), Kaduna (2000), Kano (2000), Katsina (2000), Kebbi (2000), Niger (2000), Sokoto (2000), Yobe (2001), Zamfara (2000).

[214] Yusuf, 'Managing Muslim-Christian Conflict in Northern Nigeria,' 241.

[215] Jibrin Ibrahim, 'Democracy and Minority Rights in Nigeria: Religion, Sharia and the 1999 Constitution,' *Daily Trust* (Nigeria), 22-28 February 2002.

[216] Innocent Jooji, *Mending the Cracked Pot: Perspective on Conflict Non-Violence, Social Justice and Reconciliation in Nigeria* (Ibadan, Nigeria: Daily Graphics Nigeria, 2003), 18.

interpretations affect our concept of otherness. However, it is important that policy makers engage positively with the two faith traditions to evolve strategic ways of addressing the issue of sharia and come to a compromise that will be favourable to both Christians and Muslims. Otherwise, religion will continue to divide Nigeria. The following section considers the implications of sharia for non-Muslims in Northern Nigeria.

1.5.1 THE IMPLICATIONS OF ISLAMIC SHARIA IMPLEMENTATION FOR NON-MUSLIMS IN NORTHERN NIGERIA

In this sub-section, I shall discuss the implication of sharia on non-Muslims in the region, highlighting how their fears, doubts, and suspicions have shaped their perception of the religious other.

The adoption and implementation of Islamic sharia legal system by twelve northern states in Nigeria has had both religious and political implications for non-Muslims. Christians and other minority religious groups perceived the move as a violation of their religious freedom, an infringement on their fundamental human right to practice their faith, and a violation of the secular stance of the Nigerian state.[217] Moreover, the Nigerian constitution explicitly prohibits the state adoption of a particular religion and upholds the right of every Nigerian to freedom of religion, including freedom to practice, propagate, and change religion or belief, both in public and in private.[218]

Christianity and Islam share much in common. Both religions profess monotheism, trace their ancestry to Abraham, have the Bible and the Qur'an (sacred books), prayer, and an eschatological dimension. While implementation of sharia in some northern states was perceived by some Muslim politicians as a way to legitimise their political strategies and programmes, for others it was an opportunity for an Islamic cultural revival and the restoration of the Islamic moral heritage that had been suppressed by the British colonial conquest.[219] On the other hand, non-Muslims (Christians and other minority groups) felt betrayed because their constitutional right to a fair hearing and their freedom to practise their faith were breached. They suspected an Islamic hidden agenda and an abuse of the democratic process that brought these state governors into public office.[220]

---

[217] Cf. Matthew Hassan Kukah, *The Church and the Politics of Social Responsibility* (Lagos, Nigeria: Sovereign Prints, 2007), 119-20.

[218] See *The Nigerian Constitution: 1963, 1979, 1999: A Compendium* (Lagos, Nigeria: Olakanmi & Co LawLords Publications, 2008), 326 and 341.

[219] Cf. International Crisis Group, *Northern Nigeria: Background to Conflict,* Africa Report, no. 168, December 2010, Dakar/Brussels, 15-16. http://www.crisisgroup.org

[220] Ibid.

The CBCN voiced their concern in these words:

> The reality on the ground in the states that have adopted sharia shows clearly that non-Muslims are being negatively and unjustly affected. They are being deprived of their means of livelihood. Fanatics are being encouraged to molest law-abiding citizens without cause. Under the prevailing circumstances, freedom to practice and propagate one's faith, guaranteed in our constitution, is being progressively eroded. The right of citizens to change their religion is often denied . . . Christian bodies are denied land on which to build places of worship . . . and are often denied access to the use of media of communication owned by state governments.[221]

Thus the Catholic hierarchy challenged the federal government on the constitutional provisions of equality as it affects every Nigerian, saying, 'We cannot continue along these lines and still pretend that we want a united, peaceful and prosperous nation.'[222] Although the federal government declared sharia incompatible with the constitutional guarantee of freedom of religion, the northern governors argued that the same constitution empowers states to establish their own judicial system.[223] In order to avoid inflaming religious passions, the federal government urged pro-sharia states in Northern Nigeria to exercise moderation in the application of sharia law.[224]

Sharia remains a controversial issue in North Nigerian religious politics. The fragile relationship between Christians and Muslims is strained further. Christians feel sharia is restrictive and marginalising—for example, in terms of acquiring land to build places of worship, educational and health institutions, and the ban on the public sale or consumption of alcohol. They also regard sharia as increasing general insecurity, especially with the recent bombing of some Christian places of worship.[225] Some political analysts have observed that although sharia is perceived by some Muslims as a way of achieving a just, safe, and less corrupt society, the reality, nevertheless, is that there is corruption in public service, and the Christian-Muslim

---

[221] Peter Schineller (ed.), *Pastoral Letters and Communiqués of the Catholic Bishops' Conference of Nigeria, 1960-2002: The Voice of the Voiceless* (Abuja, Nigeria: Gaudium Et Spes Institute, 2002), 146.

[222] Ibid.

[223] Cf. International Crisis Group, *Northern Nigeria*, 15-16.

[224] Ibid.

[225] Cf. Christians Association of Nigeria, 'Christians' Right Breached,' *Vanguard* (Nigeria), 5 September 2009. http://www.vanguardngr.com (Churches have been bombed in Bauchi, Jos, Madalla, Maiduguri, Suleja, Taraba and Yobe).

sharia divide has built and strengthened stereotypes which continue to polarise relations between the two faith communities.[226]

1.6 CONFLICTS IN NORTHERN NIGERIA: CONTRIBUTING FACTORS

This section expounds on factors that contribute to violent conflicts in Northern Nigeria. It examines how the government's inconsistent policies and ethnic and economic dynamics cause conflict and highlights the challenge of the *Almajiri* syndrome and the threat of the 'Boko Haram' Islamic sect to Northern Nigeria.

As an inevitable part of human existence, conflicts continue to shape and affect the ways in which people and communities relate to each other, presenting both challenges and the prospect for growth. Defined as the pursuit of incompatible interests and goals by different groups, conflict is intrinsic to human development and is normal in human relationships. Conflict can be triggered and exacerbated by numerous factors. However, understanding the causes, dynamics, and complexities of any conflict is important. It provides indications and strategies on how to respond to a particular situation and how to manage the conflict and build peace.[227] What are the contributing factors to violent conflicts in Northern Nigeria which must be understood within the context of the underlying forces that create and empower them?

1.6.1 INCONSISTENT GOVERNMENT POLICIES

In this sub-section, I shall provide insight on how inconsistent government policies have created crises, and I argue for the need for justice and fairness in policy-making. It can be stated that the various governments of Nigeria have not had clear policies about religious practices as regards the different religious traditions in the country, even though the Nigerian constitution guarantees religious freedom, security, and peaceful coexistence for all citizens.[228]

Whilst it would seem that the complex nature of the relationship between Muslims and Christians in Northern Nigeria would challenge the government to be just and fair to the particular needs of all religious groups, this has not been the case. For instance, whilst the federal government welcomed the Pope in 1982, similar hospitality was not accorded to the Rector of Al-Azhar University in Egypt when he visited Nigeria, as Kilani observes.[229] Another example is the Kano riots

---

[226]   International Crisis Group, *Northern Nigeria*, 16. For the discourse on stereotyping of otherness, see chapter 2.

[227]   See Francis, *Uniting Africa*, 63.

[228]   *The Nigerian Constitution*, 341.

[229]   Kilani, 'Issues and Trends on Religious Tolerance in Nigeria,' 276.

of 1991. The federal government of Nigeria granted permission to the Kano state branch of the Christian Association of Nigeria (CAN) to invite a famous German Christian evangelist to preach at a retreat in Kano. The same government refused permission to invite a veteran Islamic preacher to come to Nigeria from South Africa. When the Christian preacher arrived from Germany, Muslims were surprised and aggrieved, wondering why they had not been granted the same opportunity. A large number of protesters made their way to the emir's palace to register their dismay. A peaceful demonstration turned into mob violence.[230] In addition, government policy on pilgrimage to the holy lands (Mecca and Jerusalem) and the care of pilgrims has been supported by successive administrations. However, in some states, government provision for pilgrims' welfare board and the appointment of staff to the board is not always sensitive to the needs of the two faiths. This has remained a source of tension and division of one group against the other.

The experience in contemporary Northern Nigeria is that people have become very sensitive to the religious affiliation of those elected into public office (either as president or state governor), because their decisions and authority impinges on the religious sentiments of the people. For example, when a Muslim is voted into power as the chief executive, Christians feel marginalised ands vice-versa. Religious sensitivity cannot be downplayed as religion continues to play a significant role in the lives of the majority of Northern Nigerians. The manipulation of religious sentiments for political purposes has contributed immensely to fostering unfriendly relations between adherents of these faith communities. Perceived favouritism, marginalisation, and domination give rise to intense political competition and sometimes violent conflicts.[231] Unfortunately, the political class, in desperate attempts to secure power and control of resources, has at times demonstrated remarkable recklessness and total lack of restraint in manipulating religious sentiments by peddling stereotypes and prejudice against opposing religious groups with very sad consequences.[232]

Government policies have not been sensitive to the religious needs of all faith communities. Moreover, the democratic values of justice and fairness should become the hallmark of government in the interests of all religious groups in a multicultural, multireligious Nigerian society.

1.6.2 ETHNIC AND ECONOMIC FACTORS

In this sub-section, I shall consider the deep-rooted factors that play a major role in fuelling conflicts and triggers violence in the region. An ethnic group can be defined as community of people, closely united by shared experience, with a common

---

[230]   Ibid., 234-35.

[231]   Opeloye, 'Religious Factor in Nigerian Politics,' 354.

[232]   Cf. Francis, *Uniting Africa*, 78.

national and linguistic culture which includes history, tradition, myth, world-view, and origin.[233] These characteristics form a people with a unique and profound identity that differentiates them from others.[234] Ethnic identities are deeply rooted and complex. They are connected to race, language, land, resources, and religion. Conflicts that impinge on issues of ethnicity, access to recourses, power, and religion are difficult to manage. The argument in this chapter is that deeply-rooted ethnic feuds have found expression in religion and politics, leading to conflict violence in the region under study. In Northern Nigeria, ethnicity has been politicised and has become a source of tension and violence, as various ethnic groups try to assert their own identity. Politicians pursuing political office and personal ambition frame the interests of the political elite in ethnic terms in order to win support.[235] The examples include the following:

— The 1992 clash between the Hausas and the Kataf tribes in the Zangon-Kataf local government area of Kaduna.
— The 1991 and 1995 Tafawa-Balewa riots in Bauchi between the Hausa-Fulani/Jarawa and the Sayawa.
— The recurring clashes between the Hausas and the Birom ethnic groups in Jos Plateau.
— the conflict between the Tivs and the Jukuns in Taraba.

These struggles are the result of long-standing oppression and domination by the feudal Hausa-Fulani ruling class of Northern Nigeria and the discriminatory policy of government in appointments to public office. In the above instances, religion is only an incidental factor, as the Katafs, Sayawas, and Biroms are mostly Christians and the Hausa-Fulani and the Jarawas are Muslims. Furthermore, there is the contentious issue of indigenes versus settlers. There are situations where people have moved from their original home and have settled in another place for decades but are not recognised as having ownership rights in the new community—this, for example, continues to play a vital role in the conflicts in Jos Plateau state. Ethnic identity conflicts are complex and difficult to understand and manage, because ethnicity has a strong influence on the status of a community.

The socio-economic dimension of conflicts in Northern Nigeria cannot be overlooked. Ethnic conflicts are often triggered by one ethnic group attempting to

---

[233] See Godwin E. Irobi, 'Ethnic Conflict Management in Africa: A Comparative Case Study of Nigeria and South Africa,' 2005. http://www.beyondintractability.org/casestudy/irobi-ethnic; Ellis Cashmore, 'Ethnicity,' Dictionary of Race and Ethnic Relations (London: Routledge, 1996), 119-20.

[234] Cashmore, Dictionary of Race, 119.

[235] Francis, Uniting Africa, 78.

dominate and have more access to power and resources. Northern Nigeria continues to grapple with poverty, underdevelopment, unemployment, poor literacy, poor leadership, and corruption. Past and current political (and ethnic) leaders of Northern Nigeria have not done much to address economic poverty in the territory and do not seem to have concrete plans for salvaging the region from its economic woes. This presents a bleak, deplorable future for Northern Nigeria, a region challenged by insecurity, a growing population and religious fundamentalism. In addition, the wide gap between the rich and the poor and a large population of youth without employment opportunities create a vulnerable condition. These youths are ready targets for mobilisation and are used by politicians and other groups to cause chaos. Contemporary Northern Nigeria is an economically deprived region. Poor infrastructure and the collapse of the industries and the agricultural sector have dealt a devastating economic blow to the region. These socio-economic factors, coupled with deep-rooted ethnic and religious divides, are powerful contributing factors of conflict violence. Religion in most cases is only being used to perpetrate violence in the region.

1.6.3 THE CHALLENGE OF *ALMAJIRI* SYNDROME IN NORTHERN NIGERIA

In this sub-section, I shall focus on a traditional Islamic religious practice that has been challenged by lack of dynamism, poor planning, and the multicultural nature of modern society. The presence of *Almajiri* in many cities has continued to challenge the peace and security in the region. *Almajiri* is a corruption of the Arabic word *al-muhajir*, meaning 'the migrant'. *Almajiri* are migrant children who leave their homes and families with the latter's consent and travel to faraway towns and cities unknown to them or their families to attain Qur'anic education with a *Mallam* (teacher). They are taught to read the Qur'an and write Arabic.[236] This practice has been in existence for as long as Islam has been in (Northern) Nigeria. Some Nigerian Islamic scholars argue that the *Almajiri* command high respect in society because of the breadth of their Islamic knowledge and the authority that the Qur'anic system of education gives them.[237] However, colonialism relegated the Islamic system of education into the background when the western formal system of education was introduced. Consequently, Islamic scholarship took a nosedive when the colonial authorities treated it with disdain, making the influence of the *Mallam* gradually decrease.[238] Also, modernisation and a desire for western education have greatly

---

[236] See Aluaigba, 'Circumventing or Superimposing Poverty on the African Child,' 20.

[237] Cf. Muhib O. Opeloye, 'The Socio-Political Factor in the Christian-Muslim Conflict in Nigeria,' *Islam and Christian-Muslim Relations* 9, no. 2 (1998), 232-33.

[238] Ibid.

affected the Qur'anic school system because fewer resources and attention have been given to Qur'anic education.

As a result, the *Almajiri* face a number of difficulties—a life of complete poverty and destitution without any means of survival, medical care, or security. They have no steady source of income; they live by begging for food, money, and other needs. *Almajirs* are deprived; hence they roam about begging during the course of their Qur'anic studies. They do not undergo formal education as most of them are enrolled in Qur'anic schools with a *Mallam*. According to religious analyst Muhib Opeloye, the *Almajiris* do more begging than learning. They give their alms and extra food to their *Mallam* whose duty it is to train and care for them with whatever assistance he gets from their parents or the public.[239] After their morning religious instructions, the *Almajiris* beg and do menial jobs as they travel between towns and villages asking for alms. They go into public places such as car parks, railway stations, and market places where they are vulnerable to crime, drugs, violence, and danger of radicalisation by religious extremists.[240] Over the years, this situation has been exacerbated further by their lack of any useful skills or formal education due to the government's inability to integrate Qur'anic schools into the modern formal system of education.[241] The *Almajiri* are helpless, gullible, and an easy target for all kinds of nefarious activities such as being trafficked or mobilised.[242]

An outbreak of riots or public disturbance is an opportunity for looting and arson attacks. The *Almajiris* have been mobilised many times to fuel conflict violence. The *Almajiri* pose a major social, religious, and security threat that must be addressed urgently by the government, religious leaders, and the parents of these children. Public peace and order needs a political and social system to deal with vulnerable young people who are easily mobilised for conflict violence. Religion has a significant role to play in building public peace, but regrettably, as already discussed, it has been used to fuel violence. Nevertheless, proper religious education can strengthen grassroots peace building initiatives aimed at advancing better understanding between faith communities and challenge the government to address issues of poverty, education (*Almajiri* education), and social development. To achieve the above, the activities of the Interreligious Mediation Centre (directed by an imam and a pastor), the Nigerian Interreligious Council (NIREC), and the ongoing process of interreligious dialogue between Muslims and Christians are of paramount importance.

---

[239]   Ibid., 235.

[240]   Cf. Aluaigba, 'Circumventing or Superimposing Poverty on the African Child,' 19-20.

[241]   See BBC News, 'Child Beggars of Nigeria's Koranic Schools,' 2008. http://www.news. bbc.co.uk/go/pr/fr/-/1/world.africa.7796109.stm

[242]   Aluaigba, 'Circumventing or Superimposing Poverty on the African Child,' 22.

1.6.4 THE THREAT OF BOKO HARAM ISLAMIC SECT TO NORTHERN NIGERIA

In this sub-section, I shall focus on a practical example of how religious extremism and political-religious manipulation have brought about division, conflict, and insecurity.

In the last few years, Northern Nigeria has experienced an upsurge of violent attacks and bombing of public institutions (police stations, prisons, and army barracks), offices, and places of worship and continuous ethno-religious and political killings.[243] An extremist Islamic sect named 'Boko Haram' claims responsibility for most of these attacks.[244] The sect Boko Haram began in 2002 as a peaceful Islamic splinter group, committed to the propagation of the teachings of Prophet Muhammad and Jihad (Jama'atu Ahlis Sunna Lidda'awati wal-Jihad) led by Muhammad Yussuf, a young man from Yobe state in the north-east of Nigeria.[245] The sect started in Maiduguri by spreading their ideology that Western civilization, education, and values are sinful, Islamically unaccepted, and thus prohibited or forbidden.[246] This belief gradually earned the group the name 'Boko Haram', with *Boko* translating as 'western education' and *Haram* as 'sin' or 'forbidden' in the Hausa language.[247] From the outset, it seemed that the group was peaceful while propagating the teachings of Islam and the establishment of Islamic sharia law. The leader of the group, Yussuf Mohamed, established an Islamic school to teach their ideology. Many children and youths in north-eastern Nigeria and neighbouring countries like Chad and Niger attended the school and were indoctrinated in the sect's beliefs.[248]

---

[243] See David Smith, 'More than 700 Inmates Escape during Attacks on Nigerian Prison,' *Guardian* (United Kingdom), 08 September 2010. http://www.guardian.co.uk/world/2010/sep/08/Muslim-extremists-escape-nigeria-prison; Abdallah Abbah, 'Towards Lasting Peace in the North,' *Leadership* (Nigeria), 27 December 2011.

[244] Hamza Idris, 'Boko Haram Claims Responsibility,' *Daily Trust* (Nigeria), 26 December 2011.

[245] See Bala Muhammad, 'Still on Boko Haram . . .,' *Daily Trust* (Nigeria), 07 January 2012; Chinelo Obogo, 'Politics, Religion, Deaths and Boko Haram,' *The Sun* (Nigeria), 18 January 2012. http://www.sunnewsonline.com

[246] Abdulkareem Mohammed, *The Paradox of Boko Haram,* ed., Mohammed Haruna (Kaduna, Nigeria: Moving Image, 2010), 44 and 52.

[247] The argument of Boko Haram sect for denouncing western education and values is predicated on the view that the content of some subjects contradict the tenets of Islamic religion, e.g. the Big Bang theory, Darwinism, the law of conservation of matter and energy, and the views of some free thinkers and Philosophers that questions the existence of God.

[248] Obogo, 'Politics, Religion, Deaths and Boko Haram.'

However, some politicians began exploiting the group for political purposes, and the seemingly peaceful operations gradually became violent.[249] In 2009, the federal government of Nigeria launched an investigation into the group's activities, following reports that its members were arming themselves and planning to wage a religious war (Jihad) in the country.[250] The group reacted violently when Yussuf Mohamed was arrested by the army, handed over to the police, and killed in police custody.[251] Recently, the activities of the sect have turned into full-scale warfare, with many of its members engaging in suicide bombings. For instance, from 2010, various bomb attacks have rocked many parts of Northern Nigeria, killing and maiming innocent citizens (for example, the United Nations building in Abuja in which eighteen people were killed).[252] The sect claimed responsibility for many of these attacks and vowed not to give up their fight against westernisation.[253]

Some Nigerian social and political analysts have observed that Northern Nigeria is going through a violent phase because of poverty, ignorance, and severe economic hardship and despair, all of which create an environment where religion presents an alternative for purposeful living. For this reason, Boko Haram's message of a just and egalitarian society finds a ready audience among the dispossessed, unemployed, unschooled, and unskilled able-bodied young men who find a sense of purpose and mission as God's warriors aiming to cleanse society of moral impurities and establish an alternate order (sharia).[254] Unfortunately, such a radical perversion of purposeful life has become a theological innovation in the hands of extreme sects like Boko Haram who claim to create a new dynamic community of God where the martyrdom of suicide-bombing guarantees a robust and opulent afterlife far exceeding anything the Nigerian state can ever offer.[255]

Meanwhile, the growing uncertainty and insecurity caused by the threat of bomb blasts, especially in public places such as market places, schools, social events, and

---

[249] Cf. Abbah, 'Towards Lasting Peace in the North.'

[250] Obogo, 'Politics, Religion, Deaths and Boko Haram.'

[251] Cf. Tobi Soniyi, 'Army Absolves Self from Killing of Boko Haram Leader,' *This Day* (Nigeria), 25 October 2011. http://www.thisdaylive.com

[252] BBC News, 'Abuja Attack: Car Bomb Hits Nigeria UN Building,' 2011. http://www.bbc.co.uk/news/world-africa-14677957

[253] Cf. Monica Mark, 'Boko Haram Vows to Fight Until Nigeria Establishes Sharia Law,' *Guardian* (United Kingdom), 27 January 2012. http://www.guardian.co.uk/world/2012/jan/27/boko-haram-nigeria-sharia-law

[254] Jide Komolafe, 'Politicization of Religion and the Origins of Fundamentalisms in Nigeria,' 2012.http://www.nigeriaworld.com/feature/publication/jide-komolafe/011912.html

[255] Ibid.

churches, have remained the hallmark of Boko Haram.[256] People are killed almost every day.[257] And thus far, over a thousand people have been killed.[258] The seeming sophistication and the precision of attacks by the group have raised concerns about its source of funding and the possibility of the sect's affiliation with international terrorist groups. It is, however, alleged that the leader of the sect (Yusuf Muhamed) receives funds from his Salafist contact following two hajj trips he made to Saudi Arabia and donations from some wealthy Northern Nigerians.[259] In addition, robbery and illicit trafficking in drugs, vehicles, and other contraband goods has been associated with the sect.[260]

There are strong indications that suggest Boko Haram has links with terrorists groups. The Nigeria and the United States Africa Command's top military security intelligent report informs that Boko Haram has ties with Al-Qaeda in the lands of the Islamic Magreb and Al-Shabaab in East Africa.[261] These groups have training camps in Algeria, Mali, Mauritania, across the Sahel region and Somalia, for sharing funds and training in the use of explosive material.[262] Notwithstanding the above details, some Nigerian analysts and academics have argued that Boko Haram cannot be associated with global jihadist groups bent on attacking Western interests since their assault have been within Nigeria, even though the United Nations building in Abuja

---

[256] See Monica Mark, 'Nigerian Islamist Group's Leader Claims to be at War with Christians,' *Guardian* (United Kingdom), 11 January 2012. http://www.guardian.co.uk/world/2012/jan/11/nigeria-islamists-claims-war-christians

[257] David Smith, 'Nigerian "Taliban" Offensive Leaves 150 Dead: Islamic Group Opposed to Western Education, Boko Haram, Launches Attacks Across Four Northern Provinces,' *Guardian* (United Kingdom), 27July 2009. http://www.guardian.co.uk/world/2009/jul/27/boko-haram-nigeria-attacks

[258] 'Nigerian Death Toll from Boko Haram Attacks "Nears 1,000",' *Guardian* (United Kingdom), 24 January 2012. http://www.guardian.co.uk/world/2012/jan/24/boko-haram-killed-nearly-1000

[259] See Walker, 'What is Boko Haram?,' 3.

[260] Cf. Alexander Yonah, *Terrorism in North Africa & the Sahel in 2012: Global Reach & Implications* (Arlington, TX: International Centre for Terrorism Studies, 2013), 5. http://www.potomacinstitute.org/attachments/article/1358/Terrorism%20in%20North%20Africa%20&%20the%20Sahel.pdf; Kunle Falayi, 'Latin American Drug Cartels Fund Boko Haram, Ansaru-Report,' *Punch* (Nigeria), 09 March 2013. http://www.punch.com

[261] See John Thomas Didymus, 'Boko Haram Linking up with Al-Qaeda, Al-Shabaab says US Commander,' *Digital Journal* (June 2012). http://www.digitaljournal.com/article/327424; Uduma Kalu, 'Al-Quaeda-Boko Haram Links in Kano since 2009,' *Vanguard* (Nigeria), 24 December 2012. http://www.vanguard.com; 'Documents Link Boko Haram to Bin Laden,' 2012. http://www.world.myjoyonline.com/pages/nigeria/201204/85757.php

[262] Cf. Walker, 'What is Boko Haram?,' 3 and 4.

was hit in 2011.[263] Nevertheless, the existence and the activities of Boko Haram in the region remains a threat to the peace and security of (northern) Nigeria. Attempts by the federal government of Nigeria to dialogue with the sect have not yielded any fruit since Yusuf was killed and the present leadership of the sect has continued to evade the Nigerian authorities.

The question, however, remains this: why is it that Christians and their churches in Northern Nigeria have become the seeming target of attacks? Is Boko Haram a Jihad on Christians? Why are innocent people (Muslims and Christians) killed by this sect? Could it be a provocation to a religious war? What if Christians in turn attack Muslims? When are these killings and destruction going to end? What is the way for peace in Northern Nigeria? Given that the problem is both religious and political, in what ways can theology and politics collaborate to proffer solutions? This study in the following chapters will attempt to analyse these challenges and propose a way forward.

CONCLUSION

In this chapter, I have argued that the relationship between Christians and Muslims in Northern Nigeria has been marred by violent conflicts stemming from deep-rooted, ethnic, social, economic, and religious divides. Such divisions continue to influence self-understanding and the concept of community in its relationship with others. Meanwhile, Christians and Muslims are almost equal in number in the region. Religion continues to play a vital part in the lives of the people. However, religion remains a sensitive, divisive issue used by some individuals, groups, and politicians to further polarise Muslims and Christians. Poverty and a lack of development have created a breeding ground for conflict, violence, and insecurity.

Furthermore, the role played by the British colonial administration in the political-religious development of Northern Nigeria has affected the way each religious group has perceived the other politically since Nigeria's independence in 1960. In addition, the dominant influence of religion in politics makes religion a contentious issue between the two faith traditions. Religion is often blamed for every conflict, even though there are no logical and consistent ways to articulate and distinguish socio-political or ethnic ideologies with peculiar tendency towards violence from religious inclinations. The complex nature of conflict needs critical analysis of the situation as the seeming distinctions between religious, political, or secular conflict may not be helpful in understanding the intricacies of disputation, especially in a setting where, for instance, religion and ethnicity are perceived as one and the same phenomenon.

---

[263]   Ibid., 9.

Religion and politics must engage in proffering solutions. Theology as 'faith seeking understanding' must negotiate with politics to find a meaningful resolution, since neither religion nor politics have all the answers.[264] Moreover, the situation of Northern Nigeria calls for an Islamic and Christian theological hermeneutic of dialogue that negotiate peace in justice and love.[265] What are the ways to advance peace and better relations between Muslims and Christians in Northern Nigeria? The next chapter explores the theological potential for enhancing a better understanding between Muslims and Christians in the region, focusing on the theology of the Second Vatican Council (1962-65) *Nostra Aetate* which created the possibility for new conversations between religious traditions and a shift that has fostered new understanding about religious other.

---

[264] See Olle Kristenson, *Pastor in the Shadow of Violence: Gustavo Gutierrez as a Public Pastoral Theologian in Peru in the 1980s and 1990s* (Uppsala: Uppsala Universitet, 2009), 102.

[265] Ibid., 107-08.

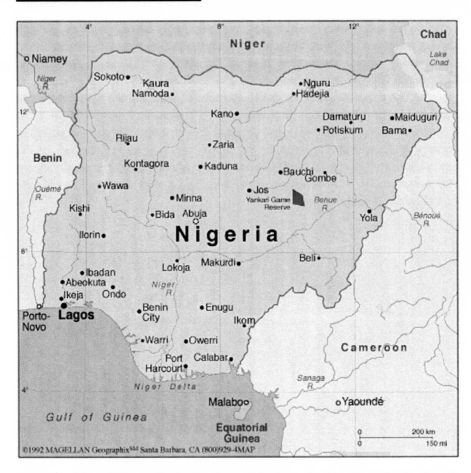

Figure 1   Map of Nigeria illustrating the section above the river Niger (north: Bauchi, Damaturu, Gombe, Jos-Plateau, Kaduna, Kano, Maiduguri, Taraba and environs) where interreligious violence is most prevalent.[266]

---

[266] Map of Nigeria, 1992. http://www.google.co.uk/search?hl=en&tbo=d&q=nigeria+states&tbm=isch&tbs=simg

Chapter 2

A Theological Analysis of the Relationship between Islam and Christianity since the Second Vatican Council

Introduction

In the preceding chapter, I provided a survey of the historical background to interreligious conflicts in Northern Nigeria. This chapter reviews relevant documents and declarations of the Roman Catholic Church (e.g. *Nostra Aetate*),[267] World Council of Churches (WCC), and the invitation to dialogue issued by the Islamic *Ummah* (community) to Christian leaders in 2007.

The *Declaration on the Relationship of the Church to Non-Christian Religions* (*Nostra Aetate*) is the official pronouncement by the Second Vatican Council of 1960-1965 of the relationship between Islam and Christianity. The aim here is to analyse and understand the position of the Roman Catholic Church's teaching with regard to other religions and Islam in particular. *Nostra Aetate* provides the theological foundation for dialogue and engagement between the Catholic Church and other religious traditions. But how far has this been effective? In what ways has this renewed perspective enhanced a positive approach to the conflicts in Northern Nigeria?

Islam and Christianity are the two largest world religions. The Qur'an contains references to Christians as 'People of the Book'.[268] At different periods and in different places, the relationship between Christianity and Islam has been marked

---

[267] 'Declaration on the Relationship of the Church to Non-Christian Religions,' 660.
[268] Qur'an 5: 14; 59-60 and 68.

both by cooperation and conflict.[269] According to Martin Bauschke, a researcher in dialogue between the three Abrahamic faiths (Christianity, Islam, and Judaism), initially Christians did not take Islam seriously since it added nothing new to what was known. The thought of a new religion was frightening as it challenged the Christian self-image of Christianity as the climax and ultimate end of God's revelation.[270] Consequently, Christians had a distorted idea of Islam, marked by ignorance, lack of understanding, and prejudice.[271] This continued for many centuries even though a few attempts were made by some Christian scholars in the Middle Ages to engage with Islam in religious dialogue. However, their achievements were minimal.[272] For centuries the position of the Roman Catholic Church was *Extra Ecclesiam Nulla Salus*, that is, there is one universal church of believers, outside of which there is no salvation.[273]

On 25 January 1959, there was a new glimmer of hope. Pope John XXIII announced to a small group of Cardinals gathered in the Basilica of St. Paul in Rome his intention to hold a general Council for the Universal Church. The aim of the Synod was to modernise the Church and its relationship to the world.[274] The Pope's motive for a Council was for the good of the Church in an attempt to address the spiritual needs of the times.[275] The Council would examine and evaluate the Church and its universal mission. Since Catholicism was on the threshold of an important

---

[269]   Tarek Mitri, 'Christian-Muslim Relations in the Arab World,' in *My Neighbour Is Muslim: A Handbook for Reformed Churches* (Geneva: Centre International Reform John Knox, 1990), 7.

[270]   Martin Bauschke, 'Islam: Jesus and Muhammad as Brothers,' in Alan Race and Paul M. Hedges (eds.), *Christian Approaches to Other Faiths* (London: SCM Press, 2008), 192.

[271]   Ibid.

[272]   Martin Bauschke, 'A Christian View of Islam,' in Lloyd Ridgeon and Perry Schmidt-Leukel (eds.), *Islam and Interfaith Relations: The Gerald Weisfeld Lectures 2006* (London: SMC Press, 2006), 142-43.

[273]   Henri Leclercq, 'Lateran Councils,' in *The Catholic Encyclopaedia*, vol. 9 (New York: Encyclopaedia Press, 1910), 18. *Note*: *Extra Ecclesiam Nulla Salus*. This was the teaching of Saint Cyprian of Carthage in the third century, upheld by the Fourth Lateran Council in 1215 and contained in the Bull of Pope Boniface VIII *Unam santam* of 1302 and reaffirmed by Pope Eugenius IV's document *Cantate Domino* of the Council of Florence in 1442.

[274]   See Guiseppe Albergo and Joseph A. Komonchak (eds.), *History of Vatican II: Announcing and Preparing a New Era in Catholicism,* vol. 1 (New York: Orbis Books, 1995), 1.

[275]   Ibid., 1-2.

historical age,[276] it was necessary to examine and update the Church's relationship with the world and other religions.[277]

The Second Vatican Council (1962-65) brought together bishops and theologians to deliberate and promote renewal in the Catholic Church. Prominent theologians such as Hans Küng, Augustine Bea, S. J, Walter Kasper, Yves Congar, O. P, Thomas Stransky, C. S. P, Karl Rahner, S. J, Edward Schilebeeckx, O. P, Hans Urs von Balthasar, Marie-Dominic Chenu, O. P, Henri-Marie de Lubac, Joseph Ratzinger, and Michael Schmaus made valuable contributions to the ideas of the bishops who took part in the debates of the Council. The Second Vatican Council document has sixteen chapters. *Nostra Aetate,* which deals with the Church's relations with non-Christian religions, has five paragraphs, the third of which deals specifically with the Catholic Church's relation to Islam.

This chapter of my thesis is divided into seven sections. The first section examines *Nostra Aetate.* It highlights the ground-breaking position of the Catholic Church in relation to other religious traditions and the efforts made since 1965 to foster better relations with Islam in particular. It further looks at other Roman Catholic Church statements about non-Christians in relation to *Nostra Aetate* and the theology of salvation in other official documents: *Dignitatis Humanae* (on *Religious Freedom)* of 1963,[278] *Redemptoris Missio* of 1990, and *Dominus Iesus* of 2000 with a survey of the Catholic Church's recent attempts in dialogue.

The second section reviews the *World Council of Churches' Guidelines on Dialogue with People of Living Faiths and Ideologies* of 1979 and further assesses recent achievements of the Council.

The third section considers the document *A Common Word: Muslims and Christians on Loving God and Neighbour* issued in 2007 by the Islamic *Ummah* to Christian leaders and the corresponding response by Christian leaders.

The fourth section examines the relationship of Christians and Muslims in Northern Nigeria since the promulgation of *Nostra Aetate.* It recognises the social, ethnic, economic, and political factors and the use of religious sentiments to fuel conflicts in the region. In addition, it focuses on the efforts of religious, governmental, and non-governmental institutions to harness available local resources in the region for peace building.

The fifth section considers the potential for Christian-Muslim dialogue. Are there common grounds for dialogue between the two faith traditions? How can common

---

[276]   Ibid., 4.

[277]   Xavir Rynne, *Vatican Council II* (New York: Orbis Books, 1999), ix.

[278]   'Declaration on Religious Freedom,' *Dignitatis Humanae,* in Walter M. Abbott (ed.), *The Documents of Vatican II,* trans. Joseph Gallagher (London: Geoffrey Chapman, 1966), 678-88.

themes such as belief in one God, revelation prayer, scriptures, and a common ethic enhance better Christian-Muslim understanding?

The sixth section reviews the efforts of Christian-Muslim dialogue since *Nostra Aetate*, highlighting the progress recorded as a result of such mutual cooperation.

The seventh section explores the theme of stereotyping and prejudice as these shape and affect how Christians and Muslims perceive each other in Northern Nigeria, contributing to sustained violent conflicts.

2.1 THE VATICAN II DECLARATION ON THE RELATIONSHIP OF THE CHURCH TO NON-CHRISTIAN RELIGIONS (*NOSTRA AETATE*)

In this section, I shall review the theology of the Second Vatican Council document *Nostra Aetate* to establish the position of the Roman Catholic Church in its relations with other faith traditions, especially Islam, and how the Church's contemporary stance is enhancing interreligious dialogue.

Nostra Aetate (*In Our Time*) was promulgated by the Second Vatican Council on 28 October 1965. It marked a significant turning point in the Church's life and attitude towards other religions, especially Islam. The Council was radical in ushering a new era and a dynamic vision. It marked a paradigm shift from a Church that was conservative to a Church that is open, receptive, and accommodating of other religious traditions. The promotion of religious freedom and dialogue with other religions is reflected in the Church's *Pastoral Constitution on the Church in the Modern World* (*Gaudium et Spes*).[279] Furthermore, in its declaration on religious freedom (*Dignitatis Humanae*), the Church states that every human person has a right to religious freedom and no one should be forced to act in a manner contrary to his or her own beliefs, nor is anyone to be restrained from acting in accordance with his or her own beliefs privately or publicly, alone or in association with others.[280] The right to religious freedom has its foundation in the very dignity of every human person as created by God. The Church admonishes that the right to religious freedom should be recognised in the constitutional law governing society and thus a civil right.[281]

Nostra Aetate is the Catholic Church's teaching on its relationship with people of other religious traditions, with particular attention to Jews, Muslims, Hindus, and

---

[279] Cf. 'Pastoral Constitution on the Church in the Modern World,' in Walter M. Abbott (ed.), *The Documents of Vatican II*, trans. Joseph Gallagher (London: Geoffrey Chapman, 1966), no. 40, 238.

[280] 'Declaration on Religious Freedom,' 678-79.

[281] Ibid.

Buddhists.[282] The Church recognised religious diversity and made a move to engage with other religions traditions.

> In our times, when every day men are being drawn closer together and ties between various peoples are being multiplied, the Church is giving deeper study to her relationship with non-Christian religions. In her task of fostering unity and love among men, even among nations, she gives primary consideration in this document to what human beings have in common and to what promotes fellowship among them.[283]

Furthermore, the document acknowledges that men and women look to various religions for answers to the perturbing questions and mysteries of the human condition and the meaning and purpose of life.[284] From ancient times until now, different peoples have recognised a certain hidden reality ever present in the course of human history. The Church acknowledges and rejects nothing of what is true and holy in these religions (no. 1).[285] The Church has high regard for these religions and calls on all Christians to engage in prudent dialogue-discussions and collaboration with members of other religions in order to foster better understanding.[286]

I now turn to how the Vatican Council viewed its relationship to Muslims (Islam) specifically. *Nostra Aetate* is very positive about Islam when it states:

> The Church has . . . high regards for Muslims. They worship God, who is one, living and subsistent, merciful and almighty, the creator of heaven and earth, who has spoken to men. They strive to submit themselves without reserve to hidden decrees of God, just as Abraham submitted himself to God's plan, to whose faith Muslims eagerly link their own. Although not acknowledging him as God, they worship Jesus as a prophet, his virgin Mother they also honour, and even at times devoutly invoke. Further, they await the day of judgement and the reward of God following the resurrection of the dead. For this reason they highly esteem an upright life and worship God, especially by way of prayer, alms-deeds and fasting.[287]

---

[282] See John McDade, 'Nostra Aetate and Interfaith Dialogue,' *The Pastoral Review* 1, no. 6 (2005), 8.

[283] 'Declaration on the Relationship of the Church to Non-Christian Religions,' no. 1, 660.

[284] Ibid., 661.

[285] Ibid.

[286] Ibid.

[287] Ibid., 739-40.

The declaration, 'the Church has high regard for Muslims', represents a remarkable change, the beginning of a new outlook on Christian-Muslim relations, and a positive attitude towards other religions. [288] The Fathers of the Council sincerely acknowledged the unpleasant, suspicious, and uncharitable relations that had existed between Christianity and Islam in the past, often characterised by hostilities, violence, and war. Consequently, the Council urges that all should forget past misunderstandings and strive to build sincere mutual relationships through dialogue.[289]

The theological basis for the Catholic Church's open and positive attitude and outreach to other religions stems from its awareness of God's love for all human beings (*Dogmatic Constitution on the Church Lumen Gentium*). God's salvation is open to all human beings, since the grace of God is active in different religions. Human beings are all invited to respond freely to God according to the dictates of their conscience, as they search for the truth.[290]

According to educationist David Creamer, *Nostra Aetate* represents a break from the traditional teaching of the Church about salvation as reflected in the Fourth Lateran Council (1215), which stated that 'there is one universal Church of believers outside of which there is no salvation',[291] and the Council of Florence (1438-1445) in the document *Cantate Domino*. It explicitly states that

> the Council firmly believes, professes, and proclaims those not living within the Catholic Church, not only pagans, but also Jews and heretics and schismatics, cannot become participants in eternal life . . . and that no one, whatever almsgiving he has practised, even if he has shed blood for the name of Christ, can be saved, unless he has remained in the bosom and unity of the Catholic Church.[292]

This was the official Roman Catholic Church's teaching and attitude towards believers in other religions until 1965. The promulgation of *Nostra Aetate* meant a new beginning and hope of fostering dialogue with Islam.[293] The document recognises and promotes points of common concern between Christianity and Islam in order to

---

[288] Michael L. Fitzgerald, 'Christian Muslim Dialogue: A Survey of Recent Developments,' 2000. http://www.sedos.org/english/fitzgerald.htm

[289] 'Declaration on the Relationship of the Church to Non-Christian Religions,' 662.

[290] 'Declaration on Religious Freedom,' 678-88.

[291] David G. Creamer, 'Nostra Aetate Building Bridges of Friendship and Cooperation Over 40 Years,' *Perspective: A Semi-Annual Examination and Application of Catholic and Ignatian Thought* 8, no. 1 (2001), 5.

[292] Ibid.

[293] Ibid., 6.

build a good relationship and respect for Islam by understanding the content of its message.[294]

The Church desires to end the long and sad history of indifference, misunderstanding, discrimination, denunciation, oppression, and violent persecution that has marked its relationship with Islam. The hope is to move from monologue to dialogue, collaboration, openness, and friendship.[295] In the document on the Church, *Lumen Gentium*, the Council expresses the belief that God's plan of salvation also includes Muslims who acknowledge the creator and the faith of Abraham. Christians and Muslims adore the one merciful God.[296] This means that Christianity and Islam have something in common, a meeting point. Hence dialogue between the two will lead to better understanding, love, and mutual respect. Such an encounter will diminish prejudice among Muslims and Christians and promote a friendlier attitude towards other people.[297]

The document prudently encourages Christians, through dialogue and collaboration, to bear witness to the Christian faith and acknowledge the spiritual and moral goodness found in Islam and other religions to promote peace for all.[298] In addition, the Church seeks to find points of common concern with other religions to establish an authentic dialogue of understanding, an attitude of respect, and a readiness to accept the truth in others.[299]

It is important to note that in spite of the success of *Nostra Aetate*, the document had a very difficult and troubled passage in the Council. Misunderstanding, intrigues, indiscretion, and fears, especially of a political nature, were part of the hurdles in the debates. Some bishops and theologians were mentally unprepared for the topic of

---

[294] Arthur Kennedy, 'The Declaration on the Relationship of the Church to Non-Christian Religions, Nostra Aetate,' in Matthew L. Lamb and Matthew Levering (eds.), *Vatican II: Renewal Within Tradition* (New York: Oxford University Press, 2008), 397-98.

[295] Bernd Groth, 'From Monologue to Dialogue in Conversation with Nonbelievers or the Difficult Search for Partners in Dialogue,' in Rene Latourelle (ed.) *Vatican II: Assessment and Perspectives: Twenty-Five years After (1962-1987)*, vol. 3 (New York: Paulist Press, 1989), 184-88.

[296] 'Dogmatic Constitution on the Church,' in Walter M. Abbott (ed.), *The Documents of Vatican II*, trans. Joseph Gallagher (London: Geoffrey Chapman, 1966), 34-35; *Catechism of the Catholic Church with Modifications from the Editio Typica* (New York: An Image Book Douleday, 1995), 242-44.

[297] Donna Orsutu, 'On the Front Line: Christifideles Laici and Lay Involvement in Interreligious Dialogue,' in Denis C. Izizoh C (ed.), *Milestones in Interreligious Dialogue: A Reading of Selected Catholic Church Documents on Relations with People of Other Religions* (Rome: Ceedee Publications, 2002), 189.

[298] 'Declaration on the Relationship of the Church to Non-Christian Religions,' 739.

[299] Kennedy, 'The Declaration on the Relationship of the Church,' 398.

'the relationship of the Church with non-Christian religions'.[300] This resulted in the document being vehemently opposed by bishops and theologians who felt that such a declaration would lead to the secularisation of Catholicism and a collapse of Church authority. Some described the action of the Council Fathers as the worst tragedy the Church had ever experienced. Others argued that the texts of Vatican II had revealed the errors of the modern world that had been repeatedly condemned by the Popes.[301]

Furthermore, *Nostra Aetate* has been criticised as being out with the Church's concern for ecumenism and against the ordinary teaching authority (magisterium) of the Church, the Councils, and the Popes.[302] Initially, *Nostra Aetate* was not intended to make a statement about other religions in general. The Church wanted to make a statement about its relationship with the Jewish people. However, a number of bishops and theologians observed that the topic of Catholic-Jewish relations was not in the ecumenical schema and advocated it should be the subject of a separate document.[303] Meanwhile, bishops from the Eastern Churches did not want the Council to say anything about the Jews for political reasons, so that the Church could not be perceived by Arab governments as favouring the recognition of the state of Israel and by implication a statement against Muslims.[304]

Nevertheless, in his book *From the Enemy to a Brother: The Revolution in Catholic Teaching on the Jews, 1933-1965*,[305] historian John Connelly observes that the Roman Catholic Church in the Second Vatican Council underwent a trial of conscience that eventually brought about persuasive transformation in the Churches' teaching regarding the Jews. The Catholic Church had for long held that the coming of Jesus (the new covenant) had nullified the Jewish religion and God's covenant with the Jewish people. Nonetheless, the Second Vatican Council was momentous

---

[300] Reinhard Neudecker, 'The Catholic Church and the Jewish People,' in Rene Latourelle (ed.), *Vatican II: Assessment and Perspectives: Twenty-Five Years After (1962-1987)*, vol. 3 (New York: Paulist Press, 1989), 283-84.

[301] Cf. Daniele Menozzi, 'Opposition to the Council (1966-84),' in Giuseppe Alberigo, Jean-Pierre Jossua, and Joseph A. Komonchak (eds.) *The Reception of Vatican II* (Washington, DC: Catholic University of America Press, 1987), 327-31.

[302] Mahmut Aydin, *Modern Western Christian Theological Understanding of Muslims since the Second Vatican Council* (Washington, DC: The Council for Research in Values and Philosophy, 2002), 22-24.

[303] Robert A. Graham, 'Non-Christians,' in Walter M. Abbott (ed.), *The Documents of Vatican II*, trans. Joseph Gallagher (London: Geoffrey Chapman, 1966), 656. The intention of Pope John XXIII was for the Council to make at statement on the Church's relationship with Jews.

[304] Kennedy, 'The Declaration on the Relationship of the Church,' 398.

[305] John Connelly, *From Enemy to Brother: The Revolution in Catholic Teaching on the Jews, 1933-1965* (Cambridge, MA: Harvard University Press, 2012).

in bringing this teaching to an end by its outright condemnation of all forms of anti-Semitic and racist creed aimed at the Jews. This shift was made possible with the contributions of Jewish-Christian convert and Catholic priest John Maria Oesterreicher, who made valuable theological inputs that influenced the debates out of which came the groundbreaking statement on the Jews.[306]

The first draft of *Nostra Aetate* was silent about other religions, including Islam. Some Council Fathers insisted that if the Council was urging Christians to show a more positive attitude towards the Jews, then a similar attitude should be encouraged towards Muslims and a large number of other religious people who are not Christians or Jews. Thus, debates about the document had to be suspended. The Pope asked the Conciliar commission headed by Augustine Bea to prepare a text on Islam. The final text which deals with non-Christian religions was presented, discussed, voted on, and finally promulgated.[307]

However, the opposition continued. Conservative bishops opposed its promulgation theologically, arguing that the text weakened the difference between Catholicism and all other religions, seeing them as of the same value, leading to non-differentiation and discouraging missionary activities. Others expressed further dissatisfaction with the document, describing it as very weak and confined to making polite remarks about other religions.[308] And more recently, Mona Siddiqui, a professor of Islamic studies, has observed that 'the declaration made by the Catholic Church at the Second Vatican Council was a groundbreaking innovation in the Church's relations with people of other faiths. Yet, in relation to Islam, the document *Nostra Aetate* is a very carefully worded text, which accords respect for Islam while withholding acknowledgment of any real legitimacy'.[309]

Despite these concerns, theologian Thomas Stransky, a participant in the Second Vatican Council, concludes that *Nostra Aetate* is optimistic. It condemns every form of discrimination and harassment due to race, colour, way of life, or religion and opened the Church to dialogue with other faith communities, respecting their

---

[306] For more discourse on the historical perspective of the significant contributions of Jewish-Christian converts to the historic teaching of the Roman Catholic Church in *Nostra Aetate,* see ibid., and John Connelly, 'Converts Who Changed the Church: Jewish-Born Clerics Helped Push Vatican II Reforms,' *The Jewish Daily Forward* (New York) 30 July 2012. *http://www.forward.*

[307] Aydin, *Modern Western Christian,* 23.

[308] Graham, 'Non-Christians,' 659.

[309] Mona Siddiqui, 'The Spirit of Declaration,' *America, the National Catholic Weekly,* 193, no. 12 (October 2005). http://www.americamagazine.org/content/article.cfm?article_id=4431

identity, rituals, and conduct.[310] Moreover, such dialogue begins with what people have in common, being created in the image of God and promoting fellowship with each other in a shared history. Nonetheless, a reading of other recent official Roman Catholic documents raises a number of questions and concerns in the light of *Nostra Aetate*. The next section examines such texts.

2.1.1   *NOSTRA AETATE* IN RELATION TO OTHER ROMAN CATHOLIC CHURCH DOCUMENTS

In this sub-section, I shall examine other relevant Roman Catholic pronouncements, such as the *Declaration on Religious Freedom (Dignitatis Humanae)* of 1963, *Redemptoris Missio* of 1990 and *Dominus Iesus* of 2000, to highlight the seeming contradictions and tensions present in these documents.

As discussed above, *Nostra Aetate* stressed emphatically the importance of interreligious dialogue and the need for the Roman Catholic Church to respect and collaborate with people of other religions traditions. However, a closer study of *Nostra Aetate* presents a number of challenges that cannot be ignored when read in the light of other Church documents such as *Dignitatis Humanae* of 1963, *Redemptoris Missio* of 1990, and *Dominus Iesus* of 2000.

In the Roman Catholic Church's document *Dogmatic Constitution on the Church Lumen Gentium* (no. 16), the Church expresses that 'the plan of salvation also includes those who acknowledge the Creator. In the first place among these there are Muslims, who, professing to hold the faith of Abraham, along with us adore the one merciful God.'[311] In *Nostra Aetate* (no. 3), the Church esteems Muslims because they adore the one living and enduring God, the maker of heaven and earth.[312] Here, the Council Fathers acknowledge the first and most important article of Muslim faith, namely the oneness of God, the worship of the only God, and life after death.[313]

However, *Nostra Aetate* is silent about Muhammad, whom Muslims revere as prophet and messenger of God. It carefully mentions 'Muslims' and not 'Islam' as a religion. Does this mean that Islam is not recognised by the Catholic Church as a religion? The document mentions Abraham as a model of faith whom Muslims strive to emulate by submitting themselves to God as he did, but it does not mention

---

[310]   Thomas Stansky, 'The Genesis of Nostra Aetate,' *America, the National Catholic Weekly* 193, no. 12 (October 2005). http://www.americamagazine.org/content/article.cfm?article_id-4431

[311]   *Dogmatic Constitution on the Church*, no. 35.

[312]   'Declaration on the Relationship of the Church to Non-Christian Religions,' 660.

[313]   Ibid., 29-30.

whether Muslims are historically linked to him (Abraham) through Ishmael.[314] Furthermore, the document does not mention the Holy Qur'an the most sacred book, 'the mother of the Book' (*umm al-kitab*), 'the word of God' (*kalimat Allah*) for Muslims,[315] which they honour as scripture, the original as well as the final revelation of God. How does the Qur'an relate to the Christian Bible? What should be the attitude of the Christian to the Qur'an, and is it to be accepted as equal to the Bible?

In the Second Vatican Council document on religious freedom (*Dignitatis Humanae*) of 1963, the Church states that every human person has the right to religious freedom. This means that in matters of religion, human beings should be free from coercion by individuals, social groups, or any authority. No one is to be forced to act in a manner contrary to his/her own beliefs, nor is anyone to be restrained from acting in accordance with his own beliefs whether privately or publicly, alone or in association with others.[316] This right has its foundation in the very dignity of the human person.[317] Therefore, religious freedom gives the right to Muslims to practise their faith and worship God in the way prescribed by Islam. In the light of *Lumen Gentium* (no. 16), God's plan of salvation includes those who acknowledge the Creator.[318] Muslims acknowledge God as creator; thus they have the right and freedom to believe and worship God according to their faith and share in the gift of eternal salvation. Does it mean that Islam is a way of salvation? Conversely, *Dignitatis Humanae* (no. 1) states that 'God himself has made known to mankind the way in which men (women) are to serve Him and thus be saved in Christ . . . We (the Catholic Church) believe that this one true religion exists in the Catholic and apostolic Church . . .' Furthermore, Pope John Paul II's declaration of 2000 *Dominus Iesus* (no. 20) presents the Roman Catholic Church as the 'Universal Sacrament of Salvation', because the Church is always united in a mysterious way to the Saviour Jesus Christ, its Head, and subordinate to him. The Church has, in God's plan, an indispensable relationship with the salvation of every one. The Pope further asserts that it is clear that it would be contrary to the Christian faith to consider the Roman Catholic Church as one way of salvation alongside other religions or seen as complementary or substantially equivalent to her, even if these are said to be converging towards the eschatological kingdom of God.[319]

---

[314]   Küng, *Islam: Past, Present and Future*, 46-49. Qur'an 2: 125.

[315]   See also Küng, *Islam: Past, Present and Future*, 64-65 and John L. Esposito, *The Future of Islam* (New York: Oxford University Press, 2010), 39.

[316]   'Declaration on Religious Freedom,'678-79.

[317]   Ibid.

[318]   'Dogmatic Constitution on the Church,' no. 35.

[319]   Pope John Paul II, *Congregation for the Doctrine of the Faith Declaration Dominus Iesus on the Unicity and Salvific Universality of Jesus Christ and the Church* (Rome Vatican City: Libreria Eitrice, 2000), no. 21. http://www.vatican.va/raman_curia/congregations/ cfaith/documents/rc_con_cfaith)doc_20000806_dominus-iesus_en.html

The Roman Catholic Church does not consider Islam and other religions as ways to eternal salvation. But how does religious freedom of the individual and other religious groups apply in this situation? On the one hand, Muslims are included in God's plan of salvation. On the other, the salvation of Muslims (and of those who are not formally and visibly members of the Catholic Church) exists in Christ in the Roman Catholic Church. Does this imply that the Christian faith is superior to other faiths? *Nostra Aetate* (no. 3) acknowledges that Christians and Muslims believe and together worship the one true God (Muslims revere Jesus as a prophet), and the Spirit of God has been working in the hearts and history of peoples, in cultures and religions (*Dominus Iesus* no.21).

In addition, the teaching of Roman Catholic Church in *Redemptoris Missio* and *Dominus Iesus* poses a challenge to genuine Christian-Muslim dialogue, because dialogue could be perceived by Muslims as an indirect process of proselitisation by the Catholic Church.[320] It is important to ask, in view of salvation (see the discussion in the next section), what the theological status of Muslims (and Islam) is in relationship to the Catholic Church? What does it mean to be a Muslim in regards to Christianity? Besides, Islamic faith teaches that salvation is a gracious gift from the merciful and transcendent God, a 'straight path leading to paradise . . . free of ambiguities, confusions, inconsistencies or mysteries and this path is revealed in the Qur'an'.[321] The believer has the responsibility to turn to the one God in faith and prayer, following the path laid down by God through the Prophet as revealed in the Holy Book (Qur'an 9: 20 and 81, 22: 78, 25: 52, 29: 69, 69: 10-13).

There is need for theological clarification and discussion of these questions by the Catholic Church. However, the Catholic Church continues to exhort Christians to prudently and lovingly enter into dialogue with Muslims (and other religions) for mutual knowledge and enrichment. Pope John Paul II's 1990 encyclical, *Redemptoris Missio* (no. 55), stresses the need for dialogue and mission. The mission here is to evangelise non-Christians, because the Catholic Church recognises the goodnes and truth in other religions only as a remote preparation for the gospel of Christ (*Notsra Aetate* no.2). Although the Catholic Church acknowledges the possibility of salvation for Muslims, the Church does not recognise Islam as a way of salvation.[322] Therefore, dialogue witnessing the values of the Christian Gospel to non-Christians remains

---

[320] Jacques Dupuis, 'Interreligious Dialogue in the Church's Evangelizing Mission Twenty Years of Evolution of a Theological Concept,' in Rene Latourelle (ed.), *Vatican II: Assessment and Perspectives: Twenty-Five Years After (1962-1987),* vol. 3 (New York: Paulist Press, 1989), 241.

[321] Riffat Hassan, 'What Does It Mean to Be a Muslim Today?' *Cross Current* 40, no. 3 (1990). http://www.crosscurrents.org/hassan.htm

[322] Aydin, *Modern Western Christian*, 39-43.

a task and a fundamental mission of the Church.[323] But how does that impact on grassroots Christian-Muslim dialogue in Northern Nigeria? How does the theological understanding of salvation in both faith traditions shape the concept of community and religious otherness? The next section focuses on salvation as an invitation to share in the eternal reign of God.

2.1.2 THE THEOLOGY OF SALVATION IN TERMS OF REDEMPTION, OR RECONCILIATION AND THE HOPE OF SHARING IN THE REIGN OF GOD

In this sub-section, I shall consider the Roman Catholic theology of salvation as it affects non-Christians (other religious traditions) vis-à-vis *Nostra Aetate*.

The theology of salvation is an invitation to reconciliation and the hope of sharing in the reign of God to which all are invited. Islam and Christianity both have an eschatological outlook. The Bible and the Qur'an both invite believers (Christians and Muslims) to faith in the one God and the promise of eternal life. Christians and Muslims mutually share in the belief in the one God, reward of heavenly bliss for the just and damnation for the unjust. The *Catechism of the Catholic Church* (no. 161) states that 'without faith it is impossible to please God, without faith no one will attain justification nor will any one obtain eternal life'.[324] What do salvation, eternal life, and redemption mean? Whose salvation, eternal life for whom, redemption from what? Is eternal life for all or for just a set of people who belong to a particular tradition of faith?[325] What does it mean when St. Paul says, 'God wants all to be saved and come to the knowledge of the truth' (1 Tim. 2: 4) and that through Jesus Christ humanity has been reconciled to God and to one another? (Rm. 5: 10; 2 Cor. 5: 18-19). What is the theological relationship between salvation and reconciliation? If salvation from a theological perspective means eternal life in God,[326] would eternal life exclude Muslims (and non-Christians)?

The messianic mission of Jesus was to reconcile humanity to God and offer the hope of sharing in the reign of God. If the death and resurrection of Jesus Christ reconciled humanity to God, the gift of salvation and eternal life must be all inclusive

---

[323] Pontifical Council for Inter-Religious Dialogue, Dialogue and Proclamation Reflection and Orientation on Interreligious Dialogue and the Proclamation of the Gospel of Jesus Christ (1) (Rome, 1991). http://www.vatican.va/roman_curia/pontifical_councils/interelg/documents/rc_pc_interelg_doc_19051991_dialogue-and-proclamatio_en.html (1991)

[324] *Catechism of the Catholic Church*, 50.

[325] Werner G. Jeanrond, 'What Salvation Do We Await? Aquinas Lecture 2010, Part 1,' *Open House*, no. 203 (June-July 2010), 7.

[326] *Catechism of the Catholic Church*, 287-90.

and all embracing.[327] This means that Christians and Muslims have been reconciled to God through Christ. The Gospel of John 14: 6, 'I am the way the truth and life', is an invitation for all to participate in the reconciling act of Christ. It is not limited and cannot be limited. No one is excluded. Everyone is invited because God's radiance draws from each one the resonance only he or she can bring in being reconciled to God and in communion with all.[328] Muslims share with Christians the hope of never-ending joy and are drawn into relationship with God. Christ has united all (Christians and Muslims) in a unique way to God. Our hope is limited within our lived experience, so there is need to liberate our hope to be transformed in support of the coming reign of God.[329] The reconciling activity of Christ is unique because it brings humanity to total union with God, an explicit sign of the presence and love of God for all.

It can be said, therefore, that all who accept God's offer of this relationship in hope, by striving to follow God's part, loving selflessly and sincerely following their conscience, are reconciled with God and have a share in the reign of God (Acts 10: 34-35, Rm. 2: 10 and Qur'an 1: 6-7; 42: 52-53).[330] Through their faith, Muslims and Christians are drawn in a deeper sense into a mystery that is multidimensional in God who is the source and coherence of who we are and are transformed in the reconciling mission of Christ, hoping that together they (Christians and Muslims) may share in the communion of the reign of God.[331] Therefore, salvation remains an invitation to be reconciled with God and one another in the hope of sharing the reign of God to which the grace of God invites all humans to partake (Matt. 20: 1-6 and *Gaudium et Spes* no.22).[332]

The future of interreligious dialogue will continue to be challenged by questions arising from eschatological debate as it affects people of other faiths in relationship to the position of the Roman Catholic Church. Bearing in mind the great commission by Jesus Christ as recorded in the Bible (Matt. 28: 18-20, Acts 1: 6-8), there is need for further critical theological investigation and discourse on the subject of 'salvation' before the Roman Catholic Church's invitation to dialogue with people of other faiths can bear genuine fruit.

---

[327] Cf. Anthony Kelly, *Eschatology and Hope* (New York: Orbis Books, 2006), 14-17.

[328] See 'Commentary on John 14 New Testament,' in *Christian Community Bible Twenty-Seventh Edition* (Diliman, Philippines: Claretian Publications, 1999), 226.

[329] Jeanrond, 'What Salvation Do We Await?' 7.

[330] See 'The Church and Other Believers,' in Richard Viladesau and Mark Massa (eds.), *World Religions: A Sourcebook for Students of Christian Theology* (New York: Paulist Press, 1994), 14-15.

[331] Kelly, *Eschatology and Hope*, 28-29.

[332] Joseph Ratzinger, 'Are Non-Christians Saved?' 2007. http://www.beliefnet.com/Faiths/Chrisitanity/Catholic/2007/01/Are-Non-Christians-Saved.aspx

In spite of the seeming contradictions examined above, the Roman Catholic Church has made some concerted effort since the promulgation of *Nostra Aetate* to reach out in dialogue to other religions, including Muslims. What achievements have been recorded in building Christian-Muslim relations (in the world) in Northern Nigeria?

2.1.3 A Survey of Recent Achievements in Christian-Muslim Relations since the Promulgation of Nostra Aetate in 1965

In this sub-section, I shall make a brief assessment of the efforts and achievements of the Roman Catholic Church in fostering interreligious dialogue from 1965 till today.

Since the promulgation of *Nostra Aetate* on 28 October 1965, the Catholic Church has made strategic efforts to implement the aspirations of the Council Fathers. A major step was taken by Pope Paul VI when he instituted the 'Secretariat for Non-Christians' that today bears the name 'Pontifical Council for Interreligious Dialogue', a part of the Vatican administrative body, the Roman Curia.[333] This Pontifical Council is responsible for promoting mutual understanding, respect, and collaboration between the Catholic Church and other religious traditions, as well as encouraging the study of religions and training in the art of dialogue.

The Pontifical Council has a specific commission to foster dialogue and relations with Muslims. This entails collaboration, analysis, promotion of mutual understanding, and information publication.[334] Also, for the purpose of study and research, a Pontifical Institute of Arabic and Islamic studies was set up in Rome in 1964. All academic and scientific activities in the institute are aimed at preparing students to meet Muslims respectfully and in mutual cooperation. This specialised formation is based upon the intensive study of the Arabic language which is essential to study of fundamental Islamic texts.[335] One of the earliest achievements of the Pontifical Council was the publication of guidelines for dialogue between Christians and Muslims in 1969 and a later revised edition in 1981. This text has been translated

---

[333] Fitzgerald, 'Christian Muslim Dialogue.'

[334] See *Bulletin of the Pontifical Council for Interreligious Dialogue* (Rome Vatican City, 1993).

[335] Denis C. Izizoh (ed.), *Milestones in Interreligious Dialogue: A Reading of Selected Catholic Church Documents on Relations with People of Other Religions* (Rome: Ceedee Publications, 2002), 428; 'Pontifical Institute for Arabic and Islamic Studies,' http://www.en.pisai.it/il-pisai-la-storia.aspx

into a number of languages, including Arabic.[336] It is a handbook and a guide for all those who engage in the process of dialogue.

The Catholic Church has continued to make great strides in its positive attitude and desire to dialogue with Muslims. For example, the visit of Cardinal König to Cairo in 1965 and his historic lecture on monotheism at Al-Azhar opened the way for exchange visits. Many Islamic spiritual leaders were invited to Rome, where they were welcomed and received by Pope Paul VI. In December 1970, a delegation from the Supreme Council for Islamic Affairs in Cairo visited Rome, and this visit was reciprocated in 1974 by Cardinal Pignedoli, Msgr. Rossano and Fr. Abou Mokh. That same year, Cardinal Pignedoli visited Saudi Arabia and met King Faysal. Later that year, a Saudi delegation of experts in Islamic law in Europe went to Rome for discussions on human rights. Working sessions were held with Vatican officials, and they had an audience with Paul VI. These visits, dialogue, and spiritual sharing have helped the relationship between Christianity and Islam to grow. This is evident in the continual exchange and the prompt response of various religious leaders to Pope John Paul II's invitation in 1986 to Assisi to pray for peace in the world. Muslims and other religious leaders honoured the invitation.[337] Furthermore, a common commitment to pray for peace was again evident in 1993 and 2002 when the Pope and the Catholic Bishops of Europe called for a special weekend of prayer in Assisi for peace in Europe and the Balkans. Muslims from nearly every country of western Europe, as well as a delegation from Bosnia, took the trouble to be present at that interfaith gathering.[338]

Since 1967, the Secretariat for Non-Christians (Pontifical Commission for Interreligious Dialogue) has developed a tradition of addressing a message of peace and goodwill to Muslims all over the world at the end of Ramadan. In recent years, care has been taken to have this message translated into the various languages used by Muslims.[339]

In the last forty years, the Pontifical Council for Interreligious Dialogue has been involved in organising dialogue between Christians and Muslims. According to Michael Fitzgerald, a past director of the Pontifical Council, in March 1969,

---

[336] Groth, 'From Monologue to Dialogue,' 184-85.

[337] Fitzgerald, 'Christian Muslim Dialogue.'

[338] *Peace: A Single Goal and a Shared Intention* (Vatican City: Pontifical Council for Interreligious Dialogue, 2002), 5-6.

[339] *Meeting in Friendship: Messages to Muslims for the End of Ramadan* (Vatican City: Pontifical Council for Interreligious Dialogue, 2003), 8-77; 'Message for the End of Ramadan 'Id al-Fitr 1429H./2008a.d. Christian and Muslims: Together for the Dignity of the Family,' *Pontifical Council for Interreligious Dialogue* http://www.vatican.va/roman_curia/pontifical_councils/interelg/documents/rc_pc_interelg_doc_20080919_ramadan2008_en.html

twenty Christians and Muslims gathered in Cartigny (Geneva), hosted by the World Council of Churches, to explore the possibilities of dialogue and plan for the future. This led to an international meeting held in Broumana (Lebanon) in July 1972, with fifty participants representing Muslims and Christians in attendance. Furthermore, meetings were held between the Secretariat for Non-Christians and the Supreme Council of Islamic Affairs, in Rome in December 1970, and in Cairo in September 1974.[340] However, Christians observed the seeming passivity of the Muslims, as most initiatives seemed to have been made by the Christians. This provoked some Muslim university lecturers in Tunisia to launch a series of Christian-Muslim seminars. Consequently, in 1974, five seminars were held in Tunisia with the theme 'Muslim and Christian Responsibility faced with the Problem of Development'. In 1976, a Christian-Muslim seminar was held in Tripoli, Libya, organised by the Muslims, with about 500 theologians and people from different walks of life present.[341]

In more recent times, dialogue has been ongoing between the World Islamic Call Society and the Pontifical Council for Interreligious Dialogue. The first preliminary meeting was held in 1989, and since then various colloquia have been held: Rome 1990, Malta 1990, Tripoli 1993, followed by a workshop in Vienna in 1994 and a meeting in Rome 1997. The Royal Academy for Islamic Civilization and Research, based in Jordan, initiated a dialogue with Christians. The first of such dialogues was arranged with the Anglican Church's commission in St. George's House, Windsor Castle, in the United Kingdom, to which various Christian denominations were invited. Prince Hassan of Jordan initiated direct dialogue with the Catholic Church. Consequently, the Pontifical Council for Interreligious Dialogue agreed to co-sponsor a series of colloquia in which the Church in Jordan participated. Six consultations have taken place between 1989 and 1997.[342] Furthermore, since 1994, a series of colloquia has been held between Tehran and Rome, organised jointly by the Pontifical Council for Interreligious Dialogue and the Secretariat of Interreligious Dialogue, Ministry of Culture and Islamic Guidance, Tehran, Iran. The most recent colloquium was held in Rome in April 2008, in which both sides agreed to promote mutual respect, the strengthening of relations, and continuous dialogue.[343]

---

[340] Cf. Fitzgerald, 'Christian Muslim Dialogue'; Akasheh Khaled, 'Nostra Aetate: 40 years Later,' *L'Osservatore Romano* (Rome) 28 June 2006. http://www.ewtn.com/library/CHISTORY/chrstnsmslms.htm

[341] Maurice Borrmans, *Interreligious Documents 1: Guideline for Dialogue between Christians and Muslims, Pontifical Council for Interreligious Dialogue* (New York: Paulist Press, 1981), 115-19; Fitzgerald, 'Christian Muslim Dialogue.'

[342] Borrmans, *Interreligious Documents*.

[343] Cf. Pontifical Council for Interreligious Dialogue: Sixth Colloquium Joint Declaration of the Pontifical Council for Interreligious Dialogue (Vatican) and the Centre for Interreligious Dialogue of the Islamic Culture and Relations Organisation (Tehran,

In many parts of the world, there have been ongoing regional interreligious meetings between Muslims and Christians, for example, in Africa, Asia, and the Middle East. The first of these meetings was held in Rome 1998. It was organised by the Pontifical Council for the countries of North Africa, Mauritania, and Egypt, with the theme 'Coexistence in the Midst of Differences'. Similar meetings were held in Ibadan, Nigeria, in 1974, 1991, and in Thailand in 1994. In 1990, the Council of Catholic Patriarchs of the East held three consecutive working sessions with their Muslim counterparts and published the proceedings in Arabic and French.[344]

Dialogue takes place continually at both national and local levels in various countries around the world. The Catholic Bishops Conferences of different countries and Catholic dioceses have set up commissions to arrange dialogues with Islam. In Nigeria, the Catholic Bishops Conference set up a Department of Mission and Dialogue within the Catholic Secretariat to organise and foster Muslim-Christian dialogue.[345]

The desire to continue the ongoing dialogue led to the formation of two joint committees between the Pontifical Council for Interreligious Dialogue and the Islamic Economic Social and Cultural Organization (ISESCO). These committees meet annually to exchange ideas on topics of common interest and to evaluate the current situation. It also provides a forum for ongoing communication.[346] Other Christian bodies such as the World Council of Churches, the Anglican Communion, and the Lutheran World Federation in Sweden work in collaboration with the Pontifical Council for Interreligious Dialogue in Rome. These bodies continue to make vital contributions through visits, seminars, conferences, symposia, lectures, workshops, and publications on different aspects of dialogue.[347]

Pope John Paul II's and Pope Benedict XVI's visits to Islamic countries and the welcome accorded them, remain significant testimonies to the progress and achievements the Church has made since the promulgation of *Nostra Aetate*. Such

---

Iran). 2008. http://www.vatican.va/roman_curia/pontifical_councils/interelg/documents/rc_pc_interelg_doc_20080430_rome-declaration_en.html

[344] Christian W. Troll, 'Catholic Teachings on Interreligious Dialogue. Analysis of some Recent Official Documents, with Special Reference to Christian-Muslim Relations,' in Jacques Waardenburg (ed.), *Muslim-Christian Perceptions of Dialogue Today* (Leuven: Peeters, 2000), 244-51.

[345] Dewan A. Danjuma, 'Mission and Dialogue Department of the Catholic Secretariat of Nigeria,' in Joseph Salihu (ed.), *Interreligious Dialogue and the Sharia Question* (Kano: Jaleyemi Group, 2005), 17-20.

[346] Fitzgerald, 'Christian Muslim Dialogue.'

[347] See Andrew White, *The Vicar of Baghdad Fighting for Peace in the Middle East* (Oxford: Monarch Books, 2009), 123-42.

visits boost relationships with Muslim leaders around the world and point to a future of genuine commitment to dialogue and peace.[348]

For Kenny, the current emphasis on Christian-Muslim dialogue is encouraging in spite of a few disappointments.[349] Each meeting seemed more daring and more promising than the previous one. However, local churches in the Middle East and Nigeria, where relationships with Muslims have not been easy, have challenged or resisted the efforts of the Pontifical Council to organise meetings with Muslims in their territory.[350] European Christians express their dissatisfaction when Muslim immigrants in Europe are given full religious liberty while Christians in Saudi Arabia are not allowed the same freedom of worship.[351] Furthermore, some Muslims are mistrustful of dialogue partly because some Islamic fundamentalists create the impression that dialogue is a new Christian missionary strategy to destabilise Islam. These concerns have led the Pontifical Council to give preference to meetings with Muslims at local levels, without publicity. Such meetings have been very fruitful in focusing on issues of religious dialogue, peace building, and collaboration.[352] Moreover, the theology of *Nostra Aetate* has stimulated other Christian traditions to be proactive in mapping the way forward to engage with people of other faith traditions.

The next section reviews the document *Guidelines on Dialogue with People of Living Faiths and Ideologies*, 1979, and further achievements of the World Council of Churches with regard to dialogue.

---

[348] Cf. John Borelli, 'Christian-Muslim Relations in the United States: Reflections for the Future after Two Decades of Experience,' *Christian-Muslim Relations in the United States* 94, no. 3 (2004), 322; Richard Owen, 'Saudi King Extends Hand of Friendship to Catholic Church,' *The Times* (Scotland), 18 March 2008; 'Turkey, November 28-1December 2006, Pope Encourages Turkish Christians to Live in Harmony with Muslims,' in Pope Benedict XVI, The Life and Works of Joseph Ratzinger 'Opening the Doors to Christ,' *A Special Publication from the Publishers of The Universe Catholic Weekly* (Washington), 2008, 52-53.

[349] Kenny Joseph Kenny, *Views on Christian-Muslim Relations* (Lagos, Nigeria: Dominican Publications, 1999), 106.

[350] Ibid.

[351] Ibid.

[352] Ibid.

2.2 THE WORLD COUNCIL OF CHURCHES: GUIDELINES ON DIALOGUE WITH PEOPLE OF LIVING FAITHS AND IDEOLOGIES, 1979

In this section, I shall review the 1979 World Council of Churches document *guidelines for dialogue with people of other faith traditions* and assess the recent achievement of the Council.

The World Council of Churches (WCC) is a fellowship of various Christian denominations. The Roman Catholic Church has a formal working relationship with the WCC but is not a member of the Council. The aim of WCC is to foster ecumenism, seek unity of purpose, and build understanding in collaboration among various Churches and communities around the world. It promotes the work of mission and evangelism and engages in Christian service by meeting human need through WCC partner agencies. It also attempts to break down barriers between people and uphold justice and peace. Its remit also includes education, ecumenical formation, and interreligious dialogue and cooperation among different faith traditions.[353] The WCC recognises the plurality of religions and emphasises dialogue as a means of building better understanding, friendship, and collaboration among faith communities.

The promulgation of *Nostra Aetate* in the 1965 gave impetus to the initiative and outreach of WCC to other faith communities to dialogue. In 1979, the WCC published *Guidelines on Dialogue with People of Living Faiths and Ideologies*. The document contends that Christians live in communities with people of other faiths. Mutual dialogue is necessary for better understanding as well as being concerned with the problems of modern socio-political, economic, and cultural life. Through dialogue, the Christian becomes aware of the goal of peace and justice for all in the wider community.[354] Moreover, interreligious dialogue offers the opportunity to deepen knowledge of the religious other and learn to respect the integrity and distinctiveness of each religious tradition.[355] Christianity has existed alongside other religions where it has been challenged by universal alternatives to the faith. This implies that theological hostility and neutrality towards these religions is no longer

---

[353]   OIKOUMENE, *An Introduction to the World Council of Churches* (Geneva: World Council of Churches, 2010), 3-5. http://www.oikoumene.org/fileadmin/files/wcc-main/2010pdfs/WCCintro_ENG.pdf

[354]   World Council of Churches, 'Guidelines on Dialogue with People of Living Faiths and Ideologies, 1979.' http://www.oikoumene.org/resources/documents/wcc-programmes/interreligious-dialogue-and-cooperation/interreligious-trust-and-respect/guidelines-on-dialogue-with-people-of-living-faiths-and-ideologies.html

[355]   Ucho Hans, Charlotte Venema, and Areane Hentsch (eds.), *Changing the Present, Dreaming the Future: A Critical Moment in Interreligious Dialogue* (Geneva: World Council of Churches, 2006), 4-5.

tenable in a world of religious pluralism.[356] However, the aim of interreligious dialogue is not to downplay other religious traditions but to foster better relationships which are only found at the deepest levels of human life and experience.

Furthermore, WCC recommends that dialogue sessions should always be planned together ecumenically, wherever and whenever it is possible.[357] Planning for dialogue necessitates regional and local guidelines. Dialogue partners should be sensitive to the religious, cultural, and ideological diversity of their local situation. It is important that partners in dialogue have the freedom to define and express themselves as they wish because dialogue is an opportunity for participants to get to know each other and their religion better thus generating a friendly attitude in the community.

Dialogue can be more fruitful when its participants actually share their lives together and develop spontaneous encounters, enterprises, and experiences. Partners in dialogue deepen their ideological and religious commitments and learn from the other while always being aware of their own cultural loyalties. When dialogue entails sharing in celebrations, rituals, worship, and meditation, it is of paramount importance that respect and honour be accorded to the ritual expressions. Dialogue will often include extending and accepting invitations to visit each other as guests and observers in family and community rituals, ceremonies, and festivals. Such occasions provide excellent opportunities to enhance mutual understanding.[358] Dialogue encounter requires mutual respect, listening, trust and confidence between parties with an open mind and a deep sense of vocation. It is with such commitment to the importance of dialogue that the Central Committee of WCC offers this Statement and Guidelines to the Churches.[359]

The World Council of Churches Dialogue with People of Living Faith (DFI), in the light and spirit of Vatican II's *Nostra Aetate,* has continued to foster dialogue relationships with other religious traditions around the world and give support to member churches involved in this process. DFI, in collaboration with the Pontifical Council for Interreligious Dialogue, Rome, organised a series of visits, conferences, lectures, symposia, and dialogue sessions with Muslims and members of other religions and made public statements supporting dialogue. At the initiative of WCC, various consultation meetings and dialogues have been held between Muslims and Christians from 1976 to 1988.[360] More dialogues have been held between 2002 and

---

[356]   Wesley Ariaraja, *The Bible and People of Other Faiths* (Geneva: World Council of Churches, 1985), 61-63.

[357]   Cf. World Council of Churches, 'Guidelines on Dialogue.'

[358]   Joseph Kenny, 'Guidelines on Dialogue with People of Living Faiths and Ideologies World Council of Churches, Geneva 1979,' *Views on Christian-Muslim Relations* (Lagos, Nigeria: Dominican Publications, 1999), 122-40.

[359]   Ibid.

[360]   Borrmans, 'Interreligious Documents,' 119.

2008. More recently, in May 2010, representatives of WCC visited Nigeria as part of its activity to promote peace through interreligious dialogue and to respond to the need for a continuous advocate for peace between Christians and Muslims in Nigeria.[361] The WCC team challenged and encouraged religious leaders in Nigeria to work for mutual peace and harmony through dialogue. The team met with the Nigerian Interreligious Council (NIREC), an initiative of Christian and Muslim leaders, to urge Muslims and Christians to live in peace with one another. They called on the government and the security agencies in Nigeria to be even-handed in their quest to build and sustain peace.[362]

The document of the World Council of Churches is, to my mind, appropriate for contemporary Nigeria, as it encourages and sets out the guidelines for dialogue. The next section focuses on the invitation to dialogue by the Islamic *Ummah* to the Christian community in the document *Common Word*.

2.3 *A Common Word*: Muslims and Christians on Loving God and Neighbour

In this section, I shall review *Common Word*, an invitation to dialogue from Islamic leaders and scholars to Pope Benedict XVI and other Christian leaders. I shall highlight the background of this call to dialogue and emphasise the Christian response to the invitation.

The Qur'an *Surah Al-'Imran* (the family of 'Imran) chapter 3: 64, reads thus:

> O People of the Book, Come to common terms as between us and you: that we worship none but Allah (God); that we associate no partners with Him; that we erect not, from among ourselves, lords patrons other than Allah. If they turn back, say: Bear witness that we at least are Muslims bowing to Allah's Will.[363]

In *Nostra Aetate*, the Catholic Church refers to bygone quarrels and dissension between Christians and Muslims and pleads that all forget the past and urges that a sincere effort be made on both sides to achieve mutual understanding through dialogue.[364] Christians and Muslims today find themselves in various historical,

---

[361] Cf. World Council of Churches, 'Overcoming Violence Churches Reconciliation and Peace: WCC Living Letters Team Calls on Religions to Work for Peace in Nigeria,' 2010. http://www.overcomingviolence.org/en/news-and-events/news/dov-news-english/article/7839/wcc-living-letters-team-c.html

[362] Ibid.

[363] Qur'an Chapter 3: 64.

[364] 'Declaration on the Relationship of the Church to Non-Christians Religions,' 740.

personal, and socio-political circumstances which call for mutual dialogue.[365] As mentioned above, this has been the task of the Pontifical Council for Interreligious Dialogue since 1965.

The speech of Pope Benedict XVI during the pontiff's visit to Regensburg, Germany, in September 2006, in which he quoted a fourteenth-century Byzantine Emperor, Manuel II Palaiologos stirred an angry reaction from the Muslim world.[366] In October 2007, the Muslim *Ummah* issued a document called *A Common Word Between Us and You*, which is an invitation and a response to the Pope's address.[367] *A Common Word Between Us and You* is a proposal, an open invitation to dialogue. It was initially launched as an open letter signed by 138 leading Islamic scholars from Egypt, Syria, Oman, Bosnia, Russia, and Istanbul, addressed to Pope Benedict XVI and world Christian denominations. The proposal is based on verses from the Qur'an and the Bible, which both share the golden commandment of paramount importance—the love of God and love of neighbour. Based on this common ground, it called for peace and harmony between Christians and Muslims.[368] The document states that Islam and Christianity are the two largest religions in the world, together making about 55 per cent of the world's population. Hence a relationship of goodwill and friendship between these two religious communities is the most important factor in contributing to meaningful interreligious peace around the world.[369]

Prince Ghazi of Jordan acknowledged that past Muslim-Christian relationships have often been marred by deeply-rooted historical, cultural, and racial misunderstanding, suspicion, prejudice, hatred, and violence. It is, therfore, important to make peace and live in harmony in the twenty-first century. Moreover, Christianity and Islam both profess to be religions of peace. The Qur'an and the Bible both enjoin worship of the one God and the commandment to love God and neighbour.[370] *A Common Word* further stresses that both the Bible and Qur'an contain the foundation

---

[365] Borrmans, 'Interreligious Documents,' 10.

[366] Bauschke, 'A Christian View of Islam,' 139.

[367] Miroslav Volf, 'A Common Word for a Common Future,' in Miroslav Volf, Ghazi bin Muhammad, and Melissa Yarrington (eds.), *A Common Word Muslims and Christians on Loving God and Neighbour* (Cambridge, UK: William B. Eerdmans Publishing, 2010), xii and 18-19.

[368] Ghazi bin Muhammad, 'On a Common Word between Us and You,' in Miroslav Volf, Ghazi bin Muhammad, and Melissa Yarrington (eds.), *A Common Word Muslims and Christians on Loving God and Neighbour* (Cambridge, UK: William B. Eerdmans Publishing, 2010), 3.

[369] John Longhurst, 'Muslim Project Invites Christians Towards Peace,' 2009. http://www. acommonword.com

[370] Muhammad, 'On a Common Word between Us and You,' 6-12.

of peace. Although there are significant differences in articles of belief, Islam and Christianity share the same divine origin and the same Abrahamic heritage.[371]

Since the advent of the *Common Word* initiative in October 2007, Christian leaders around the world have responded positively to this invitation to dialogue. Pope Benedict XVI and the Vatican expressed their deep appreciation of the initiative. While not denying the differences between Christianity and Islam, both Muslims and Christians can concentrate on what unites them as the basis for friendship and understanding. In the same vein, the Anglican Archbishop of Canterbury, Rowan Williams, welcomed the letter, stating that it is a clear reaffirmation of the potential to further develop the existing dialogue and common action between Christians and Muslims. Various other Christian groups have responded favourably to the invitation.[372]

The *Common Word* initiative has led to a number of spontaneous community dialogues in different parts of the world: Bangladesh, Britain, Canada, India, Pakistan, the United States, and South Africa. It has also become the subject of major national and international seminars, workshops, symposia, lectures, and meetings. In November 2008, the first *Common Word* Annual Catholic-Muslim Forum was held in the Vatican in Rome. In the same year, the Mediterranean Dialogue of Cultures was held. Yale University organised a series of conferences in collaboration with the Yale Centre for Faith and Culture. Much progress has been made as more institutions join in the project of the *Common Word*. Within these few years, *Common Word* has gained wide acceptance in both religious and academic circles; the main aim remains to explore the common basis for dialogue and peace building in the world.[373] Cardinal Jean-Louis Tauran, the president of the Pontifical Council for Interreligious Dialogue, observed that relations with Muslims have improved significantly in recent years. However, one of the greatest challenges at present is how to extend the greater openness shown by Muslim and Christian leaders to the ordinary Muslims and Christians.[374] Dialogue between Muslims and Christians must be built and sustained by existing bonds beginning with mutual recognition of the common elements in both faiths.[375]

A Common Word Between Us and You is timely. It provides a platform for dialogue between Christianity and Islam in Nigeria. It is a call to focus on what

---

[371] Longhurst, 'Muslim Project.'

[372] Ibid.

[373] Muhammad, 'On a Common Word between Us and You,' 12-15; Longhurst, 'Muslim Project.'

[374] See John Thavis, 'Vatican Official: Relations with Muslims Better, but Problem Remains,' 2009. http://www.catholicnews.com/data/stories.cns/0902850.htm

[375] Troll, 'Catholic Teachings on Interreligious Dialogue,' 243.

Christianity and Islam have in common while addressing issues of mistrust and suspicion and the political, social, economic, and ethnic reasons for conflicts.

2.3.1 QUR'ANIC SCHOLARS INTERPRETATION OF THE *COMMON WORD* INVITATION (*SURA AL'IMRAN 3: 64*)

Islamic historical records testify that there have been many attempts over the centuries to develop a dialogue relationship between Muslims and Christians from the time of the Prophet to the interfaith cooperation advocated by twentieth-century Muslim leaders. These endeavours, however, echo the Qur'anic invitation to the People of the Book (Christians and Jews) to come together with Muslims on a 'Common Word'. The *Common Word* initiative can be considered a continuation of an earlier Islamic tradition even though Islamic scholars and commentators have given varied interpretation of the text.

Qur'anic commentators have tried to understand and explain the meaning of the Qur'anic verse, *Come to a common word between us* (Q3: 64). Some have argued that although the Qur'an describes the *Common Word* as a mutual agreement to worship only one God, it does not limit the application of the term to a single interpretation. Any initiative that promotes better understanding and cooperation between Christians and Muslims should be understood as part of that Qur'anic invitation.[376] In the same vein, some Qur'anic scholars explore the exclusive while others the inclusive approach in their interpretations to include, for example, common themes of ethics, justice, fairness, and righteousness. Other commentators limit the invitation to the People of the book to only those who share the Abrahamic heritage while others understand it to include those of other religions other than Jews and Christians.

In addition, some Qur'anic commentators contend, how can this Qur'anic injunction be the starting point for a contemporary Muslim-Christian dialogue when the obvious meaning of the verse clearly indicates that worship be directed to the one God which constitutes a rejection of the foundational tenet of the Christian Faith.[377] Others, however, have observed in the invitation a genuine sincerity to build a good relationship between the two faith communities. They see in the phrase *Common Word* a mutual word or a mutually agreed word, a message and a statement on which Muslims and Christian can establish a theological foundation for dialogue. For instance, commentators like Ibn Jarir al-Tabari (AD 923) suggests that the People of the Book addressed in this verse are the Jews and Christians, drawing from the

---

[376] Cf. Zeki Sartoprak, 'How Commentators of the Qur'an Define 'Common Word,' in John Borelli (ed.), *A Common Word and the Future of Christian-Muslim Relations* (Washington, DC: Prince Alwaleed Bin Talal Centre for Muslim-Christian Understanding, 2009), 35.

[377] Ibid.

tradition of a group of Christians from the region of Najran who dialogued with the Prophet. However, Fakhr al-Din al-Razi (AD 1209) argues that considering the context of the verse in question, the Prophet attempted to convince the Christians in a debate about the truth of his message. The Christians were unwilling to accept his perspective. The Prophet then invited them to gather together, intending to curse them, but sensing the Prophet's honesty, they made a treaty with him instead. For him, the context of debate and the concession can be interpreted as emphasising the need to convert Christians and Jews to Islam. Hence those who do not insist on conversion are in fact distorting the meaning of the text.[378] Other Qur'anic commentators like Al-Qurtubi (AD 1273), Abu Hayyan (AD 1353), Ismail Ibn Kathir, Abd al-Rahman al-Tha'alibi (AD 1470), Mahmud al-Alusi (AD 1924), Hamdi Yazir (AD 1942), and Sayyid Qutb (1966) all suggest that the *Common Word*, given the context of dialogue between the Prophet and the Christians of Najran, is a fascinating invitation addressed to the People of the Book (Christians and Jews) which develops into a dialogue relationship between Christians and Muslims in Medina. This provides a valuable model for contemporary interfaith dialogue activities. In their opinion, such an invitation cannot be exclusive and limited to the time of the Prophet or those who debated with him. Some commentators hold that the *Common Word* is a meaningful statement of justice, fairness, equality, and a divine invitation to all previous prophets as well as Prophet Muhammad and relevant even in the present times. It is a call to dialogue on certain values shared by all human beings; hence the verse is not only a theological point of agreement between Christians and Muslims but also a set of values shared universally by all humans and an invitation to a common word where all are equal.[379]

However, scholars like Bediuzzaman Said Nursi (AD1960), the earliest twentieth-century advocate for positive Christian-Muslim relations for the future of world peace argues that the invitation in the time of the Prophet was to the *Ahl al-Kitab* (People of the Book), but in the present times it is addressed to *ahl al-maktab*, the educated people. He contends that the common root word for both *kitab* and *maktab* indicates that the Qur'an in this century speaks to people of knowledge. By issuing such an invitation, the text presents its message to those who are educated.[380] For him, Christian-Muslim dialogue should centre on themes which both traditions agree upon and avoid those areas of differences. Nursi asserts that the Qur'an does not invite the People of the Book to reject all previous faith. Instead, it calls people to build on the Scripture in their own traditions as if the Qur'an says, believe in the past prophets and the divine books and believe Muhammad and the Qur'an because the early prophet gave credence to his coming.[381] Nevertheless, Nursi

---

[378] Cf. Ibid., 38.

[379] See ibid., 39-41.

[380] Ibid., 41.

[381] Ibid., 42.

stressed the importance of Christian-Muslim dialogue with focus on common ground rather than on differences since this will be in the interests of world peace and benefit both faith traditions.

Generally, within Islamic and Christian traditions, there are those who vehemently oppose the idea of Christian-Muslim dialogue cooperation. Conversely, it can also be said that adherents of both traditions have shown great enthusiasm towards building mutual relations at local, national, and international levels. Those leaders who strongly oppose the idea of Christian-Muslim dialogue on the basis that Qur'an 3: 64 (Come to a common word between us) is distorted, ignore also the verse that reads, *Debate with the People of the Book in the most beautiful manner* (16: 125). Nevertheless, there is hope in light that those who promote Christian-Muslim dialogue are rooted in the main teaching of Islam and are exemplary within the Islamic *Ummah*. Prominent figures in this century such as Fethullah Gulen, Faisal Mawlawi, and other scholars in Egypt, Lebanon, and of course Jordan and other parts of the Arab world all continue to advocate and work towards harmonious Christian-Muslim relations. Their efforts represent a very important step to dialogue between the two faith traditions in order to foster peace through mutual understanding. The 'Common word' initiative for me is a stepping stone and a catalyst to boosting the efforts of Christian and Muslim scholars which can lead to more sustainable dialogue relations.

2.4 THE HISTORY OF THE RELATIONSHIP BETWEEN CHRISTIANS AND MUSLIMS IN NORTHERN NIGERIA SINCE *NOSTRA AETATE* (1965)

In this section, I shall focus on the historical perspective of the relationship between Christians and Muslims in Northern Nigeria since the promulgation of *Nostra Aetate*. It highlights the social, ethnic, economic, and political factors and the use of religious sentiments to fuel conflicts in the region. In addition, I will appraise the efforts of religious, governmental, and non-governmental institutions to harness the region's available local resources for peace building.

As I have discussed above in Chapter 1, Christian-Muslim relations in Northern Nigeria have not always been cordial. According to Demola Abimboye, a journalist in Nigeria, since independence in 1960 Nigeria has witnessed more than fifty religious crises, especially in the North.[382] Nigeria is a multiethnic and multireligious country. Ethnicity, religion, and politics are intricately intertwined in deceptive and destructive ways.[383] It is important to note that, although the conflict in Northern Nigeria may be termed 'religious', many factors give rise to the conflicts. Deep-rooted socio-ethnic,

---

[382] Abimboye, 'The Damages Religious Crises Have Done to the North.'

[383] Gana Abba Shettima, 'Religious Politics without Religion,' *Daily Trust* (Nigeria), 20 May 2010.

political, and economic divides, past historical colonial experience, and the manipulation of religious sentiments have strengthened stereotypes and sharpened the misconception about the other. This has continued to divide the country along political, ethnic, social, and religious lines resulting in violent conflicts.

Since independence, Nigeria has been grappling with political, social, economic, and ethnic issues of insecurity, poverty, corruption, unemployment, and underdevelopment. These concerns have contributed immensely to polarise Nigerians, resulting in frequent riots and civil unrests. The main cause of such riots may not be religious; a good example is the situation in Jos Plateau, where the cause may be ethnic or political but is manifested in religious attacks resulting in loss of life, burning, and destruction of churches.[384] Furthermore, political competition for power between the North and the South of Nigeria is aggravated by manipulation of religious sentiments. The introduction of Islamic sharia law in the Bauchi, Borno, Gombe, Jigawa, Kaduna, Kano, Katsina, Kebbi, Niger, Sokoto, Yobe, and Zamfara states of Northern Nigeria has fuelled violent religious clashes.[385] Meanwhile, suspicion and lack of trust has given rise to continual accusations and counter accusations between Christians and Muslims. Political leaders are accused of marginalising those belonging to religious traditions other than their own. For example, when a Christian is in position of authority, he or she is accused of marginalising Muslims, and vice versa.[386] The poor level of education in Northern Nigeria is often blamed on Christian missionaries, who are accused of systematic educational discrimination, aided by the British colonial imperialists.[387] All these aforementioned elements have shaped Christian-Muslim relations in the region.

However, the story of Nigeria is not just gloom, destruction, and violence. Much is being done to improve relations. *Nostra Aetate* has been a source of inspiration within the Roman Catholic Church in Nigeria, influencing religious circles in the country. Faith communities, traditional community leaders, scholars, and some politicians have taken bold steps to address the incessant recurrence of interreligious violence. The tension that has existed between the two faith communities over the years has challenged leaders to address issues of violence by collaborating with each other. For instance, in 1973, the Nigerian Supreme Council for Islamic Affairs (NSCIA) was established, with the aim of bringing Muslims together politically and

---

[384] Cf. Seriki Adinoyi, 'ECWA Laments Attacks on Its Churches,' *This Day* (Nigeria), 12 June 2010; Seriki Adinoyi, 'Jos: ECWA Calls for Sack of Army Chief,' *This Day* (Nigeria), 19 June 2010.

[385] 'Political Sharia,' 10 and 96-99.

[386] Saliu Gbadamosi, 'FOMWAN Advocates Equal Opportunity for Muslims,' *Tribune* (Nigeria), 01 May 2010.

[387] Matthew A. Ojo, 'Pentecostal Movements, Islam and the Contest for Public Space in Northern Nigeria,' *Islam and Christian-Muslim Relations* 18, no. 2 (2007), 175-88.

religiously in one organisation. The Jamalat-ul-Nasril Islam (JNI) and the Council of Ulema were established as educational, missionary, and advisory committees on Islamic affairs to the NSCIA.[388] On the Christian side, the CBCN and the Catholic Secretariat of Nigeria (CSN) have been in existence since 1956 (the CSN is the administrative base of the CBCN). In 1976, the CAN was established to bring together the different Christian denominations in Nigeria. Christian churches that constitute CAN include the Christian Council of Nigeria, Christian Pentecostal Fellowship of Nigeria (CPFN/PFN), Organisation of African Instituted Churches (OAIC), and the Evangelical Churches of West Africa (ECWA/TEKAN).[389] These Churches come together in an ecumenical dialogue with Islam.

The CSN has a department for mission and dialogue, with the sole aim to dialogue with Islam and other religions. Each Catholic diocese in Nigeria has a Diocesan Commission for Interreligious Dialogue to reach out to people of different faith traditions in a spirit of dialogue and collaboration.[390] The CSN and the Nigerian Supreme Council for Islamic Affairs (NSCIA) have had numerous meetings to address social, political, and religious concerns and collaborate together with the government in addressing the causes of conflicts in Northern Nigeria. For example, a meeting was held in Abuja in 2002 about the crisis situation in Jos. In 2005, a workshop was held in Kano and Kaduna on the question of sharia law and peaceful coexistence. In June 2010, a peace building workshop was organised for both Muslim and Christian youths and leaders in Kano.[391]

In September 1999, the Nigerian Interreligious Council (NIREC) was jointly established by Christian and Muslim leaders in Nigeria. The Council's aims are as follows:

- To foster dialogue in order to understand the true teachings of the two religions, Christianity and Islam.
- To create a permanent and sustainable channel of communication and interaction, thereby promoting dialogue between Christians and Muslims.
- To provide a forum for mutual cooperation between Muslims and Christians and to address issues of conflict violence.
- To serve as a platform to express cordial relationships among various religious groups and the government.

---

[388] Deji Ayegboyin, 'Religious Association and the New Political Dispensation in Nigeria,' *Journal for Studies in Interreligious Dialogue* 15, no. 1 (2005), 103-06.

[389] Ibid.

[390] Danjuma, 'Mission and Dialogue,' 19-20.

[391] Joseph Salihu (ed.), *Interreligious Dialogue and the Sharia Question* (Kano: Jaleyemi Group), 2005. See also Adamu Abuh, 'Praying and Working for Peace in Kano,' *Guardian* (Nigeria), 24 June 2010. http://www.guardiannewsngr.com

These aims and objective are to be achieved through continuous dialogue meetings, religious and peace education, discussions, conferences, seminars, and workshops.[392] NIREC continues a programme of seminar workshops, meetings, consultative forums, and lectures. In January 2009, a Youth Summit on Interreligious Dialogue and Peaceful Coexistence was held in Minna. Three hundred delegates attended from throughout Nigeria. The purpose was to introduce Christian and Muslim youths to dialogue and peace building strategies. In June 2010, NIREC organised a consultative meeting of African religious leaders in Abuja, Nigeria, to discuss the ways religion, theology, and politics can collaborate to advance peace, security, and interfaith harmony in Africa.[393] At the meeting, politicians were encouraged to form policies to address issues of religious and ethnic crises in Africa, highlighting the dangers of religious and ethnic manipulation for political interest. Politicians were further challenged to engage with theologians to create an atmosphere for dialogue, peace building, and harmony between faith communities.[394] As mouthpiece for dialogue and peace building, the NIREC advocates regular interfaith and inter-communal meetings to check recurring ethno-religious crises in (Northern) Nigeria. NIREC collaborates with government and security agencies to intervene in crises situations to restore peace and order.[395] The CAN and Jamalat-ul-Nasril Islam are encouraged to work with NIREC to strengthen peace between faith communities through interreligious dialogue encounter.

Another institution for Muslim-Christian dialogue and intervention is the Interfaith Mediation Centre (IMC) based in Kaduna, Northern Nigeria. The Centre was set up by James Wuye, a Christian pastor, and Muhammad Ashafa, a Muslim imam. The two had organised youth militia groups (Christian and Muslim) to plan and execute religious violence between Christians and Muslims in Kaduna and Jos. The Mediation Centre is a sign of their individual conversion, healing, and forgiveness. The pastor and imam continue to work together to promote dialogue, reconciliation, peace, and mutual coexistence between different faith communities. The Interfaith Mediation Centre aims to achieve the following:

- Mediate and encourage dialogue among youths, women, religious leaders, and the government.

---

[392] *Constitution of the Nigeria Interreligious Council* (Abuja, Nigeria: NIREC, 2001), 1-7.

[393] Nkechi Oyendika and Laolu Akande, 'African Religious Leaders Meet in Abuja to Work for Peace,' *Guardian* (Nigeria), 15 June 2010.

[394] Isa Abdulsalami and Nkechi Oyendike, 'Jonathan Blames Religious, Ethnic Crises in African Politicains,' *Guardian* (Nigeria), 16 June 2010.

[395] Michael Ishola, 'NIREC Scribe Advocate Interfaith, Inter-Communal Dialogue,' *Tribune* (Nigeria), 20 June 2010.

- Promote a culture of mutual respect and openness to religious, cultural, and historical diversity within the community.
- Propagate the values and virtues of religious harmony and peaceful coexistence.
- Serve as a resource for conflict intervention, mediation, and mitigation in and beyond Nigeria.

The Centre organises workshops, lectures, seminars, meetings, and training for various religious groups. They also network with other faith-based organisations and agencies that support dialogue and peace building.[396]

Furthermore, religious leaders, traditional rulers, individuals, government, and other stakeholders continue to be more proactive in encouraging dialogue between Christians and Muslims. The Sultan of Sokoto (and the leader of all Muslims in Nigeria), Muhammad Sa'ad Abubakar, for instance, said thus in a speech recently:

> The series of religious crises witnessed in many Nigerian cities in the last two decades, especially in the Northern states, has been very injurious to Muslim-Christian relations. These crises significantly undermined the basis of our collective existence that took generations to build and nurture. These crises have resulted in massive loss of life and material resources. However, these unfortunate incidents have neither the social base nor the religious justification in Nigerian society as many families have co-existed and continue to co-exist in peaceful harmony. Our goal must be to establish harmonious Muslim-Christian relations based on dialogue, toleration and mutual respect.[397]

In South-West Nigeria, the Muslim *Ummah* advocates religious education in all educational institutions and continuous dialogue to foster mutual understanding.[398] A Catholic nun, Sr. Kathleen, has called on Christians to never tire of loving others and building positive working relationships with Muslims. She highlighted the need to appreciate and tap into the unique contribution Muslim and Christian women

---

[396] Imam Muhammad N. Ashafa and James M. Wuye, *The Pastor and the Imam: Responding to Conflict* (Lagos, Nigeria: Ibrash Publications Centre, 1999). Interfaith Mediation Centre, http://www.imcnigeria.org/history.htm

[397] See Sultan Muhmmad Sa'ad, 'How to Achieve Peace in Nigeria,' *Vanguard* (Nigeria), 19 November 2007. Sultan Muhammad Sa'ad, 'The Quest for Peace and Religious Harmony,' *Daily Trust* (Nigeria), 09 June 2010.

[398] Sulaiman Adesina, 'MUSWEN Scribe Advocates Religious Teaching in Tertiary Institutions,' *Tribune* (Nigeria) 25 June 2010.

can bring to peace building dialogue.[399] In response to the political crises in Jos, the Nigerian Supreme Council for Islamic Affairs made a public statement which said, 'Nigerian Muslims are not at loggerheads with their Christian counterparts,' and called for peace and good relations, because Islam is against violence.[400] In the same vein, church leaders in Nigeria have committed themselves to improve relations with Muslims and encouraged all Christians to be on good terms with others. Finally, the Nigerian government has called on Nigerians to learn to live and work together in peace: 'Let us work together irrespective of our religious differences.'[401]

Nevertheless, it is not enough to invite adherents of different religious traditions to advance peaceful relations. Are there theological bases to further harmonious relations? Christianity and Islam have common ground for engagement. *Nostra Aetate,* WCC, and the *Common Word Between Us and You* invite and offer models for Muslim-Christian dialogue. What is the theological common ground for dialogue? What theological subjects can the two faiths explore in order to strengthen their common ground? How can deeper knowledge of each other strengthen and improve dialogue relations? The next section explores the theological potential for dialogue.

2.5 The Theological Potential of Meeting the Other (Abrahamic Faith: Gen. 17: 20; 21: 18-21)

In this section, I shall consider the theological possibilities for Christian-Muslim dialogue. I explore common themes in the two faith traditions that offer the prospect for interreligious engagement. Islam and Christianity both have the necessary potential for dialogue, peace building, and mutual coexistence. They are called 'Abrahamic religions' because, together with Judaism, they are monotheistic religions that are closely related in their origins and their beliefs.[402] Although their beliefs differ in some important aspects, these religions have a common origin as expressed in their holy books—Torah, Bible, and Qur'an. Abraham is a model of faith in each religion. God called and made a covenant with him to believe and worship

---

[399] Hajiya Bilkisu Yusuf, 'Agenda for Interfaith Dialogue in Northern Nigeria,' *Dailytrust* (Nigeria), 09 June 2010.

[400] Muideen Olaniyi, 'Nigerian Muslims Are Not at Loggerheads with Christians—NSCIA,' *This Day* (Nigeria), 04 February 2010.

[401] PROCMURA, 'Church Leaders in Nigeria North Re-Orientate Themselves on Growing Complexity of Christian-Muslim Relations,' *A Quarterly News Letter of the Programme for Christian-Muslim Relations in Africa,* nos. 75 and 76 (January-June 2008).

[402] John Hick and Edmund S. Meltzer (eds.), *Three Faiths—One God: A Jewish, Christian, Muslim Encounter* (London: Macmillan Press, 1989).

the one God.[403] This covenant and blessing between God and Abraham extends for generations through Isaac and Ishmael to Jews, Christians, and Muslims. [404] The most important element of the story of Abraham is his faith and obedience, as expressed in the Jewish and Christian scriptures (Holy Bible) in Genesis, and in the Muslim Qur'an.[405] Even though the Bible does not make any reference to Islam (Muslims), the Qur'an refers to Christians as 'People of the Book (Q3: 64-80)'.[406] The following theological themes are common to Islam and Christianity: belief in one God, divine revelation, prayer, sacred scriptures, and a common ethic.

2.5.1 BELIEF IN ONE GOD

Monotheism or belief in one eternal and creative God is the foundation of both the Christian and Islamic faiths. The Bible and the Qur'an both attest to the existence of one God (Deu 6: 4 and Q 21: 46). Belief in the one God is the first and the main article of faith in both religions. According to philosopher of religion Cafer Yaran, Islam is an uncompromising, pure, monotheistic religion. God is one and unique, the creator of everything in heaven and on earth.[407] In the same vein, the Christian Bible in Deuteronomy proclaims 'Yahweh our God is one' (Dt. 6: 4).[408] Also, the Nicene Creed professes belief in one God as revealed in the Bible. God is unique; there is only one God in nature, substance, and essence, the creator of heaven and earth.[409] Islam and Christianity both believe in God's providence, mercy, forgiveness, life after death, judgement, heaven (paradise), and hell.

The Qur'an reads 'our God and your God is One and it is to Him we submit in Islam' (21: 46). The Second Vatican Council documents *Nostra Aetate* (3) and *Lumen Gentium* (16) acknowledge that Muslims profess the faith of Abraham and worship the one true, merciful God, the creator of the universe. This means that Christians

---

[403] Cornelius A. Omonokhua, *Welcome to Interreligious Dialogue: A Call to Religious Tolerance and Peaceful Coexistence* (Benin: Hexagon Information Services, 2004), 8.

[404] Cf. Raymond E. Brown, Joseph A. Fitzmyer, and Murphy E. Ronald (eds.), *The Jerome Biblical Commentary the Old Testament,* vol. 1 (London: Geoffrey Chapman Publisher, 1969), 20.

[405] Genesis Chapter 22: 1. Qur'an Chapter 2: 132.

[406] 'The Interfaith Encounter,' *Grosvenor Essay*, no. 3 (Edinburgh: The Committee for Relations with People of Other Faiths and the Doctrine Committee of the Scottish Episcopal Church, 2006), 16.

[407] Cafer S. Yaran, *Understanding Islam* (Edinburgh: Dunedin Academic Press, 2007), 22-23.

[408] See David Burrell, 'Dialogue between Muslims and Christians as Mutual Transformative Speech,' in Catherine Cornille (ed.), *Criteria of Discernment in Interreligious Dialogue* (Eugene, OR: Cascade Books, 2009), 93.

[409] *Catechism of the Catholic Church*, 56-62.

and Muslims are united in important theological elements of faith. Their faith in the transcendent God challenges them to cooperation and freedom in interreligious dialogue. Abraham is the model common to both faiths of loyal submission to God and respect for each other.[410] To speak of one and the same God is not an abstraction but rather a tangible faith experience for all who try to understand each other in religious dialogue.[411] Moreover, Muslims and Christians share a common belief in God, his prophets and revelation, and moral responsibility.

2.5.2 DIVINE REVELATION

According to the *Dogmatic Constitution on Divine Revelation* (*Dei Verbum*), the Catholic Church teaches that God in His goodness and wisdom reveals Himself to humans; making known the His hidden purpose and will through Christ the word made flesh, and through whom men and women have a share in the the divine nature. Through revelation, the invisible God, out of the abundance of his love, speaks to men and women as friends and lives among them, inviting them into fellowship with himself (no. 2).[412] God in divine revelation chooses to show and communicate himself and the eternal decision of his will to men and women (no. 6).[413] God reveals fundamental truth to humankind. The knowledge that results from the act of God's self-revelation is a gift from God, not the product of human ingenuity.[414] Through revelation, God actively discloses to humanity his power and glory, his nature and character, his ways and plans.[415] Revelation is a fundamental article of faith in both Christianity and Islam, and is linked to the divine as expressed in the Bible and the Qur'an (Ex. 3: 1-15 and Sura Al-'Alaq 96: 1-4). Muslims and Christians both believe that God speaks to his people through the prophets. God always takes the initiative in calling various prophets in the Old Testament and in the Islamic account of the call of Prophet Muhammad.[416]

In Islam, God reveals his divine will so that humans can know this will and learn to live accordingly. The divine will primarily embodies the message communicated

---

[410] Pope John Paul II, 'Muslims and Christians Adore the One God,' *L'Osservatore Romano* (Holy See Rome), 5 May 1999.

[411] Bauschke, 'A Christian View of Islam,' 147.

[412] See 'Dogmatic Constitution on Divine Revelation,' in Walter M. Abbott (ed.), *The Documents of Vatican II*, trans. Joseph Gallagher (London: Geoffrey Chapman, 1966), 112-14.

[413] Ibid.

[414] Cf. 'Revelation,' *Harper's Bible Dictionary* (New York: Harpers & Row Publishers, 1985), 867.

[415] 'Revelation,' *New Bible Dictionary* (Wheaton, IL: Tyndale House Publishers, 1982), 1024.

[416] Montgomery W. Watt, *Islam and Christianity Today: A Contribution to Dialogue* (London: Routledge & Kegan Paul, 1983), 56-57.

by God through his Prophet, who conveys and translates it into a model for all to practise.[417] The divine will is revealed for guidance through God's prophets in the holy books, inviting and enabling humanity to live in peace with God and other human beings.[418] Revelation is about God's truth and the disclosure of his will to humanity. Both Christianity and Islam value the precious revelation of God within their spiritual experience. While it is believed in both religious traditions that God has spoken to humankind in various ways (such as through the prophets, Jesus Christ, and the Qur'an), it is equally important to note that Christianity and Islam differ in the ways God has revealed himself.[419] This, however, is not the focus of this study.

2.5.3 PRAYER

Prayer as an act of worship of God is common to Islam and Christianity; it is at the heart of every religious experience and a duty within these faith traditions.[420] In both religions, prayer is the most basic form of worshipping God with specifically prescribed requirements of prayer. Muslims perform ablutions while Christians compose themselves, and both address God directly in prayer. In the Qur'an, all prayers are addressed to the merciful God and (the Qur'an) contains some beautiful names for God.[421] Prayers are both a public and private religious exercise in both traditions.

The Qur'an requires a Muslim to worship God five times a day (Q 2: 238-239; 11: 114; 13: 14-15). The Bible, on the other hand, calls on Christians to pray always and to worship only the Lord our God. Moreover, Jesus teaches his disciples to pray.[422] It follows that Christians and Muslims can have an enriching spiritual encounter when they share their spiritual wealth. Mutual togetherness in prayer services, pastoral care, and praying for peace can be a starting point for building a lasting spiritual friendship. Just as Abraham offered prayers and submitted himself to the One God, Christians and Muslims can pray for each other.[423] Prayer as a common spiritual activity shows that Christians and Muslims are all created by one God and,

---

[417] Thomas B. Irving, Ahmed Khurshid, and Ahsan M. Muhammad, *The Qur'an: Basic Teachings* (Leicester: The Islamic Foundation, 1996), 2-3.

[418] Ibid.

[419] Aydin, *Modern Western Christian*, 29.

[420] Elliot N. Dorff, 'This is My God: One Jew's Faith,' in John Hick and Edmund S. Meltzer (eds.), *Three Faiths—One God: A Jewish, Christian, Muslim Encounter* (London: Macmillan Press, 1989), 21.

[421] Küng, *Islam: Past, Present and Future*, 86-89.

[422] Luke 18: 1; Matthew 4: 10; 6: 7-15; Exodus 20: 1-3.

[423] Bauschke, 'A Christian View of Islam,' 154-55.

consequently, one human family. Thus the two traditions have a common unique spiritual element which must not be ignored.[424]

In recent years (1986, 2002 and 2011), Pope John Paul II and Benedict XVI organised a symbolic activity when various religious leaders met in Assisi to pray for peace in the world. The religious leaders' positive response to the meet in Assisi is a brilliant symbol of building harmony, togetherness, and commitment to peace.[425] The experience in Assisi is of unique importance because Muslims and Christians together in prayer is a necessary condition for spiritual sharing that leads to peace, harmony, and lasting joy in the community (world). Prayer and sharing are essential to keep the community together in peace.

2.5.4 SACRED SCRIPTURES

Christianity and Islam have scriptures that are unique to their traditions. These scriptures contain the revelations of God to humanity. For Christians, it is the Holy Bible, while for the Muslims, it is the Holy Qur'an. The Bible is the word of God, revealed by God, who inspired the sacred authors to write a divinely inspired record of God's self-disclosure through their experience of the biblical authors in history, as God's love, mercy, justice, and holiness.[426] The Bible as the word of God is central to the Christian faith. As a guiding principle of life, the Bible is a vital, dynamic, and efficacious means of nourishing faith. It inspires the lives of Christians in the moral discernment of their relationship to their fellow humans.[427]

The Qur'an is the most holy book for Muslims. It is considered a declaration of the eternal word of God transmitted by an angel to Prophet Muhammad. It is a direct auditory dictation from an eternal origin which is not influenced by the Prophet. For Muslims, the Qur'an is God's final supreme word which is not dependent on any previous revelation. It is normative, unique, and immutable.[428] It is the written word

---

[424] Cf. Felix A. Machado, 'Towards Deepening Hindu-Christian Maitri,' in *Pro Dialogo* (Vaticano: Pontificum Consilium Pro Dialogo Inter Religiones, 2004), 64.

[425] Felix A. Machado, *Peace: A Single Goal and a Shared Intention Forum of Religious Representatives (Vatican City, 23 January 2002), Day of Prayer for Peace (Assisi, 24 January 2002)* (Vatican City: Pontifical Council for Interreligious Dialogue, 2002), 6-7.

[426] See Albrecht Hauser, 'Let God Be God: Christian and Muslim Understanding of God and Its Challenges in Encounter,' in *My Neighbour Is Muslim: A Handbook for Reformed Churches* (Geneva: Centre International Reform John Knox, 1990), 59.

[427] Enzo Bianchi, 'The Centrality of the Word of God,' in Giuseppe Alberigo, Jean-Pierre Jossua, and Joseph A. Komonchak (eds.), *The Reception of Vatican II* (Washington, DC: Catholic University of American Press, 1987), 115-16.

[428] Cf. Joseph Kenny, *West Africa and Islam* (Ibadan, Nigeria: AECAWA Publication, 2000), 47-49.

set down once and for all by God; it transcends all consideration of space and time. It is the main criterion of Islamic faith and action. It communicates ethical obligations, external dynamics, religious depth, and specific convictions about faith. It presents human responsibility, social justice, and Muslim solidarity with God.[429]

For Christians and Muslims, the Bible and the Qur'an are the source of the norms and guidance for life, faith, morality, and relationship with others.[430] These sacred books encourage adherents to live in peace and harmony. Both scriptures strongly reject prejudice, hatred, oppression, and persecution. They promote openness, dialogue, and cooperation between (religions) Christianity and Islam (Rm. 12: 14-21; 2 Cor. 13: 11, Qur'an 8: 61; 16: 90). Although both the Bible and the Qur'an contain texts and verses that seem to support and encourage violent conflicts, the theological interpretation of such verses has to be understood within their contextual-historical framework when considering their application to a contemporary multireligious world. Nonetheless, Christians and Muslims can be sincerely transformed by the word to become active in the promotion of justice, peace, and harmony in society.[431]

2.5.4.1 QUR'ANIC INTERPRETATION: THE IMPORTANCE OF CONTEXTUAL-HISTORICAL HERMENEUTICS

Since the Holy Qur'an emerged in the seventh century, attempts have been made by various Islamic scholars, schools of thought and commentators to study, understand and give meaning to the message contained in the classical text. The Qur'an by its nature does not provide detailed prescriptive theological guidelines for its interpretation. The fact that recognising and critically analysing the times and historical circumstances in which Muhammed appeared with his message as the prophet of God and launched his mission goes a long way in helping scholars and interpreters to articulate the message of the Holy Book.[432] The historical method of interpretation which requires that the text be examined and interpreted in accordance with the rules of grammar and the meaning of words have had is a long significant history in the development of Qur'anic exegesis.[433] Moreover, every text speaks in the language of its time. Thus the interpreter must have knowledge of language, its speakers, and context in explaining the message, while also recognising the dynamic

---

[429] Yaran, *Understanding Islam*, 29.

[430] Küng, *Islam: Past, Present and Future*, 62.

[431] See 'Synod of Bishops XII Ordinary General assembly,' *The Word of God in the Light and Mission of the Church: Lineamenta* (Abuja, Nigeria: Catholic Secretariat of Nigeria, 2007), 58.

[432] Cf. Abdulaziz Sachedina, *The Islamic Roots of Democratic Pluralism* (New York: Oxford University Press, 2001), 16.

[433] Ibid.

nature of history and society.[434] Various Islamic scholars and schools of thought have tried to assess historical forces connected with the text giving rise to divergent interpretations of God's revelation. However, these are not unrelated to the distinct views held by individual exegetes engaged in the formulation of specific lines of inquiry into the meaning of the text.[435]

According to Abdulaziz Sachedina, a scholar of religion, in the last few years, religion has re-emerged in different communities as an important source of moral imperative necessary for maintaining social cohesion in society.[436] Religion as a form of identity has not only helped to mobilise people's sense of outrage to resist autocratic governments but also plays a significant constructive role in national reconciliation and nation building. At the same time, religiously inspired nationalism and their related ethnic rivalries and conflicts have raised serious questions about the impact of religious ideology, intolerant interpretation of scripture, and extremism in a pluralistic world.[437] Meanwhile, it can be argued that Islamic revelation presents a theology that resonates with contemporary pluralistic belief that other faiths are not merely inferior manifestations of religious belief but variant forms of individual and communal responses to the presence of the divine in human life (Q 3: 198). Therefore, Qur'anic interpretation has to acknowledge the pluralistic nature of modern society and the equality of all humans as created by God.

The Qur'an presents a universal perspective of divine revelation, a Being who responds to the commitment and sincerity of humans created by God.[438] The world view of the Qur'an is overwhelmingly set within the human experience who tries to make sense of divine revelation by a positive response (faith) and to create an ethical order within human society. The challenge is to clarify the Qur'anic motivation aiming to lead the faith community to its ultimate destiny. For instance, when a verse is revealed in a particular situation and in the future another verse is revealed that seems to contradict the previous verse, what happens in such circumstance? How are such verse(s) interpreted and how can an exegete deal with such impasse?

Islamic scholars, jurists, and commentators have put forward the theory of abrogation. Abrogation is a prominent concept in the field of Qur'anic commentary and Islamic law which allows the harmonisation of apparent contradictions in legal ruling. However, understanding and analysing the principle of abrogation and applying it to the Qur'an demands a critical distinction between Qur'an as a source and Qur'an as a text. The difference being the verse removed from the text is the

---

[434]   Ibid.

[435]   Ibid.

[436]   Ibid., 4.

[437]   Ibid.

[438]   Farid Esack, *Qur'an Liberation and Pluralism: An Islamic Perspective of Interreligious Solidarity against Oppression* (Oxford: Oneworld, 1997), 146.

substance of which remains a probative source of doctrine.[439] Classical Islamic jurisprudence recognises two primary sources of legal ruling, the Qur'an and the Sunna, and two secondary post prophetic sources are acknowledged: the analogy derived from one or other of the primary sources and the consensus of qualified legal experts.[440] Nonetheless, abrogation is applicable to neither of the subsidiary sources but only to the document on which they are based. Since abrogation is surely the right of the law giver, it is argued that it must have been initiated before the demise of the Prophet who mediated the Qur'an and the Sunna.

Abrogation may be external or internal in Islam. For instance, some Muslim scholars argue that Islam abrogation of Judaism and Christianity is obvious since Islam is the last in the series of God's revelation of the Divine Will. This is defended by applying the theory of external abrogation. Internal abrogation applies when, for example, a Qur'anic verse which was previously revealed is repealed by another verse or revelation to the Prophet. Thus abrogation is claimed when one regulation is withdrawn and replaced with another or a later one even though the replaced verse remains in the Qur'anic text.

Scholars like Al-Shafii (AD 820) argue that, since the mission of the Prophet lasted over two decades, it is not surprising that a dynamic community would emphasise the idea that one of the Prophets' practices or instructions could abrogate another. On the other hand, for scholars who undertook the derivation of the law from its primary source (Qur'an and Sunna), the simplest means of disputing about an opposing view was the blunt assertion that even though the verse was correct at the time of its revelation, it has since been abrogated by a further revelation. Al-Shafii was nonetheless convinced that God had singled out the Prophet as the only one qualified to pronounce on the law. Thus he insisted on unquestionable obedience to the Prophet and affirmed that no ruling in the text be abrogated without a replacement being promulgated. Hence abrogation really means substitution.[441]

Furthermore, for some Qur'anic commentators, the idea that one verse in the text abrogates another suggests that the Divine Will is dynamic and mutable, which contravenes a basic theological tenet of revelation. Others have argued that no Muslim ever objected to the notion of abrogation; if God adapts His regulations to the different circumstances prevailing in different ages as is apparent in the alteration, God may equally adapt regulations appropriate to the initial stages of one revelation to address a present need. Meanwhile scholars like Al-Ghazali (AD 1058) and Al-Qurtubi (AD 1273) maintain that God can command and forbid whatever He wants. Divine knowledge is infinite and instantaneous and for all eternity. God knows what to command, the precise duration intended for the command, and the exact

---

[439] John Burton, 'Abrogation,' *Encyclopaedia of the Qur'an,* vol. 1 (Boston: Brill, 2001), 11.

[440] Cf. Ibid.

[441] Ibid., 13.

moment He proposes to give a further command. When abrogation occurs, people may perceive it as change, but this is only a variation from the human perspective. Moreover, there is perfect harmony between the Divine Will and knowledge which humans may not totally comprehend.[442] Scholars like Al-Tabari have objections and difficulties in accepting the theory of abrogation as worthy of the revelation of God. However, by providing variant readings for references to abrogation in the holy text, proponents of the abrogation theory claim that God was not referring to the text of the Qur'an but to the ruling conveyed by the text; in terms of beauty, no verse can be superior to another and no Sunna or Hadith is more beautiful than a verse from the Holy Qur'an.[443]

The Islamic theology of revelation as contained in the Qur'anic text and its hermeneutics is challenged today by multireligious, cultural, and social diversity. For example, the Qur'an makes reference in *Sura Al-'Imran* (chapter 3) to the People of the Book. It is obvious then that the Islamic *Ummah* dwell alongside people of other faith traditions, and thus lucid Qur'anic interpretation has to be sensitive to the multiplicity of the modern world. Islamic scholars like Farid Esack arguing from South African background, maintain that dynamic Qur'anic interpretation should stem from a Qur'anic theology of liberation that focuses on a deeper awareness of the socio-political and religious experience of the people. The interpretation should work towards liberating religion from all forms of socio-political, ethnic, and religious ideas based on structures of uncritical obedience free from all forms of injustice and exploitation of race, class, or belief.[444] This form of Qur'anic hermeneutics derives it inspiration from the Qur'an and the prophets in a process of shared analytical reflection that is critical and self-critical, engendering a positive praxis in a contemporary multireligious and social environment. To achieve such rational scriptural interpretation involves a continuous critical assessment of text, context, and historical circumstance in a reflective search of the implications of such interpretation for Muslims and non-Muslims alike.[445]

Esack proposes some criteria necessary for understanding and interpreting scripture in a contemporary multireligious diverse setting: *taqwa* meaning, an awareness of the presence of God, *tawhid*, the unity of God, *al-nas*, the people, *al-mustad'afun fi'l-ard*, the location of interpretive activity, and *jihad*, struggle.[446] These he argues are aimed at developing the standards essential for reading and theological examination of the Qur'an in general and specifically the way the text

---

[442]   Ibid., 14.

[443]   Cf. Ibid., 15-16.

[444]   Esack, *Qur'an Liberation and Pluralism*, 83.

[445]   Cf. Ibid., 86. Praxis: a conscious action undertaken by a (faith) community that has responsibility for its own socio-political, ethnic and religious determination.

[446]   Ibid.

relates to the religious other. These, however, have to be understood within specific historical context wherein the interpreter is located and bears upon the outcome of his or her interpretation, even though interpreters have the freedom to position themselves differently in relation to the situation in order to arrive at a specific interpretation.[447] The challenge with scriptural hermeneutics remains speculation and personal whim of the interpreter. According to Esack, the art of Qur'anic hermeneutic of liberation; bearing in mind the presence of God ensures that such interpretation remains free from dogmatic assertions, political reaction, and pure subjective speculation of the interpreter.[448] *Taqwa*, he further argues, facilitates the creative and spiritual balance in the life of the engaged interpreter even when such activity is approached from a socio-political perspective as the outcome of such endeavour has inference even for the (wider society) religious other.[449] Although *taqwa* is a vital source of support for the engaged interpreter in trying to understand the text of the Holy Qur'an, there is no absolute guarantee of meaning. Therefore, the interpreter has to press towards an ever increasing authentic search and a continuous critical investigation of the text in order to arrive at a viable explanation. Such a study minimises the extent to which the text can be manipulated for selfish or ideological advantage.[450]

The theology of textual hermeneutics poses further the questions of how the Qur'an relates to the religious other and how the Qur'anic interpreter should relate the message of the text to the other. The Qur'an, it can be said, presents a positive inclusivist perspective of the religious other when it makes reference to the 'People of the Book.' It goes further by inviting them to come to dialogue on a 'Common Word'. However, there are verses in the Qur'an that are potent, for example, *Surah Al-Anfal* 8: 59-60 and *Surah At-Tawbah* 9: 5. How does the interpreter relate such exhortation to wage an armed struggle against the other in a multireligious and multicultural circumstance? In such a situation, critical exploration of the text cannot be overemphasised. This allows the interpreter to discover the value of the divine message in (exegesis) contextual-historical analysis. This enables the interpreter to find a balanced approach and not isolate particular texts and understanding from the rest of scripture, but be attentive to the content and unity of the divine will in the whole of scripture.[451] While the context of individual verses dealing with the religious other is often recorded in the Qur'an, the Muslim interpreter has the duty to understand the historical setting in order to shed light on revelation within a

---

[447]   Ibid.

[448]   Ibid., 89.

[449]   Ibid.

[450]   Cf. Ibid., 90 and 111.

[451]   Cf. Catholic Bishops' Conference of England and Wales, and Scotland, *The Gift of Scripture* (London: The Catholic Truth Society, 2005), 20-22.

contemporary pluralistic milieu.[452] Furthermore, the Qur'anic interpreter must guard against the dangers of perceiving such isolated revelation to generalise denunciation of the other irrespective of the socio-historical circumstance of a particular verse, to support rejection or damnation of the other, because this fosters extremism and conflict. Moreover, the phenomenon of religious extremism becomes prevalent alongside obstinate and uncompromising attitudes of intolerance thus ruling out the need to listen to others' views and the willingness to dialogue. There are significant dangers involved in a fundamentalist approach to the scriptures which often focuses on a particular text or texts, by making absolute what is a partial and incomplete understanding of scripture.[453] Such interpretation of scripture disregards the diversity of views and the development of variety of understanding which may be found in the Qur'an and does not allow for the presence of imperfect and time-conditioned elements within scripture.[454] For a clearer understanding of a scriptural text, the exegete must fully acknowledge that it is the word of God revealed within the human historical experience. He or she must seek to discern the meaning of scripture in every age and in every society as it affects the self and the other.

Religious pluralism and scriptural interpretation also posit a unique challenge in places like northern Nigeria with a large Islamic *Ummah*, where historical records attest that shari'a law was in place in the locality until the advent of colonisation. Scholars like Abullahi Ahmed An-Na'im have argued that the historical context within which shari'a was developed and applied by the early Muslims in the seventh century could be justified because of the prevailing circumstances, which do not apply to a contemporary world of universal human rights, in a multicultural and multireligious society.[455] It is a fact that during the formative phase of shari'a the conception of human rights was not in existence anywhere in the world, so institutions like slavery and antagonism towards non-Muslims were sanctioned. However, shari'a as a practical Islamic legal system in a contemporary pluralistic world cannot disregard human rights as they apply to today's context.[456] It follows that Qur'anic interpretation in modern times must be sensitive to the religiously pluralistic nature of society on one hand and evolve an alternative form of Islamic public law on the other, one that is contextual and based on mutual equality and seeking to eliminate human rights limitations. This demands courage and

---

[452] Esack, *Qur'an Liberation and Pluralism*, 146.

[453] See Catholic Bishops' Conference of England and Wales, and Scotland, 'The Gift of Scripture,' 20.

[454] Ibid.

[455] See Abdullahi Ahmed An-Na'im, 'Shari'a and Basic Human Rights Concerns,' in Charles Kurzman (ed.), *Liberal Islam: A Source Book* (New York: Oxford University Press, 1998), 227.

[456] Ibid.

determination by Islamic scholars, jurists and exegetes to explore the possibilities of reinterpreting archaic aspects of shari'a such that Islaimic shari'a law develops humane principles compatible with humanright laws.[457] The Muslim *Ummah* and scholarship is therefore challenged to embrace and welcome such an evolutionary approach to Qur'anic hermeneutics, irrespective of the difficulty and resistance that may be encountered. This for me involves as Sachedina has suggested: analysis of literary tradition and linguistic aspect of revelation, determination of the historical context of such revelation, clarification of meaning through intra-textual reference, and explanation of passages by the use of Hadith material attributed to the Prophet as the first commentator and teacher of the Qur'an.[458]

Islam as a religion in this century must consider the religiously pluralistic nature of society. The essence of shari'a endures, but its interpretation and application must be contextual if conflict and tension with the religious other are to be weakened. Islamic scholars, jurists, and exegetes might wish to consider and promote those aspects of Islamic shari'a that are compatible with human rights in a multicultural and multireligious society. Those features that do not recognise the dignity and equality of all should be abolished. Moreover, religious pluralism presents an opportunity and a fundamental, valuable resource for different faith communities to establish justice and peaceful relations in any contemporary society. The Roman Catholic Church in *Nostra Aetate* has tried to advance this model by proposing an encounter (dialogue) between different religious traditions. Hence, Muslims and Christians in Northern Nigeria can grow in better understanding and mutual harmony to which a contextual interpretation of the sacred books remains vital and dynamic if peace building is to be sustained.

2.5.5 COMMON ETHIC BETWEEN CHRISTIANITY AND ISLAM

Islam and Christianity both believe that God has given commandments concerning the conduct of individuals in their relationship with God and other human beings where certain acts are prescribed and others are forbidden. According to the Arabic-Islamic philosopher Watt Montgomery, Christianity accepted the commandments given to Moses by God, notably the Ten Commandments; the many laws of Moses include detailed rules and general principles, such as 'love your neighbour as yourself'.[459] The Qur'an and the Bible have ideas in common in terms of moral norms, values, and the ethical tradition of the Ten Commandments (Exod. 20: 1-17, Qur'an 17: 22-37). Moreover, there is a common prophetic tradition which calls on Christians and Muslims to obey these commandments. Martin Bauschke

---

[457] Ibid., 229.

[458] Sachedina, *The Islamic Roots of Democratic Pluralism*, 18.

[459] Watt, *Islam and Christianity Today*, 72.

argues in *Jesus and Muhammad as Brothers* that Islam and Christianity tend to unite God's numerous commandments into one most significant commandment, known as the Golden Rule, known in various forms throughout the world: 'What you do not wish done to yourself, do not do to others.'[460] This is at the heart of all ethical rules and is the basis for human behaviour in both Christianity and Islam.[461] Since there is a similarity between the two religions in moral ideals and individual requirements, there should be a readiness to explore such common ground to seek a deeper understanding of each other's point of view. Above all, Muslims and Christians should live by their moral ideals.[462] The differences between the two religious traditions on how to apply God's law in human situations must not hinder cooperation and dialogue but should serve as the basis for appreciating the uniqueness of each faith tradition and a step towards mutual dialogue. Moreover, *Nostra Aetate* has encouraged Christians to dialogue with other religions.

2.6 An Appraisal of Contemporary Christian-Muslim Dialogue after *Nostra Aetate*, 1965

In this section, I shall evaluate the general process of Christian-Muslim dialogue as a result of *Nostra Aetate*. What is the outlook for the chances of fostering better understanding, and how does that contribute to peaceful negotiations in Northern Nigeria?

The Roman Catholic Church's *Declaration on the Relationship of the Church to Non-Christian Religions* (*Nostra Aetate*) is unique in creating the needed space and providing the platform and the impetus for Christian-Muslim dialogue. According to Catherine Cornille, contemporary interreligious dialogue presents itself as an essential feature of peaceful coexistence and a promise of religious growth. Dialogue between Christianity and Islam today has taken various forms, from meetings of religious leaders showing solidarity and friendship, to collaboration between people of different faiths in grassroot community projects.[463] Pope John Paul II's encyclical *Redemptoris Missio* (no. 57) emphasises that a vast field lies open to dialogue, which can assume many forms and expressions: from exchanges between experts or official representatives of various traditions, to cooperation for integral development and the safeguarding of religious values. It is through sharing their respective spiritual

---

[460] Bauschke, 'Islam: Jesus and Muhammad as Brothers,' 202-03.

[461] Watt, *Islam and Christianity Today*, 74.

[462] Joann Haafkens, 'The Direction of Christian-Muslim Relations in Sub-Saharan Africa,' in Yvonne Yazbeck Haddad and Zaidan Wadi Haddad (eds.), *Christian-Muslim Encounters* (Gainesville: University Press of Florida, 1995), 300-11.

[463] Catherine Cornille, *The Im-Possibility of Interreligious Dialogue* (New York: Crossroad Publishing, 2008), 1-3.

experiences that believers of different religious traditions bear witness to their own human and spiritual values and help each other to live according to those values in order to build a more just and fraternal society.[464]

One positive effect of the events of 11 September 2001 in the USA is that it brought some Muslims and Christians together more closely than ever before to create new opportunities for constructive dialogue and to challenge all to live in peace and harmony despite differences. It can be argued that Christians and Muslims are striving to build a culture of peace and mutual engagement within their immediate environment as in the numerous dialogue meetings taking place at grassroot level. Prejudice and stereotyping are giving way to a more positive attitude, creating a culture of dialogue where people want to learn and understand others while respecting their differences.[465] Such differences must not be perceived as a threat, but as an opportunity for mutual enrichment, to clarify, articulate, and understand the beliefs of the other. Dialogue between Christians and Muslims in Northern Nigeria must seek to promote collaboration among believers in order to achieve lasting peace. They must confront the political, social, economic, and ethnic evils that contribute to violent conflicts and together build a just and peaceful society.[466] Contemporary Christian-Muslim dialogue in Northern Nigeria must aim to form, inform, and transform believers within the two faith traditions. The success of such transformation has to begin with an intrareligious dialogue where, for example, the faith community seeks dynamic theological analysis of its self-understanding in order to relate to others in interreligious dialogue. Moreover, appropriate knowledge of the other religious tradition is beneficial for fostering mutual collaboration and tackling the threat of prejudice and stereotypes.

---

[464]   Ioannes Paulus PP. II, *Redemptoris Missio: On the Permanent Validity of the Church's Missionary Mandate* (Vaticana: Libreria Editrice, 1990). http://www.vatican.va/holy_father/john_paul_ii/encyclicals/documents/hf_jp-ii_enc_07121990_redemptoris-missio_en.html

[465]   Micheal L. Fitzgerald and John Borelli, *Interfaith Dialogue: A Catholic View* (New York: Orbis Books, 2006), 147-49.

[466]   Machado, 'Towards Deepening Hindu-Christian Maitri,' 64-70.

2.7 STEREOTYPING AND PREJUDICE OF THE DISPUTED OTHER

In this section, I shall examine the theme of stereotyping and prejudice in order to highlight Muslim-Christian perceptions of each other and how these have fuelled conflicts.

According to social-psychologist Rupert Brown, a stereotype is when a particular characteristic is attributed to a person or group and is perceived to be shared by all or most members of such a group.[467] It is a belief that all members of a given group share the same fixed characteristic.[468] Stereotype as discussed in this section is a fixed image held by one group of people about another group, an oversimplified opinion without regard for individual differences.[469] Sociologist Ellis Cashmore defines prejudice as learned beliefs and values that lead an individual or group of individuals to be biased for or against members of a particular group prior to actual experience of such a person or group.[470] In the same vein, social psychologist Allport Gordon holds that prejudice is thinking ill of others without sufficient reason: a negative or positive feeling towards a person or group without an actual experience of such a person or group.[471]

A religious stereotype can be described as particular characteristics applied to a religious group and perceived to be shared by all its members. African religious historian Julian Rukyaa argues that this leads to prejudice, which is a biased evaluation based on real or imagined characteristics, stemming, from the religious instruction, social attitudes, and ignorance of another tradition.[472] Stereotypes, bias, and prejudices built over time can cause serious harm, leading to conflicts and the inhibition of social cohesion between different religious groups.[473]

---

[467] Rupert Brown, *Prejudice: Its Social Psychology* (Oxford: Blackwell Publishers, 1995), 82.

[468] National Youth Council of Ireland, *Stereotyping of Young People Resource Pack* (Dublin, Ireland: the Equality Authority and the National Council of Ireland, 2008), 1. http://www.youth.ie/sites/youth.ie/files/STEREOTYPING%20of%20Young%20People%20RESOURCE%20PACK.pdf

[469] *Respecting One Another Religious Stereotyping Packet* (New York: Office of Interfaith Relations Worldwide Ministries Division a Ministry of the General Assembly Council Presbyterian Church, 2003). http://www.presbyterianmission.org/media/uploads/interfaithrelations/pdf/stereotyping.pdf

[470] Cashmore, 'Ethnicity,' 119-20.

[471] Gordon W. Allport, *The Nature of Prejudice* (London: Addison-Wesley Publishing, 1981), 6-7.

[472] Julian J. Rukyaa, 'Muslim-Christian Relations in Tanzania with Particular Focus on the Relationship between Religious Instruction and Prejudice,' *Islam and Christian-Muslim Relations* 18, no. 2 (2007), 189-91.

[473] Ibid.

In Northern Nigeria, negative religious stereotypes have contributed to shaping the relationship between Christians and Muslims. A Nigerian public relations analyst, Kalu Agwu, has observed that, before independence, Nigeria was divided between North and South, and the question was, 'Where do you come from?' However, with the growing prominence of religion during the 1970s, the North-South split has become a Muslim-Christian division, with the question being 'What is your religion?' Christians accuse Muslims of systematically Islamising the country, while Muslims accuse Christians of dominating in every sphere of society and promoting Christian values in Nigeria.[474] The violent religious clashes, Nigeria's membership of the Organisation of Islamic Conference (OIC), the lingering Islamic sharia controversy, plus poor religious education/formation prevalent in both religious traditions, all strengthen stereotypes further.

Nigerian scholars, critics, commentators, and some religious leaders have attributed the recurring religious crises in Northern Nigeria to ignorance and lack of proper religious education within both religious traditions. According to Arabic-Islamic historian Kenny, to honestly appreciate the other and avoid simplistic statements, every concerned Muslim and Christian should have a basic knowledge of the other faith.[475] At least some learned representatives of each faith community should have a specialised knowledge of the other's faith, history, and an up-to-date understanding of the other tradition.[476] He further argues that such basic knowledge is lacking among the adherents of the two religious traditions in Northern Nigeria. As a result, both groups have distorted and biased knowledge that has developed and is conditioned by historical experience of the other. While, for example, some Christians perceive Muslims as volatile, vicious, domineering, and violent, some Muslims see Christians as infidels, unbelievers (Kafiri), secular, and collaborators with the West which must be conquered and converted to the religion of Allah.[477] These perceptions have not promoted the spirit of tolerance and harmonious understanding.

Public preaching among Christians and Muslims is a common spiritual exercise in Northern Nigeria. Ignorance and lack of proper knowledge and respect for the other have often been manifested as outrageous and unguarded public statements by fanatical preachers of both traditions. One example is the riots in Kafanchan, March 1987. This crisis was caused by an offensive interpretation of the Qur'an and misrepresentation of Prophet Muhammad.[478] Inadequate knowledge continues to

---

[474]   Kalu Agwu, 'Nigeria,' in H.S. Wilson (ed.), *Islam in Africa: Perspectives for Christian-Muslim Relations* (Geneva: World Alliance of Churches, 1995), 79-83.

[475]   Joseph Kenny, 'Towards Better Understanding of Muslims and Christians,' *Nigerian Journal of Islam* 2, no. 1 (1971).

[476]   Ibid.

[477]   Cf. Ndiokwere, *The African Church Today and Tomorrow*, 73-80.

[478]   Opeloye, 'The Socio-Political Factor,' 234.

divide and form misleading stereotypes about the other. Additionally, such negative stereotypes have diminished and limited the potential of both sides by projecting what is not completely true about the other. It may be true that some stereotypes stem from individual bias, group experience, the media, family, friends, and the faith community, but that does not reveal the truth about the other.

Peace building in Northern Nigeria requires that Christians and Muslims realise the need for peaceful coexistence, and ask the question, 'What kind of relationship do we want to have in contemporary multireligious, multicultural Northern Nigeria?' However, to achieve better relations devoid of stereotypes and prejudice, both sides must be prepared to see the other's point of view and learn from them.[479]

CONCLUSION

In this chapter, I have argued that *Nostra Aetate* has been groundbreaking in opening up new channels of communication and building positive relations, especially between Christianity and Islam. Since 1965, a lot has been achieved in dialogue between Christianity and Islam at different levels. The commitment to dialogue on both sides is demonstrated by various ongoing dialogue activities. The *Common Word Between Us and You*, an invitation from Islamic leaders and the positive Christian response to this call, are a testimony to the extent of the mutual commitment to Christian-Muslim dialogue. Belief in God, prophets, divine revelation, moral responsibility and accountability, the value of social justice and peace, all provide common ground for a dialogue of peace between the two faith traditions.[480]

The theology of *Nostra Aetate* presents a model and lays the foundation for mutuality and positive attitudes between religions and sustain dialogue engagement. Despite the challenges that seem to weigh down the process of interreligious dialogue, Muslims and Christians are challenged to tackle the socio-ethnic, economic, political, and religious factors that lead to conflicts so as to negotiate sustainable peace. The next chapter examines the contributions of Islam and Christianity to peaceful coexistence in a religiously pluralistic society, given that both religions claim to be religions of peace and love and the challenging dynamics of living with the religious other.

---

[479] Francis Arinze, Christian-Muslim Relations in the 21st Century, 5 June 1997, A Talk given at the Centre for Christian-Muslim Understanding in Georgetown University, Washington. http://www.sedos.org/eglish/arinze.htm

[480] Esposito, 'The Future of Islam,' 38.

Chapter 3

THE CONTRIBUTIONS OF ISLAM AND CHRISTIANITY TO PEACE BUILDING

INTRODUCTION

Thus far this study has established that the theology of the Second Vatican Council in *Nostra Aetate* laid the foundation and a model for dialogue encounter between the Roman Catholic Church and other religious traditions.

In this chapter, I am arguing that Islam and Christianity have the potential to foster peace in society. The aim here is to explore and articulate the contributions of religion in peace building by critically analysing the potential of religion for peace. The focus is specifically on the resources within the Islamic and Christian traditions. Moreover, peace is a fundamental sacred value of both Islam and Christianity.[481] It is critical and indispensable to examine and strengthen the role of these religions in the promotion of peaceful coexistence.

According to religious scholar David Little and religious historian Scott Appleby, religion plays an ambivalent, paradoxical role in society.[482] Religion on its

---

[481]   Machado, *Peace: A Single Goal and a Shared Intention*, 5-6; Moses B. Owojaiye, 'Factors Responsible for Muslim-Christian Unrest in Nigeria: A Socio-Political Analysis,' 2010. http://www.pentecostalmovement.wordpress.com/?s=factor+responsible+for+Muslim+Christian+unrest+in+nigeria

[482]   David Little and Scott Appleby, 'A Moment of Opportunity? The Promise of Religious Peacebuilding in an Era of Religious and Ethnic Conflict,' in Harold Coward and Gordon S. Smith (eds.), *Religion and Peacebuilding* (Albany: State University of New York Press, 2004), 2.

own terms can underwrite both conflict and peace.[483] Religion can promote tolerance and conflict within a community.[484] However, what a religion teaches can be different from how its followers practise it. Thus religion can be manipulated to suit various interests. Throughout history religion has been used to promote discrimination, hatred, stereotyping, prejudice, political difference, ethnic conflict, and violence as witnessed in Northern Nigeria. People have been killed destroying community life and property in the name of religion. Nevertheless, religion has the potential to build and foster peace, forgiveness, contrition, reconciliation, and dialogue. Theologians and religious scholars and leaders agree that although religion can be used for violence, religious values are also a symbolic, viable option in the peace-building process.[485] How can religion contribute to sustainable peace in Northern Nigeria? What are the resources for peace-building within Christianity and Islam?

This chapter is divided into four sections. The first section focuses on the hermeneutic of religion as a powerful institution that is persuasive, motivating, and forceful in the life of an individual or a faith community. It examines critically the role of religion in faith communities to create the framework for peace-building.

The second section looks at the faith community as the nucleus that provides the supporting structure for religion and theology to thrive. It highlights the concept of community as understood from an Islamic and Christian perspective with focus on how such understanding shapes the dynamics of Christian-Muslim relations in Northern Nigeria. The third section appraises resources for peace-building in Islam and Christianity, with emphasis on scripture, religious tradition, preaching, and official documents that state clearly the position of either religious tradition on issues of peace or dialogue.

The fourth section considers the theology and praxis of love in the process of peace-building by focusing on the theology of St. Augustine, St. Thomas Aquinas, and Pope Benedict XVI in order to explore the teaching of Jesus on love of God and love of neighbour.

3.1 RELIGION AND PEACE BUILDING

In this section, the focus is on religion as a valuable institutional framework for peace-building within and between faith communities. The aim here is to buttress the fact that even though religion can be mobilised to fuel conflicts, it can also be a vehicle towards sustainable peace.

---

[483] Heather Dubois, 'Religion and Peacebuilding: An Ambivalent Yet Vital Relationship,' *Journal for Conflict and Peace* 1, no. 2 (2008). http://www.plowsharesproject.org/journal/php/article.php?issu_list_id=10&article_list_id=32

[484] Little and Appleby, 'A Moment of Opportunity,' 2.

[485] Ibid., 3.

Religion is the nexus of attitudes, convictions, emotions, gestures, rituals, belief systems, and institutions by which we come to terms with and express our most fundamental relationship with God.[486] According to theologian Richard McBrien, this relationship is disclosed by a process called revelation and thus religion is more or less the structured response to that revelation of God. Religion, however, continues to affect people and society at large in different ways.[487]

Today more than ever, the United Nations Organisation and other world bodies are recognising the vital contribution of religion to peace-building. Little and Appleby maintain that the United Nations acknowledges this contribution when it states thus:

> Having established a reputation for integrity and service through constant and direct contact with the masses, a long record of charitable work among people in need and the moral example of its core members, a religious community commands a privileged status among segments of the population.[488]

In situations of violent conflict, government, civil society organisations, and institutions have often turned to religious communities and their leaders to mediate, reconcile opposites, and assume responsibility for the welfare and common good of all. For example, it was after the joint intervention of Muslim and Christian religious leaders in September 2001 that the riots in Jos and other places in Northern Nigeria ceased, although the security forces by then had largely quelled the violence.[489] Whilst religious belief has caused violent conflict in Northern Nigeria, religion has also made an enormous contribution to the process of peace-building and conflict resolution. According to conflict mediators Johnston Douglas and Brian Cox,

> religion is becoming an increasingly obvious double-edged sword. It can cause conflict and can abate it. Even in those instances where a particular religion may be viewed as part of the problem, whether it is either central to a conflict or has allowed itself to become a mobilising vehicle for nationalist or ethnic passions, such a religion includes in the core of its tradition extensive teachings that encourage neighbourly concern and the betterment of humanity.[490]

---

[486] Richard P. McBrien, *Catholicism* (London: Geoffrey Chapman, 1984), 250.

[487] Ibid.

[488] Little and Appleby, 'A Moment of Opportunity,' 3.

[489] Hock, 'Christian-Muslim Relations in the African Context,' 54.

[490] Douglas Johnston and Brian Cox, 'Faith-Based Diplomacy and Preventive Engagement,' in: *Faith Based Diplomacy Trumping Realpolitik* (New York: Oxford University Press, 2003), 12-14.

Some religious traditions have been active in the process of peace-building, and since some are organised at both national and international levels, they offer existing channels for communication and possess transcendent authority over their adherents that political and secular leaders do not have.[491] They are a unified force for change based on their sets of expectations with the capacity to mobilise community and support the national and international peace process.[492] For political scientist Douglas Johnston, religion remains a catalyst for peacemaking instead of a basis for conflict.[493] I agree with Johnston because, in the peace-building process, religion provides a good platform for dialogue, promotes tolerance and respect, and upholds human rights, equality, and dignity of all. Furthermore, people generally listen to their religious leaders and look up to them with great respect for direction and leadership. According to religion and peace-building analyst Cynthia Sampson, in situations where peace-building requires restructuring and mediating between parties, addressing structural sources of inequalities that may be present in conflict, and transforming violent destructive conflict into constructive, peaceful relationships, religion and religious members have been most effective.[494] Since Christianity and Islam possess resources to foster sustainable peace-building initiatives, both traditions can be enriched by negotiations for peace after decades of violent conflict in the region.

Religion can provide the needed space for encounter (dialogue) with the other. It expresses the deepest feelings and sensitivities of individuals and communities. It carries deep historical memories and often appeals to universal loyalties as expressed in Islam and Christianity.[495] Although religious scholars agree that religious sentiments can be mobilised in violent conflicts, it is equally true that religion can be used to promote peace-building and reconciliation between individuals and communities. Moreover, religions have made meaningful contributions to ongoing peaceful negotiations, for example, in Plateau Nigeria (Jos, Yelwa-Shandam), and

---

[491]   Cynthia Sampson, 'Religion and Peacebuilding,' in I. William Zartman and J. Lewis Rasmussen (eds.), Peacemaking in International Conflict: Methods and Techniques (Washington, DC: United States Institute of Peace Press, 1997), 273-316. http://www. beyondintractability.org/articlesummary/10513/

[492]   Johnston and Cox, 'Faith-Based Diplomacy,' 14.

[493]   Douglas Johnston, 'The Words of the Johnston Family ICRD Founder's Address to Interfaith Audience March 2009,' http://www.tparents.org/Library/Unification/ Talks/Johnston/Johnston-090300.htm (ICRD: International Centre for Religion and Diplomacy).

[494]   Sampson, 'Religion and Peacebuilding.'

[495]   Muhammad Sammak, Peace: A Single Goal and a Shared Intention Forum of Religious Representatives (Vatican City, 23 January 2002), Day of Prayer for Peace (Assisi, 24 January 2002) (Vatican City: Pontifical Council for Interreligious Dialogue, 2002), 49.

other places in Africa (Angola, Burundi, Ethiopia/Eritrea, Liberia, Mozambique, Sierra Leone, Somalia, South Africa, and Sudan).[496] The same holds true in Latin America (Columbia, El Salvador, Guatemala, Mexico, and Peru) and other regions of the world.[497]

In his encyclical letter *Centesimus Annus* of 1991, Pope John Paul II wrote, 'I am convinced that the various religions, now and in the future, will have a pre-eminent role in preserving peace and building a society worthy of humanity.'[498] As a custodian of cultural norms and values, religion possesses the potential to address the most profound existential issues of human life, for example, morality, freedom, fear, security, and peace.[499] Religion is deeply rooted in individual and social conceptions of peace. It has developed laws and ideas that provide civilisation with cultural commitments to critical peace-related values such as empathy, love of neighbour, even strangers, suppression of unbridled ego, human rights, unilateral gestures of forgiveness, humility, reconciliation, and search for social justice. The teachings and practices of religion reveal both spiritual and moral formulations that support peace, social justice, reconciliation, and harmony between individuals and communities.[500]

According to the traditional ruler of Akure Nigeria, Oba Adebiyi Adesida, religion is an engine that can propel and move society to greater heights of peace initiatives because it provides the social, moral, and spiritual resources that hold society together.[501] This facilitates individual and communal transformative approaches to peace-building that radiates out and affects people at different levels.[502] Religion provides the basis for forgiveness and reconciliation, healing the wounds of violent conflict on individuals and communities, fully restoring damaged relationships.

---

[496] Pedro D. Jaime Goncalves, 'The Role of the Church in Conflict Resolution and Consolidation of Peace and Reconciliation in Africa,' in *Secam-Celam: Peace Fruit of Reconciliation* (Nairobi, Kenya: Paulines Publications Africa, 2001), 45-47.

[497] Rosa D. Gregorio Chavez, 'The Role of the Church in the Resolution of Conflict and in Peace Building in Central America,' in *Secam-Celam: Peace Fruit of Reconciliation* (Nairobi, Kenya: Paulines Publications Africa, 2001), 48-59.

[498] Ioannes Paulus PP. II, *Centesimus Annus* (Rome Vatican city: Liberia Editrice, 1991). http://www.vatican.va/holy_father/john_paul_ii/encyclicals/documents/hf_jp-ii_enc_01051991_centesimus-annus_en.html

[499] Religion & Peacebuilding, 'Religion and Peacebuilding Processes,' 2007. http://www.peacebuildinginitiative.org/index.cfm?pageId=1827#_ftn42

[500] Ibid.

[501] Adebayo Waheed, 'Religion: An Engine to Propel Society to Greater Heights—Deji,' *Tribune* (Nigeria), 29 October 2010.

[502] Religion & Peacebuilding, 'Religion and Peacebuilding Processes.'

According to Pope John Paul II, religious traditions possess the spiritual resources needed to heal conflict and division in a community. This is possible through persuasion and appealing to the sense of religious discipline among people to promote mutual friendship, tolerance, and respect. Order, justice, and freedom requires a priority commitment to prayer which opens hearts and minds to dialogue, listening, and commitment to God, the important well-spring of true peace.[503]

Religion addresses the spiritual as well as the conflict experience of a community, thereby providing for the spiritual needs of those affected by such conflict. Heather Dubois, a researcher in the field of religion and conflict, argues that prior to, during, and after conflict, people struggle with existential questions and suffer spiritual, physical, and psychological traumas.[504] In such situations, religious traditions, through their liturgies, rituals, prayers, and spiritual care, offer language and symbols, the needed resources and support by which people can interpret their experiences and cultivate an attitude of forgiveness, reconciliation, and healing.[505] For example, during the sharia riots of 2000-2004 in Kaduna and the religious-political crisis of 2009 and 2010 in Jos, Northern Nigerian religious groups called for the cessation of violence and offered necessary help to the victims.[506]

Furthermore, religious traditions have scriptures to guide them. Since love, respect, understanding, equality, and humility form the central message in the scriptures, especially within Islamic and Christian traditions (Bible and Qur'an), the scriptures are a valuable spiritual resource.[507] These scriptures teach the path of peace, love, and justice. However, within the Bible and Qur'an, there are texts that contradict the above and call for violence, war, and destruction of the other with the full consent of God. For example: 1 Samuel 23: 2-3: *David consulted Yahweh and asked; shall I go and fight with the Philistines? The answer was, Go and attack the Philistines;* Joshua 6: 16-21: *Shout your battle cry for Yahweh has given you the city . . . they seized Jericho and with sword in hand; they killed all the men and women, young and old*; Matthew 10: 34: *do not think I have come to establish peace*

---

[503] 'Address of His Holiness Pope John Paul II,' in *Peace: A Single Goal and a Shared Intention Forum of Religious Representatives (Vatican City, 23 January 2002), Day of Prayer for Peace (Assisi, 24 January 2002)* (Vatican City: Pontifical Council for Interreligious Dialogue, 2002), 90-91.

[504] Dubois, 'Religion and Peacebuilding: An Ambivalent Yet Vital Relationship.'

[505] Ibid.

[506] Jude Owuamanam, 'Relief Materials Pour in for Victims,' *Punch* (Nigeria), 01 February 2010; Seriki Adinoyi, 'NGO Donates Relief Material to Victims,' *This Day* (Nigeria), 17 February 2010.

[507] Harbans Singh, in *Peace: A Single Goal and a Shared Intention Forum of Religious Representatives (Vatican City, 23 January 2002), Day of Prayer for Peace (Assisi, 24 January 2002)* (Vatican City: Pontifical Council for Interreligious Dialogue, 2002), 44.

on earth. I have not come to bring peace but a sword; Qur'an 47: 4: *when you meet the unbelievers, smite at their necks at length, when you have thoroughly subdued them, bind the captive firmly;* Q. 8: 39: *and fight them on till . . . religion becomes Allah's in its entirety;* Q. 9: 5: *and when the forbidden months have passed slay the idolaters wherever you find them and take them captive, and lie in wait for them at every place of ambush.* These are verses in both scriptures I call 'violent verses'. God seems to encourage war and sanction violent conflicts, a total contradiction to the concept of peace in both Christianity and Islam. On the one hand, such verses have been used sometimes to justify war, violence, and exclusion of others. On the other hand, Christians and Muslims cannot ignore those passages within their scriptures that enunciate the message of peace, love, harmony, and togetherness among people. For instance, the Islamic community developed in the city of Mecca in Arabia, where the Prophet lived and received revelation. However, the city was assailed by cycles of tribal wars and conflicts from surrounding Byzantine and Persian empires.[508] Nevertheless, the Qur'anic injunction was that of peace and harmony. 'The Qur'an frequently and strongly balances permission to fight an enemy by mandating the need to make peace' (Q 8: 61).[509]

In most cases, complex social, political, and economic grievances are the primary triggers for violent conflicts, and of course, religion can and does provide a powerful source of motivation to legitimate the cause and mobilise popular support.[510] Nonetheless, religion does provide the framework for a guided, fair, acceptable, dynamic, and lucid interpretation of their scripture in a renewed effort to educate adherents properly on the values of their religious tradition and those of others. (Issues of religious education shall be discussed in the next chapter.) Spiritual resources in religion not only include scriptural foundations but also the example of fellow believers who, down through the ages, have taught and acted as peacemakers. Religion, therefore, can help people of different religious traditions to come together to learn from each other their shared values and to work together to build a community of justice and peace.[511]

According to sociologist Elise Boulding, peace culture maintains creative balance and enhances community bonding. She describes peace culture as a mosaic of identities, attitudes, values, beliefs, and patterns which enable people to nurture

---

[508]   Cf. John L. Esposito, *What Everyone Needs to Know About Islam* (New York: Oxford University Press, 2011), 137-38.

[509]   Ibid.

[510]   See ibid., 138.

[511]   'Spiritual Resources of the Religions for Peace 16-18 January 2003,' in *Spiritual resources of the Religions for Peace: Exploring the Sacred Texts in Promotion of Peace* (Vatican City: Pontifical Council for Interreligious Dialogue, 2003), 11-12.

one another and deal creatively with their differences while sharing their resources.[512] Religion plays an important role in the above process because religious traditions and teachings make significant contributions to shaping societies and communities and have the spiritual resources necessary to bring about a shift from preoccupation with violence to peaceful solutions to problems in the community.

However, religion is not without particular religious agents or subjects. The subjects of religious beliefs and values are human beings and adherents of religious tradition. Religious beliefs and values are expressed within the faith community and in society. In a peace-building process, religious actors are important agents who collaborate with others to resolve conflict and effect transformation within society. It is hence more advantageous if, for example, religious actors are formally trained to become advocates, mediators, and apostles of peace.[513] Such people make a valuable contribution to religious education, mobilisation for peace, and advocacy and network building for sustained dialogue in moving society towards greater integration.[514]

Religions promote positive efforts for better mutual understanding and greater collaboration between people of differing religions or cultural backgrounds in a spirit of respect and genuine understanding of the other, honouring the differences and facilitating peaceful coexistence.[515] Religion has the potential to promote, teach, and support the language and gestures of peace among believers and between communities.[516] Religion can mobilise people against conflict violence, facilitate openness to dialogue and the cooperation required of individuals and groups to sustain the peace-building process. Muslims and Christians in Northern Nigeria have the task of searching and interpreting their scriptures and religious traditions for ways that are tolerant of the other, saying no to violence and fostering mutual respect and dialogue.

In this section, I have argued that religion (Islam and Christianity) has the potential to make a unique contribution to peace-building in a conflict situation by mobilising adherents to engage with one another peacefully, using the resources

---

[512] Boulding, 'Peace Culture'.

[513] Little and Appleby, 'A Moment of Opportunity,' 5-6.

[514] Religion & Peacebuilding, 'Religion and Peacebuilding.'

[515] Francis Arinze, *Reflections by Cardinal Francis Arinze on the Day of Prayer at Assisi, 24 January 2002* (Vatican City: Libreria Eitrice Pontifical Council of Interreligious Dialogue, 2002). http://www.vatican.va/roman_curia/pontifical_councils/interelg/documents/rc_pc_interelg_doc_20020116_arinze-assisi_en.html

[516] Pope John Paul II, 'To Reach Peace, Teach Peace,' *Message of His Holiness Pope John Paul II for the Celebration of the Day of Peace, 1 January 1979* (Rome Vatican City: Libreria Editrice, 1978), no. 2. http://www.vatican.va/holy_father/john_paul_ii/messages/peace/documents/hf_jp-ii_mes_19781221_xii-world-day-for-peace_en.html

within their religious tradition to achieve harmony and coexistence in the larger society. The next section focuses on peace-building.

3.1.1 PEACE BUILDING

This section highlights the need for sustained peace building activities modelled on the theology that appreciates and respects the uniqueness of each religious tradition.

According to theologian Joanna Dewey, peace is often associated with righteousness, security, prosperity, material well-being, and safety. It is also associated with truth and a sense of faithfulness. However, within the Islamic and Christian traditions, peace is a gift from God who is the source of peace. It is a spiritual resource that exists between people and in relation to God, and is eschatological. Peace is not just the absence of war and strife among peoples, communities, and nations but complete serenity and order between individuals in a community, in a country, and the world at large.[517]

For St. Augustine of Hippo, peace among humans is the result of oneness of heart (cordia) rooted in the love of friendship. It is perfect only when a person's love is well ordered and possesses everything that it desires. Peace depends on goodwill and is truly a gift from God more than any human accomplishment. It is the essence of friendship and is possible at every level of human society. Peace among human beings begins with the experience of peace in the person. The peace of larger society flows from the peace of individuals because 'you are able to have oneness of heart in your common love of God and are at least prepared to be friends on a human level too'.[518]

Vatican II's *Pastoral Constitution on the Church in the Morden World* (*Gaudium et Spes,* no.78) declares that peace is not merely the absence of war, nor can it be understood solely as the maintenance of a balance of power between enemies. Peace is not brought about by dictatorship; instead, it is an enterprise of justice, based on the common good of humanity. Peace is never attained once and for all but must be built up continually. Peace cannot be obtained unless personal well-being is safeguarded and men and women freely and trustingly share the riches of their inner spirits and their talents with one another, with firm determination to respect the dignity of all.[519]

---

[517] Joanna Dewey, 'Peace,' in Paul J. Achtemeier (ed.), *Harpers Bible Dictionary* (San Francisco: Plaper & Row Publishers, 1985), 766.

[518] Donald X. Burt, 'Peace,' In Allan D. Fitzgerald (ed.), *Augustine through the Ages: An Encyclopaedia* (Grand Rapids, MI: William B. Eerdmans Publishing, 1999), 629-31.

[519] Austin Flannery (ed.), 'Pastoral Constitution on the Church in the Modern World,' *Vatican Council II: The Conciliar and Post Conciliar Documents* (New York: Scholarly Resources, 1975), 986-87.

In addition, peace is a value and a universal duty founded on the rational and moral order of society that is rooted in God the creator. Peace is the fruit of justice and love shared in the community. It is threatened when human dignity is not respected and religious and civil life is not directed to the common good.[520] Moreover, the defence and promotion of human rights is essential when building a peaceful society and the integral development of all peoples.[521]

In his message for the World Day of Peace 1968, Pope Paul VI described peace as a spirit which animates coexistence between peoples, a new outlook on humanity and its destiny. Peace is not just pacifism; it is a value that proclaims the highest and most universal values of life: truth, justice, freedom, love, and reconciliation.[522]

As mentioned above, both Christianity and Islam profess to be religions of peace.[523] However, religion has become a divisive and sensitive issue, constituting a flash-point of growing conflict.[524] Violent conflicts have erupted in the name of religion, people have been killed and property destroyed, as witnessed in northern Nigeria.[525] It can be argued that the violent situation in Northern Nigeria is an example of the failure of religion in promoting peace and harmony.

Although the Bible admonishes Christians to *Live in peace with one another* (Rm. 12: 16), this can be interpreted to mean living in peace with other members of the Christian community. If that is the case, how does this call affect and shape the relationship between Christians and people of other faith traditions? What is the right interpretation of this text? What is the theological implication of such an interpretation? The interpretation of such a biblical text cannot be ignorant of our common origin and the pluralistic nature of society.[526] In the same vein, the Qur'an says, *O you who believe, enter into Islam (peace) whole-heartedly* (Qur'an 2: 208). This may be interpreted to mean entering into peace with the members of Islamic community, which excludes non-Muslims. A broader interpretation means peace, love, and respect for all in the community. These are some of the tensions and

---

[520] Pontifical Council for Justice and Peace, *Compendium of the Social Doctrine of the Church* (Dublin Ireland: Veritas Publications, 2005), 231.

[521] Ibid., 232.

[522] Paulus VI. PP, *Message of His Holiness Pope Paul VI for the Observance of World Day of Peace, 1 January 1968* (Rome Vatican City: Libreria Editrice, 1967). http://www.vatican. va/holy_father/paul_vi/messages/peace/documents/hf_p-vi_mes_19671208_i-world-day-for-peace_en.html

[523] Owojaiye, 'Factors Responsible for Muslim-Christian Unrest in Nigeria.'

[524] Best, *Religion and Religious Conflicts in Northern Nigeria*, 63.

[525] Ibid., 63-65.

[526] Joseph A. Fitzmyer, 'The Letter to the Romans,' in Raymond E. Brown, Joseph A. Fizmyer, Ronald E. Murphy, and O. Carm (eds.), *The Jerome Biblical Commentary* (London: Geoffrey Chapman, 1968), 325.

contradictions inherent in the interpretation of scripture without proper guidance from exegetes. A proper hermeneutic of scripture is crucial to religious peace building.

Peace building must seek to address the causes of violent conflict and build a culture of peace on (religious) values of non-violence, respect, freedom, justice, reconciliation, solidarity, tolerance, unity, equality, dialogue, cooperation, and appreciation of our cultural and religious diversity.[527] The process is advanced effectively by initiating common activities and programmes that cut across religious traditions to engage with others in the community. This involves information sharing, planning, and support in the process. Religious members must reach out to other individuals in the community with whom they share a commitment to peaceful coexistence and mutual understanding. Each community needs to know who its potential partner might be in the peace building process.[528] In his encyclical *Pacem in Terris* of 1963, Pope John XXIII observed that the peace on earth which humanity has longed for and sought after throughout the ages can never be established or guaranteed except by diligent observance of the divinely established order of mutual love, respect, tolerance, and dialogue with the other.[529]

In my analysis, religion and the peace building process must develop models that take into consideration the unique nature of each religious tradition, appreciate the similarities, respect the differences, and build harmony on common grounds through sustained dialogue. I now propose two models of peace: a model of unity and a model of union.

The model of unity seeks to unite different faith traditions as they all seek the same truth in their own unique ways. The outlook of this model is the universality of all religions. However, this unity model does not appreciate the differences in the various religious traditions and the need for constant dialogue and negotiation to understand such differences in order to build lasting peace. It is a model of peace that will not last and cannot sustain the process of peace building in a pluralistic world.

The model of union seeks to understand the uniqueness of each religious tradition. It appreciates the differences and similarities in the various religions and advocates harmony by accepting and respecting these differences. It is a model of

---

[527] Vincent Gamut, 'Peace Education and Peer Mediation,' in Shedrack G. Best (ed.), *Introduction to Peace and Conflict Studies in West Africa* (Ibadan, Nigeria: Spectrum Books, 2005), 172.

[528] 'Building Interreligious Trust in a Climate of Fear: An Abrahamic Trialogue,' *Special Report*, no. 99 (Washington: United State Institute of Peace, 2003), 8. http://www.usip.org

[529] Michael Walsh and Brian Davies (eds.), 'Pacem in Terris,' in *Proclaiming Justice and Peace: Documents from John XXIII to John Paul II* (London: Collins Liturgical Publications, 1984), 48.

love, dialogue, and respecting otherness.[530] This model advocates a religious dialogue of hope that relationships between people will be increasingly inspired by the ideals of our common human origin and that such ideals will be shared by the different religious traditions in a way that ensures respect for human rights and sustainable peace. It advocates a religious dialogue that leads to the recognition of our diversity and fosters mutual acceptance and genuine collaboration for peace building among different faith communities.[531]

Peaceful coexistence between Muslims and Christians in Northern Nigeria is a challenge to all in the locality. Christian and Muslim leaders, scholars, and religious actors can explore the model of union described above to build peace in the region. The activities of the Interfaith Mediation Centre (IFMC) and the Nigerian Interreligious Council (NIREC) discussed in Chapter 2 are important in actualising this model. What are the peace building resources within Islam and Christianity? The next section considers the faith community as the framework where peace building activities can develop and flourish.

3.2 Faith Community and Peace Building

In this sub-section, I shall analyse faith community as the core structure in which belief systems develop.

Religious tradition provides the setting within which faith communities can explore their spiritual resources for growth to promote harmony and peace in society. According to historians Ernest Kurtz and Katherine Ketcham, a faith community is created when people seek the same spiritual values in the company of friends and fellow seekers—men and women who listen, share their experience, offer advice and support to help one another clarify questions about God, and recognise available options in making choices that help them grow towards God.[532] Thus belonging to a particular faith community is a form of identity. People come together to form communities within the larger society, creating new identities, for instance Christian, Muslim, Hindu, or Buddhist. Moreover, society provides the opportunity for people of different faith traditions to interact and experience each other in a unique way. Christians, for example, are called to bear witness to their faith in their service to others. This vocation of

---

[530] Cf. Werner G. Jeanrond, *A Theology of Love* (London: T & T Clark International, 2010), 1-4.

[531] See Pope John Paul II, 'Dialogue between Cultures for a Civilization of Love and Peace,' *Message of His Holiness Pope John Paul II for the Celebration of the World Day of Peace, 1 January 2001* (Rome Vatican City: Libreria Editrice, 2001). http://www.vatican.va/holy_father/john_paul_ii/messages/peace/documents/hf_jp-ii_mes_20001208_xxxiv-world-day-for-peace_en.html

[532] Kurtz and Ketcham, *The Spirituality of Imperfection*, 87.

witnessing within society builds an experience that can enrich and enhance theological hermeneutics by fostering a spirituality that relates to the other not just as 'the other' but as a neighbour. The discourse of Jesus on the 'Good Samaritan' is an obligation and a prime example of Christian witnessing (Lk. 10: 25-37).

In the African traditional setting, life is communitarian. Individuals make up the community, whether religious or social. However, the individual cannot exist outside the community. The community gives the individual his/her self-worth, name, social identity, and security. Community life in Northern Nigeria is organised and based on the values of unity, respect, hospitality, honesty, sincerity, accountability, hard work, sharing, care for the neighbour, tolerance, harmony, security, consultation, dialogue, and peace. Christianity and Islam also profess and promote these (African) community values.

The early Christians in the Acts of the Apostles lived in communities, caring for one another while striving to live in peace with those who did not profess the same faith (Acts 2: 42-47).[533] This tradition continues throughout the New Testament era and the early church. Unfortunately, religious wars, violent crusades, and forced conversion have punctuated the history of the church.[534] However, the Church as the body of Christ for Christians is a community of faith and an institution of love.[535] The Christian faith has always challenged those determined to follow Christ to love God and neighbour in the praxis of love as a way of life, worship, and community of discipleship.[536] Such a community is committed to peace building through catechesis, prayer, liturgical-worship, sacraments, and witnessing to the love of God by love of neighbour (Mk. 12: 29-31).[537] In Northern Nigeria, the thrust of pastoral theology is based on the conception of the 'Small or Basic Christian Community' (SCC or BCC).[538] Moreover, the vocation of living out the Christian faith is both immediate

---

[533]   Cf. Henry Chadwick, *The Early Church: The Story of Emergent Christianity from the Apostolic Age to the Dividing of the Ways between the Greek East and the Latin West* (England: Penguin Books, 1993), 1-31.

[534]   Ibid.

[535]   See Jeanrond, *Theology of Love*, 215.

[536]   Pelikan, 'Christianity,' 354-55.

[537]   Cf. Jeanrond, *Theology of Love*, 215.

[538]   See Thomas A. Kleissler, Margo A. LeBert, and Mary C. McGuinness, *Small Christian Communities: A Vision of Hope for the 21st Century* (New York: Paulist Press, 1997), 9-13. *Note*: Small or Basic Christian Community is the gathering of a small number of Christians, for example between eight and twenty people who invest time with one another for the common purpose of applying gospel values to every aspect of their lives. The aim is to create an environment in which people can grow in openness to the gospel, transforming every area of their lives and enhancing their commitment to live the mission of Christ. Cf. 111-12.

and eschatological. Thus Christian discipleship calls for witnessing to the love of God in society by the praxis of love in full anticipation of that future hope of transformation into God's unending eternity.[539] Accordingly, pastoral work is geared towards strengthening the Christian community in justice, equality, peace, love, freedom, and care for all in society (Rm. 13: 8-10; Jn 13: 34-35; 1 Jn 4: 16).

In the same vein, Islamic faith and traditions are organised and believes in a worldwide community of all Muslims, known as the Islamic *Ummah*, derived from the Arabic word *Umm,* meaning mother.[540] Before the advent of Islam, *Ummah* was used in Arabic poetry to denote a 'religious community'.[541] According to sociologist Riaz Hassan, the term *Ummah* denotes a transitional community that encompasses all Muslims, whose cohesiveness and social integration is based on the Qur'an and the commonly shared values of Islamic faith.[542] The *Ummah* is united by a religious bond that transcends all ethnic, tribal, social, cultural, and political identities (Q. 2: 143). Thus to profess Islam confers on the individual the status of membership of the world wide *Ummah*.[543] Community spirit is the driving force which impels Muslims to defend and protect other Muslims and support membership of the *Ummah* as the primary identity of all Muslims.[544] This sense of community among Muslims is essential for the unity of the *Ummah.* Muslims believe that what happens to Muslims in one part of the world affects the *Ummah* all over the world.[545] For instance, the publication of the Danish cartoons of Prophet Muhammad in February 2006 sparked riots in Northern Nigeria.[546] The task of the *Ummah* is to establish an order that thrives on the values of justice, equality, peace, love, and care for one another based on belief in one God.[547] Islam, like Christianity, is a way of life, a path to righteousness, and a hope that is eschatological, an eternal transformation in God for those who believe (Q. 45: 22).[548] Both Islam and Christianity are community-orientated. In Northern Nigeria, the two faith communities live side by side. Members of each faith community interact with each other as they go about

---

[539] Cf. Jeanrond, *Theology of Love*, 215-17.

[540] Esposito, *What Everyone Needs to Know*, 16-17.

[541] Cf. Riaz Hassan, *Faithlines: Muslim Concepts of Islam and Society* (New York: Oxford University Press, 2002), 86.

[542] Ibid., 84-85.

[543] Esposito, *What Everyone Needs to Know*, 16-17.

[544] Ibid.

[545] The Imam and the Pastor: A Documentary Film from the Heart of Nigeria, produced and directed. Alan Channer, 60 minutes, FLT films, 2006, DVD.

[546] Cf. Akaeze, 'From Maitatsine to Boko Haram.'

[547] See Hassan, 'Faithlines,' 92.

[548] Cf. Mona Siddiqui, *How to Read the Qur'an* (London: Granta Books, 2007), 31. See also Esposito, *What Everyone Needs to Know*, 5-6.

their business. Contemporary Northern Nigeria presents Christians and Muslims with the challenge of religious plurality and the need to foster mutual collaboration and friendship through peaceful cooperation of all in society.

Christians and Muslims in Northern Nigeria have common ground for such collaboration. For example, the Christian community has the Bible, the word of God that guides and orders the life of a Christian. The Muslim community has the Qur'an as a guide in the path of righteousness. These sacred scriptures are central for the two faith communities since they contain the fundamentals of the believer's relationship with God and the other.[549] These sacred books of both faith traditions are an invitation to a spiritual journey where one encounters the tender embrace and the infinite depths of the transforming grace of divine compassion lived out daily in humility, freedom, self-control, simplicity, wisdom, love, and respect for others.[550]

However, the concept of leadership and authority within these faith communities remains a challenge that needs to be analysed and understood. In the Christian tradition, leadership stems from the Bible: in some church denominations, this is ordered hierarchically under a single authority. For example, the Catholic Magisterium (the teaching authority of the Church) consists of the Pope and Bishops, who govern the Roman Catholic Church.[551] The Archbishop of Canterbury heads the worldwide Anglican Communion, and presently, Olav Fykse Tveit is the current president of the World Council of Churches (WCC). The CBCN, the Primate of the Church of Nigerian Anglican Communion (Rev. Nicholas Okoh), the National President Pentecostal Fellowship of Nigeria (PFN, Pastor Ayo Oritsejafor), and the Prelate of the Methodist Church Nigeria (Rev. Ola Makinde) are responsible for leading the various Christian denominations in Nigeria. On many occasions they have spoken in one voice through the CAN. These local Churches work in collaboration with the existing authority of their worldwide denominations in matters of theological hermeneutics, social, political, and general administration.

In contrast, the Islamic *Ummah* does not have a universal existing authority that regulates matters of theological hermeneutics and general administration. The Qur'an has central authority on issues of faith and life within the *Ummah*. According to philosopher of Arabic literature Kister J. Meir, each Islamic community should have a leader (an imam) whose duty it is to keep the unity of the Muslim *Ummah* firmly in his charge, to listen, obey, and adhere closely to the *Ummah* and guide it in the

---

549   Siddiqui, *How to Read the Qur'an*, 15.

550   Cf. Martha Ann Kirk, *Women of Bible Lands: A Pilgrimage to Compassion and Wisdom* (Collegeville, MN: Liturgical Press, 2004), 36-40.

551   Cf. William G. Most, 'The Magisteruim or Teaching Authority of the Church,' http://www. ewtn.com/faith/teachings/chura4.htm; see also Luke 10: 16; *Catechism of the Catholic Church*, 251-58; and John Salza, *The Biblical Basis for the Papacy* (Huntington, WV: Our Sunday Visitor, 2007).

right path to Allah (God).[552] He adds that there is need for a community consensus about the person(s) who have the responsibility of leading the *Ummah*. The faithful must obey their imam while the imam has the responsibility of leading and guiding the community in the way of righteousness. The *Ummah* reciprocates by praying, listening, and collaborating with the imam.[553]

In Nigeria, the Sultan of Sokoto, His Eminence Alhaji Muhammad Sa'ad Abubakar III, is the leader of the Nigerian Islamic community. He speaks on matters of faith and the social and political life of Muslims in the country. However, issues of theological and scriptural hermeneutics are left to the various Islamic sects, schools of thought, and individual imams.[554] Nevertheless, the thrust of the two faith traditions in Northern Nigeria is towards building a strong vibrant faith community. This, of course, does not happen without tensions and misunderstandings between the two. The challenge remains thus: what can the two faith communities learn from each other? The next section analyses the potential in Islam and Christianity for sustained peace building in Northern Nigeria.

3.3 RELIGIOUS RESOURCES FOR PEACE BUILDING

In this section, I shall focus on the resources within religion for peace building. The emphasis is on harnessing the various spiritual assets in Christianity and Islam that foster mutual harmony.

According to conflict analysts Judy Carter and Gordon Smith, Islam and Christianity uniquely possess and offer a rich abundance of guidance and insight into peace building.[555] A close reflection on their teachings reveals a striking similarity in their ethical foundations and underlying principles for peace and cooperation. These religious traditions preach peace and advocate a social code that admonishes adherents to love and respect the other. 'Do unto other as you would have them do unto you' (the Golden Rule).[556]

Both Christianity and Islam have scriptures (Bible and Qur'an) and have developed an impressive spiritual tradition. They regard faith in God, kindness, charity, compassion, honesty, justice, fairness, equality, sincerity, tolerance, respect, humility, non-violence,

---

[552] Cf. Kister J. Meir, 'Social and Religious Concepts of Authority in Islam,' *Jerusalem Studies in Arabic and Islam*, no. 18 (1991), 102-06.

[553] Ibid., 108-09.

[554] See Lateef Abdul Adegbite, 'Unity of the Nigerian Ummah: An Imperative for the 21st Century,' 2008. http://www. Islamicforumng.org/FWI/Chapter%202

[555] Judy Carter and Gordon S. Smith, 'Religious Peacebuilding: From Potential to Action,' in Harod Coward and Gordon S. Smith (eds.), *Religion and Peacebuilding* (Albany: State University of New York Press, 2004), 279-81.

[556] Ibid.

forbearance, self-discipline, moderation, prayer, forgiveness, reconciliation, and peace as virtues. The founders of these religions preached peace and lived in peace within their communities. These religions have remained the source of peace and strength for believers, a way of finding meaning to life, communal interaction, dialogue, and meeting the spiritual needs of individuals and the community at large.[557]

Religion has and will continue to play a vital role in the process of peace building if the spiritual wealth of peace and harmony within religion is properly harnessed for unity, tolerance, dialogue, and peaceful coexistence. Christianity and Islam offer Christians and Muslims ample resources to address issues of violence, religious stereotypes, the use of aggressive language, and utter disrespect of the other. Moreover, the potential for peace and harmony in these religions is of justice, equality, and respect for the rights and dignity of others.[558] The Islamic and Christian traditions possess the potential to resolve conflicts, address hostilities, and build peace in Northern Nigeria. This is achievable by a process of sustained interreligious dialogue meetings and willingness to meet and engage with the other, resulting in greater understanding, acceptance, and appreciation of differences and similarities within these religious traditions. However, the cooperation and solidarity of adherents of these religious traditions are essential if conflict issues are to be addressed. We shall now focus on Islam to explore its potential for peace building.

3.3.1 ISLAM

In this segment, I examine Islam to consider the resources for peace within the Islamic religious tradition with focus on the Qur'an and Hadith. 9/11, a tragic attack on the twin towers in New York, intensified and sharpened the socio-political debate about peace and security and the teachings and contributions of religion to sustainable peace. Critics who perceived the attack as a religious Jihad wondered whether a call for violence is central to Islamic faith.[559] Those who read the attacks as an act of terrorism continue to question, analyse, and assess the contributions of Islam to peace.

---

[557] Adenike Yesufu, 'And Peace for All,' *Vanguard* (Nigeria), 25 July 2010. http://www. vanguardngr.com/2010/07/25and-peace-forall/

[558] See Francis Arinze, 'Religions Witnessing to Justice and Peace,' in *Peace: A Single Goal and a Shared Intention Forum of Religious Representatives (Vatican City, 23 January 2002), Day of Prayer for Peace (Assisi, 24 January 2002)* (Vatican City: Pontifical Council for Interreligious Dialogue, 2002), 13-14.

[559] Hisham Soliman, 'The Potential for Peace Building in Islam: Towards an Islamic Concept of Peace,' *Journal of Religion Conflict and Peace* 2, no. 2 (2009). http://www. plowsharesproject.org/journal/php/article.php?issu_list_id=12&article_list_id=39

According to political scientist Hisham Soliman, much research has focused on the relationship between Islam and violence, leaving the relationship between Islam and peace building largely unexplored. He argues that broadening the horizon to include the relationship between Islam and peace building is very critical, as Islam can be a resource for peace. Moreover, highlighting the peaceful insights of Islam improves the outlook on Islamic faith and strengthens dialogue and peace initiatives with other religious traditions.[560]

Islamic traditions, scholars, and adherents present Islam as a religion of peace and harmony, in obedience and submission to the will of God. According to philosopher of religion Cafer Yaran, Islam teaches peace and harmony and requires all Muslims to seek peace and happiness through submission to the will of God.[561] Islam preaches a universal message of peace for the whole of humanity. Qur'an 2: 208 teaches, *O ye who believe enter into Islam whole-heartedly* . . . The Qur'an invites believers to peace by submission to God, a way of life for Muslims and peace towards others.[562] Humans are created by God in a state of harmony and peace, and therefore peace shall be the eschatological destiny of all (Qur'an 10: 25).[563]

In the same vein, Islamic scholar Asghar Ali Engineer affirms that Islam is a religion of peace and does not allow for violence in any form. He argues that even when the Qur'an permits war, it is only to defend and protect the rights of the oppressed and exploited and not for achieving prominence over others.[564] Imam Zaid Shakir agrees and further argues that Islam is a religion of peace. However, the understanding of the true meaning of peace is eschatological, associated with a transformed world. Islam encourages Muslims to live in peace in the *Ummah* and peace in society.[565] He concludes that living in peace with one another and extending peace to those in the wider community demonstrate that Islam is a religion of peace.[566]

Nevertheless, some scholars, religious leaders, critics, and analysts have quoted Qur'anic sources saying that Islam is committed to Jihad, war, and violence, and thus the claim that Islam is a religion of peace is untrue.[567] Many non-Muslims, and even

---

[560] Ibid.

[561] Yaran, *Understanding Islam*, vii-1.

[562] Hassan, 'What Does It Mean to Be a Muslim Today?'

[563] Ibid.

[564] Asghar Ali Engineer, *On Developing Theology of Peace in Islam* (New Delhi: Stering Publishers, 2003), 115.

[565] Cf. Imam Zaid Shakir, 'The Concept of Peace and Justice in Islam,' 2011. http://www.irfi.org/articles2/articles_3051_3100/The%20Concept%20Of%20Peace%20and%20Justice%20in%20Islam.htm

[566] Ibid.

[567] See Kamran Sayed Mirza, 'An Exegesis of Islamic Peace,' 2002. http://www.faithfreedom.org/Articles/SKM/Islamic_peace.htm

Muslims, are of the opinion that Islam is inherently against any form of friendliness towards non-Muslims. Some assume that Islam prescribes that the normative relationship between Muslims and non-Muslims is one of violence, war, and intolerance.[568] Meanwhile, peace and conflict analyst Ayse Kadayifci Orellana argues that, even though some groups and individuals within the Islamic tradition have resorted to extreme forms of violence in the name of Islam, the Islamic principle of peace goes back to the Qur'an, which promotes non-violence.[569] The Islamic tradition is rich in values and practices that encourage tolerance, peacemaking, and dialogue. Peace building activities take place in mosques, in sermons, in religious education in schools and madrassas, and at informal gatherings and meetings.[570]

The Qur'an and Hadith are a major source of peaceful collaboration in Islam. QUR'AN: the Islamic Holy Scripture is a vital spiritual source within Islam. It is the word of God in Islam and a guide for Muslims. It contain themes such as love (Qur'an 28: 56), mercy (3: 157-158), goodness (23.96; 4: 86), compassion, justice (4: 58; 135; 16: 90), peace (2: 208; 10: 10; 8: 61; 56: 25-26), respect, forgiveness (4: 64; 106), equality (49: 13), reconciliation (49: 10), and trust (3: 75).

HADITH: a report, a tradition of remarks or actions of the Prophet. It is a collection of the sayings and deeds of Prophet Muhammad.[571] These are authoritative statements about rituals and the moral and religious concerns of Muslims. Hans Küng upholds that the Prophet has a saying for all important aspects of the life of a Muslim. For example, questions of faith, life, morals, family, relationships, and justice are addressed.[572] In the Hadith, Muslims can find specific examples and rules for any circumstance in life which the Qur'an has not mentioned. Muslims are guided by the Hadith because there they have the explicit teachings of the Prophet. The Hadith is the second source of Islamic law after the Qur'an.[573]

Accordingly, Muslim leaders, Islamic scholars, exegetes, and preachers are responsible for interpreting these texts and making this knowledge available. Since the Qur'an is the abiding foundation of Islamic life and principles, its values must be read,

---

[568] Cf. Islamic Education Trust, Train the Trainers Course (TTC) in *Islam and Dialogue for Peaceful Coexistence Basic Module 101* (Minna, Nigeria: Da'wah Institute of Nigeria, 2010), 64.

[569] Ayse S. Kadayifci-Orellana, 'Among Muslims, Peace Building Takes on Its Own Distinct Forms,' *Harvard Divinity Bulletin* 35, no. 4 (2007). http://www.thecmcg.com/index.php?/archives/6-Among-Muslims,-peace-building-takes-on-its-own-distinct-forms html—34k

[570] Ibid.

[571] Marston Speight, 'Christians in the Hadith Literature,' in Lloyd Ridgeon (ed.), *Islamic Interpretations of Christianity* (London: Curzon Press, 2001), 30-31.

[572] Küng, *Islam: Past, Present and Future*, 263.

[573] Ibid., 263-65.

understood, appreciated, and applied in the peace building process.[574] Furthermore, attempts must be made to reinterpret historical symbols, stories, and other events in the Islamic tradition that legitimise shunning violence in all its forms. Qur'anic sources that condemn violence and war should be emphasised. Those verses that encourage tolerance and kindness towards all people without exception should be highlighted (Q 5: 64 and 16: 90).[575] Muslims must expound on the religious values of these themes and reach out so that that there is peace and harmony with non-Muslims.

In his article 'Islam and Peace building: Continuities and Transition', Islamic historian Frederick Denny argues that for decades, western stereotypes have perceived Islam as an aggressive religion. This has come from the experience of the crusades. Medieval critics continue to focus on Prophet Muhammad as the architect of all that is evil and violent in Islam. These critics seem to know very little about Muhammad, the Qur'an, and Islamic law.[576] Meanwhile, the Qur'an emphasises tolerance and kindness towards other people without exception. For instance, *God commands you to treat (everyone) justly, generously and with kindness* (Qur'an 16: 90).

For Islamic leaders such as Imam Salih Yucel, Islam, and the majority of Muslims disapprove of violence and fanaticism. Political ideas or violent actions of marginal groups have often been presented throughout the world as the real Islam. Some academics, writers, and preachers have analysed Islamic principles and traditions and conclude that Islam is not a religion of violence but one of tolerance and peace. However, their voices have often been unheard. He further argues that Islam is often singled out as being violent, warlike, a 'religion of the sword'. It is true that in the Qur'an (and the Bible) there are verses that seem to encourage violence and war. Such verses are circumstancial and must be read and interpreted within their historical context.[577] Those scriptural passages that do not encourage harmony and peace need to be re-examined in a renewed effort to educate adherents in plurality of religions and the values of peace and harmony.[578] Moreover, the Qur'an accepts the plurality of religions when it expresses, in a number of ways, a

---

[574] Ibid., 66.

[575] Mohammad Abu-Nimer, 'The Miracle of Transformation through Interfaith Dialogue: Are You a Believer?' in David R. Smoke (ed.), *Interfaith Dialogue and Peacebuilding* (Washington, DC: United Institute of Peace, 2007), 230.

[576] Denny, 'Islam and Peace Building,' 134-41.

[577] Imam Sali Yucel, 'Qur'an and Tolerance,' *Islamic Movement for Non-Violence.* http://Islamnon-violence.org/en/Qur'an-and-tolerance/

[578] 'Final Declaration of the Participants in the Symposium on Spiritual Resources of the Religions for Peace Rome, 16-18 January 2003.' http://www.vatican.va/roman_curia/pontifical_councils/interelg/documents/rc_pc_interelg_doc_20030211_religions-peace_en.html

fundamental tolerance for the earlier religions whose faith centers on the one and only God (Qur'an 29: 46).[579]

The Prophet's example enjoins Muslims to peace and tolerance, and respect for non-Muslims remains paramount. This is demonstrated when the Prophet received a delegation of sixty Christians from Najran in the year 10 A. H. They ate, slept, and were permitted to pray in the Prophet's mosque in Madinah. This exemplifies the respect the Prophet had for these Christians' right to practise their faith.[580] Islamic tradition also indicates that the Prophet received some pagans of Banu Thaqif from Taif in his mosque in 9 A. H.[581] In the Meccan period of the Prophet's life (610-622 C.E.), he lived a life of non-violent resistance, as is reflected in his teachings, focusing on values of patience and steadfastness even in the face of oppression.[582] Besides, the Hadith of the Prophet challenges Muslims to exercise love, kindness, mercy, charity, and trust in Allah (God).[583]

Islamic scholars and preachers are challenged to evolve a theology of peace building based on the Qur'an and the Hadith, that is a theology that is sensitive to the diverse nature of society, a theology that seeks to encourage Muslims to a genuine encounter with the religious other. Understanding the faith of others requires not only the knowledge of the sacred sources of a religion but also an awareness of what people actually believe and practise.[584] The Qur'an and Hadith are the guide for Muslims in Northern Nigeria to work with Christians to build a community of love, justice, peace, and togetherness—a community of neighbours living in peace and respecting their religious differences.

3.3.2 CHRISTIANITY

In this sub-section, I shall consider the Christian faith as a spiritual resource for the cultivation of harmonious coexistence with people of other faith traditions, despite seeming contradictions.

The central message of the life and ministry of Jesus centres on love, peace, forgiveness, and respect of the other. Even though the author of the gospel of Matthew 10: 24-36 seems very ironic when he presents Jesus as saying, 'Do not think I have

---

[579] Shihab, *Christian-Muslim Relations*, 71.

[580] 'Islamic Education Trust,' 78.

[581] Ahmad Imtiaz, 'Friendship with Non-Muslims,' Quoted in Islamic Education Trust, 78.

[582] Abu-Nimer, 'The Miracle of Transformation,' 230.

[583] A.I. Rahman Doi, *Hadith: An Introduction* (Ile-Ife, Nigeria: Kazi Publications, 1980), 83-109.

[584] See also Esposito, 'The Future of Islam,' 5.

come to establish peace on earth. I have come not to bring peace, but a sword.'[585] Also, in the Old Testament, there is a seeming justification for violence and war in the law of revenge, *lex talionis* (Ex. 21: 24), in the plan of God for his people.[586] However, according to conflict analyst Andrea Bartoli, Jesus's pronouncement, 'I have come not to abolish the law but to fulfil it', refers to the law of love and peace. He argues that Jesus's own life is an example. Although Jesus was crucified, he did not use violence against his adversaries. Instead he preached a radical message of peace, forgiveness, and reconciliation with enemies.[587]

The theology of the Second Vatican Council teaches that, in bearing witness to the message of Jesus, Christianity has recognised diversity in the world. 'True pluralism is impossible unless communities of different origins and culture undertake dialogue.'[588] Although Christianity possesses valuable resources for peace, throughout history, Christianity has at various times generated and fuelled violent conflicts, for example, the Crusades. Nevertheless, Christianity has made some remarkable contributions to peace building by drawing inspiration from the Bible, which contains a wealth of instructions about living in peace and harmony.[589]

Within the Christian tradition, the Bible is the major resource for peace building. 'Blessed are the peace makers for they shall be called the children of God' (Matt. 5: 9). St. Paul and other New Testament writers have urged Christians to do their best and live in peace with everyone (Rm. 12: 18; 1 Cor. 7: 15; Heb. 12: 14; 1 Pet. 3: 11). Peace is not just the absence of war and conflict. According to scripture scholar John McKenzie, Christians are called to a vocation of interior calm and harmonious relations in the community.[590] In the Biblical tradition, *shalom*, 'peace', is a gift from God, a positive concept. It indicates well-being, prosperity, and integrity. It implies physical health, economic security, and sound social relationships. It is part of the covenant relationship between God and his people. It is to be cultivated and preserved as part of the universal order. Peace in the Bible is comprehensive. It goes hand in hand with justice and righteousness. The prophet Isaiah says that in order

---

[585] Ralph Martin Novak, *Christianity and the Roman Empire Background Texts* (Harrisburg, PA: Trinity Press International, 2001), x.

[586] Michael Amaladoss, *Peace on Earth* (Bombay: St. Paul Press, 2003), 19-20.

[587] Andria Bartuli, 'Christianity and Peacebuilding,' in Harold Coward and Gordon S. Smith (eds.), *Religion and Peacebuilding* (Albany: State University of New York Press, 2004), 148-58.

[588] Austin Flannery (ed.), 'Church in the Modern World,' *Vatican Council II: The Conciliar and Post Conciliar Documents* (New York: Scholarly Resources, 1975), 1002-03.

[589] Ingo Baldermann, 'The Bible as a Teacher of Peace,' in H. Gordon and L. Grob (eds.), *Education for Peace: Testimonies from World Religions* (New York: Orbis Books, 1987), 76.

[590] McKenzie, *Dictionary of the Bible*, 652.

to obtain peace we must practise justice in all spheres of life (Is. 32: 17).[591] In the Christian tradition, Jesus is the prince of peace. He brought peace by reconciling humanity to God. (Eph. 2: 14-17). In practical terms, what does this mean for Christians in Northern Nigeria? How are Christians to bear witness to their faith in peace among Muslim neighbours? What does the incarnation of Jesus (the prince of peace) mean to the Christian in an ongoing violent situation? How do you build peace and good relations with Muslim brothers and sisters and people of other faith traditions?

Peace building in Northern Nigeria challenges the Christian to a deep faith commitment that reaches out to the other in love, even in the face of opposition, conflict, and violence. It is a faith that seeks to preach peace, reconciliation, harmony, and a sincere willingness to engage with people of other religious traditions. For the Christian, the incarnation of Jesus is a unique invitation to humanity to be reconciled to God and one another. Christians are called by their faith to social actions and attitudes that restore the value of being created in the image and likeness of a loving, peaceful, and merciful God.[592] Christians believe in the gift of peace bestowed by Christ after his resurrection ('My peace I give to you' (Jn. 14: 27)), and thus must proclaim the same peace in bearing witness to their faith.[593]

In the religiously pluralistic world of today, Christians are called to bear witness to truth, justice, love, and freedom. This is because truth and justice will build peace if every individual sincerely acknowledges not only personal rights but also his or her duty to others. Love will build peace if people regard the needs of others as their own and share what they have with them, especially the values and the spirit of God's gift of peace. Freedom builds peace and makes it grow if, in making daily choices, people act according to reason and assume responsibility for their own actions, while

---

[591]   Esther Mombo, 'Reflections on Peace in the Decade to Overcome Violence,' *The Ecumenical Review* 63, no. 1 (2011), 73. http://onlinelibrary.wiley.com/ doi/10.1111/j.1758-6623.2010.00095.x/full

[592]   See Patriarch H.B. Daniel, 'Peace: A Divine Gift and Human Responsibility,' 30 June 2009, A Speech Addressing the IEPC Consultation on 'Peace Ethics in Orthodoxy,' Bucharest.http://www.overcomingviolence.org/en/resources-dov/wcc-resources/ documents/presentations-speeches-messages/peace-a-divine-gift-and-human-responsibility.html

[593]   Cf. Samuel Kobia, 'Overcoming Violence: An Ecumenical Task,' 27 October 2005, A Speech given at an International conference on Violence and Christian Spirituality, Boston. http://www.overcomingviolence.org/en/resources-dov/wcc-resources/documents/ presentations-speeches-messages/overcoming-violence-an-ecumenical-Christian-task. html

respecting the freedom of others.[594] Moreover, the peace of Christ entails respect for the dignity of each person, accepting others as they are and offering a hand of friendship and reconciliation. As church historian Esther Mombo puts it, 'overcoming the enemy that is in me so that the other, seeing my outstretched hand, can overcome an enemy.'[595] To achieve the above, I am convinced that interreligious dialogue and cooperation is critical to create the opportunity for better understanding and harmony among religions. Christians in Northern Nigeria can champion the process of peace building collaboration

Other resources for peace building within the Christian tradition include church documents and pronouncements on peaceful coexistence, for example, documents from World Council of Churches, Papal Encyclicals, and message for World Day of Peace. Furthermore, documents on Catholic Social Teaching and Pastoral letters from Bishops' Conferences and Church leaders in Nigeria calling for peace between Christians and Muslims. These are valuable and treasured resources that will help Christians understand, appreciate, and discern the ideals of peace.[596]

I propose that Christian belief and practice in Northern Nigeria need to develop the hermeneutics of the biblical themes of mercy, goodness, compassion, justice, peace, respect, forgiveness, and reconciliation: a theological interpretation that is open, inclusive, and affirming of others and not threatened by the difference of the other. This is a hermeneutic of proper self-assurance that comes from knowing that we all belong to a greater whole and are diminished when others are humiliated or when their dignity is not respected. This entails seeing life through the eyes of others, while being aware that we are fully ourselves only in relation to others.[597] Christian witnessing in Northern Nigeria requires Christians to foster the process of

---

[594] See Pope John Paul II, 'Pacem in Terris: A Permanent Commitment,' *Message of His Holiness Pope John Paul II for the Celebration of the World Day of Peace, 1January 2003* (Rome Vatican City: Libreria Editrice, 2002), no. 9. http://www.vatican.va/holy_father/ john_paul_ii/messages/peace/documents/hf_jp-ii_mes_20021217_xxxvi-world-day-for- peace_en.html

[595] Mombo, 'Reflections on Peace,' 74.

[596] Cf. Agbonkhianmeghe E. Orobator, 'Catholic Social Teaching and Peacemaking in Africa: A Tale of Two Traditions,' in Elias O. Opongo (ed.), *Peace Weavers Methodologies of Peace Building in Africa* (Nairobi, Kenya: Paulines Publications Africa, 2008), 32-38; see also Schineller (ed.), *Pastoral Letters and Communiqués of the Catholic Bishops' Conference of Nigeria 1960-2002: Voice of the Voiceless* (Abuja, Nigeria: Gaudium Et Spes Institute, 2002), 225, 352 and 381.

[597] See World Council of Churches, 'Christian Discipleship in a Broken World,' 11-16 May 2008, A Statement on Peace Building by Participants of the Seminar, "Religion: Instruments of Peace or Causes of Conflict?",' Bossey. http://www.overcomingviolence. org/fileadmin/dov/files/iepc/expert_consultations/statement.pdf

peace building through dialogue activities that engender reconciliation and healing in communities torn apart by violent conflict.[598] Most Christian denominations in Nigeria have institutions and ministries of justice, peace, and reconciliation departments within their structures. For example, the Anglican Church has a well-staffed department dealing with interfaith and ecumenical matters; it also has a Centre for the Study of Islam and Muslim-Christian Relations.[599] The Catholic Bishops Conference (and the CSN) has a department for Mission and Dialogue (further discourse on these institutions will be addressed in the next chapter). The capacity of these institutions has to be strengthened for the task of building peaceful relations with people of other faith traditions. The Bible and the Christian tradition are the guide for Christians to work towards achieving healing and harmony between Christians and Muslims in Northern Nigeria.

3.4 THEOLOGY OF LOVE AND PEACE BUILDING (LK. 10: 25-37; MATT. 5: 43-44)

In this section, I shall examine the theology and praxis of love in an attempt to understand the teaching of Jesus on love of God and love of neighbour. I shall consider some definitions of love by theologians and analyse the biblical teaching on love. I will then focus on teachings of St. Augustine, St. Thomas Aquinas, and Pope Benedict XVI in order to comprehend the praxis of love and its implication for peaceful coexistence in Northern Nigeria.

In the Gospel of Luke's discourse between Jesus and the teacher of the Law, the teacher asks Jesus, *Master, what must I do to inherit eternal life?* Jesus asks in return, *What is written in the Law?* The teacher answers, *You shall love the Lord your God with all your heart, with all your soul, with all your strength and with all your mind. And you shall love your neighbour as yourself.* Jesus gives credit to the teacher for this response and the teacher asks, *And who is my neighbour?* To answer the question, Jesus tells the story of the Good Samaritan (Lk. 10: 25-37). Jesus's teaching on love in the Gospel of Matthew is very significant in understanding the Christian theology of love as it relates to violent conflicts and peace building. *You have heard that it was said: Love your neighbour and hate your enemy. But I say this to you: Love your enemies, and for those who persecute you.* (Matt. 5: 43-44).

The Bible teaches in 1 John 4: 16 that *God is Love.* What does this mean? What does this say about God in relation to humans, whom he has created in his own image

---

[598] Ibid.

[599] Eyene Okpanachi, 'Building Peace in a Divided Society: The Role of Civil Society in Muslim-Christian Relations in Nigeria,' 4-6 June 2008, A Paper Presented at SHUR International Conference on 'Human Rights in Conflict: The Role of Civil Society,' Rome. http://www.shur.luiss.it/files/2009/06/okpanachi.pdf

and likeness (Gn. 1: 26-27)? What is the theological implication of *God is Love* to the Christian faith and praxis in a religiously pluralistic world? How does this strengthen the process of interreligious dialogue and peaceful coexistence in Northern Nigeria, which is the focus of this thesis? To begin this analysis, it is important to ask the question—what is love?

Love can be described as a strong feeling of affection towards another (either subject or object). According to theologian Werner Jeanrond, human experience, knowledge, and wisdom lead us to approach love as a relationship that affirms a subject or object, appreciate and acknowledge its value, and motivate us to further explore that subject-object of one's attention.[600] Love as a relationship is often inspired by an intense desire to seek some sort of union with the other, to enter into a deeper communion with the other, and perhaps to become one.[601] Love may also involve the desire for something one does not have and considers to be good.[602] Moral theologian Livio Melina describes love as an approval of the goodness and existence of the other, an approval that unites the human acts of love with the gaze and the intention of the creator.[603]

The New Testament biblical understanding of love is described using the Greek word *agape,* which denotes a special relationship between the divine (God) and humanity, created in the image and likeness of God and also reveals the nature of God as love. For scripture scholar Bruce Long, *agape* designates the self-emptying love of God manifested singularly in his generous act of sending his son Jesus Christ to free humanity from sin and to live eternally in God's love.[604] Moreover, the core of New Testament understanding of love stems from the Old Testament Deuteronomic code: *you shall love your God with all your heart, with all your soul and with all your strength* (Dt. 6: 5), and Leviticus 19: 18: *you shall love your neighbour as yourself.* This forms the background of Jesus's own message: to love God with all your heart and soul without reservation and love your neighbour as yourself. However, the source and inspiration of this love of God and neighbour (*agape*) is unsought by humankind but is a gift freely bestowed by God.[605]

For Augustine of Hippo (354-430), God is and should be the central point of our love, even though humans are incapable of loving God because of the consequence

---

[600] Jeanrond, *Theology of Love,* 2.

[601] Ibid.

[602] Miroslav Volf, *Allah: A Christian Response* (New York: HarperOne, 2011), 154.

[603] Livio Melina, 'Love: The Encounter with an Event,' in Livio Melina and Carl A. Anderson (eds.), *The Way of Love Reflections on Pope Benedict XVI's Encyclical Deus Caritas Est* (San Francisco: Ignatius Press, 2006), 22.

[604] Bruce P. Long, 'Love,' in Mircea Eliade (ed.), *The Encyclopedia of Religion*, vol. 9 (New York: Simon & Schuster Macmillan, 1986), 38.

[605] Ibid.

of original sin. This fall was so great that human nature has been impaired and such weakness is transmitted from generation to generation.[606] For Augustine, human love is considered from the point of view of what God does through humans. God is everything, and human beings are weak and nothing and cannot love perfectly.[607] Augustine affirms that all humans are created in the image of God, whose truth and love are eternal and true.[608] God is the eternal Being that can love perfectly.[609]

Augustine was influenced by Platonic philosophy in his early life and spent a great deal of time in search of worldly possessions and pursuit of pleasure. In his *Confessions*, he writes, 'Late have I loved Thee, O Beauty so ancient and so new; late have I loved Thee. For behold Thou were with me . . . and I sought Thee outside and in my unloveliness fell upon those things that Thou hast made. Thou were with me and I was not with Thee.'[610] He argues that original sin changed the course of human history and caused a dramatic weakening of the human will.[611] Consequently, human beings have lost control of their bodily passions and the ability to love genuinely. However, humans should aspire to love God, the highest good. God is worthy of our love because the nature of God is love and is immutable; therefore, God rightly deserves our love. When, as humans, we love genuinely, it is God we love in our acts of loving.[612] Furthermore, since God is the highest good, it follows that God alone is the true goal of our life and only God is deserving of our love and attention.[613]

St. Paul, writing on the virtues of faith, hope, and love in his first letter to the Corinthians, says that love is the greatest and most enduring gift of all. He urges the Christian community to persevere in bearing witness through love (1 Cor. 13: 1-13). Augustine teaches that love is the most eminent commandment, since love unites us with the object of our love (God) in a stronger way than faith and hope. Through love, our likeness to God grows, as love brings us nearer to God. Although we will not become fully like him, the greater our likeness to God the more our love will

---

[606] Vernon J. Bourke, 'Introduction,' *Saint Augustine: The City of God* (New York: Image Books, 1958), 295.

[607] Jeanrond, *Theology of Love,* 45-46.

[608] Philip Schaff (ed.), *Nicene and Post-Nicene Father of the Christian Church: St. Augustine's City of God and Christian Doctrine*, vol. 2, trans. Marcus D.D. Dods (Edinburgh: T & T Clark, 1997), 221.

[609] Ibid.

[610] *Confessions of St. Augustine*, trans. F.J. Sheed (London and New York: Sheed & Ward, 1960), 188 (xxvl1).

[611] Cf. Peter Brown, *Augustine of Hippo: A Biography* (London: Faber and Faber, 1967), 365.

[612] Jeanrond, *Theology of Love*, 51-52.

[613] Ibid.

increase and the clearer we will see God. Therefore, the grace of God dwells in us, for only God can lead us to God.[614]

The command to love God and neighbour for Augustine calls for a radical commitment on the part of the Christian: a sincere commitment and desire to love God above all things, and to love the neighbour for the sake of God, because every genuine relationship is an opportunity to build a stronger relationship with God. Hence loving the neighbour and of course one's self, ultimately becomes a function of one's love for God.[615] Consequently, Christians have to love with the love bestowed on them by the Holy Spirit. Our love must be inspired by divine love and ought to mirror it, because love as a divine gift endows men and women with the desire to strive for divine truth, wisdom, justice, and love.[616] Therefore since God is love, he has endowed humans with the grace and desire to love him and to love the neighbour, imaging love as self-giving, since God's love is unconditional.[617]

The Dominican friar Thomas Aquinas (1225-1274), influenced by Aristotelian philosophy and the Augustinian tradition, teaches that every form of genuine love must relate to God, who is the ultimate origin and aim of love. He argues that human beings are capable of loving, since we are created in the image and likeness of God.[618] He describes love as passion, which is a natural dimension of human life. Human beings are created by God with the faculties and desire to love God, which make them friends of God. Love then propels humans to seek union with their desired object of love (God).[619] For Aquinas, a thing is said to be loved when the desire of the lover regards it as his good. Thus we love each thing in as much as it is for our good. Therefore humans ought to love God more than themselves or any other created thing, since God is the supreme good.[620]

On the Christian praxis of love of God and love of neighbour, Aquinas teaches that love of God cannot be separated from the love of neighbour. Charity for him means that one loves God and one's neighbour, seeing them in relation to the one common supreme good (God).[621] We ought to be friends with God and neighbour; therefore, the love of God ought to include the love of neighbour. He affirms too

---

[614] Von Tarsicius J. Barvel, 'Love,' in Allan D. Fitzgerald (ed.), *Augustine through the Ages: An Encyclopaedia* (Grand Rapids, MI: William B. Eerdmans Publishing Company, 1999), 509-15.

[615] Jeanrond, *Theology of Love,* 53.

[616] Barvel, 'Love,' 515.

[617] Cf. Jim McManus, *I Am My Body: Blessed Pope John Paul's Theology of the Body* (Hants: Redemptorist Publications, 2011), 29-34.

[618] Jeanrond, *Theology of Love,* 77.

[619] Ibid., 77-78.

[620] Long, 'Love,' 39.

[621] Jeanrond, *Theology of Love,* 79-81.

that the scriptures do not command us to love the enemy as an enemy but to love them as fellow humans created by God, whose essence is love and who cares for all (Matt. 5: 43-48).[622] Thomas Aquinas further acknowledged the connection between love, forgiveness, and peace. When love and forgiveness are central to the individual and the community, peace ensues. Moreover, peace flows from the praxis of love, and love requires engagement and self-investment. Peace requires acts of sincere forgiveness if it is to flourish.[623]

In his encyclical letter *Deus Caritas Est* (God is Love), Pope Benedict XVI expresses God's love as understood in the New Testament tradition of *agape*, which is God's love for his people and the love and care people should have for one another. It is a love which seeks the good of the loved one by willingness to sacrifice oneself for the other (no. 5).[624] This is central to the Christian faith and is a reflection of how God invites all humans to participate in God's creative and reconciling project of love.[625] God's love (*agape*) is a free gift given to humans and is not earned. God's passionate love for his people is at the same time a forgiving love that reconciles all to him (no. 10).[626] The Pope reminds the faithful of their primary vocation—the ardent desire to love God and the neighbour.[627] The incarnation of Christ manifests that God is love (1 Jn. 4: 8) through whom we discover Christian love and life which leads to God who is love (no. 12-16).[628] He stresses that loving God and one's neighbour is a Christian responsibility.[629] The Christian is called to love God and neighbour with a mature love that deepens engagement with the other. In the visible manifestation of God's love in the other, we experience being loved, causing us to reach out in a unique way even if the other is considered an enemy (no. 17-18).[630] Furthermore, regarding the Christian praxis of love of God and love of neighbour, Jesus's story of the Good Samaritan (Lk. 10: 25-37) remains the universal standard for the Christian's relationship to the other. Love must be at the heart of Christian individuals and communities (Rm. 12: 9-18;

---

[622] Ibid. See also 'Love of Enemies,' Commentary on Matthew 5: 38-48 New Testament, in *Christian Community Bible Twenty-Seventh Edition* (Diliman, Philippines: Claretian Publications, 1999), 18-19.

[623] Jeanrond, *Theology of Love*, 253.

[624] Desmond O'Donnell, *God Is Love: A Simplified and Abridged Version of Deus Caritas Est. An Encyclical Letter from Pope Benedict XVI* (Dublin, Ireland: Columba Press, 2005), 6-7.

[625] Jeanrond, *Theology of Love*, 161.

[626] O'Donnell, *God Is Love: A Simple and Abridged Version of Deus Caritas Est*, 8.

[627] Jeanrond, *Theology of Love*, 161.

[628] O'Donnell, *God Is Love: A Simplified and Abridged Version of Deus Caritas Est*, 9-10.

[629] David L. Schindler, 'The Way of Love in the Church's Mission to the World,' in Livio Melina and Carl A. Anderson (eds.), *The Way of Love Reflections on Pope Benedict XVI's Encyclical Deus Caritas Est* (San Francisco: Ignatius Press, 2006), 33.

[630] O'Donnell, *God Is Love: A Simplified and Abridged Version of Deus Caritas Est*, 10-11.

14: 19; Gal. 6: 10).[631] Jesus in the parable explains graphically who our neighbour is and how love should be extended to the other, even if he/she is considered an enemy.[632] The Pope further describes love as a light which illuminates a world grown dim, a light that gives hope. Moreover, love gives us the needed courage to keep living and working. Humans are able to practise love because God is love, and we are created in the image and likeness of God (39).[633]

How does the praxis of love of God and love of neighbour apply to the situation in Northern Nigeria, where tension, mistrust, and violent conflicts have continued to affect the relationship between Christians and Muslims as described in Chapter 1 of this thesis? How can these two faith communities love and be neighbours to each other? The Bible and the Qur'an play a significant role in the daily life of Muslims and Christians in Northern Nigeria. Scripture provides the guide for social, moral, and human interaction, giving the background for both individual and group identity and also providing hope for the eschatological reign of God in both faith communities.[634] For instance, Qur'an 49: 13 reads, *O mankind, we created you from a single (pair) of a male and female and made you into nations and tribes that you may know each other . . .* , while the Bible in Acts of the Apostles 17: 26 reads, *From one stock God created the whole human race to live together throughout all the earth . . .* These scriptural passages acknowledge the fact that Muslims and Christians are of the same origin, created by God; thus they are neighbours and ought to love and respect each other. Although mutual love and respect for the other does not deny the possible differences, there is a challenge to see others as human beings and loving and treating them as one would desire to be treated. Therefore, being neighbours to each other necessitates continuous education on the praxis of love and peace, a spirit of tolerance built on mutual respect, recognising that the human family is multicultural, consisting of individuals and groups who have the right and freedom to be different.[635]

For me, this is the hope for Christians and Muslims in Northern Nigeria. 'Hope' here implies a trustful and confident movement towards a brighter future of fruitful cooperation and dialogue between both faith communities.[636] Moreover, the Islamic

---

[631] Ibid., 13.

[632] 'Parable of the Good Samaritan,' in Jose Maria Casciaro (ed.), *The Navarre Bible: Gospels & Acts: Text and Commentaries, Reader's Edition* (Dublin, Ireland: Scepter Publisher, 1999), 399-401.

[633] O'Donnell, *God Is Love: A Simplified and Abridged Version of Deus Caritas Est*, 19.

[634] See Eliza Griswold, *The Tenth Parallel Dispatches from the Faultline between Christianity and Islam* (London: Penguin Books, 2010), 71.

[635] 'International Day for Tolerance,' *Tribune* (Nigeria), 17 November 2010. http://tribune.com.ng

[636] Kelly, *Eschatology and Hope*, 1.

and Christian faiths both point to a future hope of sharing in the reign of God, a future that focuses on what is truly important and each of us carrying the image and likeness of a loving God. This future hope begins in this life through a process of openness, sincerity, and dialogue with the other. This implies the willingness to understand the others' beliefs from their point of view and to acknowledge the truth in them, even if at first such beliefs and practices seem meaningless and abhorrent.[637] Hope is dynamic and cannot be limited. It spurs people on to look to the future with confidence; it opens out towards the future, sustaining life with its potency.[638] The greatest sign of hope for Northern Nigeria is in the many levels of dialogue and peace building activities taking place, where people are striving for a deeper understanding of what it means to be a neighbour. This process of dialogue must continue to work for greater mutual comprehension and collaboration among different faith traditions, as all look towards a future of communion in eternal life.[639]

In both Christianity and Islam, love of God and love of neighbour are essential characteristics of faith in God. There can be no true faith in God without the love of neighbour.[640] Thus theology of love and peace building challenges Christians and Muslims to respect each other as humans with dignity and integrity, to be neighbours to each other through listening, sharing, and being considerate. The praxis of love involves a sincere willingness to risk and sacrifice for the other. It is worthy of note that during violent crisis in Kaduna and Jos, many Muslims gave protection to Christian families and individuals whose lives were in danger, and vice-versa. According to Nigerian Islamic scholar Shaikh Musa Ibrahim Menk, the Hadith which clearly explains the Islamic obligation to live in peace and harmony with neighbours as demanded by the Qur'an and tradition also includes non-Muslim neighbours, who also have a claim on the kindness and sympathy of Muslims.[641] A Christian is a neighbour to a Muslim, and a Muslim is a neighbour to a Christian. Christians and Muslims will continue to live side by side in Northern Nigeria. Therefore, both should consider using their privileged position in the region to influence and encourage mutual understanding that will transform the conflict situation into a more

---

[637] Cf. Josiah Fearon-Idowu, 'No Peace in Nigeria without Dialogue between the Muslims and the Christians,' *Leadership* (Nigeria), 28 May 2011. http://www.leadership.ng

[638] Jean Duplacy, 'Hope,' in Xavier Léon-Dufour (ed.), *Dictionary of Biblical Theology* (London: Geoffrey Chapman, 1973), 239-40.

[639] See Kelly, *Eschatology and Hope*, 15-17.

[640] Ghazi bin Muhammad, 'A Common Word between Us and You,' in Miroslav Volf, Muhammad bin Ghazi, and Melissa Yarrington (eds.), *A Common Word Muslims and Christians on Loving God and Neighbour* (Cambridge, UK: William B. Eerdmans Publishing, 2010), 30-46.

[641] Musa Ibrahim Menk, 'Islam Demands Good Neighbourliness,' *Daily Trust* (Nigeria), 18 April 2011. http://www.dailytrust.com

humane and dynamic society, where both communities can coexist in peace, treating each other with the dignity they deserve, respecting and negotiating the differences that will always be present.

I propose that the praxis of love of God and love of neighbour be reflective, personal, and effective. It must not discriminate against persons; it must be holistic and sincere, transforming us into the likeness of God, who is the source of love (Jn. 3: 17-18; 4: 7-20). The love of God is incomplete without a genuine love of neighbour. Neighbours have to accept and trust each other. Unfortunately, in Kaduna, Northern Nigeria, Christians who live in the Muslim-dominated northern part of the city are moving to the primarily Christian southern part of the city, and vice versa.[642] This challenges the praxis of love. I suggest that Islamic and Christian communities in Northern Nigeria must develop a hermeneutics that recognises the other as neighbour and come to understand their interdependence in fostering justice, equality, and freedom in addressing the conflict issues in the region.[643] Sincere love must be interested in the dynamics of genuine encounter with the neighbour, which leads to an eschatological openness to God and the hope of individual transformation.[644] However, the question will always remain—who is my neighbour?

CONCLUSION

In this chapter, I have argued that religion possesses the potential to advance peace and harmony in society, even as religion can be manipulated to promote conflict. Moreover, religion continues to affect and shape the lives of people in many different ways. However, it is equally true that religious traditions (Christianity and Islam) as institutions of peace in the community represent significant channels for communication and action.[645] When engaged, these will enable religious believers to function as powerful agents of conflict transformation, advancing human development through interreligious cooperation in multireligious efforts. Such collaboration breaks down barriers between various groups and creates horizontal connections between faith communities, helping them to function as common

---

[642] Cf. Imam Imam, 'Nigeria: Kaduna's Jerusalem and Mecca,' *This Day* (Nigeria), 10 April 2010. http://www.allafrica.co/stories/201004130074.html; and Christiana T. Alabi, 'Lemu Panel: Community Demands State for Southern Kaduna,' *Daily Trust* (Nigeria), 30 June 2011. http://www.dailytrust.com

[643] See William F. Vendley, 'The Power of Inter-Religious Cooperation to Transform Conflict,' *Cross Currents* 55, no. 1 (2005). http://www.thefreeelibrary.com; cf. also Cornille, 'Introduction: On Hermeneutics in Dialogue,' xi-xvii.

[644] Jeanrond, 'Towards an Interreligious Hermeneutics of Love,' 52-53.

[645] Ibid.

stakeholders in peace building efforts, thereby reducing the temptation to manipulate religion for selfish interests.[646]

Peaceful coexistence in Northern Nigeria requires an enduring Christian-Muslim dialogue encounter. Interreligious dialogue provides the moral coalition needed for better understanding and change.[647] Whenever Muslims and Christians collaborate for peace as neighbours in the region, they demonstrate the true nature of their faith community and the importance of religion in shaping the socio-cultural value of peace in society. The next chapter examines the process of Christian-Muslim dialogue in Northern Nigeria as a strategy for negotiating peace. Moreover, religion as a contributing factor to conflict can shape the emotional character of adherents to create the needed space to foster a culture of dialogue for peace.

---

[646]   Ibid.

[647]   Ibid.

Chapter 4

DIALOGUE AND PEACE BUILDING IN CONTEMPORARY NORTHERN NIGERIA

INTRODUCTION: INTERRELIGIOUS DIALOGUE REVISITED

This chapter examines significant aspects of contemporary Christian-Muslim dialogue in Northern Nigeria. I argue that sustained interreligious dialogue is paramount for peaceful coexistence. The aim is to critically explore dialogue activities in the region and suggest measures for upholding such endeavours.

Dialogue is an important activity for fostering community relations. It helps people of different social, cultural, political, and religious traditions to come to a better understanding of each other. Dialogue can be defined as a conversation, a frank discussion between two or more parties with the aim of learning and understanding each other's point of view.[648] It is a conversation on a common subject between two or more people with differing views, so that each participant learns and enriches each other.[649] Dialogue can be revolutionary when it fosters discipline, planning, continuous learning, diversity, conflict exploration, decision-making, problem solving, and leadership.[650] For interreligious dialogue analyst Leonard Swidler, dialogue is about expanding our capacity for attention, awareness, learning with and from each other, and exploring what it means to be human in a pluralistic

---

[648] Emefie Ikenga-Metuh, 'Dialogue with African Traditional Religions (ATR): the Teaching of the Special Synod on Africa,' 1994. http://www.afrikaworld.net/afrel/metuh.htm

[649] Leonard Swidler, 'The Dialogue Decalogue Ground Rules for Interreligious, Interideological Dialogue,' *Journal of Ecumenical Studies* 20, no. 1 (1983). http://www.sacredheart.edu/pages/13027_the_dailogue_decalogue_by_leonard_swidl

[650] Gerard Glenna and Ellinor Linda, *Dialogue: Rediscovering the Transforming Power of Conversation* (Hoboken, NJ: John Wiley & Sons, 1998).

environment.[651] According to philosopher and social scientist Alberto Quattrucci, dialogue is patient listening to one another, understanding and recognising the human and spiritual make-up of the other. He argues that dialogue must transcend the limited world of specialists to involve people in the community.[652] Moreover, the dynamics of religious encounter demand that dialogue be initiated to achieve cooperation between individuals, groups, and communities who may differ in terms of religious, political, social, or cultural ideologies. For Christians and Muslims in Northern Nigeria, interreligious dialogue is essential for negotiating peaceful coexistence and religious growth in both faith communities.[653]

The Christian Bible (as the word of God) can be described as a dialogue account between God and his people. A critical study of the life and ministry of Jesus in the Gospels reveals that Jesus was in constant dialogue with the people around him. For example, Jesus is continuously engaged in dialogue with his disciples and individuals (the Samaritan woman at the well (Jn. 4: 1-30), the Canaanite woman (Matt. 15: 21-28) and the Syrophoenician woman (Mk. 7: 24-30), and the Pharisees (Matt. 19; Mk. 12: 13; Lk. 20: 41). Moreover, in the first letter of Peter, Christians are admonished to be ready always to answer questions with respect, gentleness, and reverence, while keeping a clear conscience. (1 Pt. 3: 15).[654] Similarly, the Qur'an explicitly calls on Muslims to engage with believers who are their associates and not dispute with the 'people of the book' (Q 29: 46-47).[655] The Prophet further encouraged Muslims to invite people to the way of the Lord with wisdom and good example and to dialogue with them in the best and most gracious ways (Q 16: 125).[656]

The Second Vatican Council declaration in *Nostra Aetate* (no. 2-3) and *Gaudium et* Spes (no. 92) urges Christians to dialogue with prudence and charity with members of other religions in an atmosphere of mutual esteem, reverence, and harmony.[657]

Islamic history and tradition acknowledges pluralism in culture and religion as an undeniable fact; hence dialogue between Islam and other religions is first and

---

[651]   Ibid.

[652]   Alerto Quattrucci, in *Peace: A Single Goal and a Shared Intention Forum of Religious Representatives (Vatican City, 23 January 2002), Day of Prayer for Peace (Assisi, 24 January 2002)* (Vatican City: Pontifical Council for Interreligious Dialogue, 2002), 67-68.

[653]   Cf. Cornille, *The Im-Possibility of Interreligious Dialogue*, 1.

[654]   Borrmans, 'Interreligious Documents,' 28.

[655]   Ibid.

[656]   Ibid.

[657]   'Pastoral Constitution on the Church in the Modern World, Vatican II Gaudium et Spes, 7 December 1965,' in Austin Flannery (ed.), *Vatican Council II: The Conciliar and Post Conciliar Documents* (New York: Costello Publishing, 1975), 999-1000.

foremost a necessary and vital re-establishment of contact with the world.[658] Muslims are encouraged to engage in honest and respectful dialogue with the 'people of the book' who are recognised by the Qur'an as fellow monotheists.[659] For Muslims, the motivation for interreligious dialogue is based on the imperatives of the Qur'an and the practice of Prophet Muhammad, who in the year AD 630 engaged in dialogue with a Christian delegation from Najran.[660]

The Roman Catholic Church's Document *Dialogue and Proclamation* (no. 42) and scholars in the field of interreligious dialogue, such as John McDade, Michael Fitzgerald, John Borelli, and the Nigerian religious analyst Bauna Peter Tanko, differentiate dialogue into the following typologies:

Information Seeking Dialogue: The aim is to transmit information from one party to another.

Dialogue of Negotiation: The aim is for both parties to strike a deal, come to an agreement or compromise through bargaining over an issue, conceding some interests and insisting on others.

Dialogue of Inquiry: In this process, the aim is for the participants to collectively prove a particular position according to given standards of proof.

Dialogue of Life: This is where the participants strive to live in an open neighbourly spirit, sharing the challenges of life that come their way and supporting one another.

Dialogue of Action or Dialogue of Deed: Each participant and the group collaborate to seek the integral liberation and development of all people. Such conversation and action includes, for example, addressing issues of social justice, poverty, and community development. The goal of collaboration is humanitarian, social, economic, or political in nature, for the benefit of all in the community.

Dialogue of Theological Exchange: This is a forum for specialists to share, draw from each other and seek to deepen their understanding of their own religious perspective, and learn to appreciate the spiritual heritage and values of the other.

---

[658] Muhammad Talbi, 'Islam and Dialogue Some Reflections on a Current Topic,' in Joseph Kenny, *Views on Christian-Muslim Relations* (Lagos, Nigeria: Dominican Publications, 1999), 141-42.

[659] Asma Afsaruddin, 'Discerning a Qur'anic Mandate for Mutually Transformational Dialogue,' in Catherine Cornille (ed.), *Criteria of Discernment in Interreligious Dialogue* (Eugene, OR: Cascade Books, 2009), 101. See also Kilani, 'Issues and Trends on Religious Tolerance in Nigeria,' 273-74; Mustapha Sani Salih, *Muhammad Rasulullah and the People of the Book: His Benevolence, Kindness, Large-Heartedness and Quest for Peace* (Kaduna, Nigeria: Essam International, 2010), 83-87.

[660] Salih, *Muhammad Rasulullah and the People of the Book,* 83-87.

Dialogue of Religious Experience: Here people of different religious traditions come together to share their spiritual riches, such as prayer, to deepen understanding, friendship, and respect for each other. This could also be referred to as interreligious dialogue.[661]

Dialogue for peace building requires Muslims and Christians to embrace their fundamental call to dialogue so that the dynamism and will to interact with each other in dignity and freedom may flourish. This demands genuine interest in another religious tradition, its teachings, ritual-practices, and life of faith experience, since the purpose of dialogue includes mutual enrichment and growth in the truth.[662] Dialogue can facilitate peace building activities, conflict resolution, and reconciliation among peoples and communities. It builds trust and sustains confidence among individuals and groups. Dialogue—be it cultural, social, political, or religious—has the potential to build understanding, peace, and harmony.[663]

To advance this objective, the Catholic Bishops' Conference of Nigeria has challenged Christians in Nigeria to continuous dialogue, especially with the Islamic community, and has established a department for dialogue and mission within the CSN.[664]

However, the success of interreligious dialogue is impeded by a number of obstacles; insufficient grounding in one's own religious faith knowledge coupled with insufficient understanding of the belief and practices of other religious traditions, results in a lack of appreciation of their significance and misrepresentation.[665] Other impediments are a lack of conviction about the value of interreligious dialogue, self-sufficiency, and the need for openness, which leads to defensive or aggressive behaviour and suspicion about the motives of others. Intolerance (associated with

---

[661] Typologies of dialogue: see 'Dialogue and Proclamation Reflection and Orientations on Interreligious Dialogue and the Proclamation of the Gospel of Jesus Christ (1),' *Pontifical Council for Interreligious Dialogue* (Vatican City: Libreria Editrice, 1991), no. 42. http://www.vatican.va/roman_curia/pontifical_councils/interelg/documents/rc_pc_interelg_doc_19051991_dialogue-and-proclamatio_en.html (1991); McDade, 'Nostra Aetate and Interfaith Dialogue,' 11; Fitzgerald and Borelli, *Interfaith Dialogue: A Catholic View*, 28-34; and Bauna Peter Tanko, *The Christian Association of Nigeria and the Challenge of the Ecumenical Imperative* (Jos, Nigeria: Fab Anieh Nig, 1991), 33-39.

[662] Cornille, 'Introduction: On Hermeneutics in Dialogue,' xiii-xvii.

[663] E. J. Fisher, 'The Interreligious Dimension of War and Peace,' in H. Gordon and L. Grob (eds.), *Education for Peace: Testimonies from World Religion* (New York: Orbis Books, 1987), 18.

[664] Cf. Peter Schineller (ed.), *The Church Teaches: Stand of the Catholic Bishops of Nigeria on Issues of Faith and Life* (Abuja: Gaudium Et Spes Institute, 2002), 45-51 and Danjuma, 'Mission and Dialogue,' 19-20.

[665] 'Dialogue and Proclamation,' nos. 51-52.

ethnic, social, economic, political, and racial factors), lack of reciprocity, religious indifference, religious extremism, lack of self-criticism, and lack of respect, all create confusion and give rise to new challenges that inhibits dialogue process.[666]

The chapter is divided into eight sections. The first section is an appraisal of ongoing dialogue activity in Northern Nigeria. It highlights the efforts of institutions engaged in fostering dialogue and considers the challenges and the prospects for contemporary Muslim-Christian dialogue in the region.

The second section focuses on the use of language and symbols to weaken stereotypes and acknowledges the central role of communication in the process.

The third section discusses peace building activities in Northern Nigeria. It explores the efforts of peace institutions and evaluates the effectiveness of their achievements by reviewing events, using the 2002 peace training workshop and the 2009 Nigerian Youth Summit as case studies.

The fourth section analyses Christian-Muslim dialogue initiatives in Northern Nigeria. It highlights joint dialogue efforts and their evident achievements in the various communiqués featured in this work.

The fifth section concentrates on parliamentary dialogue enterprise. It examines and assesses the attempts by federal and state governments to support and advance the cause of sustained dialogue and peaceful negotiations in Northern Nigeria.

The sixth section is a theological evaluation of the effectiveness of both parliamentary and Christian-Muslim interreligious dialogue projects. It considers the difficulties and complexities of dialogue in the region and future hope.

The seventh section discusses the interplay between politics and religion in Northern Nigeria. The aim is to stress on how politics is influenced greatly by religion and argue that theological values can transform and advance politics for peace in the region.

The eighth section delves into the history of education in Nigeria before the advent of Christian missionaries and the introduction of the western system of education. It examines the challenges and confrontation that ensued between the traditional system of Islamic religious education prevalent in Northern Nigeria and the western style of learning aimed at evangelisation. It further reviews the limitations of religious and interreligious education in the region and argues for the need for a robust system of religious education that enhances social cohesion and peace.

---

[666] See Arinze, 'Christian-Muslim Relations in the 21st Century; Talbi, Islam and Dialogue,' 143-44.

4.1 Muslim-Christian Dialogue in Northern Nigeria Today

In this section, I shall appraise Muslim-Christian dialogue activities by examining the efforts of institutions responsible for fostering dialogue encounter, with focus on its challenges and prospects in the region.

Interreligious dialogue has been going on in Nigeria since the late 1970s. Muslim and Christian leaders in Northern Nigeria have continued to appreciate the need to create the space for continuous and sustained peace building activities. The tension and conflicts that have existed between the faithful of the two communities have challenged religious leaders to come together in dialogue.

The CBCN and the CSN were formed in 1956. The Nigerian Supreme Council for Islamic Affairs (NSCIA) was created in 1973, and Jamalat-ul-Nasril Islam (JNI), the Council of Ulema, and the CAN were formed in 1976. The role of these organisations is to respond to the various religious, social, political, cultural, and missionary challenges within Nigeria post independence.[667] These bodies operate at national, state, and local government levels.

The leaders of these groups in Northern Nigeria are responsible for engaging with each other in the process of dialogue. They meet, discuss, and issue joint statements addressing affairs of common concern in the region. To enhance the process of dialogue, seminars, symposia, and conferences are organised, experts are invited to facilitate, and joint actions for peace are proposed and considered for implementation. For example, the Nigerian Youth Summit on Interreligious Dialogue and Peaceful Coexistence was held in 2009 (for further discussion on the Nigerian Youth summit, see below, no. 4.4.7). However, each faith community is chiefly responsible for grassroots implementation of such projects. Furthermore, each group at state level is responsible for inviting the religious other to dialogue in order to foster friendship and understanding in conflict issues. The Nigerian Interreligious Council (NIREC) and the Interfaith Mediation Centre (IFMC), for instance, have continued to champion the course of peace building between faith communities in a sustained process of interreligious dialogue.[668]

The recurring violent situation challenges religious leaders and other stakeholders to condemn violent conflict and be more proactive in exploring avenues of lasting peace in the region.[669] They speak collectively as advocates of peace,

---

[667] Ayegboyin, 'Religious Association,' 103-06.

[668] Okpanachi, 'Building Peace in a Divided Society.'

[669] Cf. Hakeem-Apanpa Qudirat, 'Muslim Clerics Condemn Jos Crisis,' *Tribune* (Nigeria), 05 December 2008. *http://www.Tribune.com*; Joseph Bege, 'CAN Condemn Attacks,' *The Sun* (Nigeria), 28 July 2009. http://www.sunnewsonline.com; 'Muslim Leaders Condemn Mayhem,' *Daily Trust* (Nigeria), 05 August 2009. http://www.dailytrust.com; see also

stressing the need to avoid all forms of hostile confrontation. For example, the Sultan of Sokoto and the leader of Muslims in Nigeria, Muhammad Sa'ad Abubakar, in a recent speech admonished Christians and Muslims

> not to allow present-day politics of hatred and injustice to consume us and tear apart the strong bond of unity and tolerance that once existed between us. Nigerians should embrace peaceful dialogue and avoid acts of violence in the interest of the stability and orderly development of the nation.[670]

In the same vein, the Catholic Archbishop of Jos Nigeria, Ignatius Kaigama, cautioned that the future of Nigeria depends largely on mutual cooperation between Christians and Muslims. Arguing that if they are engaged merely in competing for numerical strength, geographical expansion, and claim to superiority, they will do much harm to the corporate social existence of all in the country.[671] The CAN and Jamalat-ul-Nasril Islam (JNI) have been challenged to collaborate in fostering harmony through dialogue.

According to theologian Hans Küng, there can be no world peace without peace among religions, no peace among religions without dialogue between religions, and no dialogue between religions without accurate knowledge of one another.[672] I agree with Küng and add that there can be no peace in Northern Nigeria without sustained dialogue between Christians and Muslims in the region. Interreligious dialogue has been very effective in bringing together religious leaders to explore how each faith tradition can contribute to peaceful coexistence. Consequently, the desire to build peace and harmony through dialogue challenges Christians and Muslims to condemn indiscriminate attacks and promote working with all agencies and persons of goodwill for the common good.

The efforts to dialogue keeps growing. Muslims and Christians have developed joint organisations working for peace and cooperation between their communities; these are notable for example in Kaduna, Minna, Jos, and other

---

Martins Oloja, Lawal Iyabo, and Musa Njadvara, 'Sultan, Onaiyekan, Sheriff Decry Boko Haram Crisis,' *Guardian* (Nigeria), 13 August 2009. http://www.ngrguardiannews. com; Nzeshi Onwuka, 'Sultan, Onaiyekan Condemn Killings,' *This Day* (Nigeria), 22 January 2010. http://www.thisdayonline; Muhammad, 'Religious, Traditional Rulers Urge Christians and Muslim Unity.'

[670] Charlse Coffie Gyam, 'Sultan Appeals for Calm,' *Guardian* (Nigeria), 30 November 2008. http://www.ngrguardiannews.com

[671] CAFOD, 'Faith in Nigeria,' 2010. http://www.cafod.org.uk

[672] Hans Küng, 'Christianity and World Religions: Dialogue with Islam,' in Leonard Swidler (ed.), *Muslims in Dialogue: The Evolution of a Dialogue* (Lewiston, NY: Edwin Mellen Press, 1992), 161-62. http://www.global-dialogue.com/swidlerbooks/Muslim.htm

northern communities.[673] Issues discussed at dialogue sessions range from ways of strengthening bonds of friendship and harmony between faith communities, to evolving practical modes to address problems of conflict, violence, poverty, unemployment, ethnicity, underdevelopment, politics, and policy-making as these affect religion and peaceful coexistence.[674] Other bridge-building activities on the dialogue agenda include visits to the local chiefs, exchange of congratulatory messages at religious festivities, joint support to speak out against common societal ills, and united efforts to initiate and sustain community projects.[675]

A significant achievement in the process of peace building through interreligious dialogue is that participants have identified the urgent need for education and training of religious preachers, leaders, and teachers. They agree that proper training for religious leaders is of paramount importance to address issues of stereotypes, conflict, and violence. Properly trained religious leaders will appreciate the true values of religion and lead their communities to a better understanding of the meaning of religious tolerance and respect. On the other hand, poorly formed religious leaders in most cases exploit religion for personal ends which fuels conflict and violence. Therefore, it is pertinent for religious authorities to be responsible for training religious leaders to prevent incompetent men/women from preaching and teaching, as sometimes happens in the region[676] (for further discourse on education and training, see Chapter 5).

---

[673] See Joseph Kenny, 'Interreligious Dialogue in Nigeria: Personal Reminiscence of 40 years,' in Anthony A. Akinwanle (ed.), *All that They Have to Live on. Essays in Honour of Archbishop Onaiyekan and Msgr. John Aniagwu* (Ibadan, Nigeria: Dominican Institute, 2004), 184-91. http://www.josephkenny.joyeurs.com/onaiyekan.htm

[674] Cf. Sam Eyoboka, 'Sultan, CAN Leaders Propose Pathway to Lasting Peace in Jos,' *Vanguard* (Nigeria), 07 December 2008. http:www.vanguardngr.com/content/view23495/24/; Samuel Aruwan, 'Emir Task Religious Leaders on Peaceful Coexistence,' *Leadership* (Nigeria), 08 August 2010. http://www.leadership.ng/nga; Ibrahim A. Yusuf, 'Okogie Preaches Love among Nigerians,' *The Nation* (Nigeria) 26 June 2011. http://www.thenationonline.net

[675] See Yusuf, 'Agenda for Interfaith Dailogue,' 'Okotie Greets Muslims at the end of Ramadan, Urges Peaceful Coexistence,' *Newsdaily* (Nigeria), 01 September 2010. http://www.nigerianewsdaily.com; 'CAN, Okogie Greet Muslims at Ramadan,' *Vanguard* (Nigeria), 15 August 2010. http://www.vanguardngr.com; and Abdulraheem Aodu, 'ACF, CAN Congratulates Muslims on Eid-el-Kabir,' *Daily Trust* (Nigeria), 08 December 2008. http://www.newsdailytrust.com

[676] See also Francis Ugwoke, 'Boko Haram: Islamic Leaders to Vet Clerics,' *This Day* (Nigeria), 08 April 2009. http://www.thisdayonline.com/nview.php?=150620

4.1.1 THE CHALLENGES OF INTERRELIGIOUS DIALOGUE IN NORTHERN NIGERIA TODAY

In this segment, I shall focus on highlighting the challenges that continue to impede the process of interreligious dialogue in the region under study.

Although remarkable progress has been made in sustaining the process of Christian-Muslim dialogue in Northern Nigeria, evaluating how effective it has been is not an easy exercise, as it involves social, economic, political, ethnic, cultural, historical, and religious concerns. However, it is believed that success depends very much on how committed religious leaders and participants in dialogue are willing to explore new ways of addressing these questions.

A major challenge is a missing link: grassroots community participation in the process of dialogue. Dialogue as understood in this work is an invitation for partners to come together to share the wealth of each religious tradition, with the aim of building better understanding and peaceful cooperation. However, in my experience, it seems that interreligious dialogue in Northern Nigeria takes place almost exclusively at the level of the elite—religious leaders and other experts—without participation at the grassroots community level. This means that the experiences, feelings, concerns, and aspirations of ordinary people do not feature in dialogue sessions. As Islamic philosopher Tariq Ramadan affirms:

> To be involved in dialogue between two religions while being completely cut off from the believers of one's own religion is problematic and can be counterproductive. Many 'specialists' in interreligious dialogue move from conference to conference totally disconnected from their religious community as well as the grassroot realities.[677]

I agree with Ramadan because in such situations there is little or no feedback to and from the grassroots community where all the action and interaction of day-to-day living takes place. This implies that community dialogue for peace building is more or less non-existent or not strengthened, as is evident for instance in the violent conflicts where faith communities attack each other in the name of religion. Consequently, this lack of consistent contact with grassroots communities means that very little progress is recorded as far as interreligious dialogue is concerned. Moreover, it is the duty of those who take part in a formal dialogue setting to ensure that there is free flow of information to and from their communities. It is also their responsibility to encourage members of their faith community to dialogue in their day-to-day interactions, respecting the dignity of all.

---

[677] Ramadan, *Western Muslims and the Future of Islam*, 209.

Furthermore, very few women take active part in the dialogue process, perhaps due to lack of education, encouragement, and the male-dominated structure of society. However, women play an important role in the community, especially in the home. There they have a unique but subtle way of keeping peace and building mutual understanding in the family. Their almost non-participation in the formal dialogue process means a great deal of experience is being lost. It is imperative for leaders to explore ways of encouraging women's active participation in the dialogue process.

Other factors that continue to mar the efforts and progress of genuine Christian-Muslim dialogue in Northern Nigeria include misconceptions, mistrust, suspicion, lack of equality among participants, prejudices, stereotypes, ethnicity, anger, selfishness, lack of respect, frustration, fear, and political bias. All these counter the honest, open, and trusting attitude necessary for interreligious relations. Politics is greatly influenced by religion, so that relations between the two faith communities are characterised by competition, tension, and rivalry.[678] Religious sentiments are employed on both sides to foster political, economic, social, and ethnic discrimination. Access to the corridors of power means political and social favours for one's faith community at the expense of the common good. For example, public funds are used to build places of worship and to pay for Muslim and Christian pilgrimages.

Often dialogue takes place between participants who know little about the other faith. Although participants (religious leaders) share with each other, their understanding remains very shallow, and ways of expression and perceptions differ. This sometimes leads to anger, frustration, and lack of interest.[679]

Past historical events and experiences continue to influence the image and perception of the other. Violent conflicts over the years have soured relationships between the two faith communities; past hurt and pain affect the trust-building process. Christians and Muslims judge each other in the light of their experiences and form opinions which in turn affect the sincere commitment to explore ways to forgive and be reconciled.[680] Each group thinks and feels that the issues discussed remain

---

[678] 'Ex-Minister Decries Religious Politics,' *Punch* (Nigeria), 18 April 2011. http://www.punchng.com; see also Ibrahim Shuaibu, 'Shema: Don't Use Religion, Ethnicity to Create Disunity,' *This Day* (Nigeria), 13 May 2011. http://www.thisdayonline.com/

[679] Cf. Matthew Hassan Kuka, 'The Church's Mission and Dialogue in a Pluralistic Society,' in *The Church in Nigeria: Family of God on Mission. ACTA of the First National Pastoral Congress* (Lagos, Nigeria: Catholic Secretariat of Nigeria Publication, 2003), 149-53. See also Matthew A. Ojo and Folaranmi T. Lateju, 'Christians-Muslim Conflicts and Interfaith Bridge-Building Efforts in Nigeria,' *The Review of Faith & International Affairs* 8, no. 1 (2010), 34-35.

[680] See Ataullah Siddiqui, *Christian-Muslim Dialogue in the Twentieth Century* (London: Macmillan Press, 1997), 50.

at the dialogue stage and do not affect general life in society. This becomes evident in times of conflict when issues quickly degenerate into violence and the perceived hurt is avenged by one group on the other. These deep wounds of the past hinder the efforts to build trust, making it difficult for the two to accept each other as equals.

In addition, the lack of sustained dialogue between adherents of the same faith tradition and their leaders who participate in the dialogue process impedes progress. Sustained information sharing, catechesis, and interaction between members of the same faith tradition and their leaders is necessary to enhance better understanding of their own faith and encourage good relations with those of other faith traditions. Intra-faith dialogue provides an opportunity to teach the faith and provide and receive feedback to the dialogue session.[681] Furthermore, sometimes the valuable support and cooperation of religious, political, and social leaders is not constant, making it difficult to access the resources needed to enhance dialogue. This stifles the effort of those who mobilise people for interreligious dialogue.[682] However, amidst all these challenges, is there any hope for sustainable peace building through interreligious dialogue in Northern Nigeria? The following section evaluates the prospect of progress.

4.1.2 THE PROSPECT OF INTERRELIGIOUS DIALOGUE IN NORTHERN NIGERIA

This section discusses the potential for interreligious dialogue for furure peace in the region and the need for faith communities to collaborate if this vision is to come to fruition.

The hope for Christian-Muslim dialogue in Northern Nigeria depends on the willingness of the two faith communities to concede sincerely that the love and providence of God extends to all human beings equally, irrespective of religious, cultural, and ethnic identity. Both must strive to accept each other's faith on their own terms and recognise that there is truth in both the Qur'an and the Bible.[683] Hence the ultimate goal and hope of religious dialogue is in the ability of Christians and Muslims to hear God speaking to them within their own faith experience and humbly listen to the same voice speaking to both faith traditions in the process of dialogue (Q 5: 48 and 1 Jn. 3: 2).[684] Accordingly, accepting and respecting the religious freedom of others means being involved in a mutual dialogue of understanding and

---

[681] See Ramadan, *Western Muslims and the Future of Islam*, 209.

[682] Cf. 'Empower Inter-Religious Councils on Tolerance—CAN,' *Leadership* (Nigeria), 10 July 2011. http://www.leadersgip.ng

[683] Mahmoud Ayoub, 'A Muslim View of Christianity,' in Omar A. Irfan (ed.), *Essays on Dialogue* (New York: Orbis Books, 2007), 69.

[684] Cf. Ibid.

cooperation, one that seeks to respect the religious beliefs of others and the freedom to choose and practise their faith. Such dialogue demands, as Quattrucci put it, patient listening to one another in order to understand each other.[685] The dynamics of the model of dialogue described above provides the background to the 'union' model of peace building suggested in Chapter 3, a model that recognises religious diversity and seeks to understand the uniqueness of each religious tradition. However, this does not mean that Christians and Muslims become religiously neutral or subservient, watering down their own faith. Rather, it challenges all to be deeply religious, honest, and patient in their encounters, respecting the identity and freedom of each other.

The future of building peaceful coexistence in Northern Nigeria consists of extending the hand of friendship to the other and opening sustained channels of communication, such as visits and support in times of need. The long history of mistrust and violence must not be a barrier to reconciliation. Muslims and Christians in Northern Nigeria must commit to paving the way to harmony by mutual respect in order for peace to flourish. Religion must be the platform for building good and enduring friendships by exploring in dialogue the common ground in Islam and Christianity. There has to be a conscious and creative effort on the part of religious leaders and those who participate in interreligious dialogue to build sound relationships in their own faith communities and have a solid theological knowledge of their faith. Without this effort there is a danger that those involved in interreligious dialogue may slip away from their own faith communities to become a closed circle of intellectuals who speak mostly to and for themselves and do not promote the concerns of the faith community in the peace building process.[686]

The future of interreligious dialogue presupposes religious education about the other. Basic knowledge of the other fosters openness, understanding, respect for the truth, and sincerity of purpose. Religious dialogue in Northern Nigeria must encourage the education of the younger generation so that they grow with the basic knowledge and understanding of the religious other. Furthermore, religious organisations must work in collaboration with each other, that is, the CAN, Jamatu Nasril Islam (JNI), the Muslim Students' Society (MSS), Catholic

---

[685] See Quattrucci, *Peace: A Single Goal*, 67-68.

[686] Cf. Josiah Fearon-Idowu, 'Interfaith Relations and Community Development: How Feasible? What Are the Obstacles? How Do We Surmount Them?' 22-24 January 2009, A Paper Presented at BBA Workshop with FBOs and NGOs from Plateau State, Kaduna, Nigeria. http://www.anglicandiocesekaduna.com; Ramadan, *Western Muslims and the Future of Islam,* 211; Fearon-Idowu, 'No Peace in Nigeria without Dialogue,' and Anastasios Yonnoulatos, 'Problems and Prospects of Inter-Religious Dialogue,' *The Ecumenical Review* 52, no. 3 (2000). http://www.findarticles.p/articles/mi_m2065/is_3_52/ai_66279075

Women Organisation (CWO)/Christian Mothers, and Federation of Muslim Women Association of Nigeria (FOMWAN).

Much could be achieved in peace building at the grassroot community level. Moreover, what is needed is not simply religious tolerance but something much more positive and proactive, a conscious mutual respect, dialogue, and solidarity among peoples. This may be achieved through creative cooperation, a common project that brings people together to address a particular need in society, for example, digging a well for the provision of portable water. Such steady efforts towards social harmony and genuine acts of love and support for each other are necessary for the future peace in Northern Nigeria. Religious leaders, politicians, and government must do everything within their power to encourage interreligious dialogue for peace. To abandon such ventures would mean giving new impetus to the formation of ghettos, ethnic and religious violence, and development of various new expressions of religious fanaticism and chaos.[687] This is not what Nigeria needs in this millennium.

4.2 DISMANTLING RELIGIOUS STEREOTYPES IN NORTHERN NIGERIA

In this section, I shall address the challenge of religious stereotypes by suggesting practical ways to weaken them. In this thesis I have identified religious stereotyping, prejudice, bias, and lack of understanding as contributing factors to conflicts in Northern Nigeria. I have argued that religious stereotypes evolve as a result of poor religious education, instruction, and preaching. Other causes are lack of understanding, fear, misconception, marginalisation, discrimination, and lack of education.

Thus to adequately address religious stereotypes in Northern Nigeria, I propose a process of sustained deorientation and reorientation of adherents within both faith communities in order to bring about change of attitudes. This involves a conscious effort by leaders and preachers of both religious traditions to debunk false impressions about the other that are acquired or passed on and to replace them with the truth.

A change of attitude can be achieved through education and re-orientation when adherents are properly instructed in the truth about the other. Hence each religious tradition ought to consider formation in true religious knowledge about the other. Believers must be formed and informed so that the desired transformation for peace and harmony can take place. This is done through catechesis, instruction, and preaching at home, in schools, seminaries, Qur'anic schools, and Madrasas. Religious stereotyping leads to hate, fanaticism, and violent conflict. To avoid such struggles, Christians and Muslims must accept religious freedom and respect the right of the

---

[687] Yonnoulatos, 'Problems and Prospects.'

other to be different.[688] The cultivation of sincere respect for the religious belief of one's neighbour and the freedom to practise it is a social necessity. This calls for dialogue of life, which makes social interaction, creativity, progress, and development among peoples possible.

Dismantling religious stereotypes further challenges Muslims and Christians to a deep faith commitment that reaches out to the other in love even in the face of opposition and violence, a faith that seeks to preach peace, reconciliation, and harmony. All must accept pluralism, condemn fanaticism, and reach out in friendship in dialogue characterised by mutual acceptance, respect, cooperation, and elimination of negativity. It demands proper education, appropriate training for religious leaders, teachers, religious instructors, and preachers. Moreover, preaching remains a vital means of breaking down religious stereotypes.

Christianity and Islam both profess to be religions of peace.[689] In order to create peace and mutual understanding, I further propose that Christian and Muslim leaders might consider meeting and working regularly with each other. They must strive together to create the necessary space for meeting where people feel safe enough to be open and honest. I am convinced that in such an environment, stereotypes, fears, hurts, and hopes can be safely expressed. In addition, kindness and hospitality towards the other builds trust and weakens stereotypes. Christians and Muslims should be hospitable to one another, be good neighbours, and give wholehearted support to each other. Both should be open to talk and share about each other's faith with respect and dignity and accept the differences. Social activities such as sports, National Day celebrations, naming ceremonies, weddings, festivals, and harvest thanksgivings are events that bring people together to socialise. These are informal opportunities for people to get to know each other better and strengthen ties of mutual peace and social cohesion. When stereotypes are weakened, mutual trust and welcoming attitudes among neighbours flourish.

---

[688] See 'Declaration on Religious Freedom,' no. 2, 678.

[689] Owojaiye, 'Factors Responsible for Muslim-Christian Unrest in Nigeria.' *Note*: For this work, peace is defined as tranquillity of order, a situation of justice, rightly ordered social relationships that are marked by respect for the rights of others which provides favourable conditions for integral human growth and harmonious coexistence. See chapter 3 for more discuss on peace.

4.2.1 THE USE OF LANGUAGE AND SYMBOLS IN PEACE BUILDING

In this sub-section, I shall focus on the importance of language and symbols in the process of peace building, by highlighting the vital place of communication in nurturing human relations.

Humans communicate through the use of language, which may be spoken, written, verbal, or non-verbal. It includes gestures, signs, and symbols.[690] Language connects humans to one another by expressing heartfelt thoughts and, when used positively, enhances peaceful relationships between people and communities.[691] Symbols, gestures, signs, actions, emblems, icons, and body language may represent or convey a particular message of peace. I argue that positive use of language and symbols can contribute to peaceful coexistence in Northern Nigeria.

We communicate using language, signs, and symbols to express ourselves. According to conflict mediator Marshall Rosenberg, language allows us to reveal our inner selves, relate to others, and give and receive messages. It allows our natural tendencies like compassion, love, and care to flourish. He argues that the positive use of language and symbols communicates compassion and peace towards others.[692] This begins by working on our own mindset, on the way we perceive ourselves, our needs, and the other.[693] He further notes that speaking peacefully in our use of language is challenging because it requires honesty, sincerity, and openness, developing a certain literacy of expression, while overcoming deeply ingrained stereotypes, bias, judgement, fear, and shame.[694] The primary purpose of communication is to connect people and communities and to foster smooth interactions. When our use of language in communication is positive, it enhances better understanding, collaboration, and friendship and diminishes conflict tendencies, tension, and mistrust. On the other hand, when language is used negatively, it breeds mistrust, tension, enmity, conflict, and violence. However, a heart devoted to peace desires to listen and understand, respect others, and use language to promote truth and peace.[695] This challenges leaders, communities, and people to the careful use of language to promote peace and respect for the other.[696]

Peace building between Christians and Muslims in Northern Nigeria requires the use of positive language that conveys mutual friendliness, respect, and compassion.

---

[690] Marshal B. Rosenberg, *Speak Peace in a World of Conflict: What You Say Next Will Change Your World* (Encinitas, CA: Puddle Dancer Press, 2005), 9-10.

[691] Ibid.

[692] Ibid.

[693] Ibid., 10-11.

[694] Ibid.

[695] John Paul II, 'To Reach Peace, Teach Peace.'

[696] See ibid.

Christians and Muslims in the region must cultivate and sustain an affirming attitude and speak peace using language to further integration. Constructive, non-violent, and non-abusive use of language enhances peaceful coexistence.[697] It demands a commitment to encouraging attitudes of respect, collaboration, and treating the other with a generous heart. Moreover, to foster change, people must respect the dignity of the other by exploring more humane ways of collaborating despite differences. It is important that children and the younger generation be taught the use of positive language to build good relationships. Practice of peace leads to peace and teaches those searching for peace that this treasure is attainable by commitment to peace building by sharing and collaboration with others.[698] For example, to describe the other as an infidel or an unbeliever (*kafir*) is hurtful and diminishes good relations. The use of language in peace building is a gradual process of changing opinions, eroding old stereotypical barriers, and gradually introducing new structures to encourage peaceful relations.[699]

Language and symbols go together in the peace building process. Symbols/ gestures of peace are culturally bound. A symbol or gesture that signifies peace in one culture may not be the case in another. Gestures of peace spring from the lives of a people who foster peace, first of all, in their own hearts and towards others (blessed are the peacemakers, Matt. 5: 9). The values and vision of peace are expressed in language and gestures of peace. Without such gestures, budding convictions vanish, and the language of peace quickly becomes a discredited rhetoric. Symbols/gestures of peace enhance growth when people appreciate fully the community dimension of their lives; then they can grasp the meaning and consequences of events in their own communities and in the world at large.[700]

Additionally, gestures of peace create a tradition, an environment, and a culture of peace. Religion plays a vital role in fostering gestures and consolidating conditions for peace. It exercises this role all the more effectively when adherents of a religious tradition strive to bring the values of peace forward, to promote universal brotherhood and celebrate our common origin in God (Gn. 1: 27). Religious symbolic gestures express the desire to nurture peace by spreading a spirituality and culture which strengthens our inter-connectivity and stimulates collaboration and mutual interest in upholding the dignity and freedom of the human person.[701]

---

[697] Cf. Rosita Iwuanyanwu, 'Interreligious Dialogue Organised by the Nigerian Conference of Women Religious, December 2008.' http://www.sndden.wordpress.com

[698] John Paul II, 'To Reach Peace, Teach Peace,' no. 3.

[699] Cf. Ibid., and 'Rosenberg, Speak Peace,' 128-31.

[700] Pope John Paul II, 'Pacem in Terris: A Permanent Commitment, http://www.vatican.va/ holy_father/john_paul_iimessages/peace/documents/hf_jp-ii_mes_20021217_xxxvi-world-day-for-peace_en.html

[701] Cf. Ibid.

In Northern Nigeria, symbols of peace include water (drunk from the same calabash), a handshake, a smile, a gift, the gift of kolanut, and asking others for forgiveness and reconciliation using language. These have religious, cultural, and traditional symbolism. Offering the other any of these gestures, especially in conflict resolution, is a powerful symbol of peace and desire for reconciliation. In some situations, it may even require series of meetings and discussions about the issues at stake. I am convinced that these can be explored and analysed to become stepping stones to better collaboration in strengthening the process of interreligious peace building. The potential for peace has to be cultivated in such a way that even in tensions and conflicts people will find the breathing space necessary to develop fruitful fraternal resolutions by using language and symbols/gestures of peace. To achieve the above, religious/dialogue leaders, preachers, families, parents, and educators are responsible for helping people, especially young people and children, to appreciate language and gestures of peace everywhere—in mosques, churches, other places of worship, at home, at school, at play with friends, during social interactions, in team work, in competitive sports, and in the many ways in which friendship can be established and nurtured.[702] Positive use of language and symbols of peace will stimulate better relations to enhance peace building. *Happy are the peace makers for they shall be called the children of God* (Matt. 5: 9).

4.3 Concrete Ongoing Peace Building Initiatives in Northern Nigeria

In this section, I shall explore ongoing peace building attempts in Northern Nigeria. I focus on the efforts of the Interfaith Mediation Centre/Muslim-Christian Dialogue Forum (IFMC/MCDF) and the Nigerian Interreligious Council (NIREC) to appraise these endeavours. The aim here is to highlight a glimmer of hope for a future of peace in sustained mutual negotiations.

4.3.1 The Interfaith Mediation Centre (IFMC), Kaduna

This segment is a brief history of the events that led to the establishment of the Interfaith Mediation Centre in Kaduna, Northern Nigeria. The centre was set up by Imam Muhammad Ashafa, a scholarly Muslim, and Pastor James Wuye, a charismatic Pentecostal Christian. These are two clerics who harboured deep-rooted hatred and desire for revenge towards each other. They were both commanders of two militia youth groups, one Christian, the other Muslim. Each organised and led their group in conflict and violence. For example, they personally contributed to the escalation

---

[702]   See also John Paul II, 'To Reach Peace, Teach Peace,' no. 3.

of the conflict in Zangon-Kataf and Plateau state in the 1990s.[703] It was not until both experienced personal tragedy that their ferocity and militancy was transformed into revolutionary humility. The pastor lost his hand, and the imam's spiritual father and his brother died in the conflict. They both nursed a desire for revenge for their loss. However, through the study of their scriptures (Bible and Qur'an) and listening to preaching, they each began to question the cost of violence. Both found texts and traditions which helped them to develop a more peaceful interpretation, leading to their individual conversion and personal transformation, with the courage to sincerely forgive each other and be reconciled.[704]

Their first encounter in 1995 was characterised by uncertainty, doubt, and suspicion; nevertheless, the desire to make peace was stronger. This impelled both to learn to trust each other, and in time, bitterness gave way to forgiveness, reconciliation, and peace.[705] The pastor and the imam are a living proof that people can be transformed, and the urge for revenge can be changed into an urge to foster reconciliation, peace, and harmony in a conflict situation.[706] The experience of the pastor and the imam inspired them to build a relationship of interpersonal reconciliation and to work for reconciliation between communities ridden with stereotypes, hate, conflict, and violence. They set up the Interfaith Mediations Centre and the Muslim-Christian Dialogue Forum. They believe that peace will be achieved through education and dialogue. They began a process of deorientation, change of attitude, forgiveness, and reconciliation within their militia groups. They believe that education and highlighting the pains and evils of violent conflicts can lead to reconciliation between the two groups. The mediation centre is based in Kaduna; it reaches out to youths, women, and religious, political, and community/traditional leaders at different levels with the aim of building peace and harmony.[707]

---

[703] See Ashafa and Wuye, *The Pastor and the Imam: Responding to Conflict*, 154.

[704] James M. Wuye and Muhammad N. Ashafa, 'The Pastor and the Imam: The Muslim-Christian Dialogue Forum in Nigeria,' in *People Building Peace II* (Hague, the Netherlands: European Centre for Conflict Prevention, 2009), 1-2. http://www. peoplebuildingpeace.org; see also Renee Garfinkel, 'Personal Transformations: Moving from Violence to Peace,' *Special Report* (Washington: United States Institute of Peace, 2007), 3-4.

[705] Cf. Little, 'Peacemakers in Action,' 261-264.

[706] Garfinkel, 'Personal Transformations,' 1.

[707] *Note*: The aims and objectives of the Interfaith Mediation Centre are already discussed in chapter 2.

4.3.2 ACTIVITIES OF THE INTERFAITH MEDIATION CENTRE/THE MUSLIM-CHRISTIAN DIALOGUE FORUM

This segment highlights the efforts of the Interfaith Mediation Centre through the use of available local resources for peace building. The major aims of IFMC/ MCDF are to promote mutual respect, openness to religious, cultural, and historical diversity within communities through dialogue and to propagate the values and virtues of religious harmony and peaceful coexistence in Northern Nigeria. The target groups are faith communities, youths, women, and leaders in the community (traditional, social, economic, ethnic, and political leaders). The method used in the peace building process is a multitrack approach, using different techniques to study, analyse, and address issues of communal, inter-communal, and intra-communal conflicts and to proffer solutions. This is achieved by a process of education via workshops, seminars, and symposia. For example, such workshops are conducted using two approaches: the illustrative approach, where participants are exposed to the causes, dangers, and evils of violence, and the ventilation approach, where warring parties have the opportunity to vent their anger, pain, and frustration by telling their stories, analysing conflicts, and negotiations. Other methods used by IFMC/MCDF include the use of scripture to diffuse tension and suspicion, storytelling, personal life stories (e.g. the film *The Imam and the Pastor*),[708] media advocacy, peace building stories around the world, trauma counselling techniques, and reference to the spiritual values that appease people. Additional methods include the use of rituals (i.e. having conflict parties write down hurts, pains, and frustrations and the scripts burnt), mending trust by getting people to apologise and ask for forgiveness, trust building, prayers, peer mediation, drama, and children's playtime while parents/adults partake in the mediation-reconciliation process.[709] What are the resources available for the effectiveness of these methods?

The IFMC/MCDF uses the local resources in the region where the mediation process is taking place, such as stories, proverbs, sayings, and traditional methods of conflict resolution. The centre has trained facilitators for conflict resolution, dialogue, and mediation and has developed and printed resource material for the effective implementation of its aims and objectives.[710] The centre networks with the Nigerian Supreme Council for Islamic Affairs (NSCIA), CAN, Jama'atu Nasril Islam (JNI),

---

[708] The Imam and the Pastor: A Documentary Film from the Heart of Nigeria, produced and directed. Alan Channer, 60 minutes, FLT films, 2006, DVD.

[709] James M. Wuye, Kaduna, Interview by author, 15 January 2011.

[710] Ibid. The printed material include: *Students for Peace: Peace Building Modules, Student Guidebook and Peace Education Manual for Senior Secondary Schools in Christian and Islamic Knowledge* (1998) for schools and institutions. Others are: *Community Conflict in Nigeria* (1998), *The Pastor and Imam Responding to Conflict* (1999), *Forgiveness and*

Conflict Management Stakeholders Network, other non-governmental organisations (NGOs), and faith-based organisations (FBOs).[711] The centre also networks with international institutes engaged in peace building activities, for example, the United States Institute for Peace (USIP), USA, European Centre for Conflict Prevention, Netherlands, and Responding to Conflicts (RTC), United Kingdom.[712] These networks provide the centre with the use of a variety of resources to enhance the peace building process, with remarkable success in Northern Nigeria.

4.3.3 The Effectiveness of IFMC/MCDF Mediation Process

This segment is an appraisal of the activities of the Interfaith Mediation Centre and the Muslims-Christian Dialogue Forum, in which I critically highlight particular events that have proved to be success stories.

Evaluating the effectiveness of IFMC/MCDF is not easy because a lot of groundwork has been done by Pastor James and Imam Ashafa since the opening of the centre. Although significant progress has been recorded in peace building, nevertheless there has been a relapse into violent hostilities in the region, which demonstrates that peace cannot be achieved in one day. The centre continues to address the challenges of peace building using a faith-based approach to promote the acceptance of religious, cultural, gender, and social differences in a pluralistic society. Religion is part and parcel of the life of the people of Northern Nigeria, and nearly everyone in the region belongs to one religion or another. Religion has a powerful influence on people; therefore, religious values have been most effective in the ongoing peace building process.[713]

A recent achievement of the IFMC/MCDF is the mediating and negotiating of a peace process in Kaduna, which led to the formation of 'Kaduna Peace Committee' and the adoption of the Kaduna Peace declaration on 22 August 2002 (for the full text of Kaduna Peace Declaration of Religious Leaders, see documentation 1). Since the signing of the Kaduna Peace Declaration, grassroot efforts to maintain peace have been going on but not without challenges: in November of the same year, there was much tension and protest over a newspaper article in Nigeria connecting Prophet Muhammad to the Miss World beauty contest being hosted in the country.

Reconciliation: Islam and Christian Perspective (2001), *Training Manual on Interfaith Guide for Good Governance* (2003), and *Faith-Based Advocacy on the Rights of Women.*

[711] Interfaith Mediation Centre, 'Committed to Building Peace, Building Interfaith Cooperation and Good Governance,' 2009. http://www.imcnigeria.org/history.htm

[712] Ibid.

[713] See 'Interfaith Mediation Centre of Muslim-Christian Dialogue Forum (IMC-MCDF).' 2007. http://www.changemakers.com/comprtition/entrepreneuring-peace/entries/interfaith-mediation-cntre-Muslim-Christian-dialogue-f

The pastor, imam, and other religious leaders had to appeal for calm among religious communities through the media and public forums. The prompt intervention to contain a volatile situation was possible because of the commitments made by religious leaders in the Kaduna Peace Declaration.[714] To further stem the tide of violence, the centre and the signatories of the Kaduna Peace Declaration embarked on a programme of conflict resolution training for religious instructors in schools and other educational institutions.[715] A similar peace building initiative was undertaken in Plateau state after the violent conflict that engulfed the state. IFMC/MCDF mediation in a peace process led to the signing of 'Yelwa-Shendam Peace Affirmation' on 19 February 2005 (for the full text of the Yelwa-Shendam Peace Affirmation, see documentation 2).[716] The centre has facilitated peace negotiations among the Pan and Goemai communities in 2006 and the Dillimi-Kwang communities, which led to the rebuilding of the community market destroyed during the crises of 2006.[717] Other significant activities include a Coexistence Training Workshop for Peace Networks in Kaduna state, a Peace Building and Reorientation for Religious Community Youth Leaders in Jos, and Metropolitan Areas Workshop held in Jos Plateau State in May 2010, in response to the ongoing Plateau crises.

Since these major events took place, the above-named communities have lived in relative peace and harmony. However, there are challenges in maintaining the relative peace in these communities, just as there are ongoing activities to sustain the peace building process in the region to mitigate future conflicts. There are regular dialogue meetings between the faith communities, training programmes for leaders to promote good governance and accountability, and the establishment of peace constituencies that seek to bring elected representatives, the electorate, and religious representatives to dialogue. Furthermore, the establishment of faith institutions, the Bureau for Religious Affairs, and State Interreligious Council in Kaduna and Plateau states are efforts showing positive results. Also, the establishment of the State Interfaith network in Kano, the formation of peace clubs in schools, and the development of a peace curriculum for schools and colleges in (Northern) Nigeria are commendable.[718] These projects aim to dispel stereotypes, foster reconciliation, and build trust and lasting mutual harmony in the region. I now focus on the Peace Training Workshop for Christian and Muslim Youth Leaders in (Northern) Nigeria as a case study example.

---

[714] Cf. Wuye and Ashafa, 'The Pastor and the Imam,' 5.

[715] Ibid.

[716] See Okpanachi, 'Building Peace in a Divided Society,' 21-22.

[717] 'Interfaith Mediation Centre of Muslim-Christian Dialogue Forum.'

[718] Ibid.

4.3.4 THE PEACE TRAINING WORKSHOP FOR CHRISTIAN AND MUSLIM YOUTH LEADERS

In this segment, I shall analyse critically a peace training workshop as an example of how stereotypes and misunderstanding about the religious other can fuel conflicts and to stress the need for constant dialogue engagement.

The training workshop was organised by IFMC/MCDF and held in Kaduna in 2002, as part of the preparation to ensure peace and security during the 2003 national elections. Economic deprivation, poor leadership, and the use of religious/ethnic slogans to recruit and mobilise unemployed youths into militia groups was the early warning sign of the threatening crisis. The centre, in collaboration with the CAN, Jama'atu Nasril Islam (JNI), and United States Institute of Peace (USIP), developed a proactive strategy to prevent this potential catastrophe by helping youth leaders confront and possibly revise their stereotypes, bias, misconceptions, and prejudices.[719]

The workshop was aimed at transforming Christian and Muslim youths from being vanguards of violence into instruments of peace by educating and exposing them to the pains and evils of violence and the need for peace through conflict resolution. The plan was to improve relations between the two religious communities by better understanding, respect, and cooperation. A dialogue forum was initiated to open a peace network, leading to grassroot peace actions and also to establish an early warning mechanism for the nation. Hence, participants were carefully selected from different states of the nation. Some held positions of influence among their peers, with the power to escalate or de-escalate conflict situations within their constituencies. Others were commanders in religious groupings who were respected by both religious and political leaders.[720]

The workshop began after preliminaries with scriptural references from the Bible and the Qur'an, quoting religious commands for peace and harmony. Participants were able to appreciate these values and unanimously condemn the culture of violence, killing, and maiming in the name of religion. An intra-religious dialogue session was introduced, during which Christians and Muslims met separately. Discussions were centred on the concept of neighbour, the right and freedom of the other to choose and practise their faith, and respect for religious minorities and their beliefs and practices. This was followed by intra-religious reorientation and discussions. It gave the participants in the two groups the opportunity to discuss freely and honestly, expressing their fears and expectations about meeting the religious other. Fears of insincerity, ignorance, misunderstanding, confusion, violent

---

[719] David R. Smock (ed.), *Religious Contributions to Peacemaking: When Religion Brings Peace, Not War* (Washington: United Institute for Peace, 2006), 21.

[720] Cf. Ibid.

disagreements, discord, animosity, and lack of respect were expressed on both sides. Facilitators dealt with this positively, allaying these fears by explaining the need to engage in religious dialogue by referring to the holy books. They further encouraged participants to live by the dictates of their religious values of mercy, compassion, love, peace, and respect for the other. They were admonished to listen and speak the truth with respect as they expressed the concerns of their faith community. Both groups further expressed the fears of their faith communities such as ignorance, pride, unfaithfulness, a domineering attitude, hypocrisy, lack of obedience, illiteracy, and poverty. These had to be addressed within the religious circle through education and social responsibility as it affected the group (Christian or Muslim). Imam Muhammad Ashafa led the team that facilitated the Muslim group, while Pastor James Wuye led the Christian group.

The interreligious conference session brought the two groups together in a dialogue assembly. The remote preparation for this session involved moving all participants from their separate hostel accommodation to a single hostel with adjacent rooms to boost community spirit through interaction. Some participants were afraid of being attacked during the night; others had mixed expectations about having a joint session.[721] At the meeting, ground rules were set and ice-breaking exercises were introduced. It was also agreed that the Muslim prayer times be allowed and respected.

The dialogue session began with the facilitators stating the positive and negative sentiments of one group towards the other, discussing misconceptions, stereotypes, bias, and prejudice and identifying further steps for productive dialogue. This opened with discussions where each group expressed their thoughts about the other, for example, Christians said Muslims respect and cherish their Islamic faith and culture with a sense of unity, prayer, generosity, and impressive foresight. On the negative side, Muslims are thought of as self-centred, aggressive, lazy, and domineering sycophants. The Muslims on the other hand perceived Christians as cooperative with each other, having vision and foresight, well-organised, industrious, and economically enterprising. On the negative side, Christians are said to have a deep hatred of Muslims, blackmailing them deliberately, uncompromising, and opposing Islamic views. Both groups were amazed to hear what the other said about them. This interactive dialogue generated more discussion with the facilitators, addressing common misconceptions and stereotypes. At the end, participants identified conditions for effective dialogue; these include striving to learn the basic tenets of each other's faith, being sensitive and respecting the religious values of the other, being open to learning from the other, and speaking the truth sincerely.[722] A joint communiqué was issued at the end of the workshop (for the full text of the Muslim-Christian joint Communiqué, see documentation 3).

---

[721]   Ibid., 23.

[722]   Ibid.

This training workshop succeeded in bringing to light the hidden perceptions, stereotypes, tensions, fears, and pains. Peaceful relationships cannot be built on stereotypes and suspicion. A sustainable peace building process has to connect with the salient experiences and feelings towards the other and deal positively with them in order to enhance growth and better understanding. The workshop helped tremendously to create the chance to confront these doubts and build trust and confidence in the youths, giving them renewed vigour for an optimistic engagement with each other. The fact that youth leaders in turn organised further dialogue workshops for youths of different faiths to interact in order to reduce hostility in conflict prone areas, indicates that the peace training workshop was successful.

For me one of the greatest achievements of IFMC/MCDF is in the area of trauma counselling and healing of emotional injuries. Experience of excessive violence and gross violations of human rights in and between faith communities involved in the conflicts, leave people traumatised and suffering deep emotional injuries. The loss of loved ones and property and painful memories of conflicts cause deep emotional and psychological stress to victims. The IFMC/MCDF has given renewed hope and strength by healing emotional injuries and traumas in counselling, thus making a major contribution to peace building and reconciliation between communities torn by violence. Moreover, religion provides the emotional, psychological, and spiritual resources needed for such healing.[723] It is essential for the centre to continue to collaborate with religious institutions. I shall now examine the activities of the Nigeria Interreligious Council (NIREC).

4.3.5   THE NIGERIA INTERRELIGIOUS COUNCIL (NIREC)

In this segment, I shall examine the Nigeria Interreligious Council (NIREC), highlight its aims and activities, and stress the vital role and achievements of NIREC in Christian-Muslim dialogue.

NIREC is the brainchild of Muslim and Christian leaders, with the support of the Federal Government of Nigeria. It is an independent organisation made up of fifty members (twenty-five Christians and twenty-five Muslims), representatives of the two major religions in Nigeria, Christianity and Islam. NIREC was inaugurated in September 1999. The establishment of NIREC was occasioned by the incessant ethno-religious conflicts in Northern Nigeria. It provides religious and traditional leaders with a variable forum to promote greater interaction and understanding among religious groups. NIREC's aims to have a positive influence on the Muslim

---

[723]   Cf. Tsejeard Bouta S. Ayse Kadayifci-Orellana and Muhammad Abu-Nimer, *Faith-Based Peace-Building: Mapping and Analysis of Christian, Muslim and Multi-Faith Actors* (Hague: Netherlands Institute of Iinternational Relations Clingendael, 2005), 36. http://www.salaminstitute.org/FaithBasedActors.pdf

and Christian religious faithful, enhance religious tolerance and promote peaceful coexistence and good governance in Nigeria.[724] (For the discourse on NIREC, see Chapter 2.) NIREC holds regular quarterly meetings to dialogue, analyse, and evaluate their activities. At such meetings, the perennial issues of harmony, tolerance, and security are discussed.[725] Communiqués are issued for information, action, and implementation. These communiqués address not just matters of religion but also fundamental issues about governance, development, equity, justice, security, and anything the NIREC considers to be part of the root cause of conflicts in Nigeria. For instance, at the end of the November 2008 meeting, NIREC issued a communiqué urging governments at all levels, civil society, and faith-based organisations to build a systematic platform for peace and religious harmony by promoting socio-economic justice, transparency, and good governance.[726]

This communiqué further highlights the perverse effects of corruption, poverty, marginalisation, youth unemployment, injustice, and inequity as triggers of conflicts. The government was asked to address the situation urgently. In order to enhance national security and further reduce inter-communal conflicts in Nigeria, NIREC suggested taking government measures to curb the proliferation of small arms which creates a culture of violence and is a major source of crime.[727] NIREC also recognised 'reckless religious preachers' as dangers to peace in Nigerian society and resolved to caution those who preach inciting sermons insensitively which foment religious misunderstanding and violence. NIREC has further called for capacity building for religious organisations in constant interfaith dialogues, emphasising the common values of religious belief that create mutual understanding and respect for differences.[728] (For the highlights of the communiqué, see documentation 4a-b).

The major function of NIREC is to foster peace by being proactive in creating awareness, education, and intervention in crisis situations. This is accomplished through advocacy, seminars, conferences on dialogue, symposia, and religious education in collaboration with religious bodies, the media, NGOs/FBOs, and the government. NIREC has nine standing committees, two of which are dedicated to

---

[724] See 'Nigeria Inter-Religious Council (NIREC),' 2009. http://www.nirecng.org/hisoty.html

[725] Ibid.

[726] Cf. 'NIREC Quarterly Communiqué November 2008,' http://www.nirecng.org/docs/ NIREC_COMMUNIQUE_AT_KANO_MEETING.pdf

[727] Ibid. See also Salisu N. Dambatta, 'NIREC Calms Religious Frayed Nerves,' *Daily Trust* (Nigeria), 22 June 2008. http://www.dailytrust.com

[728] 'NIREC Quarterly Communiqué November 2008.' See also Okpanachi, *Building Peace in a Divided Society,* 17-18.

interreligious dialogue and public enlightenment, peace building, and conflict resolution.[729]

NIREC has made a significant breakthrough in the peace building process and is becoming increasingly relevant in championing the cause of peaceful coexistence, religious tolerance, and harmony. During a religious crisis in Bauchi in December 2007, the chairmen of NIREC visited Bauchi State and addressed Christians and Muslims on the essence of religious tolerance and peace. This intervention was unprecedented in the history of conflicts in Northern Nigeria. The effect of their action was immediate: cessation of hostilities on both sides. Furthermore, the crisis in Jos Plateau State did not spread to neighbouring states because of the role played by the co-chairmen of NIREC (the Sultan of Sokoto Muhammad Sa'ad Abubakar and the Catholic Archbishop of Abuja John Onaiyekan).[730]

NIREC has ushered in a new dawn in Christian-Muslim relations, building trust and good neighbourliness. For example, in Shendam, Plateau State, a Christian cleric, noticing that a mosque was to be torched by some hooligans, risked his life to stop the arsonists and was injured by the attackers. In a similar gesture, a group of Muslims, on noticing that a church building was on fire rushed to contain it before the Christian community got to the scene.[731] These actions are symbolic of healing divisions and creating an atmosphere of peace and harmony.

The NIREC has continued to educate and guide the public in the challenges of religious diversity, tolerance, respect, and peaceful coexistence, by having public lectures, meetings, advocacy, dialogue seminars, communiqués, addresses, and paper presentations. This channel of communication and dialogue has created a growing mutual understanding that received a boost in January 2009 at the Muslim-Christian youth summit in Minna Niger, with participants from all over the country. A further move has been made by NIREC to initiate a joint interfaith project to address the menace of malaria, HIV/AIDS, and poverty. Public awareness of the need for all stakeholders to collaborate on these issues is growing. The NIREC also makes recommendations to all tiers of government on matters that will assist in fostering peace and harmony and the integral development of the nation.[732]

---

[729] 'NIREC Standing Committees,' http://www.nirecng.org/docs/NIREC_STANDING_COMMITTEES.pdf; Constitution of the Nigerian Inter-religious Council (NIREC), 11 and 13.

[730] Nigeria Inter-Religious Council (NIREC), 'Our Achievements,' http://www.nirecng.org/achieve.html; see also Eyoboka, *Sultan and CAN Leaders.*

[731] Cf. 'Jos Violence: Everyone Lives in Fear of His Neighbour,' *People's Daily* (Nigeria), 17 April 2011. http://www.peoplesdaily-online.com

[732] Michael Ishola, 'NIREC Scribe Advocates Interfaith, Inter-Communal Dialogue,' *Tribune* (Nigeria), 20 June 2010.

However, in spite of these achievements, violent conflicts remain a challenge, especially in the northern region. NIREC is only an advisory body on issues of security and can only make recommendations to the government and relevant agencies. NIREC has no judicial powers to prosecute perpetrators of violence in Nigeria. Moreover, the security of Nigeria is the responsibility of the national government. It is unfortunate that no one has ever been charged for the violent loss of life and property; nevertheless, NIREC remains committed to collaborating with religious groups and institutions to build peace and harmony. I shall now examine the Muslim-Christian Youth Summit.

4.3.6 THE NIGERIAN YOUTH SUMMIT ON INTERRELIGIOUS DIALOGUE AND PEACEFUL COEXISTENCE, MINNA, NIGER STATE, 2009

In this section, I shall review an activity of NIREC—the Nigerian Youth Summit on Interreligious Dialogue, and discuss the highlights of the seminar.

One of the recent activities and achievements of NIREC was the successful hosting of a Youth Summit. The NIREC, having evaluated the causes of conflicts, and in a bid to put in place necessary measures to ensure sustainable harmony, organised a summit of Christian-Muslim youth representatives in Nigeria. The aim was to educate and foster better understanding among young people of different religious traditions. The five-day seminar-workshop was tagged 'Nigerian Youth Summit on Interreligious Dialogue and Peaceful Coexistence' held in Minna, Niger State, Nigeria.[733] I participated as an observer, representing CAN and the Catholic Secretariat. There were 250 participating youths, consisting of 100 Christians, nominated by the CAN, and 100 Muslims, nominated by the Nigerian Supreme Council for Islamic Affairs (NSCIA), as well as twenty-five Christians and twenty-five Muslims nominated by the host state (Niger). Resource persons, reporters, logistics officers, and representatives of religious organisations, NGOs/FBOs, traditional rulers, and the government also attended, totalling about 300 participants.[734]

The summit focused on issues and effects of interreligious conflicts in Nigeria by presenting scenes of violence, chaos, and devastation in Northern Nigeria resulting from religious conflict. This aroused curiosity among participants, who asked questions. For example, two people asked if there are verses in the Bible or Qur'an that permitted any one to kill a neighbour. References were made to verses in the Qur'an and the Bible to affirm that neither religion advocates killing another

---

[733] See 'Summit on Inter-Religious Dialogue and Peaceful Coexistence by the Nigerian Inter-Religious Council (NIREC) Held on 21-25 January 2009 at Minna, Niger State,' http://www.nirecng.org/home/docs/youth_summit_report.pdf

[734] Ibid.

person. In a further response to the question, it was stressed that killing the other is unacceptable in both Christianity and Islam.

The lectures and paper presentations revealed the evils of conflicts and violence vividly and the need for conflict resolutions for peaceful coexistence. Group discussions explored contentious issues to find the root causes of the violent conflicts. For instance, the conflict cycle in Jos Plateau State was critically analysed without apportioning blame. Three points were articulated: the history of the conflict, the issues and causes of the conflict, and parties in the conflict. The fact that land resources and religion are sources of conflict came out strongly: religion should be a way to peace but is used to ferment conflicts. It was, however, agreed that these conflicts are more complex than they seem, and efforts must be geared towards a better understanding of them. Therefore, addressing these issues through proper information dissemination and clarification play a very significant role in peace building.

The following resolutions were made at the end:

- To continue a peace building process by collaboration in addressing issues leading to conflict in the community, to respect the values of others, and be open to interreligious dialogue opportunities with other youths;
- To establish NIREC chapters at state levels coordinated by the participants of the summit, who in turn reach out to educational institutions and the National Youth Service Corps (NYSC, a one-year service programme compulsory for all graduates in Nigeria) to build better understanding and peace through interreligious dialogue.
- To respect the religious values of the other and the freedom to choose and practise their faith.
- To be committed to becoming ambassadors of peace and harmony in their communities through collaboration with other youths and agencies for purposeful interfaith ventures.

The youth summit was successful in bringing together young people from different parts of Nigeria to interact and build a relationship of understanding and collaboration through dialogue. It was the first of its kind, cutting across religious, ethnic, and social barriers and exposing the dangers of violent conflicts. The aim of the summit was achieved by reiterating the reality of the multicultural and multireligious nature of contemporary Nigeria and the need for a system of religious education that seeks to teach and learn about other religious traditions. There were disagreements and lack of compromise on some of the issues discussed at group interactions, such as gender and Islamic sharia as practised in some northern states in Nigeria.[735] However, it was agreed that these issues need greater awareness and education at different levels of society. The summit finally closed with a communiqué which challenged religious leaders and the government to develop a system of religious education that teaches adherents the religious values of the other to bring better understanding, peace, and development to Nigeria (for the highlights of the communiqué, see documentation 5).

4.4 INTERRELIGIOUS DIALOGUE INITIATIVES IN NORTHERN NIGERIA

In this section, I shall focus on the dialogue ventures of different Christian denominations (Catholic, Anglican, and Lutheran Churches) in Northern Nigeria and those of Jama'tu Nasril Islam (JNI) and the Federation of Muslim Women Association of Nigeria (FOMWAN). The aim here is to analyse and understand the attempts made by these religious groups to engage in dialogue for peace building.

4.4.1 CATHOLIC CHURCH INITIATIVES IN NORTHERN NIGERIA

The CBCN has always stressed the need for Christians in Nigeria to dialogue with other religions, especially with Islam. This desire has been strengthened with the establishment of a department for dialogue and mission within the CSN. Catholic ecclesiastical provinces and dioceses have taken up the challenge to dialogue with our Muslim brothers and sisters and have established commissions to achieve this aim. This received a boost in 2003 when the Interreligious Dialogue Commission of the Association of Episcopal Conferences of Anglophone West Africa (AECAWA) organised its annual dialogue workshop study session in Kaduna on the theme of 'Offer Forgiveness and Receive Peace: A Challenge to a Multi-Religious Society'.[736] The reason for the choice of the venue was the militant and violent character of Kaduna and its environs.

The workshop gathered together religious (Christian, Muslim, and traditional) leaders, participants, government representatives, and opinion leaders. A Muslim and a Christian each presented a paper on the need for dialogue and peace at the workshop. After each paper, the willingness of participants to engage in discussions was remarkable, emphasising the importance of the workshop. It was also evident, judging from the level of engagement, that participants were well prepared for interreligious discussions. At the end, a communiqué was issued condemning violence and stressing the need for forgiveness, reconciliation, and peace. The

---

[735]   Ibid.

[736]   Cf. Denis Chidi Isizoh, 'Nigeria: Report of a Visit 10-14 November 2003,' in *Pro Dialogo* (Vaticano: Pontificium Consilium Pro Dialogo Inter Religiones, 2004), 74.

government was challenged to be proactive in tackling poverty, injustice, and violence. The meeting recommended that education on the principles of interreligious coexistence and dialogue be taught at grassroot level: homes, schools, communities, churches, and mosques (for the full text of the communiqué, see documentation 6). The workshop ended with a commitment to foster collaboration in the promotion of justice, peace, and dialogue among people.[737] In this work, I limit my analysis to the Catholic Ecclesiastical Provinces of Kaduna and Jos in Northern Nigeria.

Kaduna Ecclesiastical Province: This province consists of seven dioceses in north-west Nigeria, within the sharia states.[738] In June 2005, Kaduna Provincial Interreligious Commission organised a dialogue workshop on the 'Implication of Islamic sharia in Northern Nigeria for Christians'. The seminar was attended by participants from the dioceses, as well as three representatives of JNI. The Christians spoke vehemently of the injustices and oppression they experience in the northern states and their misgivings about sharia law. The Muslim speaker (Hajiya Bilkisu Yusuf) argued that the expansion of the sharia criminal code is not equal to the establishment of sharia in the region. He emphasised the social mission of sharia and the need to compel public leaders to be accountable.[739] At the end of this seminar, a communiqué was issued. The drafting of the communiqué on the implications of sharia was very challenging for Christians. The Muslim participants insisted that sharia does not apply to Christians, while the Christians expressed a contrary opinion forcefully. However, it was eventually agreed that further discussions are necessary for Christians and Muslims to listen to each other's views and clarify misconceptions (for the complete text of the communiqué, see documentation 7).

Jos Ecclesiastical Province: In the 1980s and 1990s, the Pastoral Institute in Bukuru-Jos was a place where friendship and collaboration developed between Christians and Muslims of that region. This was due to the establishment of a Christian-Muslim secretariat, where extensive research was conducted on the development of Islam/Muslim-Christian relations in (Northern) Nigeria. The outbreak of conflict and violence in 2001 challenged the Justice Development and Peace Commission (JDPC) to organise a dialogue/reconciliation workshop in

---

[737]   Ibid., 77.

[738]   Kaduna Archdiocese (Kaduna metropolis), Kafanchan Diocese (southern Kaduna state), Kano Diocese (Kano and Jigawa states), Kontagora Vicariate (Niger and Kebbi states), Minna Diocese (Niger state), Sokoto Diocese (Sokoto and Kebbi states), and Zaria (northern Kaduna and some part of Kano and Katsina states).

[739]   Hajiya Bilkisu Yusuf, 'Sharia and Non-Muslims Fears and Expectations,' in Joseph Salihu (ed.), *Interreligious Dialogue and the Sharia Question* (Kano: Jaleyemi Group Publications, 2005), 58-68. See also Kathleen McGarvey, *Muslim and Christian Women in Dialogue the Case of Northern Nigeria* (Lagos, Nigeria: Die Deutsche Bibliothek, 2009), 259-60.

which Muslims and Christians participated. In 2005, Jos Ecclesiastical Province Commission for interreligious dialogue organised a training workshop for Christians from Jos, Maiduguri, and Yola (north-eastern Nigeria). The aim was to empower participants with dialogue skills and encourage Christians to reach out to their Muslim brothers and sisters. Most participants felt that dialogue is risky because both Christians and Muslims react strongly to even constructive criticism. Fears were expressed about insincerity, lack of trust, and tolerance. It was, however, agreed that dialogue is imperative for peace and harmony.[740]

There are ongoing peace building initiatives geared towards harmony and peace at the grassroot level in the various Catholic dioceses. For example, in 1996, the Diocese of Kano established a Centre for Comparative Religions to foster better understanding through Christian-Muslim dialogue. Activities at the centre included seminars, workshops, and conferences. Three conferences were held between 1996 and 1997. However, during the third conference, angry words were exchanged between some fundamentalist Christians and fanatical Muslims which almost resulted in violent riots.[741] Dialogue activities and other local events were suspended due to that negative experience deepening mistrust in the faith communities.

By 2004, the centre was renamed 'Centre for Religious Coexistence', and participation in conferences was restricted to those who would abide by the ground rules set to guide dialogue sessions. In 2005, a seminar was held to discuss the implications of sharia for non-Muslims in Kano.[742] Recently Christians and Muslims came together to pray and brainstorm on conflict management in Kano and its environs. There has been no violent conflict in Kano in the last seven years, proving the success of dialogue meetings.[743] Similarly, in the Diocese of Minna, dialogue forums were organised between 2004 and 2006. In April 2009, a violent conflict erupted between Muslim and Christian youths. Religious and traditional leaders had to intervene to quell the riot. In November 2009, a dialogue meeting with youths and religious and community leaders of both faiths was held to explore ways to foster peace, forgiveness, and reconciliation.[744] It was a success story because there is now a growing harmony and better cooperation between the faith communities.

In December 2008, the Nigerian Conference of Women Religious organised a peace building dialogue forum for both Christian and Muslim women in Kaduna, on

---

[740] McGarvey, 'Muslim and Christian Women in Dialogue,' 260-61.

[741] Ibid., 258.

[742] Ibid.

[743] See Abuh, 'Praying and Working for Peace in Kano'; Yusuf, 'Agenda for Interfaith Dialogue.'

[744] Cf. 'Religious Violence in Niger State,' *Punch* (Nigeria), 26 April 2009. http://www.punchng.com

the theme of 'Made in the Image and Likeness of God'.[745] This offered participants the opportunity to dialogue on the causes of conflict and violence from the women's perspective as it affects the family. A communiqué was issued condemning violence and reaffirming the need for peaceful coexistence and religious peace education (for the full text of the communiqué, see docummentation 8).

4.4.2 THE JOINT DIALOGUE INITIATIVES OF THE ANGLICAN AND METHODIST CHURCH IN NORTHERN NIGERIA

The Anglican and Methodist Church in Nigeria formed the Islam in Africa Project (IAP) in 1958 to motivate Christian Churches to study and understand the Islamic faith.[746] This project today is a pan-African organisation known as Project of Christian Muslim Relations in Africa (PROCMURA). The purpose is to improve Christian-Muslim relations in Northern Nigeria and Africa and to encourage Christian churches to deepen their knowledge of the Islamic tradition.[747] The Anglican Bishop of Kaduna is the president of the northern area committee and has established an institute for the study of Islam and Christian-Muslim relations. This institute and PROCMURA organise dialogue conferences, seminars, and interfaith training to improve public understanding of the teachings and practices of the two faiths. PROCMURA provides support and counselling for victims of violence and cooperates with other peace building agencies.[748] In October 2010, PROCMURA hosted a workshop on conflict prevention/management, peace building, and reconciliation in Kaduna. Christians and Muslims from five northern states participated.[749] Their thoughts, hurts, and resolutions are articulated in a communiqué that was issued at the end of the workshop (for the complete text of the communiqué, see documentation 9).

4.4.3 THE EFFORTS OF THE LUTHERAN CHURCH IN NIGERIA

In 1993, the Lutheran Church in Nigeria initiated the Association for Christian-Muslim Mutual Relations in Nigeria (ACMMRN). The thrust of the activities of ACMMRN centres is on openness to other faiths, dialogue, and

---

[745] Iwuanyanwu, 'Interreligious Dialogue.'

[746] Cf. PROCMURA, 'Church Leaders in Nigeria'; Ojo and Lateju, 'Christian-Muslim Conflicts,' 35.

[747] McGarvey, *Muslim and Christian Women in Dialogue*, 255.

[748] See Ojo and Lateju, 'Christian-Muslim Conflicts,' 36; Okpanachi, 'Buiding Peace in a Divided Society,' 15.

[749] States that participated in the October 2010 Conflict Prevention and Management Seminar includes: Bauchi, Kaduna, Kano, Kogi and Plateau states.

reconciliation. They organise dialogue conferences, encouraging Muslims and Christians to make every effort to reach out to each other. Between 1993 and 2002, five dialogue conferences were organised, with Muslims and Christians participating. The resulting communiqués highlight the need for constant dialogue within and between religions to foster peace, respect, forgiveness, and reconciliation. Muslims and Christians are asked to make a sincere effort to teach the truth about the other[750] (for the complete text of communiqués, see documentation 10).

4.4.4 The Efforts of Jama'tu Nasril Islam (JNI) and Federation of Muslim Women's Association in Nigeria (FOMWAN)

Jama'atu Nasril Islam (JNI), in collaboration with NIREC and CAN, organised dialogue seminars to which Christians were invited. In February 2000, a dialogue conference on Islamic sharia was organised, which included paper presentations and discussions with arguments and counter-arguments on the topic. This was sensitive, revealing, and educational. However, it was inconclusive in the sense that further consultation on the issues was necessary. The government went ahead with the adoption and implementation of Islamic sharia as a state law.[751] FOMWAN is a Muslim women's organisation which aims to articulate Muslim women's concerns and give them a voice in society. FOMWAN engaged in a dialogue conference with the Christian Women Organisation (CWO), to share their concerns and to build better understanding for peace. These meetings were held in 1990. However, not very much has been achieved. Due to religious tensions in Northern Nigeria in 1990, the dialogue meetings between FOMWAN and CWO did not continue.[752]

---

[750] Cf. Kathleen McGarvey, 'Where Are the Women in Interfaith Dialogue? The Church and Christian-Muslim Relations in Africa: In Service to Reconciliation, Justice and Peace,' *The Catholic Voyage*, vol. 8 (2011), 87; McGarvey, 'Muslim and Christian Women in Dialogue,' 253-55.

[751] Cf. Ogba Oche, 'Religion and Politics: Nigeria's Kaduna State Ignited a Powder Keg When It Adopted Sharia Law,' *Conflict Trends* (March 2003), 28-31. http://www.accord. org.za

[752] See McGarvey, 'Muslim and Christian Women in Dialogue,' 166-80 and 247. Due to the tension between Muslims and Christians in Nigeria in 1990, the dialogue meetings between FOMWAN and CWO did not continue.

4.5 THE PARLIAMENTARY DIALOGUE INITIATIVES

In this section, I shall focus on government-sponsored peace initiatives. It highlights the efforts of the government to work with religious leaders and peace institutes in peace negotiations between religious traditions.

The federal and state governments of Nigeria support the activities of NIREC and the Institute for Peace and Conflict Resolution (IPCR).[753] At the state level, Kaduna established a Bureau for Religious Affairs that works in collaboration with CAN and JNI on dialogue issues and peace building. Other states have their own similar establishments.[754] An example of a government peace initiative is the Plateau Peace Program.

The 2002/2004 violent clashes in Plateau state (Yelwa-Shendam) challenged the government to initiate the 'Plateau Peace Program' to restore peace in the region.[755] Its central component is dialogue between religious, ethnic, and community leaders to prevent further violence. Dialogue activities are structured in three phases: dialogue between the government and the people, dialogue between the people, and a peace conference involving the whole state. The emphasis is on challenging communities directly affected by the violence in order to analyse the causes and proffer solutions. Central to this peace initiative is handing in weapons in exchange for a financial reward and a government promise not to prosecute anyone for illegal possession of weapons.[756]

This project has been successful in bringing Christian and Muslim leaders (CAN and JNI) to dialogue. They submitted a peace agreement to the government which promised, among other things, cooperation in the peace initiatives. They admitted that religion had been used and exploited for selfish political interests. They resolved to adopt measures to prevent further violence by calling on ethnic groups in the state to mutual respect, tolerance, and peace with each other.[757] This was followed by a peace conference to discuss the main issues of the conflict and the way forward.

---

[753] Nigeria, 'Institute for Peace and Conflict Resolution,' 2002. http://www.ipcr.gov.ng/publi. html

[754] Josiah Fearon-Idowu, 'Conflict and Cooperation between Christians and Muslims in Nigeria,' 16 February 2005, Paper Presented at the Fourth Borderlands Lectures St. Johns College Durham. http://www.dur.ac.uk/resources/johns/publications/conflict.pdf

[755] 'Revenge in the Name of Religion: The Cycle of Violence in Plateau and Kano States,' 49.

[756] See ibid., 49-52.

[757] Ibid.

4.6 THE EFFECTIVENESS OF THESE INITIATIVES

This section is an appraisal of both interreligious and parliamentary dialogue initiatives, asking if these dialogue endeavours have contributed to peace in Northern Nigeria.

A theological evaluation of the effectiveness of the discussed dialogue activities is not easy, due to the vastness of the northern region and other socio-political and economic factors that contribute to the conflicts. However, the efforts of different religious organisations and the various government attempts to deal with violent conflicts and insecurity have been successful in creating awareness of the need for peace and security. These initiatives have provided the necessary space for meetings, discussions and analysis so that peace building activities can be challenged, evaluated and improved. These efforts have been effective in curbing the menace of conflict and violence.

Although much has been accomplished, the recent threat of Boko Haram in Northern Nigeria presents a complex situation that requires urgent attention. Nevertheless, I am convinced that if dialogue efforts are sustained, there is hope for greater achievements, especially through (religious) education and government policy, emphasising the need for religious dialogue.

4.7 THE INTERPLAY BETWEEN RELIGION AND POLITICS IN PEACE BUILDING IN NORTHERN NIGERIA

In this section, I shall discuss the interplay between religion and politics in Northern Nigeria. It highlights the tension in the Nigerian political scene in a religiously sensitive environment. I argue that religious values can enhance and transform politics to build peace, harmony, and better collaboration in Northern Nigeria.

As discussed in Chapter 1, the religious-political history of Nigeria has been bedevilled by ethno-religious sentiments which continue to prohibit a national life of equity, fairness, peace, and security for every citizen. From colonial times, the inherited division between the so-called Muslim north and Christian south affects almost every facet of life. Some Nigerian scholars have argued that the imposition of an Islamic ethos in Northern Nigerian politics makes it difficult for non-Muslims to climb the political ladder.[758] In as much as I do not entirely agree with the above submission, I want to note that Northern Nigeria must be appreciated within the presence of Islamic political structures that existed for many centuries before colonialism. Northern Nigeria has always had challenges in terms of education and skill acquisition, exacerbated by colonial preference, which has not helped the development of a viable northern region.

---

[758] Cf. Kukah, *The Church and the Politics*, 102-03.

The Sokoto Caliphate, as discussed in Chapter 1, remains a symbol of both religious (Islamic) and political dominance in Northern Nigeria. For instance, after Nigeria's independence in 1960, the overriding political party in the north was the Nigerian People's Congress (NPC), led by the Sardauna Sir Ahmadu Bello, who was also a religious leader. NPC wished to enhance the political influence of the north over the south, which was more developed in terms of Western learning and skill acquisition and to preserve the northern religious and cultural identity inherited from the Caliphate era, despite being disrupted by colonisation.[759]

To achieve the above, the Sardauna introduced a crash training programme to equip northern civil servants with the necessary qualifications to assume greater control of government at both regional and federal levels.[760] This policy was aimed at fostering unity in the north. Minority Christian groups benefited from it due to their high level of missionary school education. However, it is argued that Ahmadu Bello did not undertake a corresponding administrative reform to respond to the long-standing demands of minority groups in the region for local autonomy from emirate rule.[761] Instead, opposition parties that served as the rallying point for minority groups, such as the Middle Zone League (MZL) and the United Middle Belt Congress (UMBC), were suppressed. A political aristocratic class was imposed to promote the ideals of the Islamic faith both as a unifying factor and a means of preserving the unique cultural and religious identity of the region.[762] This project, supported by the government and led by the Sardauna himself, gave rise to many Islamic organisations (such as JNI), Islamic sects, and the conversion of many non-Muslims to Islam in places like Bida and Zaria in the Niger province.[763] Consequently, some Muslims were deployed to manipulate politics in order to return to Islamic principles and demand the implementation of Islamic sharia. This has led some Nigerian religious-political analysts to argue that there is a thin line between religion and politics in the Islamic tradition because religious leaders have such a strong political influence, and vice-versa.[764] Moreover, the Muslim vision of religion and politics is based on the interpretation of the Qur'an as well as the historical role of Prophet Muhammad as a religious and community-political leader in Mecca and

---

[759] Cf. International Crisis Group, *Northern Nigeria*, 7-9.

[760] Ibid.

[761] Ibid., 7.

[762] Ibid.

[763] Ibid.

[764] See also ibid., 9; Kukah, *The Church and the Politics,* 40 and 101-02; 'We Fear that Nigeria Might Become Islamised, says Primate Okoh of the Anglican Church of Nigeria,' *Sahara Reporters* (Nigeria), 21 August 2011. http://www.saharareporters.com; Muhammad M. Nasran, 'The Concept of an Islamic State,' http://www.arts.ualberta.ca; Yaran, *Understanding Islam*, 6.

Medina. Thus Muslims describe Islam as a 'total way of life' and believe that religion cannot be separated from social and political life, since religion permeates every facet of Muslim life (Q 2: 30; 1: 165).[765]

The conflict of religious mistrust, rivalry, and subtle competition is expressed in politics so much that politics seem to follow religious lines in (Northern) Nigeria. Politicians tend to play up to the ethnic and religious sentiments of the people, capitalising on their ignorance while using religion as a weapon for political achievements. Some politicians use inflammatory rhetoric, promoting religious and ethnic differences to gain political power. This creates tension among the populace, leading to violent conflicts.[766] Such trends heighten the feeling of marginalisation, expressed in accusations and counter accusations. For example, the government makes political appointments to public office from which Christians feel excluded, while Muslims think they are not fairly represented in the process of governance.[767]

Peace building in this situation demands a theological approach that recognises political leadership as service to the people irrespective of their religious-political and social affiliations. Religious values of peace, harmony, love, respect, and personal freedom apply as much in politics as elsewhere. Moreover, the God of creation and the God Christians and Muslims worship is the same God in politics who blesses all (Matt. 5: 45). Discrimination in politics promotes a negative solidarity, which divides rather than unites the people. Peace building challenges Christians and Muslims to insist on justice, fairness, and equality, holding leaders accountable for their actions.[768] This demands religious education for the common good and a religious-theological engagement with politics in peace building. The conflict situation in Northern Nigeria is religious, political, and ethnic. Peace as a fundamental good involves respecting and promoting essential human values.[769]

---

[765]   Cf. Esposito, *What Everyone Needs to Know*, 180-81.

[766]   See Emeka Mamah, 'Makarfi Lists Northern Region's Woes,' *Vanguard* (Nigeria), 1 August 2011. http://www.vangurdngr.com

[767]   'Yar'Adua's Appointments Call for Concern, Says CAN Scribe,' *Guardian* (Nigeria), 31 July 2009. http://www.ngrguardiannews.com. See also Abdulmalik, 'Myth of Northernization of Nigeria (II),' *Guardian* (Nigeria), 11 August 2009. http://www.ngrguardiannews.com; Shettima, 'Religious Politics without Religion.'

[768]   Cf. Kelvin Ebiri, 'Why Conflict Persists in Nigeria, by Kukah, Mbillah,' *Guardian* (Nigeria), 1 October 2010. http://www.ngrguardinnews.com; John Shiklam, 'Kukah Blames Ethnic, Religious Clashes on Military Rule,' *This Day* (Nigeria), 26 June 2011. http://www.thisdayonlime.com

[769]   Pope John Paul II, 'Believers United in Building Peace,' *Message of His Holiness Pope John Paul II for the XXV World Day of Prayer for Peace* (Rome Vatican City: Libreria Editrice, 1991). http://www.vatican.va/holy_father/john_paul_ii/messages/peace/documents/hf_jp-ii_mes_08121991_xxv-world-day-for-peace_en.html

Therefore, religion and politics must address both ethnic and social issues for peace and development. For me, the starting point is education.

4.8 THE INTERPLAY OF EDUCATION AND RELIGION IN NIGERIA

In this section, I shall briefly review the history of the establishment of a Western or formal system of education in Nigeria. I consider the traditional African method of education and the introduction of the Western system of learning to highlight further the challenges within the educational sector in contemporary Nigeria.

Education can be described as a process through which knowledge is transmitted by means of teaching, learning, training, acquisition of skills and awareness formally or informally.[770] Education (formal and informal) has contributed immensely to the development of contemporary society and remains the catalyst for growth and expansion in the world. However, the approaches and goals of education differ from place to place; every society has its own system of training and educating young people.[771]

Before the advent of missionary enterprise in Africa (Nigeria), societies had a traditional-indigenous system of education by participation, apprenticeship, and observation.[772] This is a system where children and adults engaged in participatory education in ceremonies, rituals, initiations, recitations, folklore, stories, singing, proverbs, and demonstrations to impart moral, spiritual, and societal values in the growing child.[773] For instance, within a community, a warrior or a hunter, or a person who combined good character with specific skills, was judged as well-educated and well-integrated citizen of the community and could teach these skills to children. The role of the family in traditional African society was paramount; it was considered the primary and indispensable cell of society and the primary base to impart life values to the younger generation. Parents and elders played significant roles in this process of formation.

The traditional African educational system, while generally informal, was a process of induction into society and a preparation for adulthood with much emphasis on social responsibility, respect, honesty, collaboration, accountability, dialogue, and

---

[770] Aduljeleel Solahudeen, 'Islam and Child's Right to Education,' *Tribune* (Nigeria), 3 June 2011. http://www.tribune.com.ng

[771] Cf. Daniel Edevbaro, 'Promoting Education within the Context of a Neo-Patrimonial State: The Case of Nigeria,' *The United Nations University World Institute for Development Economies Research*, no. 123 (1997), 8-9. http://www.wider.unu.edu/publications/working-papers/previous/en_GB/wp-123/_files/82530852629257468/default/WP123.pdf

[772] Ibid.

[773] Ibid.

peace in the community.[774] Accordingly, evaluating the impact of the indigenous African system of education has to take into account the fact that such an educational system was an important transmitter of cultural identity and a means to train children in the skills and attitudes appropriate for their social roles as male and female in society.[775] This was achieved by the use of native language, meeting with elders, and the use of examples both within and outside the home. African (Nigerian) indigenous education responded to the needs of the local community; political leaders as well as ordinary farmers were educated with a sense of citizenship in the community.[776] In modern-day Nigerian society, the informal method of education still transmits traditional community values and customs, in spite of the strong influence of the formal Western system of education.

The history of the formal Western system of education in Nigeria dates back to 1848, when Christian missionaries began to educate as part of their evangelising mission in Nigeria.[777] Southern Nigerians were the first to benefit from this project. The thrust of education was the promotion of industrial-agricultural skills, training of teachers for mission schools, and to produce graduates with the competence needed by the colonial administration to serve British commercial interests in the region.[778] However, from 1859 to 1923, grammar schools were established in Lagos, Ibadan, Onitsha, and other south-eastern cities in Nigeria, with a curriculum covering various aspects of academic life.[779]

While all these developments were underway in south-eastern Nigeria, Islamic schools and the Qur'anic system of education was operational in Northern Nigeria. As discussed in Chapter 1, Islam has a long history as part of the religious culture of Northern Nigeria, including the system of Qur'anic education.[780] Both the formal and informal structure of Islamic education emphasised recitation of the Holy Qur'an in the Arabic language, the teaching of religious ethics and Islamic theology.[781] The colonial government in Northern Nigeria was anxious to ensure stability in the territory and with the support of the traditional authorities was reluctant to promote modern Western-style education. They feared that Western education would lead to disenchantment with the system of Indirect Rule and, in due course, with the political

---

[774]   Ibid., 9.

[775]   Ibid., 10.

[776]   Ibid.

[777]   Sanneh, *West African Christianity*, 151.

[778]   See Edevbaro, 'Promoting Education,' 12.

[779]   Sanneh, *West African Christianity*, 151-54.

[780]   Cf. Hyacinth Kalu, *The Nigerian Nation and Religion* (Bloomington, IN: iUniverse, 2011), 30-36.

[781]   Edevbaro, 'Promoting Education,' 12.

system.[782] Consequently, Christian missionaries were restricted from setting up Western education in schools in the region.[783] Some Nigerian analysts have argued that such constraints have been responsible for the low standard and backward nature of formal Western education in Northern Nigeria.[784]

Nigeria's independence in 1960, however, became an opportunity for the new government to decide the future of education in the country. A National Conference on Education was held in 1969, which led to the introduction of a National Policy in 1976 but failed to develop a basic religious education curriculum in schools.[785]

Currently, the standard of education in Nigeria is very low, and this is due to poor planning, poor infrastructure, and lack of proper funding. Other drawbacks are a lack of a dynamic educational curriculum, probity, poor training of teachers/ lecturers, little commitment by government, policy makers, and students plus poor encouragement from some parents and religious bodies.[786] There is not a comprehensive syllabus for imparting religious and interreligious education, especially in public institutions. These challenges need to be addressed; however, this is not the focus of this thesis.

Nevertheless, the importance of education in fostering better understanding in a pluralistic society cannot be overemphasised. It can be argued that the Western style of education inherited in Northern Nigeria did not lay the needed foundation for dialogue and harmony. The aim was more to enhance commerce and evangelisation than building social cohesion. However, peace building needs some level of education to continue to thrive. Education is necessary to advance any form of dialogue. It provides a level ground between participants, especially in a formal dialogue process and guards against indoctrination. Participants in dialogue require basic education to dispose them to understand correctly the modern mind in order to engage in dialogue

---

[782] O'Connor, *From the Niger to the Sahara*, 105.

[783] Cf. T.M. Bray and R.G. Cooper, 'Education and Nation Building in Nigeria since the Civil War,' *Comparative Education* 15, no. 1 (1979), 34.

[784] See ibid. Nwachukwu Orji, 'Eat and Give to Your Brother: The Politics of Office Distribution in Nigeria,' *In-Spire Journal of Law, Politics and Societies* 3, no. 2 (2008), 131.

[785] Emmanuel Edukugho, 'Reviving an Ailing Education Sector,' *Vanguard* (Nigeria), 10 November 2010. http://www.vanguardngr.com; see also Mohammad Abubakar, 'Jonathan Bemoans Failure of Education Policies,' *Guardian* (Nigeria), 5 October 2010. http://www.ngrguardiannews.com

[786] Cf. Rotimi L. Oyekanmi, 'Borno's Education Sector Suffers Neglect,' *Guardian* (Nigeria), 28 October 2010. http://www.ngrguardiannews.com; see also Saliu Gbadamosi, 'Don Laments Muslim's Lackadaisical Attitude to Education,' *Tribune* (Nigeria), 17 September 2010. http://www.tribune.com.ng; Innocent Oweh, 'Towards Effective Education System,' *Daily Independent* (Nigeria), 10 October 2010. http://www.independentngonline.com

with their contemporaries.[787] Additionally, the participants need to be familiar with the subject under discussion; not only their own opinion but also relating to the subject matter of such dialogue is paramount. However, the low standard of education and poor religious knowledge impede the progress of interreligious understanding. Renewed consensus is required on the part of government, religious leaders, and parents to strengthen education in order to facilitate a better interreligious understanding in the future.

4.8.1 THE IMPACT OF RELIGIOUS EDUCATION IN NORTHERN NIGERIA

This segment discusses the need for religious education to build effective peace in Northern Nigeria. It focuses on the limitations of poor religious education and emphasises efforts to enhance better religious and peace education.

Religious education is essential for sustained peace to end hostilities, mutual segregation, and stereotyping. Unfortunately, the religious challenges in contemporary Northern Nigerian society are not tackled effectively by the formal system of education or by learning institutions for religious studies.[788] Religious education refers to knowledge and understanding the nature of religious experience, as well as the concepts, practices, and complexities of a religious tradition.[789] It further entails critical engagement with religious language, rituals, and basic hermeneutics for necessary knowledge of a religious tradition.[790] However, since independence, religious education in Northern Nigeria has not prioritised harmonious relationships between the faith traditions. The curriculum for Islamic/ Christian religious knowledge in both primary and secondary schools is exclusively Islamic or Christian, with no interreligious knowledge. Each religious tradition is responsible for instructing and forming their adherents; in most cases, the formation is religiously stereotyped or without reference to the other. The method of imparting knowledge in the Qur'anic schools and Christian Sunday schools excludes even the basic tenets of the other faith tradition. Hence it can be said that the so-called religious unrest in Northern Nigeria is partly due to ignorance about other faiths and the spiritual values that Christianity and Islam have in common. In my opinion,

---

[787] Cf. Austin Flannery (ed.), 'Decree on Ecumenism,' *Vatican Council II: The Conciliar and Post Conciliar Documents* (Leominster Hrefords, England: Fowler Wright Book, 1981), 1013.

[788] See 'Da'wah Institute of Nigeria,' *The 2008 Prospectus of Da'wah Institute of Nigeria* (Minna, Nigeria: Da'wah Institute of Nigeria, 2008), 2.

[789] Cf. James C. Conroy and Robert A. Davis, 'Citizenship, Education and the Claims of Religious Literacy,' Paper Presented at a Colloquium on Religion and Public Life, 8 March 2010, Theology and Religious Studies Department, University of Glasgow.

[790] Ibid.

there can be no effective peace building in Northern Nigeria without basic religious education about the other. Who will champion the cause of religious education in Northern Nigeria?

Religious leaders and clerics, who are respected by the people, are responsible for championing religious education by being proactive in forming the minds of young adherents in the Qur'anic schools and Christian Sunday schools. They must take government and policy makers to task about the need to develop a curriculum for religious education, teacher training, and peace education. Effective peace building in Northern Nigeria requires robust religious and peace education in our schools, seminaries/madrasas, churches, and mosques. Religious traditions must be responsible for training their leaders, religious instructors, and preachers properly in peace building dialogue and have a basic knowledge of the other faiths. Moreover, peace must always be negotiated and consensual. Peace building is not a one-off thing; it is an ongoing one. Relationships must be established based on harmonious interactions aimed at achieving mutual goals while being dependent on each other's resources through dialogue.[791] Sustained religious education and training is paramount in achieving peace.

Islamic and Christian scriptural hermeneutics demand religious instruction. The Bible says *teach this to your children* (Dt. 6: 7), and *teach them to fulfil all that I have commanded* (Matt. 28: 20). The Qur'an also says *we have revealed the book to you in truth for instructing mankind* (Q 39: 41). The emphasis here is on teaching scriptural exegesis and appreciating the need to educate the other in the basics of faith. I agree with Catherine Cornille when she advocates a dialogue of religious education for mutual enrichment, understanding, and growth in the truth.[792] This is because proper religious education leads to better understanding, positive interdependence and relationships, harmony, and peaceful coexistence.[793]

A significant move has been made by the Catholic Church and some Islamic madrasas (Da'wah Institute of Nigeria (DIN)) to include training in dialogue and basic studies in Islamic and Christian traditions respectively in their programme of formation. The aim is to prepare religious leaders adequately for interreligious engagements. This broadens the vision beyond religious, ethnic, and cultural horizons and strengthens the potential for peace in the region.[794]

---

[791]   David W. Johnson and Roger T. Johnson, 'Essential Components of Peace Education,' *Theory into Practice* 44, no. 4 (2005), 282-83.

[792]   Cf. Cornille, 'Introduction: On Hermeneutics in Dialogue,' xvii.

[793]   Ibid., 283.

[794]   Michael L. Fitzgerald, *A Guide for Teaching African Traditional Religion, Islam, Interreligious Dialogue in Catholic Major Seminaries, Houses of Religious Formation and Institutes of Higher Learning in Sub-Saharan Africa* (Vatican City: Pontifical Council

(For the complete text of the Catholic and Da'wah Institute teaching guides, see documentation 11 and 12.)

Religious education must go hand in hand with peace education—a philosophy that teaches non-violence, love, compassion, and reverence for all. According to education, policy, and community analysts Ian Harris and Mary Lee Morrison, peace education confronts indirectly the forms of violence that dominate society by providing teaching about its causes and giving knowledge of alternatives.[795] Peace education seeks ways to transform and be proactive in addressing conditions and structures that give rise to conflict and violence. As part of ongoing peace building efforts in Northern Nigeria, I recommend that peace education be included in the educational curriculum and taught in churches, mosques, and schools as a compulsory subject along with religious education. This demands developing a syllabus, teacher training, and provision of necessary resources. (For more practical suggestions in the subject, see the next chapter.)

CONCLUSION

In this chapter, I have argued that dialogue between Muslims and Christians in Northern Nigeria is paramount for harmony and peace to flourish. The theology of interreligious dialogue challenges Christians and Muslims to promote dialogue initiatives by stimulating collaboration on topics of mutual interest such as freedom, the dignity of every human person, and the quest for the common good, peace, and development.[796] This is possible through sustained dialogue of understanding and cooperation between the two religious groups. Contributing factors to conflicts must be articulated and analysed in order to seek ways to address the social, economic, and religious challenges adequately in contemporary Northern Nigeria.

The dialogue of everyday living among adherents of both religions plays a significant role in creating respect, esteem, and the courage to reach out to the other as neighbour. Peaceful coexistence can be negotiated by using language and gestures that promote solidarity and respect. In this regard, the contribution of the pastor and imam and other peace building institutions, reinforces the need for positive engagement between Christians and Muslims in the region. The two seminars considered in this chapter remain exemplary. Furthermore, the importance

---

of Interreligious Dialogue, 2004), 11-12; Francis Arinze, 'Education for Dialogue: A Duty for Christians and Muslims,' *L'Osservatore Romano* (Rome), 20-27 December 2000.

[795] Ian M. Harris and Mary Lee Morrison, *Peace Education* (Jefferson, NC: McFarland & Company, 2003), 9.

[796] Cf. Benedict XVI. Pope, 'Address the Great Challenges that Mark the Post-Modern Age,' Papal Message on Cultural and Religious Dialogue, 3 December 2008, Rome Vatican City. http://www.zenit.org

of religious and peace education cannot be overemphasised in the peace building process. Education generally creates awareness and a sense of responsibility among people; it leads to development, dialogue, and other bridge-building activities. For me, interreligious dialogue remains fundamental if Christians and Muslims in Northern Nigeria are to come to a better understanding of each other's religious tradition to build mutual tolerance and respect. The following chapter examines the difficulties of Christian-Muslim dialogue activities and suggests some practical recommendations for shared peace building ventures in Northern Nigeria. Understanding the dynamics of interreligious engagement provides indicators and strategies of how to sustain a peace building process competently.

Chapter 5

THE COMPLEXITIES OF ENGAGING IN INTERRELIGIOUS DIALOGUE IN NORTHERN NIGERIA

INTRODUCTION

This chapter considers the complexities of engaging in interreligious dialogue in northern Nigeria. It analyses the complications, possibilities, challenges, and prospects for dialogue and offers concluding recommendations for a sustained process of interreligious dialogue for peaceful coexistence. The purpose is to link theology and politics in peace building.

The history of Northern Nigeria is shaped by the legacy of British colonial rule, the nineteenth-century Islamic Jihad led by Uthman dan Fodio and the Christian missionary enterprise. These have been influential in shaping the religious-political history of the region and the relationship between Christians and Muslims.[797] One of the challenging tasks for religious and political leaders in contemporary Northern Nigeria is to find workable ways for Christians and Muslims to be true to their faith convictions and the interpretation of that experience in a faith community while living together in peace and harmony in the same political and social milieu.[798]

The volatile conflict situation in Northern Nigeria demands that Christians and Muslims work together to achieve peace. In a Christmas day broadcast in 1959, a northern political leader and premier of Northern Nigeria Alhaji Sir Ahmadu Bello said:

---

[797]   Ojo, 'Pentecostal Movements,' 175.

[798]   Cf. Volf, *Allah: A Christian Response*, 13-14.

> Here in the northern Nigeria we have people of many different races, tribes and religions who are knit together in a common history, common interest and common ideas; the things that unite us are stronger than the things that divide us. I always remind people of our firmly rooted policy of *religious tolerance*. We have no intention of favouring one religion at the expense of another. Subject to the overriding need to preserve law and order, it is our determination that everyone should have absolute liberty to practise his belief according to the dictates of his conscience . . . [799]

Regrettably, this vision of tolerance and togetherness has been overtaken by decades of doubts and violent confrontations. The region is further challenged by poverty, a high level of unemployment, poor religious education, corruption, and poor political leadership. Religion has been used to express deep-rooted historical, social, cultural, and ethnic divides and called to serve ignorance, prejudice, contempt, abuse, and violence.[800] Although religion has failed and is disfigured, it can, nonetheless, make a valuable contribution to peace. Peace building is one of the greatest tasks of theology and politics in this millennium. Religious and political leaderships must engage in addressing squarely the issues of violence in the region.

Both Christianity and Islam claim to be religions of peace, love, mercy, compassion, prayer, kindness, hospitality, respect, forgiveness, and hope that is eschatological (Matt. 25: 31-36; Lk. 10: 27; Rm. 12: 12-19, Ep 2: 17-17; Q 1;1-6; 5: 70; 6: 32, 22: 78; 49: 10).[801] These, I am convinced, are common grounds and stepping stones for a sustainable peace process. The theological explanation of these religious concepts can be contentious when trying to comprehend their real interpretation from an Islamic or Christian perspective. Nevertheless, these present an opportunity for interrligious dialogue encounter.

However, is there theological potential for peace in the region? What is the role of Christian and Islamic theology in fostering peaceful coexistence in Northern Nigeria? What is the way forward? What are practical ways of developing a sustained spirituality, peace dialogue, and transformation based on scriptures (Bible and Qur'an)? For taken on their own terms, neither theology nor politics have all the answers, yet both must engage to proffer solutions. Hence, the peace building project in Northern Nigeria must be multifaceted—religious, social, and political, with

---

[799] See Abubakar Iya, 'Citation on Sir Ahmadu Bello Sardauna of Sokoto,' 2006. http://www.arewaonline-ng.com/sardauna/citation.html; and 'Ahmadu Bello,' in *New World Encyclopedia,* 2008. http://www.newworldencyclopedia.org/entry/Ahmadu_Bello

[800] Cf. John L. Allen, 'Benedict XVI Sets New Papal Record for Mosque Visit,' 2009. http://www.ncroline.org/news/vatican/benedict-xvi-sets-new-papal-record-mosque-visits

[801] Cf. G. Theriault M. Afr (ed.), *Introduction to Islam* (Ibadan, Nigeria: AECAWA/IRDC Publications, 1999), 79-97; Esposito, *What Everyone Needs to Know*, 77.

education as the foundation. The focus of this work is more religious than social or political.

This chapter is divided into eight sections. The first section examines the complex nature of dialogue in Northern Nigeria. It analyses the difficulties of dialogue engagement and challenges religious leaders, politicians, and peace building institutions to commit to the process of peace building.

The second section explores the necessity of forgiveness and reconciliation for the healing of memories, using the model of Genesis and the teaching of Jesus in the Gospels to advocate a hermeneutic of healing that involves all parties in the conflict.

The third section discusses the significance of tolerance and respect in building harmonious relations in a religiously pluralistic contemporary society. It highlights symbolic actions of some renowned religious leaders to exemplify the future hope for peace in the region.

The fourth section emphasises the need for religious and peace education as a necessary condition for peace. It stresses the importance of developing a curriculum and teaching and training of teachers and religious instructors for effective learning in matters of faith and schooling. It further deals specifically with the education of *Almajiri* as an urgent requirement for building community of peace.

The fifth section addresses the question of policy making and governance. It emphasises the necessity for institutional reforms to tackle the socio-economic conditions that breed conflicts and the role of theology in the political sphere.

The sixth section examines and highlights the role of clerics, religious leaders, and preachers in fostering peace in the region. It focuses on the value of training, collaboration, and support among religious leaders for dialogue and the advancement of peace.

The seventh section attempts to answer the question, what can faith communities do to foster mutual relations? It further considers what individuals and families can contribute to harmonious existence and finally explores the role of women in advancing peace.

The eighth section deals with the need for non-governmental and faith-based organisations to network in articulating ideals for peace. It highlights improved awareness and joint projects as essential steps in achieving social cohesion.

5.1 THE NEED FOR INTERRELIGIOUS ENGAGEMENT AND DIALOGUE IN DAY-TO-DAY INTERACTION

In this section, I shall examine critically the complex nature of interreligious dialogue. I am arguing that dialogue in day-to-day engagement is vital for peace. It highlights the difficulties and risks involved and concludes by affirming that much can be achieved through collaboration to surmount the challenges.

The thrust of the theology of *Nostra Aetate* provides a model for interreligious engagement. As discussed in Chapter 4, dialogue is a conversation, a frank discussion between two or more parties to learn to understand each other's point of view.[802] However, such informed mutual understanding can be influenced by historical and political, as well as religious, experiences. In contemporary Northern Nigeria, the Christian-Muslim dialogue relationship is marred by significant past and recent events that seem to impede peace building by interreligious dialogue. The recurrence of violent clashes, killing people, and destroying property and places of worship, remain a distressing experiences that spoil the ideals of interreligious peace building activities. The violence of the extreme Islamic sect 'Boko Haram' in the recent past has challenged the willingness and sincerity of ordinary Christians to trust and engage meaningfully with Muslims. It is true that not every Muslim is an extremist, but when a so-called religious sect terrorises people in word and deed, insists on legalising sharia in the country, vows to destroy Christians, threatens the government and entire security of the nation, rejoicing in exclaiming *Allahu'akbar* (God is great),[803] many questions are asked. Is that the true representation of the religion of Islam? How can Christians trust Muslims in dialogue? How can dialogue flourish in these circumstances? Even when Muslim leaders and scholars condemn such attacks and disown the actions of such a group in the name of Islam, the reality is that harm has been inflicted and people suffer, thus the dialogue process is stifled and the prospect of peace shattered. Furthermore, one would expect that Muslim leaders, clerics, and the entire Islamic *Ummah* to be consistent in condemning the actions of such a group vehemently and even go the extra mile to try to identify the perpetrators of such heinous acts. But when all seems quiet, the lives of ordinary people are snuffed out in the name of religion and the religious group does not respond sypathetically, it leaves much to be desired. Is that faith community complacent or indifferent to the situation?

Dialogue in this situation becomes a risky venture, if not impossible. This is because the mutual trust and sincerity which is the basis of dialogue is replaced by suspicion, doubt, and fear, making it difficult to engage openly in authentic dialogue. It exposes our vulnerability of having to ask for pardon and the forgiveness of the other. So how may we build and sustain the confidence needed between dialogue partners if dialogue is to be fruitful? Besides, who are the participants in a formal dialogue venture? What learning do they have? Do they have good knowledge of their own faith tradition? Can they be trusted by other dialogue partners? What are the hidden political agendas of participants on both sides? We may not be able to find the answers to these questions; nonetheless, it brings to fore the intricacies of engaging in interreligious dialogue in Northern Nigeria; neither religion nor politics

---

[802]   Metuh-Ikenga, 'Dialogue with African Religions.'

[803]   Cf. Emeka Mamah and Sam Eyoboka, 'Boko Haram Threatens Jonathan,' *Vanguard* (Nigeria), 13 April 2012. http://www.vanguardngr.com/2012/04/boko-haram-threatens-jonathan/

can provide the needed solutions, but an engagement with both is necessary for a peaceful future. What is needed is a religious-political strategy that seeks to separate religious issues from political concerns so that theology addresses religious questions and politics attends to social needs, security, and matters of governance in the state.

Peace, as defined in this work, is tranquillity of order, justice, and good social relationships that respect the rights of others thus providing favourable conditions for integral human growth and harmonious coexistence.[804] It is essential, therefore, that religious and community leaders collaborate with experts in the field of interreligious dialogue to develop a theology of patient listening in order to understand the other with respect and dignity (see Chapter 4). Achieving this goal requires the concerted effort of both religious and political leaders to create the needed space for dialogue.

Religious leaders must be resolute in dialogue to engage with all concerned in addressing causes of tension and division between faith communities. Frequent grassroot community interaction, listening, and sharing information strengthens dialogue, especially with the religious other. This entails regular catechesis that promotes peace and harmony. In most of our communities, religious leaders are highly respected and extremely influential figures, and people listen to them. They enjoy a privileged position of leadership and exercise authority in society. Peace building in religiously sensitive Northern Nigeria requires religious leaders to respond effectively to check extremism and the religious excesses of their faithful. They must ensure that religious beliefs are not used to justify any form of violent aggression, intolerance, or political mischief. Awareness of what goes on within the community is vital in curbing religious fundamentalism. Furthermore, intra-religious dialogue, consultations, sharing, and evaluation of the activities of the subgroups within the larger faith community will check excesses. The Catholic Bishops' Conference of Nigeria challenged Islamic leaders to identify members of the sect Boko Haram:

> [S]ince their perpetrators belong to the house of Islam, the house of Islam
> has a responsibility to itself and to our collective security to explore ways
> of checking the activities of this group which claims to be acting in the
> name of Islam.[805]

Dialogue in day-to-day activities is the most frequent form of dialogue as people engage with one another in the daily interactions of life. However, in a situation of stereotyping, conflict, and misunderstanding without trust and respect, it is impossible for this form of dialogue to flourish. Nevertheless, building relationships between

---

[804] Cf. Arinze, *Reflections by Cardinal Francis Arinze*, 2.

[805] Cf. Okechukwu Jombo, 'Catholic Bishops Back Call for New Constitution,' *Nigerian Pilot* (Nigerian), 07 March 2012. http://www.nigerianpilot.com

people in such circumstances is at the heart of peace building. Respect for and the recognition of the rights and freedom of the other are the basic values required along with the empowerment of individuals to manage conflict maturely.[806] Christian and Muslim leaders and the faithful must be committed to improving relations with each other in their everyday life. Open and sincere encounter with the other, interest in the basic tenets of each other's faith, and respect for the dignity of the neighbour are vital to good relationships. True dialogue happens when people strive to have an open, neighbourly spirit and share their joys and sorrows in support of each other.[807] Creating such a spirit means overcoming stereotypes and ignorance. Good neighbourliness is strengthened by visits to one another's homes, offering a helping hand when someone is in need, and sharing the joys of marriages and births, or the sadness of bereavements. Such activities are important to establish good relationships and unite people in peace.

The sincere willingness to engage with one's neighbour fosters what theologian Valson Thampu refers to as dialogue of neighbours.[808] This form of dialogue begins with the realisation that people in the same locality are strangers who need to become neighbours. Barriers begin to crumble and the spirit of friendship and peace is established the moment we begin to chat and engage with the other. Thampu argues that this is a defining aspect of neighbourliness; it means 'being with'—not just a physical or geographical presence but a mental and spiritual disposition to dialogue with the neighbour.[809] Religious plurality adds to the beauty of interreligious dialogue where neighbourliness means reaching out in love and friendship, while respecting the freedom to be religiously different. I agree with Thampu, the goal here is to overcome the barriers of living our faith with others, whether Christians or Muslims. Dialogue with neighbours diminishes stereotypes and transforms a neighbourhood into a community of love, respect, listening, and service. The teaching of Jesus, *unless you become like little children you will not enter the kingdom of heaven* (Matt. 18: 3) is very significant for peace building; children in any neighbourhood interact freely without being conditioned by religion or stereotypes; they symbolise the freedom to be different and the interaction that ought to exist between individuals and (faith) communities.[810] Moreover, living together transforms the image of the other from a stranger to a neighbour, sharing common values, concerns, and goals

---

[806] Lisa Schirch, *Ritual and Symbol in Peacebuilding* (Bloomfield, NJ: Kumarian Press, 2005), 151.

[807] See *Pontifical Council for Inter-Religious Dialogue, Dialogue and Proclamation*, no. 42.

[808] Valson Thampu, 'Models of Interreligious Dialogue,' in Hans Ucko, Charlotte Venema and Ariane Hentsch (eds.), *Changing the Present, Dreaming the Future: A Critical Moment in Interreligious Dialogue* (Geneva: World Council of Churches, 2006), 39-41.

[809] See ibid., 40.

[810] Ibid.

that must be accepted and respected.[811] I am convinced that we can learn to build peace by reaching out to a potential friend in a neighbour.

The media have a significant role to play in promoting dialogue in the day-to-day interaction between people to diminish religious stereotypes. Radio, television, newspapers, and the Internet can be used positively to confront religious stereotypes. I strongly urge that the 2006 documentary film *From the Heart of Nigeria: The Imam and the Pastor* be shown publicly on the National Network of the Nigerian Television Authority (NTA). Muslim and Christian leaders should collaborate with all branches of the media so that religious programmes and reporting educate, enrich, and strengthen faith communities. A group should be responsible for censoring religious programmes on radio and television to avoid misrepresentation; such broadcasts should aim to break down religious stereotypes and encourage dialogue.

Furthermore, community events which bring people together to celebrate and interact with each other are important, for example, market interactions, community meetings, end of farming season, and harvest celebrations. Festivals such as the Argungu fishing festival, family celebrations, naming/christenings, wedding ceremonies, religious feasts, Christmas, Easter, Eid-ul-fitr, Sallah, sport activities, and cultural celebrations bring people together.[812] These are opportunities to celebrate with neighbours in the spirit of peace and love. Moreover, Christians and Muslims in Northern Nigeria are responsible for promoting citizenship, shared values, and the common good by addressing causes of discrimination, stereotypes, and extremism. The Nigerian Supreme Council for Islamic Affairs (NSCIA) has called for a consensus effort to dialogue, reconciliation, and reintegration between faith communities.[813]

The CAN, Jamalat-ul-Nasril Islam (JNI), and other faith-based organisations should appreciate and value the contributions of the Interfaith Mediation Centre/ Muslim-Christian Dialogue Forum (IFMD/MCDF), Nigeria Interreligious Council (NIREC), and other peace building institutions and collaborate with them to sustain the ongoing peace building activities.

Christians and Muslims in the region have to work together to bring about the divine gift of peace. They must confront the difficulties and challenges of diversity of religious beliefs and not allow exploiters of religion for political and selfish motives to cause conflict and division. Moreover, the greatest challenge in interreligious

---

[811] Aram I. His Holiness, 'Our Common Calling,' in Hans Ucko, Charlotte Venema and Ariane Hentsch (eds.), *Changing the Present, Dreaming the Future: A Critical Moment in Interreligious Dialogue* (Geneva: World Council of Churches, 2006), 14.

[812] Cf. Fanen Ihyongo, 'Peace Talks as Jukun Celebrate,' *The Nation* (Nigeria), 24 August 2011. http://www.thenationonlineng.net

[813] Hajiya Bilikisu Yusuf, 'Building an Interfaith Bridge of Peace,' *Leadership* (Nigeria), 5 June 2008.

dialogue is to honest believers to have the courage to unite to make their voices heard when they sense that religion is being abused, exploited, misinterpreted, and misappropriated to cause conflict.[814] Dialogue in daily interaction is both a risk and a blessing; a blessing because it leads to mutual understanding, tolerance, and harmony and a risk since in asking for forgiveness we have to deal with the pain we have caused the other. Hence dialogue in daily interaction is imperative for peace and security in Northern Nigeria.[815]

5.2 THE NEED FOR FORGIVENESS, RECONCILIATION, AND HEALING

In this section, I shall discuss the vital place of forgiveness and reconciliation in peace building, using the model of Joseph and his brothers in Genesis and the teaching of Jesus in the Gospels.

The long history of Christian-Muslim conflict has created a rift that needs to be healed. As argued in Chapter 3, both Islamic and Christian teachings condemn intolerance and the horrendous violence often perpetrated in the name of religion. Although Christians and Muslims in Northern Nigeria have hurt one another, they have to continue to live side by side as neighbours. The praxis of the teaching of Jesus, *you shall love your neighbour as yourself* (Matt. 22: 39), requires that we know and respect our neighbour; if one's neighbour is hurt or wounded because of one's actions and choices, the love of neighbour demands that we seek forgiveness and reconciliation.[816] The question then is who is my neighbour? The temptation is to think one's neighbour as a fellow believer within one's faith tradition; however, it goes beyond such an assumption. (For the purpose of this work, Muslims are neighbours to Christians and vice-versa.) In the contemporary Northern Nigerian experience, neighbours have hurt themselves. There is a great need to explore the possibilities of reconciliation.

Genesis chapters 43 to 45 provides a model of dialogue for reconciliation. It is a story about Joseph and his brothers, who meet again after a painful history of jealousy, betrayal, guilt, and grief.[817] His brothers sold him into slavery, and after many years, they are sitting face to face in dialogue for reconciliation (Gn. 43: 33).[818]

---

[814] See Machado, 'Towards Deepening Hindu-Christian Maitri,' 70.

[815] Cf. Hamzat Baba, 'Only Dialogue Can Return Peace to Nigeria,' *Leadership* (Nigeria), 16 July 2011. http://www.leadership.ng

[816] Cf. Leo Lefebure, 'Healing Interreligious Relationships,' 2009. http://www.dicid.org

[817] See Jesper Svartvik, 'Geschwisterlichkeit: Realizing that We are Siblings,' in *Kirche und Synagoge: Ein Lutherisches Votum* (Herausgegeben von Folker Siegert: Vandenhoeck & Ruprecht, 2012), 325-26.

[818] Ibid.

In the same vein, the painful history of Christian-Muslim conflicts in Northern Nigeria can be seen another way—one of dialogue which seeks to spread knowledge, oppose stereotypes, and contempt by exploring the possibilities for forgiveness, reconciliation, and healing. Moreover, it is by granting and receiving forgiveness that the traumatised individuals and communities experience healing; in turn, this helps divided families and communities to rediscover harmony and peace.[819] Sincere reconciliation overcomes crises, restores the dignity of individuals, and opens up the path to development and lasting peace between peoples at every level.[820] Hence there is need to develop a spirituality of peace by forgiveness and reconciliation among neighbours. Dialogue creates the opportunity for those in dispute to listen to one another and learn from each other's hopes, dreams, fears, needs, and anxieties. Parties are able to acknowledge and share each other's pain and losses, forgive and ask for forgiveness, and begin the healing process. Dialogue activities can facilitate discussions of mutual concern and a creative vision for the future.[821] It offers the opportunity for personal/interpersonal and community transformation required for peaceful coexistence.[822]

Jesus's teaching and example on the need for forgiveness, reconciliation, and peace is revolutionary: *And if you remember your brother/sister has something against you . . . go at once and make peace . . .* (Matt. 5: 23-24); *Father forgive them for they do not know what they do* (Lk. 23: 34) and Vatican II *Nostra Aetate* (no. 3) . . . *Over the centuries many quarrels and dissension have arisen between Christians and Muslims. The sacred Council now pleads with all to forget the past and urges that sincere efforts be made to achieve mutual understanding . . .* [823] These statements provide the theological hermeneutic for mutual reconciliation and healing which play a significant role in helping people come to terms with their traumatic, violent experiences. Additionally, the scriptures enable believers to reflect and understand that each person is created in the image and likeness of God, and thus the message of scripture promotes reconciliation and healing.

---

[819] See Benedict XVI. Pope, 'Africae Munus,' *Post-Synodal Apostolic Exhortation of His Holiness Pope Benedict XVI to the Bishops, Clergy, Consecrated Persons and the Lay Faithful on the Church in Africa in Service to Reconciliation, Justice and Peace* (Benin Republic: Libreria Editrice Vaticana, 2011), no. 21. http://www.vatican.va/holy_father/benedict_xvi/apost_exhortations/documents/hf_ben-xvi_exh_20111119_africae-munus_en.html

[820] Ibid.

[821] Carter and Smith, 'Religious Peacebuilding,'290-99.

[822] Ibid.

[823] Cf. Flannery, 'Declaration on the Relationship of the Church to Non-Christian Religions,' no. 3, 740.

Faith communities responsible for seeking practical ways to dialogue in order to bring about reconciliation and healing. It is important to apologise for the hurt, killing, maiming, and destruction of property to evoke cultural ways of showing remorse for hurtful actions. To seek forgiveness involves going to the other to ask for pardon. I am convinced that is the way towards reconciliation and healing. Recently in Pakistan, for example, two Muslim leaders publicly apologised to the Christian community and asked for pardon for the outbreak of violence against Christians in Punjab's Gojra city.[824] This goes a long way to heal the wounds of broken relationships. Similarly, Christians and Muslims in Northern Nigeria can do the same by organising interreligious services of peace and reconciliation; people can express those deep-seated feelings of violence, betrayal, resentment, anger, and hatred against each other. This ritual offers the opportunity for apologies and peacemaking with the other.

Faith communities in Northern Nigeria need to initiate ways to bring healing and peace. Within the Islamic and Christian traditions, community prayer is a vital spiritual exercise and an essential part of the journey to forgiveness, reconciliation, healing, and renewal. Peace building by reconciliation would involve reading from scripture, prayers, music, symbols, and reflection on a particular theme that brings consolation, healing, support, and renewal to those who have experienced pain and loss.[825] It is important that interfaith reconciliation services become occasions of welcome, listening, support, and care for those who have suffered the physical and emotional pain of violence and abuse. Moreover, listening with openness, care, and sensitivity fosters the healing and reconciliation process. Faith communities are responsible for reflection and planning to bring this social, pastoral, spiritual, and liturgical resource to others; it is an important way to give practical care in the process of reconciliation, healing, and renewal.[826]

Reconciliation and peace with the other is ongoing in the life of a Christian. Jesus continually refers to the need for reconciliation in the parables (Matt. 18: 15-17; Lk. 17: 3-4) and makes reconciliation and forgiveness central to the 'Lord's Prayer' (Matt. 6: 9-15). The great events of the crucifixion and resurrection of Jesus signify breaking down of walls of division and hatred and bringing healing,

---

[824]   See John Pontifex, 'Muslim Leaders Apologise for 2009 Attacks on Christians,' 2011. http://www.indcatholicnews.com

[825]   See Irish Catholic Bishops' Conference, 'Towards Healing and Renewal,' *A Pastoral Response from the Irish Catholic Bishops' Conference to Mark the First Anniversary of the Publications of the Pastoral Letter of the Holy Father Pope Benedict XVI to the Catholics in Ireland* (Dublin, Ireland: Veritas Publication, 2011), 5-7.

[826]   Ibid., 9.

peace, and renewal to all (Gal. 3: 26-29; 2 Cor 5: 17-21).[827] To forgive and be truly forgiven involves letting resentful feelings go along with and the thoughts that underlie the feeling of being hurt. Surrendering a view of self as victim and making a sincere physical and spiritual effort to forgive and be forgiven brings a sense of renewal—a shift where blaming others is dispelled and the courage to reach out in a new relationship of friendship and peace is found.[828] Forgiveness, reconciliation, and healing are part of a slow process which takes a long time; there are no quick fix solutions.[829] This also shows how vulnerable both humans and the process can be, because how can one be sure that the person who asks for pardon will not repeat the same hurtful action again? How can one trust that the other is genuine and sincere? What about restitution—who fixes the damage?[830] Nevertheless, parish and mosque communities have to be committed to provide opportunities for victims to tell and listen to their stories, if survivors are to experience the desired healing and peace.

5.3 TOLERANCE, ACCEPTANCE, AND THE NEED TO RESPECT THE OTHER

In this section, I shall analyse the importance of tolerance in a pluralistic environment and the need to respect the right and the freedom of the other to be different. I highlight the vivid example of some prominent religious leaders to demonstrate how faith communities can transcend exclusive tendencies to adopt a more open attitude towards religious others.

The United Nations Declaration of Principles on Tolerance defines tolerance as respect, acceptance, and appreciation of the rich diversity of our world's cultures, forms of expression, and ways of being human.[831] Tolerance is fostered when we respect the dignity of our differences by openness to diversity, knowledge, communication, freedom of thought, conscience, and belief.[832] Tolerance promotes harmony despite differences and a culture of peace.[833] Sometimes tolerance can be

---

[827] Cf. Michael Bennett, 'Reconciliation,' *Africa—St Patrick's Missions* 76, no. 6 (2011), 14-15.

[828] Cf. Kurtz and Ketcham, *The Spirituality of Imperfection*, 222.

[829] Bennett, 'Reconciliation,' 14.

[830] Cf. Jim Consedine, *Restorative Justice Healing the Effect of Crime* (Lyttelton, New Zealand: Ploughshares Publications, 1995), 169-79.

[831] UNESCO, 'Declaration of Principles on Tolerance Proclaimed and Signed by the Member State of UNESCO on 16 November 1995,' http://www.unesco.org

[832] See Jonathan Sacks, *The Dignity of Difference: How to Avoid the Clash of Civilization* (London: Continuum, 2002), 45-67.

[833] See UNESCO, 'Declaration of Principles on Tolerance.'

an attitude of merely putting up with the other, not genuinely interested in them but choosing to endure in spite of dislike for them.

Nevertheless, tolerance is not concession, condescension, or indulgence; it is the recognition that every human being has the right to freedom of thought, conscience, and religion. This right includes freedom to practise or change one's religious belief either alone or with others, in public or private, and the right to manifest one's religious belief in teaching, practice, worship, and observance.[834] Tolerance is an active attitude prompted by recognition of the rights and freedom of all.[835] Religious tolerance recognises that everyone is free publicly or privately, to profess religious belief in teaching, worship, and observance.[836] Moreover, human beings are created by one God with the ability to know God. Both the Qur'an and the Bible recognise the diversity of religion (Q 2: 140; Acts 17: 22-23).

The Nigerian 1999 Federal Constitution recognises the right and freedom of religious belief when it states that

> [e]very person shall be entitled to freedom of thought, conscience and religion, including the freedom to change his (her) religion or belief and freedom either alone or in community with others, and in public or in private to manifest and propagate his (her) religion or belief in worship, teaching, practice and observance.[837]

The diversity of religious beliefs in contemporary Northern Nigeria necessitates tolerance and respect for religious differences. The increase in urban population and changing social patterns shown in diversity of life and religious beliefs demands understanding for peace and harmony. Religious tolerance challenges Christians and Muslims to accept and respect the integrity and right of the other to be different. Developing an attitude of mutual listening and interest in the religious other fosters peace. Diversity provides opportunities for positive encounters, friendships, and collaboration. In addition, symbolic acts and gestures are significant in fostering harmonious encounters. For instance, the visit of Pope John Paul II in May 2001 to Omayyada Mosque in Damascus[838] and Pope Benedict XVI's visit to the Blue Mosque

---

[834]   Ibid.

[835]   Cf. Ibid.; 'United Nations Universal Declaration on Human Rights,' 1998. http://www.un.org

[836]   Ibid.

[837]   *The Nigerian Constitution*, 341.

[838]   Pope John Paul II, 'Meeting with the Muslims Leaders Omayyad Great Mosque, Damascus,' Address of the Holy Father. 2001. http://www.vatican.va/holy_father/john_paul_ii/speeches/2001/documents/hf_jp-ii_spe_20010506_omayyadi_en.html

in Istanbul in November 2006 and the Mosque in Amman Jordan in May 2009[839] were positive gestures. The visit of the Archbishop of Canterbury Dr Rowan William to Dawoodi Mosque in May 2010[840] and the visit of the Archbishop John Onaiyekan to the National Mosque in Abuja, Nigeria,[841] were symbolic historical gestures bringing hope, courage, and strength to peace building efforts. Other events, such as meetings of leaders of various religious traditions at both national and international level, are opportunities for religious leaders in Nigeria to enrich grassroot efforts for peace and harmony.

Violent conflict in the name of religion will diminish in northern Nigeria when tolerance, friendship, trust, and acceptance are the thrust of reaching out in mutual appreciation of the other. Christians and Muslims must make sincere efforts to understand each other's religious beliefs by being hospitable and open to faith sharing. There is a long way to go to boost the confidence needed to overcome stereotypes and build trust. On the other hand, hospitality is central in both Islamic and Christian faith. The model of Abraham in the Qur'an (51: 24-27) and the Bible (Gn. 18: 1-9) is the basis for promoting a theology of hospitality and friendship in the two faith traditions. Hospitality between people of different religious traditions who are neighbours has the potential to cultivate friendship and respect and stabilise society especially in times of need, conflict, or chaos. Friendship based on hospitality builds the social cohesion and support necessary for peace and security.

Scripture (Bible and Qur'an) has a significant role to play in bringing about the inner transformation that leads to a future of peace and tolerance in Northern Nigeria, for example, Romans 12: 16; 1 Peter 3: 11; Luke 6: 27-29 and Qur'an 2: 256; 8: 61; 42: 40. As discussed in Chapter 4, the imam and the pastor were able to forgive each other and create a friendship of respect and acceptance because they listened to the word of God in their own faith traditions. Their scriptures had a major role to play in their conversion. Thus much can be achieved in religious peace building through the study of scripture with guided interpretation. Moreover, the authority of the sacred texts (Bible and the Qur'an) has enormous influence on believers engendering virtues of hospitality, tolerance, and peace. The media has a significant role to play in facilitating mutual respect and acceptance between faith communities. Radio,

---

839 Cf. Richard Spencer, 'Pope Benedict XVI Visits Jordan Mosque in Effort to Heal Vatican's Rift with Islam,' 2009. http://www.telegraph.co.uk/news/worldnews/europe/vaticancityandholysee/5300283/Pope-Benedict-XVI-visits-Jordan-mosque-in-effort-to-heal-Vaticans-rift-with-Islam.html

840 Cf. 'Archbishop's Visit to Dawoodi Bohra Mosque and Jain Temple,' 2010. http://www.archbishopofcanterbury.org/articles.php/989/archbishops-visit-to-dawoodi-bohra-mosque-and-jain-temple

841 See 'Archbishop Onaiyekan Visits National Mosque, Seeks Peace, Mutual Respect,' *Leadership* (Nigeria), 19 January, 2012. http://www.leadership.ng

television, newspapers, and the Internet provide opportunities to promote positive constructive values of acceptance and freedom to be different. These are necessary ingredients for sustainable peace building in Northern Nigeria.

5.4 THE SIGNIFICANCE OF RELIGIOUS AND PEACE EDUCATION IN NORTHERN NIGERIA

In this section, I shall discuss the importance of religious and peace education for peace and security in contemporary Northern Nigeria. I stress the need for a policy and curriculum on religious and peace education, teacher training, and funding for a peaceful future.

Education is a process through which knowledge is transmitted by means of teaching, learning, and training, acquisition of skills and awareness which may be formal or informal.[842] Accordingly, religious education is essential to peace building, since it provides understanding of the nature of religious experience, concepts, practices, and complexities of a religious tradition.[843] In the same vein, peace education confronts indirectly the forms of violence that dominate society by teaching about its causes and offering alternatives that seek to transform changing social structures and thought patterns that seem to sustain conflict.[844] Dialogue in daily life is helped by a system of religious and peace education that empowers people to think for themselves, dispel ignorance, and encourages respect for the freedom to be different. The United Nations Educational Scientific and Cultural Organisation (UNESCO) maintains that educating people about their shared rights and freedoms is the most effective means of preventing intolerance.[845] An effective educational system that trains people to think, become responsible, independent, and open minded is imperative in addressing issues of deep-rooted social, cultural, economic, political, ethnic, and religious intolerance.

Good and qualitative (religious) education is important to sustain peace and harmony (not only) in Northern Nigeria. Christians and Muslims are obliged to educate their adherents to be respectful, polite, genuinely friendly, and civil towards people of other faiths in the promotion of peaceful coexistence. It is imperative that religious leaders, parents, and policy makers (including the Nigerian government) put in place a dynamic policy on religious and peace education and develop a curriculum to improve the standard of education. Such a programme of study should include learning about plurality of religion, conflict, dialogue, and the need for peace while addressing questions of prejudice, stereotypes, and biases that lead to conflict.

---

[842]   Solahudeen, 'Islam and Child's Right to Education.'

[843]   Cf. Conroy and Davis, 'Citizenship, Education and the Claims of Religious Literacy.'

[844]   Harris and Morrison, 'Peace Education,' 9.

[845]   Cf. UNESCO, 'Declaration of Principles on Tolerance.'

Furthermore, such a policy should have Islam included in all parts of the religious curriculum in Christian schools and catechetical education centres. Similarly, the teaching of Christianity should be part of the entire curriculum in Islamic schools and *madrasa* (Islamic learning centres). The approach should be a positive focus on understanding different faith traditions. This programme of religious education should counter influences leading to fear and exclusion of others and helping young people develop independent critical judgement and reasonable ethical thinking.[846] Such an educational model should be the prototype for schools and be evaluated constantly to assess the progress being made. In addition, peace education should form part of the school curriculum from nursery school to the tertiary institutions and be the base of all religious catechesis in churches and mosques. As Arabic and Islamic historian William Watt argues, 'It is possible for one to be educated in either the Christian or Islamic traditions without losing one's own religious identity.'[847]

I, therefore, recommend reforms in the structure of education. This would include adequate funding, provision of resource materials (books and other equipment), and training and retraining of teachers in religious and peace education. This is vital for the development of education, peace, and security in Nigeria.[848] Education for peace building has to be both formal and informal. Formal education takes place in schools (primary, secondary, and tertiary). These institutions can become transformative establishments that guard against indoctrination by forming free and independent minds, while taking responsibility for justice and peace in society. (For discussion on informal form of education for peace building, see 5.7.1.) Furthermore, constant supervision and evaluation of schools by the relevant agency responsible for implementing the programme of education will check and maintain required standards. I propose that religion and peace education be integrated in the history, culture, and language curricula as a compulsory syllabus in general education. Children of different religious backgrounds can be taught together, focusing on the diversity of religion. As educational psychologists David Johnson and Roger Johnson have argued, peace can only develop when positive relations are established between members of disputing parties.[849] I agree, and further argue, that integrating the teaching of religion and peace education gives students of diverse cultural and religious backgrounds the opportunity to learn and appreciate the values of tolerance, respect, dialogue, and peace.

---

[846] Ibid.

[847] Watt, *Islam and Christianity Today*, 172.

[848] Cf. Muhammad Ibrahim, 'Teachers Training Key to Attainment of Millennium Development Goals,' *New Nigeria* (Nigeria), 26 July 2011. http://www.newnigeriannews. com

[849] Cf. Johnson, 'Essential Components of Peace Education,' 284-85.

Government, religious leaders, and other stakeholders in the Nigerian educational sector must develop a framework for religious education that guarantees every student the chance to learn about different religions other than their own. For example, in northern Nigeria, Muslim and Christian students could be taught together by two teachers teaching Islamic and Christian religious knowledge. This will encourage students to develop basic and critical knowledge of both religious traditions, helping them to appreciate the diverse nature of contemporary Nigerian society, as well as learn to respect their differences. It would provide further opportunities for encounter and dialogue between students and a chance to confront stereotypes. Moreover, the educational system needed for peace in Northern Nigeria should encourage students' interaction through common projects, living together, group work, assignments, and sharing of experiences. Negative stereotyping can be weakened further if educational programmes include mutual study exchange, regional cooperation among educators and students, and the strengthening of the Nigerian National Youth Service Corps (NYSC), where, for example, student graduates from the south are sent to the north for service and vice-versa. The objective of the above project is to support mutual exchange and build bridges of peace, dialogue, and understanding. The success of the above scheme demands knowledge and skills on how to deal with religious and human diversity; hence the need for the teacher training in religious and human differences and interreligious dialogue. However, Muslim and Christian parents may resist their children learning about other faiths for the fear of conversion would be significant. It is a genuine fear, but considering the high price Northern Nigerians are paying for ignorance of the religious other, it is worth the risk.

I support whole-heartedly the practice of public preaching and religious instruction and education in churches and mosques. However, I want to suggest that this be done with the utmost respect for the religious other. Hence religious preachers and teachers in Qur'anic schools and Sunday schools ought to be properly trained and licensed by the leadership of their religious traditions. The training of clerics should include proper formation in Islam, Christianity, and religious dialogue, with the provision, for example, that a trained Muslim teaches Islam in a Christian seminary and a trained Christian teaches Christianity in an Islamic *madrasa*. Furthermore, in the parish or in the mosque community, when religious lessons are taught, a Muslim could be invited to share about the Qur'an and Islamic faith to the Christian faithful; a Christian could be invited to talk about the Bible and Christian faith to the Muslim faithful. The emphasis here is on sharing and getting to know about the other faith; it is not about conversion, arguments, or debate. The focus is on increasing knowledge of the other faith tradition.

Additionally, a day, for example, 16 November, the annual International Day for Tolerance,[850] could be an open day in all mosques and churches. Such a day provides

---

[850]   UNESCO, 'Declaration of Principles on Tolerance.'

the opportunity for people to visit the mosque or church within their area. It offers the Christian and Muslim faithful a unique experience of the other. It weakens stereotypes further and builds trust and friendship that leads to peace. In Germany, for instance, 3 October every year is an Open Day for Mosques,[851] and people are encouraged to make visits; religious leaders in northern Nigeria could do the same.

The hope here is that learning and sharing in community religious education will foster the values of peace, love, and harmony that both Islam and Christianity share and motivate adherents to increase their knowledge of the other's faith; such sharing would develop love and friendship and discern the values that lead to peace and harmony in society.[852]

5.4.1 QUR'ANIC SCHOOLS AND THE EDUCATION OF ALMAJIRI IN NORTHERN NIGERIA

This segment deals specifically with the need to educate *Almajiris*. I argue that educating *Almajiri* in the region is essential for a future of peace and harmony. Current statistics show that between 7 and 9.5 million children (*Almajiris)* roam the streets of Northern Nigeria, attending Qur'anic schools and begging for food and other means of livelihood.[853] As discussed in Chapter 1, these children have no formal education and have left their homes and families to attend Qur'anic schools without any financial support. Thus they resort to begging to live.

Therefore, providing holistic, educational, and social development for these children is fundamental to sustain peace and security in the locality. Parents and Islamic authorities in Northern Nigeria must be responsible for giving these children both religious (Qur'anic) and modern education that helps them develop open, independent minds and equip them for a productive future. Improving the educational standard of *Almajiris* is an urgent challenge to parents, Islamic religious authorities, and the government.

Education, both religious and conventional, is necessary for a future of peace, development, and security in the region; the *Almajiri* phenomenon challenges that prospect. The government must provide a functional system of education that

---

[851] Cf. Stefan Herrmann, 'Open Mosque Day Welcomes Non-Muslims in Germany,' 2011. http://www.presstv.ir/detail/202584.html

[852] See Micheal McGrath, 'Religious Education and Having Faith in Our Schools,' *Scottish Catholic Observer* (Scotland), 19 August 2011.

[853] See Aluaigba, 'Circumventing or Superimposing Poverty on the African Child,' 20; Ibrahim A. Yushau, 'Sultan to Establish Almajiri Foundation,' *Daily Trust* (Nigeria), 21 February 2011. http://www.dailytrust.com; Attahiru Ahmed, '1.2 Beggars Roaming Zamfara Streets-Gov Yari,' *The Sun* (Nigeria), 5 October 2011. http://www.sunnewsonline. com

obliges parents and religious organisations to promote the importance of learning. The integration of existing Qur'anic schools with the conventional system of modern education is a way forward for Northern Nigeria. In addition, the conference of the Northern Governors' Forum can back this project by mobilising support and channelling resources into the educational sector in the North. Successful *Almajiri* education entails training and retraining of *Mallams* (teachers) and the provision of necessary infrastructure and a robust curriculum with constant evaluation.[854] Some Nigerian scholars and analysts observed that the educational backwardness in Northern Nigeria is due to the resistance and non-receptive attitude of some Islamic leaders and communities to the modern Western system of education. It is considered secular in nature without any provision for the spiritual upbringing of children in the Islamic tradition.[855] This point of view has affected the region negatively in terms of security, development, mutual harmony, and peace. Northern Nigeria remains deprived, impoverished, and underdeveloped. Nonetheless, some progress is being made in appreciating the strategic importance of modern education, science, and technology, yet some Muslim parents still mistrust the value of modern education and send their children to the traditional *Madrasas*.[856]

Religious leaders, government, and the media can make a significant contribution by educating parents to develop the capacities of their children and acquire skills by modern education. Policy makers can contribute by enacting laws that prohibit the large migration of children from one village to another and a complete ban on street begging.[857] However, this is possible only if the government makes the necessary provision for compulsory religious and modern education for children in their local schools, equipped with the essential facilities. Furthermore, fusing traditional Qur'anic schools with modern education can be encouraged with the assistance and establishment of private scholarship schemes, educational foundations, and endowment funds to cater to the needs of those who may not have the means to access education. This would go a long way in encouraging poor parents to inspire their children to be educated for the development, peace, and security of the northern region.

---

[854] Cf. Aluaigba, 'Circumventing or Superimposing Poverty on the African Child,' 22-23; Adelowo Oladipo, 'Nigeria's Education Sector Needs Revolution,' *Tribune* (Nigeria), 14 September 2011. http://www.tribune.com.ng

[855] See Sultan Abubakar, 'Islam and Peace Building in West Africa (1) Imperatives of Knowledge, Justice and Anti-Corruption,' *Vanguard* (Nigeria), 10 October 2011. http://www.vanguardngr.com; Aluaigba, 'Circumventing or Superimposing Poverty on the African Child,' 22; Abdulmalik, 'Re: Almajiri Education,' *The Nation* (Nigeria), 05 April 2010. http://www.thenationonlineng.net.

[856] Sultan, 'Islam and Peace Building in West Africa.'

[857] Cf. Aluaigba, 'Circumventing or Superimposing Poverty on the African Child,' 23.

5.5   Government and Policy Making in Nigeria

In this section, I shall discuss governance and policy making in Nigeria. I highlight the value that educated politicians bring to policy making, institutional reforms, and good governance. It further explores politics as a vocation of service and an opportunity for collaboration between politicians and theologians in the public sphere.

The government of Nigeria has the constitutional responsibility to guard and protect the rights of every citizen and ensure an atmosphere of peace and security for all. The first step towards ensuring security is for the government to address squarely issues of poor education, unemployment, poverty, and lack of development. Secondly, the government should put in place a national policy to be the guiding principle for peace, security, and the constitutional rights of everyone.[858] The success of the above requires an independent judicial system that is able to hold people accountable for their actions together with reforms in the security agencies (army, police, and state security service). It also demands the provision of resources for proper training, retraining, and ongoing formation of security agents/personnel in the subjects of human rights, security, and good community relations. In addition, there must be a dialogical relationship between politicians and theologians. Politicians should engage with theologians to develop clearly new ways to deal with the complexity of the situation. Theologians should inform politicians whose responsibility it is to implement social reforms. Since religious issues may be sensitive, opinionated, and bigoted, addressing conflicts in the region under study necessitates the collaboration of theology and politics to proffer solutions.

Furthermore, government, through the National Legislative Assembly must pass laws to protect people—for example, make it a criminal offence to use hired violence in politics and bring to justice those who contravene the law or breach security. In the last thirty years, there has been ongoing violence in the North, and no one has ever been prosecuted or held accountable. There is no law in Nigeria, for instance, to punish anyone who burns a mosque or a church.[859] Successive governments have failed to implement the recommendations of several committees set up at various times to investigate civil disturbance.[860] Enacting a law and enforcing it will deter the perpetrators of violence and enhance peace and security in the region.

Democracy cannot thrive without educated leaders committed to serve the people. Nigeria has a huge population. It is imperative to have well-educated leaders,

---

[858]   Cf. Chris Agbambu, 'Lack of National Security Policy, Nigeria's Major Problem,' *Tribune* (Nigeria), 01 August 2011. http://www.tribune.com.ng

[859]   Adeyemi Muyiwa, 'Kukah Blames Nigeria's Woes on Conscription of Office Holders,' *Guardian* (Nigeria), 12 October 2011. http://www.ngrguardiannews.com

[860]   'Lemu Report on Election Violence,' *Guardian* (Nigeria), 25 October 2011. http://www. ngrguardiannews.com

politicians, and policy makers to provide the kind of leadership that is enabling, accountable, just, and fair to all. Those elected to serve in public office should have basic education and be open to ongoing formation in politics, policy making, and the art of good governance. Nigeria and Nigerians have suffered from poor governance and the misfortune of being ruled by unprepared leaders.[861] The result is abuse of power, poor service, poverty, underdevelopment, corruption, lack of accountability, and the use of religion for political ends. Moreover, educated politicians are able to develop the democratic ethic of accountability, respect for the rule of law, and the proper use of resources at their disposal. Education is fundamental to the growth of democracy and good governance. The Nigerian National Assembly must enact and enforce laws to hold those in public office accountable in order to address corruption in Nigeria. I suggest that it should become mandatory for all public office holders to declare their assets and punish those who appropriate public resources. Furthermore, a Nigerian constitutional review should address these issues properly—ethnic domination, inequality, and indigene versus settler syndrome that have challenged peace and security.

The support of the federal government of Nigeria for the establishment of the Nigeria Interreligious Council (NIREC) is commendable. It provides dialogue space for religious leaders, theologians, and politicians to collaborate in addressing conflicts. Dialogue, reconciliation, and the pursuit of peaceful coexistence among all religious groups is fundamental to national stability, development, peace, and security in Nigeria.[862] The government, for its part, must remain committed to strengthening Christian-Muslim dialogue and desist from favouring one religion over other—for example, in matters such as pilgrimages, building places of worship, access to public media, and religious instruction in schools.[863] Politicians, on the other hand, should refrain from playing on people's religious sentiments in canvassing for political support, knowing how easily this can erupt into violence.[864]

It is vital for government to collaborate with the private sector to invest in job creation, infrastructural development, and a vibrant economy that supports the population.[865] Poverty, unemployment, underdevelopment, and low literacy levels have been identified in this study as contributing factors to conflict. Nigeria has a large growing population of which, arguably, 50 per cent are young people below the

---

[861] See Femi Makinde, 'Kukah Blames Nigeria's Problems on "Accidental" Leadership,' *Punch* (Nigerian), 14 October 2011. http://www.punchng.com

[862] See Bisi Oladele, 'Why Dialogue with Boko Haram Is Tough, by Kukah,' *The Nation* (Nigeria), 04 October 2011. http://www.thenationonlineng.net

[863] Schineller, *The Church Teaches*, 203.

[864] Ibid.

[865] Cf. Okonjo Iweala, 'Nigeria Needs Critical Infrastructure to Support Job Creation,' *Guardian* (Nigeria), 30 August 2011. http://www.ngrguardiannews.com

age of thirty-five.[866] It is, therefore, imperative that government addresses issues of poverty and unemployment so that youths are engaged productively. The northern governors and political leaders must make a commitment to achieve economic growth in the region to address the underlying problems that cause violent conflicts.[867] This is possible through education, skill acquisition, and job creation for the general well-being of the people.

Moreover, Islamic and Christian theology considers politics a vocation to service. For instance, the words of Jesus, *you are the salt of the earth . . . you are the light of the world* (Matt. 5: 13-14), and *give to Caesar what belong to Caesar and God what belongs to God* (Matt. 22: 21-22), inspire (Christian) politicians to serve God and humanity. As good stewards, they must be diligent in discharging their duties (Matt. 25: 14-23). The example of Jesus, who came to serve and not to be served (Lk. 22: 27; Matt. 20: 28), is the model for all public servants. Thus Nigerian politicians and public office holders must strive to be just, fair, and transparent in discharging their duties, irrespective of ethnic, social, religious, and political affiliation. They must encourage goodwill to promote peace initiatives by appreciating the central role of religion in society. They must think carefully about integrating religion into political and civil life as a means to peace while taking into account its sensitive nature when making and executing policies. Furthermore, such policies should consider the fears and anxieties of all stakeholders (religious groups) after due consultation. It is important that the government collaborates with religious and community leaders to build and sustain peace through dialogue and avoid using religion to cause rancour, division, and disharmony.[868] However, the question remains, are politicians willing to interact with theologians? Many times they seem to be in support of dialogue—they may even initiate it—but they hijack the process to political advantage. Nevertheless, as St. Paul says, let us look for what strengthens peace and mutual understanding (Rm. 14: 17).

---

[866] Yusuf Alli, 'Why Federal Government Must Create Jobs, Expand Economy,' *The Nation* (Nigeria), 26 October 2011. http://www.thenationonlineng.net

[867] See Tayo Lewis, 'Poverty: UN's Timely Warning,' *Tribune* (Nigeria), 28 October 2011. http://www.tribune.com

[868] Cf. Carter and Smith, 'Religious Peacebuilding,' 292.

5.6 THE RESPONSIBILITY OF RELIGIOUS LEADERS AND PREACHERS IN FOSTERING PEACE IN NORTHERN NIGERIA

In this section, I shall examine the role of religious leaders, clerics, and preachers in fostering peace in the region under study. I focus on the value of training, collaboration, and support among religious leaders for the advancement of dialogue and peace.

Muslim and Christian religious leaders and preachers in Northern Nigeria are responsible for fostering peace in the region by cultivating a sincere willingness to engage and work with each other as peace intermediaries—for example, the simple effort of finding out who the local priest, pastor, or imam within ones vicinity are; then reaching out in friendship to these leaders goes a long way to establish channels of communication. Religious leaders must lead their communities towards peace building by recalling and emphasising the virtues and principles of tolerance and non-violence as taught by their faith traditions.[869] They can and should prevent and resolve violent conflict by reminding their adherents of their duty of peace and harmony in society.[870] In times of crisis, they must avoid any action that would aggravate the situation. By preaching a message of tolerance and mutual understanding and striving to reinforce the advantages of working together, they can engender greater peace among people.[871] Sustainable peace building requires that religious leaders remain proactive in responding effectively to the excesses of their co-believers. Addressing extremist fundamentalist tendencies that promote intolerance, hatred, and violence must ensure that their faith is not used to justify any form of violence or aggression. Those responsible must be held accountable for the harm they do.[872]

Religious leaders and preachers can advance the cause of peace within their faith communities when they are educated and trained in their own faith and other faith traditions. Being educated in the principles of dialogue and peace education, they become effective peace negotiators in society. They can guard against violence when they notice that religion has been exploited for political interest by speaking out vehemently against it and caution their followers to hold on to the true teachings of the faith.

Clerics and preachers play a vital role in the life of a faith community. The prospects of fostering better understanding will be better if, for instance, they are

---

[869] See ibid, 294.

[870] Ibid.

[871] Cf. Stanley Nkwocha, 'Sultan Cautions Oritsejafor on Buhari,' *Leadership* (Nigeria), 27 April 2011. http://www.leadershipeditors.com

[872] Ibid.

educated in the art of communication, the use of language, the history of religions, and dialogue for peace. Public preachers must use language in a constructive way to encourage tolerance, respect, and harmony in society. Preachers have a wonderful opportunity to speak about their faith. They can educate their congregation, weaken stereotypes, and encourage mutual friendship.[873] Hence training for religious preachers is crucial for peace building. The Catholic Bishops Conference, the Anglican, Lutheran, Methodist, and the Pentecostal fellowship movement and the Nigerian Supreme Council for Islamic Affairs (NSCIA) in the region are responsible for ensuring that those who preach in the name of their traditions are properly trained. The established Christian seminaries and Islamic *madrasas* provide an opportunity for the proper formation of religious preachers.

Generally, the Muslim and Christian faithful listen to their leaders and preachers with respect and reverence. It is imperative that leaders be proactive in setting a good example of inclusivity and openness, reaching out in dialogue, and speaking out publicly against violence, injustice, discrimination, and arousing negative religious sentiments.[874] Some examples are worthy of note: the pastor and imam (whose peace building activities are both national and international) have mediated in the conflict in Kaduna and Jos; the Anglican Bishop of Kaduna, Josiah Fearon-Idowu, promotes peace through religious education; the Catholic Archbishop of Jos, Ignatius Kagama; the Catholic Bishop of Sokoto, Matthew Hassan Kukah; and the Sultan of Sokoto, Muhammad Sa'ad Abubakar, are commendable for their tireless efforts and collaboration for peaceful coexistence. These leaders are champions of conflict resolution using dialogue. They have visited various Christian and Muslim communities in (Northern) Nigeria to bring the message of peace, harmony, and reconciliation.[875] Other religious leaders can take a cue from the above examples and work to bring people of different religious faiths together for dialogue. The aim is not to debate or argue but to enhance mutual understanding and harmony.

Furthermore, the Christian and Muslim faithful will be challenged and encouraged when they see their spiritual leaders coming together publicly to pray for peace. Prayer in common reiterates a religious vision of peace and mutual respect. The recent gathering of world religious leaders in Assisi (27 October 2011) for a 'Day of Reflection, Dialogue and Prayer for Peace and Justice in the World'

---

[873] Cf. Joseph Cardinal Ratzinger, *Truth and Tolerance: Christian Belief and World Religions* (San Francisco: Ignatius Press, 2004), 106; and Esposito, 'The Future of Islam,' 166.

[874] Cf. John Pontifex, 'Nigeria: Bishop Blames Renegade Politicians, Corrupt Police for Attacks on Churches,' 2011. http://www.indcatholicnews.com; see also Schineller, *The Church Teaches*, 217-19.

[875] Joseph Kenny, 'The Bishop and Sultan in Sokoto,' *Guardian* (Nigeria), 23 October 2011. http://www.ngrgurdiannews.com; see also Fearon-Idowu, 'No Peace in Nigeria without Dialogue'; and Kaigama, *Dialogue of Life*, 73-74.

is a significant example that religious leaders in Northern Nigeria can emulate.[876] For instance, the Nigerian national day celebration, beginning of a new year, and other national festivities are occasions when religious leaders can come together in prayer for peace and harmony. As spiritual leaders, they must continue to stretch out a hand of friendship to one another and stand together for peace; even when difficulties and tensions arise they must remain the salt of the earth and the light of the world (Matt. 5: 13-14).[877]

5.7 THE ROLE OF FAITH COMMUNITIES IN ADVANCING PEACE IN NORTHERN NIGERIA

In this section, I shall discuss the role of faith communities in nurturing peaceful coexistence. I highlight collaboration, teamwork, and dialogue as key elements in the promotion of peace.

Islam and Christianity as communities of faith in Northern Nigeria will continue to exist side by side. Those who profess either of these faiths interact in a contemporary pluralistic society as neighbours. As discussed in this work, religion touches upon deeper levels of human identity, and people are sensitive in matters of religious beliefs, which sometimes generates fear and tension.[878] Consequently, mutual understanding is essential for conflict prevention and resolution. Faith communities can be proactive in fostering a spirit of trust when leaders guide their communities to perceive the other as neighbour and reach out constructively. Furthermore, by deepening our knowledge of the religious other, meeting in dialogue and respecting differences, faith communities are able to build trusting relationships that motivate people to collaborate for the common good. Therefore, initiating an interfaith programme of social action designed to increase tolerance and respect within these communities fosters a spirit of collaboration.[879] For example, a community project that is beneficial to all gives the opportunity for interaction between people of different religious and cultural backgrounds.

---

[876] See Benedict XVI. Pope, 'Day of Reflection, Dialogue and Prayer for Peace and Justice in the World 'Pilgrims of Truth, Pilgrims of Peace'' *Address of His Holiness Benedict XVI at the Meeting for Peace in Assisi* (Rome Vatican City: Libreria Editrice, 2011), http://www.vatican.va/holy_father/benedict_xvi/speeches/2011/october/documents/ hf_ben-xvi_spe_20111027_assisi_en.html

[877] Cf. Ian Dunn, 'Faith Leaders in Scotland Pray for Peace,' *Scottish Catholic Observer* (Scotland), 04 November 2011; see also Stephen Reilly, 'Religious Leaders Promote Pathway to Peace,' *Scottish Catholic Observer* (Scotland), 04 November 2011.

[878] See Abu-Nimer, 'The Miracle of Transformation,' 17.

[879] Cf. 'Peace Building Initiatives,' 2007. http://www.peacebuildinginitiative.org

Faith communities can make a meaningful contribution to peace when young people are taught the importance of respect for the other. This is achieved by working closely with youth leaders, teachers of religious instruction, and ministers who preach. The pastor and the imam working with Christian and Muslim youths is an example of reorientation for young people. Through education and preaching, youths realise the inherent evil in violent conflicts, torching of places of worship, destruction of property, and the killing and maiming of people. Furthermore, faith communities can team up with the government, non-governmental organisations, and individuals to initiate youth empowerment schemes for the alleviation of poverty by skill acquisition.[880] For instance, the Catholic Diocese of Jos put in place an Interfaith Youth Vocational Training Centre, located at Hai-Hung, in Bokkos Plateau state.[881] Such programmes help young people to become self-reliant and contribute positively to the development of the region.

Christians and Muslims both suffer pain and losses in conflicts; these communities can bring about healing and peace by supporting each other during crises; after such incidents, communities are left to deal with the trauma, the pain of their loss, and the struggle to recover from the experience. For instance, after the April 2011 crisis in Jos, in Dadin-Kowa neighbourhood, a reprisal attack in which six people were killed and houses and places of worship were destroyed,[882] the Christian community (with Pastor Declan Onyebuchi) and the Muslim community (with Imam Abdul Aziz Suleiman) agreed to support each other and protect their neighbourhood by preventing intruders from causing violence.[883] These are opportunities to reach out to each other. Another example is how the Evangelical Church of West Africa (ECWA) sent material support with a message of peace to both Muslim and Christian communities affected by the May-June 2011 post-election violence in Kafanchan.[884] In a similar move in Dogo-Dutse Jos, the Islamic cleric Sheikh Muhammad sent relief material to victims of both faith communities,[885] and recently a faith-based Christian

---

[880] See Emmanuel Jose Ohize and Muhammad Jebba Adamu, 'Case Study of Youth Empowerment Scheme of Niger State, Nigeria in Poverty Alleviation,' *AU Journal of Technology* 13, no. 1 (2009), 47. http://www.journal.au.edu/au_techno/2009/jul09/journal131_article07.pdf

[881] Cf. Catholic Arch Diocese of Jos Nigeria, 'Kaigama Opens Interfaith Youth Vocational Centre,' 2011. http://www.archjosnigeria.org/archjosnews.php?id=1

[882] See Ray Walker, 'Jos Violence: Everyone Lives in Fear of His Neighbour,' *BBC News*, 07 April 2011.http://www.bbc.co.uk/news/world-africa-12985289

[883] 'Jos Violence: Everyone Lives in Fear of His Neighbour.'

[884] Cf. Yusuf Aminu, 'Relief Comes for Violence Victims,' *The Nation* (Nigeria), 27 August 2011. http://www.thenationonlineng.net

[885] See 'We Care for Both Needy Christians, Muslims says Sheikh Muhammad,' *People's Daily* (Nigeria), 03 August 2011. *http://www.peoplesdaily-online.com*

organisation, the Jos branch of Christian Women for Excellence and Empowerment in Nigerian Society, donated material to the Federation of Muslim Women Association of Nigeria (FOMWAN) in Jos, to support the Eid-el-Kabir Islamic religious festival, with a message of peace and love.[886]

These gestures strengthen the relationship between faith communities in peace building. Moreover, achieving peace is a collective responsibility that begins with individuals willing to live in peace with those of other faith traditions. It is a process of transformation that takes time, based on the religious values of peace and harmony, expressed and extended to the people of other faiths in respect, tolerance, and dialogue. Hence sustainable peace in Northern Nigeria requires the sincere collaboration of the two faith communities and the goodwill to live with each other in harmony as neighbours.

5.7.1 THE ROLE OF INDIVIDUALS AND FAMILIES IN FOSTERING PEACE IN NORTHERN NIGERIA

In this segment, I shall consider what individuals and families can contribute to peaceful relations in the area under study. I focus on grassroot interactions that will engender harmonious existence.

Islamic and Christian theological hermeneutics ask the faithful to be kind and generous, treating everyone justly, since all are created by the one true God (Q 16: 40; 49: 13; Matt. 5: 43-48; Rm. 12: 18). As individual believers, Christians and Muslims can deepen their faith and contribute significantly to a peaceful Northern Nigeria by becoming examples of peace in their communities. Achieving this objective entails personal transformation in response to the God who has loved us first. This love is expressed in service to others, living in peace and open to a relationship that seeks to deepen the knowledge of our faith and that of the other. Such transformation is possible if sustained by one's faith convictions and supported by genuine catechesis.[887] In addition, individual transformation challenges the person to mutual respect, tolerance, and willingness to extend a hand of self-giving friendship to others.

Religion is not just an individual phenomenon. It has a social dimension that offers each believer a sense of belonging to a community of fellow believers. With its reference to a transcendent source of truth, and codification of shared norms and values, religion serves as the link between the individual and their faith community, within a religiously pluralistic society.[888] The challenge nonetheless is to foster social

---

[886] Marie-Therese Peter, 'Christian Women Donate to Muslims,' *The Nation* (Nigeria), 07 November 2011. http://www.thenationonlineng.net

[887] Benedict XVI, 'Africae Munus,' no. 32.

[888] *Peace Building Initiatives.*

cohesion. Northern Nigeria, as a multicultural and multireligious society, presents an opportunity for individuals (Muslims and Christians) to make concerted efforts to live in peace, even in the face of conflicts.

The family is an important organ of society, the nucleus of every community. God wishes humanity to live in harmony and peace and laid the foundations for this in the very nature of the human being, created in his image and likeness (Gn. 1: 27).[889] This divine image develops not only in the individual but also in that unique communion of persons formed by God and united in love, which binds all people together irrespective of tribe, race, or religion.[890] The family, as a group of closely related individuals, is the first and most indispensable teacher of peace and a means for transmitting the religious and cultural values which help the person to acquire his or her own identity.[891] It is the best setting for learning and applying the culture of forgiveness, peace, and reconciliation. We experience these fundamental elements of peace, justice, forgiveness, and love between parents, brothers, and sisters in a family.[892]

Hence, the family setting is crucial to the promotion of peace. It is fundamentally an essential educating nucleus, where religious, cultural, and community values are passed on, helping each member to acquire his or her own identity.[893] The family contains in itself the very future of our society, contributing effectively to peace when children are taught the African values of community life, respect for the dignity of everyone (young and old), tolerance, hospitality, collaboration, honesty, sincerity, and peace with one another. Parents are the first teachers in the family. It, however, follows that these values, as well as being taught in family circles, must be, as Pope John Paul II puts it, 'witnessed to in the family setting by showing that self-giving love to others, accepting those who are different, responding to their needs and demands and allowing them to share family benefits'.[894] These domestic virtues, based upon profound respect for human life and dignity, are practised in understanding, patience, mutual encouragement, and forgiveness, enabling the small community of the family to live out the first and most fundamental experience of peace making in society.[895]

---

[889] Pope John Paul II, 'The Family Creates the Peace of the Human Family,' *Message of His Holiness John Paul II for the XXVII World Day of Peace January 1994* (Rome Vatican City: Libereria Editrice, 1993), no. 1. http://www.vatican.va/holy_father/john_paul_ii/messages/peace/documents/hf_jp-ii_mes_08121993_xxvii-world-day-for-peace_en.html

[890] Ibid.

[891] Ibid., no. 2.

[892] Benedict XVI, 'Africae Munus,' no. 43.

[893] See John Paul II, 'The Family Creates Peace,' no. 2.

[894] Ibid.

[895] Ibid.

Moreover, an enduring peaceful order needs institutions which express and consolidate the values of peace. The family is an active agent for peace by the values it expresses and transmits within itself and in the participation of each of its members in the life of community.[896] Consequently, the future of sustainable peace in Northern Nigeria challenges families to impart the traditional values of listening, respect, neighbourliness, and peace to their children and young people. Parents must take this responsibility seriously to become models of peace and love themselves in the family and in society.

5.7.2 THE ROLE OF WOMEN AS AGENTS IN THE PROMOTION OF PEACE IN NORTHERN NIGERIA

This segment focuses on women as agents for advancing peace in Northern Nigeria. It considers the unique role of women in nurturing the family and how such skills can contribute to building a homogeneous society.

At least 50 per cent of most communities and settlements around the world are women.[897] Women have made significant contributions to the development of their communities. Although their role as mothers, nurturers, teachers, peace makers, helpers, and home makers may not be publicly recognised and appreciated, often due to the patriarchal nature of society, their initiatives and contributions, however, towards building peaceful coexistence in the home and the community cannot be overlooked. For example, this is evident in the recent award of the 2011 Nobel Peace Prize to three African women, Ellen Johnson Sirleaf (President of Liberia), Leymah Gbowee (a Liberian), and Tawakkol Karman (from Yemen) for their non-violent contributions to peace building in their immediate communities.[898] This shows the skills and talents women can bring to a process of peace building.

In many societies, power relations between men and women are gender specific.[899] Traditionally established gender roles in several cultures ascribe the private domestic sphere to women, in the home, family, and relational community concerns.[900] It can be said that such a domestic role gives women the unique opportunity to develop skills of nurturing, care, and fostering peaceful relationships in the home.[901] Having learnt the values of steadfastness and focus from childhood, they remain docile and submissive while the patriarchal social order induces

---

[896] Cf. Ibid., no. 6.

[897] See McGarvey, 'Where Are the Women in Interfaith Dialogue,' 75.

[898] Cf. 'The Nobel Peace Prize 2011.' http://www.nobel_prizes/peace/laureates/2011/

[899] See Cynthia Cockburn, 'The Continuum of Violence: A Gender Perspective on War and Peace,' in Wenona Giles and Jennifer Hyndman (eds.), *Sites of Violence Gender and Conflict Zones* (Los Angeles: University of California Press, 2004), 35.

[900] McGarvey, 'Gender, Peace and Religious Coexistence,' 66-67.

[901] Ibid.

women to pay attention to minor details in the family.[902] Yet, in a situation of violent conflict, women often become victims of such violence because of their domestic roles. However, some analysts and sociologists have argued that women may not be as docile, subservient, and peaceful as society perceives them; statistical records attest that women have been involved in violence as suicide bombers in Lebanon, Sri-Lanka, Chechnya, Israel, Turkey, and Somalia.[903] In northern Uganda, Sierra-Leon, and Liberia, women took an active part in armed conflict as combatant soldiers who killed, maimed, and caused pain and destruction in their communities.[904]

Nonetheless, if women are empowered and given the opportunity, they are effective agents in the promotion of peace and reconciliation in the community. Their traditional function of homemaking offers them the chance to imbibe cultural, religious, traditional, and social values of peace, which they in turn pass on to their children in the home. Thus women are teachers of culture, values, language, and models of peace in the community. Their motivation is to promote peace by helping people and families cope with the pain and emerging socio-economic struggles resulting from conflict.[905] For instance, after the 2008 crisis, women in Dadin Kowa in Jos played a major role in keeping peace in the community by voicing their fears about potential future violence. As a result, pastors, imams, and several elders met and agreed on a peace declaration that was read out to the community.[906] In Liberia, women have been active promoters of peace, even in overwhelming conflict situations. They achieve this by using music, songs, story-telling, folklore, proverbs, sayings, symbols, rituals, communication, and support in times of crisis.[907] Their

---

[902]   See Oluwakemi Ajani, 'Women Need to Take Their Future in Their Hands,' *Guardian* (Nigeria), 15 April 2012. http://www.ngrguardiannews.com

[903]   Cf. Debra Zedalla, *Female Suicide Bombers* (Honolulu: University of Hawaii Press, 2004), 3; 'Female Suicide Bomber Kills Somali Sport Chiefs,' *Vanguard* (Nigeria), 04 April 2012. http://www.vanguardngr.com/2012/04/female-bomber-kills-somali-sports-chiefs/

[904]   See Susan McKay, 'Girls as "Weapons of Terror" in Northern Uganda and Sierra Leonean Rebel Fighting Forces,' *Studies in Conflict and Terrorism* 28, no. 5 (2005), 385-97.

[905]   Cf. Agustiana T. Endah, 'Women and Peace-Building Central Sulawesi and North Maluku,' 2004. http://www.internal-displacement.org/8025708F004CE90B/(httpDocuments)/63E26 21B492E7276C12577F8003710EA/$file/Indonesia_-_Thematic_Assessment,_Women_ and_Peace-Building.pdf

[906]   Cf. Jana Krause, 'A Deadly Cycle: Ethno-Religious Conflict in Jos, Plateau State, Nigeria,' *Executive Summary Working Paper* (June 2011), 3. http://www.genevadeclartions/ fileadmin/docs/regional-publications/GD-ES-deadly-cycle-jospdf

[907]   See Aj Jackson, 'African Women in Conflict: More Than Only Helpless Victims,' *The Academic Journal of New York University's Centre for Global Affairs* 5, no. 1 (2010). http://www.perspectivesonglobalissues.com/archives/fall-2010-conflict/africa-women-in-conflict/

initiatives and contributions are distinctive as women, because their experience of conflict is different from that of men.[908]

Women in African society are active promoters of a culture of peace and harmony by playing key roles in the family and the community.[909] They teach religious and societal values of collaboration, tolerance, honesty, hospitality, and respect for the other, thus making a positive contribution to the development of children.[910] Furthermore, they enhance peace building by reaching out and sharing in the painful experiences of others; they listen, console, encourage, and support each other by being hospitable, thus maintaining balance in society.[911]

In the same vein, Muslim and Christian women in Northern Nigeria are reliable peace emissaries in the home and the community. They strive to build bridges of peace and share many common concerns in the region.[912] These include conflict violence, inequality, discrimination, insecurity, poverty, illiteracy, vulnerability, lack of opportunity, and inability to assert their rights as women. Nevertheless, their care, conciliatory attitude, and ability to negotiate and further peace in the home is invaluable in society.[913] They have the commitment, perseverance, and passion to mobilise other women in peaceful demonstrations for peace and the cessation of hostilities.[914] Their experience as women provides the platform for dialogue. They bring with them their grief as well as stories of atrocities and loss.[915] Muslim and Christian women in dialogue can voice their views unanimously regarding violent conflicts in the region as members of their faith communities and society.

Furthermore, peace awareness campaigns and peace education rallies are ways women can muster the support of other stakeholders to join in the process of sustainable peace building. Older, experienced women can take on the role of peace envoys by drawing attention to the great potential for reconciliation and peace through

---

[908]   Katherine Marshall, Susan Hayward, Claudia Zambra, Esther Breger, and Sarah Jackson, 'Women in Religious Peacebuilding,' *Peaceworks*, no. 71 (2011), 6. http://www.usip.org

[909]   Cf. Miriam Agatha Nwoye, 'The Role of Women in Peace Building and Conflict Resolution in African Traditional Societies: A Selective Review,' in *Resources for Peace in Traditional Religions: Acts of the Colloquium Rome, 12-15 January 2005 Pro Manusripto* (Vatican City: Pontifical Council for Interreligious Dialogue, 2005), 97.

[910]   Ibid., 99.

[911]   Ibid.

[912]   McGarvey, 'Gender, Peace and Religious Coexistence,' 77.

[913]   Cf. Gerard J. DeGroot, 'A Few Good Women: Gender Stereotypes, the Military and Peacekeeping,' in Loise Olsson and Tornnl Tryggested (eds.), *Women and International Peacekeeping* (London: Frankcass Publishers, 2001), 24.

[914]   Leymah Gbowee, 'Peace Protest in Liberia,' Telephone Interview by Adam Smith (Oslo: 07 October 2011). http://www.nobelprize.org/mediaplayer/index.php?id=1639&view=1

[915]   Krause, 'A Deadly Cycle,' 3.

dialogue.[916] This is possible through advocacy visits to religious leaders, political office holders, and opinion leaders in the locality. Moreover, for generations women have served as agents in the promotion of peace in their families and society, despite not being recognised; yet they have proved instrumental in building bridges and imparting values of peace.[917] They have their fingers on the pulse of the community, playing a significant role in mobilising their communities towards reconciliation and rebuilding relationships when hostilities have ended.

Consequently, sustainable peace in Northern Nigeria requires the full participation of women and men at all stages of the process. It is essential that religious leaders, experts in dialogue and peace building institutions (e.g. the Interfaith Mediation Centre) within the region engage with women's organisations such as the Federation of Muslim Women Organisation of Nigeria (FOMWAN), Christian Women Organisation (CWO), the Dorcas Band, Women Opinion Leaders Forum (WOLF), and Women's Right Advancement and Protection Alternative (WRAPA) empowering them to further peace in the territory. These organisations seek to promote and protect the interests of women by making their peace building contributions felt in society. Accordingly, engaging with these organisations will give women the opportunity to work for peace in society, to build new ties, and offer fresh impetus and a chance for communities to move beyond stereotypes towards a spirit of collaboration, better understanding, friendship, and respect for the other.

5.8 THE ROLE OF NON-GOVERNMENTAL AND FAITH-BASED ORGANISATIONS IN FOSTERING PEACE IN NORTHERN NIGERIA

In this section, I shall consider the role of non-governmental and faith-based organisations in advancing peace in Northern Nigeria. I emphasise networking, advocacy, and collaboration as central to achieving harmony in the region.

Non-governmental and faith-based organisations are independently constituted civil and religious organisations that build, analyse, and promote development in society.[918] Such organisations have played vital intermediary roles in encouraging peace building activities in Africa and the world at large. They have tapped into available local resources for sustainable peace building projects in conflict regions.

NGO/FBOs make a significant contribution to the peace process in Northern Nigeria by strengthening channels of communication between faith communities. They facilitate interfaith communications and discussions to restore trust and social

---

[916] See Nwoye, 'The Role of Women in Peace Building,' 109.

[917] CF. Kofi Annan, 'The Vital Role of Women in Peace Building.' http://www. huntalternatives.org/pages/460_the_vital_role_of_women_in_peace_building.cfm

[918] Francis, 'Peace and Conflict Studies,' 25.

interaction in peace-building seminars and workshops. Learning about religious teachings on peace creates positive results in faith communities, easing out tensions and finding common ground that Christians and Muslims can explore in dialogue.[919] Such communication channels are developed further by visits and contact with opinion and traditional community leaders among young people. Moreover, an effective contribution to conflict prevention requires a credible presence in the region and a sound impartial grasp of the historical, political, and social needs of the different communities.[920] NGO/FBOs encourage the quest for the common values of peace, harmony, and dialogue, while emphasising the need for faith communities to collaborate.

Additionally, NGO/FBOs provide the needed space for fruitful dialogue between faith communities by mediation. Faith communities can articulate their doubts and anxieties, negotiate peace, and build trust by engaging with the other. Furthermore, these organisations foster peace building and the reconciliation process by initiating joint projects, bringing people together from different religious affiliations in a cooperative endeavour, such as youth empowerment peace building training programmes. Such projects have the positive effect of weakening stereotypes, building tolerance, friendship, and mutual dependence and hopefully a future relationship that will address conflicts.

NGOs/FBOs champion the cause of peace by appealing to government agencies to tackle economic, social, and ethnic factors that have remained the source of violent conflicts in the region. In collaboration with religious leaders, they raise awareness by challenging government agencies to create a favourable environment for economic growth, strategic development, and security. The poor security in Northern Nigeria is an area where non-governmental agents can work with government to raise awareness; for instance, initiate a project that focuses on curbing the proliferation of small arms and light weapons in the region. A 'buy-back' programme that seeks to retrieve illegal arms and enhance local power by education and skill acquisition could be put in place.[921] In addition, awareness and training in conflict prevention and management would ensure that individuals and groups with legitimate interests take responsibility for their communities to encourage positive change that results in future peace and security.

To sustain the peace building process in Northern Nigeria, it is imperative that civil society and faith-based organisations network with other peace building

---

[919] Cf. Carter and Smith, 'Religious Peacebuilding,' 298-99.

[920] See Reychler, 'Religion and Conflict.'

[921] See Dorcas Onigbinde, 'Arms Trafficking in West Africa: The Role of Civil Society in Security Sector Reform,' *ACCORD—Conflict Trends* (2008), 47. http://www. humansecuritygateway.com/documents/CONFLICTTRENDS_ArmsTrafficking_ WestAfrica.pdf

institutions, women, and faith groups in the region. These are, for example, the Interfaith Mediation Centre/Christian-Muslim Dialogue Forum (IFMC/CMDF), Nigeria Interreligious Council (NIREC), Institute for Peace and Conflict Resolution (IPCR), and socio-political groups like the Northern Elders Forum (NEF) and Arewa Consultative Forum (ACF). In addition, there are women's organisations such as the Federation of Muslim Women Organisation of Nigeria (FOMWAN), Christian Women Organisation (CWO), and faith groups like the CAN, Jamalat-ul-Nasril Islam (JNI), and the ACMMRN. Continuous collaboration between these groups and persistent engagement with government will help to find solutions to violent conflicts in the region. However, the vast nature of Northern Nigeria challenges these groups to initiate and coordinate community dialogue projects to engage diverse faith communities not in abstract talks about peace but in concrete actions that stimulate peace through mutual support.[922] The recent conference organised in December 2011 by the Arewa Consultative Forum (ACF), to analyse the threat of violent conflicts in the region, is commendable and exemplary.[923] The key to the success of such cooperation and future hope is peace initiatives using information sharing and collaboration and all available resources for sustained political, as well as interreligious, engagement.

CONCLUSION

Due to its complex nature, undertaking the project of interreligious dialogue for peace building in Northern Nigeria seems daunting and bleak. However, there is a glimmer of hope when seen from the perspective and use of available local socio-cultural, political, educational, and religious-theological resources.

Islamic and Christian leaders in the locality have to cooperate with each other and the government in harnessing and efficiently putting to use every opportunity to sustain dialogue engagements. This includes dialogue of day-to-day interaction, tolerance, respect, forgiveness, and reconciliation. Moreover, grassroots dialogue encounter is efficient in advancing positive relations, because it springs from the experience of living as neighbours with the religious other, and such enterprise can challenge each person to recognise the value of the other, and be open to listen to, learn from, and share with the other for mutual enrichment. Peace building can further be enhanced through continuous religious and peace education as a necessary condition for any sustainable peace.

---

[922] Cf. Ajayi Rotimi, 'Carrot: New Violence Solving Mechanism in the North,' *Vanguard* (Nigerian), 06 November 2011. http://www.vanguardngr.com

[923] See Kunle Akogun, 'Restore Peace in the North, Mark Tells ACF,' *This Day* (Nigeria), 18 November 2011. http://www.thisdaylive.com

Moreover, peace building institutions might wish to intensify their efforts at networking in order to create a dialogue prospect between communities. Furthermore, they might wish to engage, for instance, with women (organisations) in an effort to muster all the needed support for unrelenting peace building endeavours.

General Conclusion

In the pages of this book, I have argued that theology, understood as the critical and self/critical reflection on religious faith, is fundamental in addressing interreligious conflicts in contemporary Northern Nigeria. Religion, as a powerful impulse, plays a paradoxical role in the region. It is both part of the problem and central in proffering solutions. The fact that Northern Nigerians subscribe to one religion or another (Christianity, Islam, traditional African religion) is indicative of the significant influence of religion in the socio-political and economic lives of the people and central in creating conflicts.

This study reveals that the conflict situation in Northern Nigeria is a conglomeration of diverse causes that are historical, social, ethnic, economic, political, and religious. These factors characterise a major challenge that is theological, socio-political, and economic, needing urgent attention if peace, security, and harmony in the region are to be secured. The use of religious sentiments in politics impinges on deep-rooted historical, ethnic, and cultural divides, sustained by mutual social, political, and religious exclusion. In addition, religious stereotyping and poor religious and peace education simultaneously fuel disharmony. At the same time, manipulation of religion to enforce questions of identity, ethnicity, and political differences underpins the division between the two faith communities studied here, that is, Islam and Christianity.

Meanwhile, the intensity of violent conflicts in Northern Nigeria calls into question the claims of Islam and Christianity to be religions of peace and harmony, given that in the name of religion, life and property have been destroyed. Nevertheless, a critical study of religion reveals that even though religion can be mobilised in the promotion of violent conflicts, religion is equally central in our understanding and establishment of peace within society. This study impresses the fact that Christian and Islamic scriptures and traditions possess rich valuable resource for peace building.

The theology of the Second Vatican Council (*Nostra Aetate*) is momentous in putting forth a new interreligious understanding by recognising the truth in other religious traditions and offering the possibility of dialogue between religions. This shift is tremendous, ecumenical, inclusive, and significant in fostering deeper intrareligious as well as interfaith dialogue, as a central value for peace and human development. Such a theological model recognises religious otherness as a potential for better self-understanding in building a society where tolerance, freedom, respect, and peace become the principles for living together. Moreover, Islam and Christianity do possess an integrative theological perspective necessary for the advancement of dialogue. It is, therefore, critical and indispensable to examine and strengthen the role of these religions in the promotion of peace.

Chapter 1 examined the contextual religious-political history of interreligious conflict in Northern Nigeria and concludes that the conflict situation in Northern Nigeria is a medley of diverse causes that are historical, social, ethnic, economic, political, and religious, exacerbated by poverty and poor litaracy. At the same time, the dynamics of the spread of Islam and Christianity in Northern Nigeria and the politics of colonial administration in the region prepared the breeding ground for violent interreligious conflicts.

Chapter 2 is a theological analysis of the relationship between Islam and Christianity since the Second Vatican Council and concludes that *Nostra Aetate* marked a significant turning point in the Roman Catholic Church's attitude towards other religious traditions. It provided the first theological model for dialogue engagement between Christianity and other religions in mutual understanding, creating the possibility for new conversation between different religions. It further provoked a shift that fostered new encounter between Islamic and Christian traditions in general and possibilities and difficulties of dialogue between Muslims and Christian in Northern Nigeria in particular.

Chapter 3 focused on the contributions of Islam and Christianity to peace building and concludes that Islamic and Christian traditions have the potential to foster peaceful coexistence since both faith traditions profess to be religions of peace. Religion, as a powerful impulse in human existence, can underwrite conflict and peace in society. Hence, articulating and strengthening the resources for peace within these religions can engender a culture of mutual respect, tolerance, dialogue, and the needed harmony for peace in Northern Nigeria.

Chapter 4 considered dialogue and peace building in contemporary Northern Nigeria and concludes that Christian-Muslim dialogue is critical for sustainable peaceful coexistence in the region. Such interreligious engagement is essential to explore, educate, and strengthen mutual religious understanding as a valuable step for peace. Moreover, interreligious dialogue provides the opportunity to address factors that causes interreligious conflict, and peace building institutions have the challenge of networking with faith communities and government to sustain peace building initiatives.

Chapter 5 examined the complexities of engaging in interreligious dialogue in Northern Nigeria and concludes that undertaking the project of interreligious dialogue engagement in the locality is a daunting task, due to the socio-political, historical, ethnic, religious, educational, and developmental poverty characteristic of the region. Nevertheless, peace building efforts have to be multifaceted and sustained through dialogue encouter. Religious leaders and clerics may wish, therefore, to consider cooperating with each other to engage with government and peace building institutions in the venture of peaceful negotiations.

The study, therefore, proposes that contemporary Christian-Muslim dialogue is indispensable for sustainable peaceful coexistence in Northern Nigeria. Interreligious dialogue has to explore and strengthen mutual religious understanding as an essential step for peace. Hence, grassroots dialogue encounter should be efficient in advancing positive relations when it springs from the experience of living as neighbours with the religious other. Such an engagement requires that each person recognises the values of the other, be open to listen to, learn from, and share with the other for mutual enrichment.

Northern Nigerian Muslims and Christians in mutual dialogue of day-to-day interaction have the opportunity to verbalise their traumatic and painful conflict experiences by telling their story in the hope of reconciliation and peace. Furthermore, in view of the fact that no religion or religious leader can resolve purely political and administrative challenges of law enforcement, justice, and security, peace building in Northern Nigeria has to be multifaceted, modelled on a critical theological hermeneutics of engagement between religion and politics. Christian and Muslim leaders have to engage critically and self-critically with the politics of the region to adequately proffer both theological and political solutions to the persistent conflicts.

The role of education is strategic in this quest for an enduring peace. Thus, an effective peace process demands good and efficient learning (formal or informal) that humanises and challenges the mind to positive thinking and responsibility. Quality religious education of children and young people ought to strive for the proficiency to improve awareness, break down social and religious barriers, and aim at stimulating growth and greater cooperation in society. The task of education begins with the responsibility of parents and, with them, the families and institutions of learning, as well as those responsible for religious, cultural, economic, and social education. It is, however, pertinent that government and religious institutions collaborate earnestly on the course of education to develop a methodical system of religious and peace education aimed at weakening religious stereotypes and to advance better understanding between different faith traditions. Besides, balanced knowledge about religious otherness has the propensity to dispel ignorance and promote tolerance.

It is imperative for religious leaders and clerics, in cooperation with politicians, to champion a peace building process that addresses squarely the causes of conflicts in the region. As the Hausa maxim says, *Ba a chin gari sai da dan garin*, meaning

it is impossible to conquer a city except with the help of the citizen of such a city.
Religious and political leaders in the region have the primary responsibility of
leading Northern Nigeria towards peace, in being proactive in establishing and
promoting mutual relationships which create the social space for building trust
and dialogue for peace. Religious leaders and clerics ought be conscious of their
role as leaders of their faith communities and not mislead their people by preying
on the insecurity induced by a weak state whose predilection with corruption has
created an environment for impunity to thrive. They have to be exemplary, beyond
reproach, always apt for peace and unity, and desist from provocative and misleading
statements, whilst having a firm stand on religious extremism.

Government, politicians, and those at the helm of affairs in Northern Nigeria
must display the values of justice, fairness, and good governance. Peace in the region
necessitates efficient and effective service delivery, social justice, and development,
as well as protection and advancement of people's rights and freedom. Political
leaders have to be open to the promotion of dialogue and listen to and interact with
religious leaders to initiate joint actions for peace in the region.

Accordingly, Islamic and Christian theological hermeneutics has to critically
reflect the praxis of love, even in a situation characterised by suspicion, mistrust, and
violence. Christians and Muslims in Northern Nigeria have to be witness, in dialogue
with each other as neighbours, to their experience of pain and desperation. This is
because peace in Northern Nigeria requires a new ethic, a fresh outlook established
on the virtues of respect, tolerance, and religious freedom. The role of religion in
achieving this vision cannot be underestimated. Religion creates the needed space for
a constructive culture of dialogue which must be strengthened. In the same vein, the
task of religious leaders and clerics as interpreters of scripture and religious tradition
demands scholarship and training. Academic scholarship and proper learning in
theological hermeneutics and principles of dialogue is necessary if religious leaders
are effectively to guide their communities to be open minded, kind, and welcoming
to fellow seekers of the truth in other religions, in order to engender peaceful
coexistence, rather than exclusive attitudes, enmity, and violence. Equally, increasing
efforts towards learning from each other and collaboration for the interest of peace
signifies the willingness of Muslims and Christians to complement each other in the
venture of building a peaceful and harmonious Northern Nigeria.

Finally, Christians and Muslims in Northern Nigeria might be able to overcome
the sad memories of violent conflicts for a purposeful future of openness and
mutual cooperation in dialogue and peaceful negotiations. This study represents one
attempt to contribute to this process. At the same time, it opens up numerous further
questions: what more can be done to build friendship, confidence, and trust between
communities polarised by violent conflicts and challenged by religious extremism?
What are the economic impacts of conflicts in the region? What is the role of religion
in fostering good governance in Northern Nigeria? What are the contributions of
religion to the development of Northern Nigeria? What are the prospects of stories

and narratives and their reconciliation in peace building? How do we develop an educational curriculum for effective religious and peace education? I am convinced that further research in these areas will intensify and advance the cause of dialogue for peace, and the critical and self-critical practice of religion is fundamental in the process.

Bibliography

PUBLISHED SOURCES

Abu-Nimer, Muhammad. 'The Miracle of Transformation through Interfaith Dialogue: Are You a Believer?' David R. Smoke (ed.). *Interfaith Dialogue and Peacebuilding*. Washington, DC: United Institute of Peace, 2007.

'A Communiqué Issued by the Association of Episcopal Conferences of Anglophone West Africa (AECAWA) Inter-Religious Dialogue Commission.' In *Proto Dialogo*. Vaticano: Pontificum Consilum Pro Dialogo Inter Religiones, 2004.

'Address of His Holiness Pope John Paul II.' In *Peace: A Single Goal and a Shared Intention Forum of Religious Representatives (Vatican City, 23 January 2002), Day of Prayer for Peace (Assisi, 24 January 2002)*. Vatican City: Pontifical Council for Interreligious Dialogue, 2002.

Adebayo, Ibrahim R. 'Ethno-Religious Crises and the Challenges of Sustainable Development in Nigeria.' *Journal of Sustainable Development in Africa* 12, no. 4 (2010): 213-25.

Afr, Theriault G.M. (ed.). *Introduction to Islam*. Ibadan, Nigeria: AECAWA/IRDC Publications, 1999.

Afsaruddin, Asma. 'Discerning a Qur'anic Mandate for Mutually Transformational Dialogue.' Catherine Cornille (ed.). *Criteria of Discernment in Interreligious Dialogue*. Eugene, OR: Cascade Books, 2009.

Agwu, Kalu. 'Nigeria.' S. H. Wilson (ed.). *Islam in Africa: Perspectives for Christian-Muslim Relations*. Geneva: World Alliance of Churches, 1995.

Albergo, Giuseppe and Joseph A. Komonchak (eds.). *History of Vatican II: Announcing and Preparing a New Era in Catholicism*. Vol. 1. New York: Orbis Books, 1995.

Allport, Gordon W. *The Nature of Prejudice*. London: Addison-Wesley Publishing, 1981.

Amaladoss, Michael. *Peace on Earth*. Bombay: St. Paul Press, 2003.

Anastasios, Archbishop. *Peace: A Single Goal and a Shared Intention: Forum of Religious Representatives (Vatican City, 23 January 2002), Day of Prayer for Peace (Assisi, 24 January 2002)*. Vatican City: Pontifical Council for Interreligious Dialogue, 2002.

Anderson, Mary B. *Do No Harm How Aid Can Support Peace-or War*. London: Lynne Rienner Publishers, 1999.

An-Na'im, Ahmed Abdulahi. 'Shari'a and Basic Human Rights Concerns.' Charles Kurzman (ed.). *Liberal Islam: A Source Book*. New York: Oxford University Press, 1998.

Aram, His Holiness I. 'Our Common Calling.' Hans, Ucko, Charlotte Venema, and Ariane Hentsch (eds.). *Changing the Present, Dreaming the Future: A Critical Moment in Interreligious Dialogue*. Geneva: World Council of Churches, 2006.

Ariaraja, Wesley. *The Bible and People of Other Faiths*. Geneva: World Council of Churches, 1985.

Asante, Kate Molefi. The History of Africa: The Quest for Eternal Harmony. New York: Routledge, 2007.

Ashafa, Muhammad N., and James M. Wuye. The Pastor and the Imam: Responding to Conflict. Lagos, Nigeria: Ibrash Publications, 1999.

Ashafa, Muhammad N., and James M. Wuye. 'Warriors and Brothers.' David Little (ed.). *Peace Makers in Action Profiles of Religion in Conflict resolution*. New York: Cambridge University Press, 2007.

Aydin, Mahmut. *Modern Western Christian Theological Understanding of Muslims since the Second Vatican Council*. Washington, DC: The Council for Research in Values and Philosophy, 2002.

Ayegboyin, Deji. 'Religious Association and the New Political Dispensation in Nigeria.' *Journal for Studies in Interreligious Dialogue* 15, no. 1 (2005): 101-13.

Ayoub, Mahmoud. 'A Muslim View of Christianity.' Omar A. Irfan (ed.). *Essays on Dialogue*. New York: Orbis Books, 2007.

Baldermann, Ingo. 'The Bible as a Teacher of Peace.' H. Gordon and L. Grob (eds.). *Education for Peace: Testimonies from World Religions*. New York: Orbis Books, 1987.

Bartuli, Andria. 'Christianity and Peacebuilding.' Harod Coward and Gordon S. Smith (eds.). *Religion and Peacebuilding*. Albany: State University of New York Press, 2004.

Barvel, von Tarsicius J. 'Love.' Allan D. Fitzgerald (ed.). *Augustine through the Ages: An Encyclopaedia*. Grand Rapids, MI: William B. Eerdmans Publishing Company, 1999.

Bauschke, Martin. 'Islam: Jesus and Muhammad as Brothers.' Alan Race and Paul M. Hedges (eds.). *Christian Approaches to Other Faiths*. London: SMC Press, 2008.

Bauschke, Martin. 'A Christian View of Islam.' Lloyd Ridgeon and Perry Schmidt-Leukel (eds.). *Islam and Interfaith Relations: The Gerald Weisfeld Lectures 2006*. London: SMC Press, 2006.

Best, Gaya Shadrack. 'Religion and Religious Conflict in Northern Nigeria.' *University of Jos Journal of Political Science* 2, no. 3 (2001): 63-81.

Bianchi, Enzo. 'The Centrality of the Word of God.' Giuseppe Alberigo, Jean-Pierre Jossua, and Joseph A. Komonchak (eds.). *The Reception of Vatican II.* Washington, DC: Catholic University of American Press, 1987.

Borelli, John. 'Christian-Muslim Relations in the United States: Reflections for the Future after Two Decades of Experience.' *Christian-Muslim Relations in the United States* 94, no. 3 (2004): 321-33.

Borrmans, Maurice. *Interreligious Documents 1: Guideline for Dialogue between Christians and Muslims, Pontifical Council for Interreligious Dialogue.* New York: Paulist Press, 1981.

Bourke, Vernon J. 'Introduction.' *Saint Augustine: The City of God.* New York: Image Books, 1958.

Bray, T.M., and R.G. Cooper. 'Education and Nation Building in Nigeria since the Civil War.' *Comparative Education* 15, no. 1 (1979): 33-41.

Brown, Peter. *Augustine of Hippo: A Biography.* London: Faber and Faber, 1967.

Brown, Raymond E., Joseph A. Fitzmyer, Ronald E. Murphy, and O. Carm (eds.). *The Jerome Biblical Commentary the Old Testament.* Vol. 1. London: Geoffrey Chapman Publisher, 1969.

Brown, Rupert. *Prejudice: Its Social Psychology.* Oxford: Blackwell Publishers, 1995.

Browning, W.R.F. 'Religion.' *Oxford Dictionary of the Bible.* New York: Oxford University Press, 1997.

Bulletin of the Pontifical Council for Interreligious Dialogue. Rome Vatican City, 1993.

Burrell, David. 'Dialogue between Muslims and Christians as Mutual Transformative Speech.' Catherine Cornille (ed.). *Criteria of Discernment in Interreligious Dialogue.* Eugene, OR: Cascade Books, 2009.

Burt, Donald X. 'Peace.' Allan D. Fitzgerald (ed.). *Augustine through the Ages: An Encyclopedia.* Grand Rapids, MI: William B. Eerdmans Publishing, 1999.

Burton, John. 'Abrogation.' *Encyclopaedia of the Qur'an.* Vol. 1. Boston: Brill, 2001.

Carter, Judy and Gordon S. Smith. 'Religious Peacebuilding: From Potential to Action.' Harold Coward and Gordon S. Smith (eds.). *Religion and Peacebuilding.* Albany: State University of New York Press, 2004.

Cashmore, Ellis. *Dictionary of Race and Ethnic Relations.* London: Routledge, 1996.

Catechism of the Catholic Church. New York: An Image Book Doubleday, 1995.

Catholic Bishops' Conference of England and Wales, and Scotland. *The Gift of Scripture.* London: The Catholic Truth Society, 2005.

Cavanaugh, William T. *The Myth of religious Violence: Secular Ideology and the Roots of Modern Conflict.* New York: Oxford University Press, 2009.

Chadwick, Henry. *The Early Church: The Story of Emergent Christianity from the Apostolic Age to the Dividing of the Ways between the Greek East and the Latin West.* England: Penguin Books, 1993.

Chavez, Gregorio Rosa D. 'The Role of the Church in the Resolution of Conflict and in Peace Building in Central America.' *Secam-Celam: Peace Fruit of Reconciliation.* Nairobi, Kenya: Paulines Publications Africa, 2001.

Cockburn, Cynthia. 'The Continuum of Violence: A Gender Perspective on War and Peace.' Wenona Giles and Jennifer Hyndman (eds.). *Sites of Violence Gender and Conflict Zones.* Los Angeles: University of California Press, 2004.

Commentary on John 14 New Testament, in *Christian Community Bible Twenty-Seventh Edition.* Diliman, Philippines: Claretian Publications, 1999.

Confessions of St. Augustine. Trans. F.J. Sheed. London and New York: Sheed & Ward, 1960.

Congregation for the Clergy. *General Directory for Catechesis.* Vatican City: Libreria Editrice Vaticana, 1997, pp. 28-32.

Connelly, John. *From Enemy to Brother: The Revolution in Catholic Teaching on the Jews,* 1933-1965. Cambridge, MA: Harvard University Press, 2012.

Consedine, Jim. *Restorative Justice Healing the Effect of Crime.* Lyttelton, New Zealand: Ploughshares Publications, 1995.

Constitution of the Nigeria Interreligious Council. Abuja, Nigeria: NIREC, 2001.

Cornille, Catherine. *The Im-Possibility of Interreligious Dialogue.* New York: Crossroad Publishing, 2008.

Cornille, Catherine. 'Introduction: On Hermeneutics in Dialogue.' Catherine Cornille and Christopher Conway (eds.). *Interreligious Hermeneutics.* Eugene, OR: Cascade Books, 2010.

Creamer, David G. 'Nostra Aetate: Building Bridges of Friendship and Cooperation Over 40 Years.' *Perspective: A Semi-Annual Examination and Application of Catholic and Ignatian Thought* 8, no. 1 (2001): 4-15.

Danjuma, Dewan A. 'Mission and Dialogue Department of the Catholic Secretariat of Nigeria.' Joseph Salihu (ed.). *Interreligious Dialogue and the Sharia Question.* Kano: Jaleyemi Group Publications, 2005.

Da'wah Institute of Nigeria. *The 2008 Prospectus of Da'wah Institute of Nigeria.* Minna, Nigeria: Da'wah Institute of Nigeria, 2008.

'Declaration on the Relationship of the Church to Non-Christian Religions.' Walter M. Abbott (ed.). *The Documents of Vatican II.* Trans. Joseph Gallagher. London: Geoffrey Chapman, 1966.

'Declaration on the Relationship of the Church to Non-Christian Religions Vatican II, Nostra Aetate 28 October 1965.' Austin Flannery (ed.), *Vatican Council II: The Conciliar and Post Conciliar Documents.* New York: Scholarly Resources, 1975.

'Declaration on Religious Freedom.' Walter M. Abbott (ed.). *The Documents of Vatican II.* Trans. Joseph Gallagher. London: Geoffrey Chapman, 1966.

DeGroot, J. Gerard. 'A Few Good Women: Gender Stereotypes, the Military and Peacekeeping,' in Loise Olsson and Tornnl Tryggested (eds.), *Women and International Peacekeeping.* London: Frankcass Publishers, 2001.

Denny, Frederick M. 'Islam and Peace Building.' Harold Coward and Gordon S. Smith (eds.). *Religion and Peacebuilding*. Albany: State University of New York Press, 2004.

Dewey, Joanna. 'Peace.' Paul J. Achtemeier (ed.). *Harpers Bible Dictionary*. San Francisco: Plaper & Row Publishers, 1985.

'Dogmatic Constitution on the Church.' Walter M. Abbott (ed.) *The Documents of Vatican II*. Trans. Joseph Gallagher. London: Geoffrey Chapman, 1966.

'Dogmatic Constitution on Divine Revelation.' Walter M. Abbott (ed.). *The Documents of Vatican II*. Trans. Joseph Gallagher. London: Geoffrey Chapman, 1966.

Doi, Rahman A.I. *Hadith: An Introduction*. Ile-Ife, Nigeria: Kazi Publications, 1980.

Dorff, Elliot N.I. 'This is My God: One Jew's Faith.' John Hick and Edmund S. Meltzer (eds.). *Three Faiths—One God: A Jewish, Christian, Muslim Encounter.* London: Macmillan Press, 1989.

Duplacy, Jean. 'Hope.' Xavier Léon-Dufour (ed.). *Dictionary of Biblical Theology.* London: Geoffrey Chapman, 1973.

Dupuis, Jacques. 'Interreligious Dialogue in the Church's Evangelizing Mission Twenty Years of Evolution of a theological Concept.' Rene Latourelle (ed.). *Vatican II: Assessment and Perspectives: Twenty-Five Years After (1962-1987)*. Vol. 3. New York: Paulist Press, 1989.

D'souza, Diane. 'Creating Spaces: Interreligious Initiatives for Peace.' Harold Coward and Gordon S. Smith (eds.). *Religions and Peacebuilding*. Albany: State University of New York Press, 2004.

Ecumenical Considerations for Dialogue and Relations with People of Other Religions. Geneva: WCC Publications, 2003.

Engineer, Asghar Ali. *On Developing Theology of Peace in Islam*. New Delhi: Stering Publishers, 2003.

Esack, Farid. *Qur'an Liberation and Pluralism: An Islamic Perspective of Interreligious Solidarity against Oppression*. Oxford: Oneworld, 1997.

Esposito, John L. *The Future of Islam*. New York: Oxford University Press, 2010.

Esposito, John L. *What Everyone Needs to Know About Islam*. New York: Oxford University Press, 2011.

Falola, Toyin and Biodun Adediran. *Islam in West Africa*. Ile-Ife, Nigeria: University of Ife Press, 1983.

Fazing, Vincent N. 'Religiosity without Spirituality: The Bane of the Nigerian Society.' *Jos Studies*, vol. 12 (2003): 12-19.

Fisher, E.J. 'The Interreligious Dimension of War and Peace.' H. Gordon and L. Grob (eds.). *Education for Peace: Testimonies from World Religion*. New York: Orbis Books, 1987.

Fitzgerald, Michael L. *A Guide for Teaching African Traditional Religion, Islam, Interreligious Dialogue in Catholic Major Seminaries, Houses of Religious*

Formation and Institutes of Higher Learning in Sub-Saharan Africa. Vatican City: Pontifical Council of Interreligious Dialogue, 2004.

Fitzgerald, Michael L., and John Borelli, *Interfaith Dialogue: A Catholic View.* New York: Orbis Books, 2006.

Fitzmyer, Joseph A. 'The Letter to the Romans.' Raymond E. Brown, Joseph A. Fizmyer, Ronald E. Murphy and O. Carm (eds.). *The Jerome Biblical Commentary.* London: Geoffrey Chapman, 1968.

Flannery, Austin (ed.). 'Pastoral Constitution on the Church in the Modern World.' *Vatican Council II: The Conciliar and Post Conciliar Documents.* New York: Scholarly Resources, 1975.

Flannery, Austin (ed.). 'Church in the Modern World.' *Vatican Council II: The Conciliar and Post Concilia Documents.* New York: Costello Publishing, 1975.

Flannery, Austin (ed.). 'Decree on Ecumenism.' *Vatican Council II: The Conciliar and Post Conciliar Documents.* Leominster Hrefords, England: Fowler Wright Book, 1981.

Francis, Arinze. 'Religions Witnessing to Justice and Peace.' In *Peace: A Single Goal and a Shared Intention Forum of Religious Representatives (Vatican City, 23 January 2002), Day of Prayer for Peace (Assisi, 24 January 2002).* Vatican City: Pontifical Council for Interreligious Dialogue, 2002.

Francis, Arinze. *A Call for Solidarity to the Religions of the World Religions for Peace.* New York: Doubleday, 2002.

Francis, David J. *Uniting Africa: Building Regional Peace and Security Systems.* Aldershot: Ashgate, 2007.

Francis, David J. 'Peace and Conflict Studies: An African Overview of Basic Concepts.' Shedrack G. Best (ed.). *Introduction to Conflict Studies in West Africa.* Ibadan, Nigeria: Spectrum Books, 2005.

Gaiya, Maigamu Philip. *Religion and Justice: The Nigerian Predicament.* Kaduna, Nigeria: Espeep Printing and Advertising, 2004.

Gamut, Vincent. 'Peace Education and Peer Mediation.' Shedrack G. Best (ed.). *Introduction to Peace and Conflict Studies in West Africa.* Ibadan, Nigeria: Spectrum Books, 2005.

Garfinkel, Renee. 'Personal Transformations: Moving from Violence to Peace.' *Special Report.* Washington: United States Institute of Peace, 2007.

Geertz, Cliffortd. *The Interpretations of Cultures: Selected Essays.* New York: Basic Books, 1973.

Glenna, Gerard and Ellinor Linda. *Dialogue: Rediscovering the Transforming Power of Conversation.* Hoboken, NJ: John Wiley & Sons, 1998.

Goncalves, Jaime Pedro D. 'The Role of the Church in Conflict Resolution and Consolidation of Peace and Reconciliation in Africa.' *Secam-Celam: Peace Fruit of Reconciliation.* Nairobi, Kenya: Paulines Publications Africa, 2001.

Graham, Robert A. 'Non-Christians.' Walter M. Abbott (ed.). *The Documents of Vatican II.* Trans. Joseph Gallagher. London: Geoffrey Chapman, 1966.

Griffiths, Ieuan. 'The Scramble for Africa: Inherited Political Boundaries.' *The Geographical Journal* 152, no. 2 (1986): 204-16.

Griswold, Eliza. *The Tenth Parallel Dispatches from the Faultline Between Christianity and Islam.* London: Penguin Books, 2010.

Groth, Bernd. 'From Monologue to Dialogue in Conversations with Nonbelievers or the Difficult Search for Dialogue Partners.' Rene Latourelle (ed.). *Vatican II: Assessment and Perspectives: Twenty-Five Years After (1962-1987).* Vol. 3. New York: Paulist Press, 1989.

Haafkens, Johann. 'The Direction of Christian-Muslim Relations in Sub-Saharan Africa.' Yvonne Yazbeck Haddad and Wadi Zaidan Haddad (eds.). *Christian-Muslim Encounters.* Gainesville: University Press of Florida, 1995.

Harris, Ian M., and Mary Lee Morrison. *Peace Education.* Jefferson, NC: McFarland, 2003.

Hasting, Adrian. *The Church in Africa, 1450-1950.* Oxford: Clarendon Press, 1994.

Hassan, Riaz. *Faithlines: Muslim Concepts of Islam and Society.* New York: Oxford University Press, 2002.

Hauser, Albrecht. 'Let God Be God: Christian and Muslim Understanding of God and Its Challenges in Encounter.' *My Neighbour Is Muslim: A Handbook for Reformed Churches.* Geneva: Centre International Reform John Knox, 1990.

Hick, John and Edmund S. Meltzer (eds.). *Three Faiths—One God: A Jewish, Christian, Muslim Encounter.* London: Macmillan Press, 1989.

Hickey, Raymond. *The Growth of the Catholic Church in Northern Nigeria 1907-2007.* Jos, Nigeria: Augustinian Publications, 2006.

Hock, Klaus. 'Christian-Muslim Relationship in the African Context.' *The International Journal for the Study of Christian Church* 3, no. 2 (2003): 36-57.

Imokhai, C.A. 'Evolution of the Catholic Church in Nigeria.' A.O Makozi and Afolabi G. J. Ojo (eds.). *The History of Catholic Church in Nigeria.* Lagos, Nigeria: Macmillan Nigerian Publishers, 1982.

Irish Catholic Bishops' Conference. 'Towards Healing and Renewal.' *A Pastoral Response from the Irish Catholic Bishops' Conference to Mark the First Anniversary of the Publications of the Pastoral Letter of the Holy Father Pope Benedict XVI to the Catholics in Ireland.* Dublin, Ireland: Veritas Publication, 2011.

Irobi, Godwin E. *Ethnic Conflict Management in Africa: A Comparative Case Study of Nigeria and South Africa.* Boulder, CO: The Beyond Intractability Project, University of Colorado, 2005.

Irving, Thomas B., Ahmed Khurshid, and Ahsan M. Muhammad, *The Qur'an: Basic Teachings.* Leicester: The Islamic Foundation, 1996.

Isichei, Elizabeth. 'The Maitatsine Rising in Nigeria 1980-85: A Revolt of the Disinherited.' *Journal of African Religion* 17, no. 3 (1987): 194-208.

Isizoh, Denis Chidi (ed.). *Milestones in Interreligious Dialogue: A Reading of Selected Catholic Church Documents on Relations with People of Other Religions.* Rome: Ceedee Publications, 2002.

Isizoh, Denis Chidi. 'Introduction.' Micheal L. Fitzgerald (ed.). *A Guide for Teaching African Traditional Religion, Islam, Interreligious Dialogue in Catholic Major Seminaries, Houses of Religious Formation and Institutes of Higher Learning in Sub-Saharan Africa*. Vatican City: Pontifical Council of Interreligious Dialogue, 2004.

Isizoh, Denis Chidi. 'Nigeria: Report of a Visit 10-14 November 2003.' *Pro Dialogo*. Vaticano: Pontificium Consilium Pro Dialogo Inter Religiones, 2004.

Jeanrond, Werner G. *A Theology of Love*. London: T & T Clark International, 2010.

Jeanrond, Werner G. 'Towards an Interreligious Hermeneutics of Love.' Catherine Cornille and Christopher Conway (eds.). *Interreligious Hermeneutics*. Eugene, OR: Cascade Books, 2010.

Jeanrond, Werner G. 'Belonging or Identity? Christian Faith in a Multi-Religious World.' Catherine Cornille (ed.). *Many Mansions? Multiple Religious Belonging and Christian Identity*. New York: Orbis Books, 2002.

Job, B.J. 'Religion.' *New Bible Dictionary*. Vol. 2. Leicester: Inter-Versity Press, 1962.

Johnston, Douglas and Brian Cox. 'Faith-Based Diplomacy and Preventive Engagement.' *Faith Based Diplomacy Trumping Realpolitik*. New York: Oxford University Press, 2003.

Johnson, David and Roger Johnson. 'Essential Components of Peace Education.' *Theory into Practice* 44, no. 4 (2005): 280-92.

Jooji, Innocent A. *Mending the Cracked Pot: Perspective on Conflict Non-Violence, Social Justice and Reconciliation in Nigeria*. Ibadan, Nigeria: Daily Graphics Nigeria, 2003.

Kaigama, Ignatius A. *Peace, Not War: A Decade of Interventions in the Plateau State Crises (2001-2011)*. Jos, Nigeria: Hamatul Press, 2012.

Kaigama, Ignatius A. 'An Address Presented to the Prefect of the Congregation for the Evangelisation of Peoples, by the 2nd Group of the Catholic Bishops' Conference of 'Nigeria on the Occasion of the AD LIMINA VISIT to Rome 24 February 2009.' Michael Ekpenyong (ed.). *The Threshold of the Apostles*. Abuja, Nigeria: Catholic Secretariat of Nigeria, 2009.

Kaigama, Ignatius A. *Dialogue of Life: An Urgent Necessity for Nigerian Muslims and Christians*. Jos, Nigeria: Fab Educational Books, 2006.

Kaigama, Ignatius A. 'Nigeria . . . Religion Is Not the Cause of the Clashes,' *Irish Missionary Union*, no. 2 (2010).

Kalu, Hyacinth. *The Nigerian Nation and Religion*. Bloomington, IN: iUniverse, 2011.

Kastfelt, Niels. 'Rumours of Maitatsine: A Note on Political Culture in Northern Nigeria.' *African Affairs* 8, no. 350 (1989): 83-90.

Keating, Joseph. 'Christianity.' *The Catholic Encyclopaedia*. Vol. 3. New York: The Encyclopedia Press, 1913.

Kelly, Anthony. *Eschatology and Hope*. New York: Orbis Books, 2006.

Kennedy, Arthur. 'The Declaration on the Relationship of the Church to Non-Christian Religions, Nostra Aetate.' Matthew L. Lamb and Matthew Levering (eds.). *Vatican II: Renewal Within Tradition.* New York: Oxford University Press, 2008.

Kenny, Joseph. *West Africa and Islam.* Ibadan, Nigeria: AECAWA Publication, 2000.

Kenny, Joseph. 'Guidelines on Dialogue with People of Living Faiths and Ideologies World Council of Churches, Geneva 1979.' *Views on Christian-Muslim Relations.* Lagos, Nigeria: Dominican Publications, 1999.

Kenny, Joseph. *Views on Christian-Muslim Relations.* Lagos, Nigeria: Dominican Publications, 1999.

Kenny, Joseph. *The Church and Islam in West Africa in the 20th Century: With Particular Reference to Nigeria.* Rome: Istituo per le Scienze Religiose and L'Ecole Francaise, 1998.

Kenny, Joseph. 'Sharia and Islamic Revival in Nigeria.' E. Metuh (ed.). *The Gods in Retreat: Continuity and Change in African Religion.* Enugu, Nigeria: Forth Dimension Publishers, 1986.

Kenny, Joseph. 'Christians and Muslims in Nigeria: A Case of Competitive Sharing.' *Nigerian Dialogue,* no. 4 (1982): 5-8.

Kenny, Joseph. 'Towards Better Understanding of Muslims and Christians.' *Nigerian Journal of Islam* 2, no. 1 (1971): 51-53.

Kenny, Joseph. 'The Challenge of Islam in Nigeria,' *West African Journal of Ecclesial Studies,* no. 4 (1992): 46-58.

Kilani, Abdul Razaq O. 'Islam and Christian-Muslim Relations in Niger-Delta (Nigeria).' *Journal of Muslim Minority Affairs* 20, no. 1 (2000): 131-36.

Kilani, Addul Razaq O. 'Issues and Trends on Religious Tolerance in Nigeria: The Contemporary Scene.' *Journal of Muslim Minority Affairs* 16, no. 2 (1996): 273-78.

Kirk, Ann Martha. *Women of Bible Lands: A Pilgrimage to Compassion and Wisdom.* Collegeville, MN: Liturgical Press, 2004.

Kleissler, Thomas A., Margo A. LeBert, and Mary C. McGuinness. *Small Christian Communities: A Vision of Hope for the 21st Century.* New York: Paulist Press, 1997.

Kristenson, Olle. *Pastor in the Shadow of Violence: Gustavo Gutierrez as a Public Pastoral Theologian in Peru in the 1980s and 1990s.* Uppsala: Uppsala Universitet, 2009.

Kukah, Hassan Matthew. *The Church and the Politics of Social Responsibility,* Lagos, Nigeria: Sovereign Prints, 2007.

Kukah, Hassan Matthew. 'Religious Liberty in a Plural Society: The Nigerian Experience.' *A Theme for Christian-Muslim Dialogue.* Vatican City: The Pontifical Council for Interreligious Dialogue the Commission for Religious Relations with Muslims, 2006.

Kuka, Hassan Matthew. 'The Church's Mission and Dialogue in a Pluralistic Society.' *The Church in Nigeria: Family of God on Mission. ACTA of the First National Pastoral Congress.* Lagos, Nigeria: Catholic Secretariat of Nigeria Publication, 2003.

Kukah, Hassan Matthew. *Religion, Politics and Power in Northern Nigeria.* Kaduna, Nigeria: Spectrum Books, 1993.

Küng, Hans. *Islam: Past, Present and Future.* Oxford: Oneworld, 2007.

Kurtz, Ernest and Katherine Ketcham. *The Spirituality of Imperfection Story Telling and the Journey of Wholeness.* New York: Bantam Books, 1994.

Leclercq, Henri. 'Lateran Councils.' *The Catholic Encyclopaedia.* Vol. 9. New York: Encyclopaedia Press, 1910.

Lederach, John Paul. *The Little Book of Conflict Transformation Clear Articulation of the Guiding Principles by a Pioneer in the Field.* Intercourse, PA: Good Books, 2003.

Little, David (ed.). *Peacemakers in Action Profiles of Religion in Conflict Resolution.* New York: Cambridge University Press, 2007.

Little, David and Scott Appleby. 'A Moment of Opportunity? The Promise of Religious Peacebuilding in an Era of Religious and Ethnic Conflict.' Harold Coward and Gordon S. Smith (eds.). *Religion and Peacebuilding.* Albany: State University of New York Press, 2004.

Loimeier, Roman. 'Boko Haram: The Development of Militant Religious Movement in Nigeria.' *Africa Spectrum* 47, nos. 2-3 (2012): 137-55.

Long, Bruce P. 'Love.' Micea Eliade (ed.). *The Encyclopedia of Religion.* Vol. 9. New York: Simon & Schuster Macmillan, 1986.

'Love of Enemies.' Commentary on Matthew 5: 38-48 New Testament, in *Christian Community Bible Twenty-Seventh Edition.* Diliman, Philippines: Claretian Publications, 1999.

Machado, Felix A. 'Towards Deepening Hindu-Christian Maitri.' *Pro Dialogo.* Vaticano: Pontificum Consilium Pro Dialogo Inter Religiones, 2004.

Machado, Felix A. *Peace: A Single Goal and a Shared Intention Forum of Religious Representatives (Vatican City, 23 January 2002), Day of Prayer for Peace (Assisi, 24 January 2002).* Vatican City: Pontifical Council for Interreligious Dialogue, 2002.

McBrien, Richard P. *Catholicism.* London: Geoffrey Chapman, 1984.

McDade, John. 'Nostra Aetate and Interfaith.' *The Pastoral Review* 1, no. 6 (2005): 8-13.

McDonald, Kevin. 'Christians in a Multi-Faith Society.' *Pro Dialogo.* Vaticano: Pontificum Consilium Pro Dialogo Inter Religiones, 2004.

McGarvey, Kathleen. 'Where Are the Women in Interfaith Dialogue? The Church and Christian-Muslim Relations in Africa: In Service to Reconciliation, Justice and Peace.' *The Catholic Voyage,* no. 8 (2011): 75-95.

McGarvey, Kathleen. 'Gender, Peace and Religious Coexistence: Insight from Nigeria.' *Joras Journal of Religion and Society*, no. 1 (2011): 54-74.

McGarvey, Kathleen. *Muslim and Christian Women in Dialogue the Case of Northern Nigeria*. Lagos, Nigeria: Die Deutsche Bibliothek, 2009.

McKay, Susan. 'Girls as "Weapons of Terror" in Northern Uganda and Sierra Leonean Rebel Fighting Forces.' *Studies in Conflict and Terrorism* 28, no. 5 (2005): 385-97.

McKenzie, John L. 'Peace.' *Dictionary of the Bible*. London: Geoffrey Chapman, 1968.

McManus, Jim. *I Am My Body: Blessed Pope John Paul's Theology of the Body*. Hants: Redemptorist Publications, 2011.

Meeting in Friendship: Messages to Muslims for the End of Ramadan. Vatican City: Pontifical Council for Interreligious Dialogue, 2003.

Meir, Kister J. 'Social and Religious Concepts of Authority in Islam.' *Jerusalem Studies in Arabic and Islam*, no. 18 (1991): 102-06.

Melina, Livio. 'Love: The Encounter with an Event' Livio Melina and Carl A. Anderson (eds.). *The Way of Love Reflections on Pope Benedict XVI's Encyclical Deus Caritas Est*. San Francisco: Ignatius Press, 2006.

Menozzi, Daniele. 'Opposition to the Council (1966-84).' Giuseppe Alberigo, Jean-Pierre Jossua, and Joseph A. Komonchak (eds.). *The Reception of Vatican II*. Washington, DC: Catholic University of America Press, 1987.

Mitri, Tarek. 'Christian-Muslim Relations in the Arab World.' *My Neighbour Is Muslim: A Handbook for Reformed Churches*. Geneva: Centre International Reforme John Knox, 1990.

Mohammed, Abdulkareem. *The Paradox of Boko Haram*. Mohammed Haruna (ed.). Kaduna, Nigeria: Moving Image, 2010.

Muhammad, bin Ghazi. 'On a Common Word between Us and You.' Miroslav Volf, Ghazi bin Muhammad and Melissa Yarrington (eds.). *A Common Word Muslims and Christians on Loving God and Neighbour*. Cambridge, UK: William B. Eerdmans Publishing, 2010.

Nasr, Hossein S. 'Islamic-Christian Dialogue: Problems and Obstacles to be Pondered and Overcome.' *Islam and Christian-Muslim Relations* 11, no. 2 (2000): 213-27.

Ndiokwere, Nathaniel I. *The African Church Today and Tomorrow: Prospects and Challenges*. Vol. 1. Onitsha, Nigeria: Effective Key Publishers, 1994.

Neudecker, Reinhard. 'The Catholic Church and the Jewish People.' Rene Latourelle. (ed.), *Vatican II: Assessment and Perspectives: Twenty-Five Years After (1962-1987)*. Vol. 3. New York: Paulist Press, 1989.

Novak, Martin Ralph. *Christianity and the Roman Empire Background Texts*. Harrisburg, PA: Trinity Press International, 2001.

Nwosu, V.A. 'The Growth of the Catholic Church in Onitsha Ecclesiastical Province.' A.O. Makozi and Afolabi G.J. Ojo (eds.). *The History of Catholic Church in Nigeria*. Lagos, Nigeria: Macmillan Nigeria Publishers, 1982.

Nwoye, Agatha Miriam. 'The Role of Women in Peace Building and Conflict Resolution in African Traditional Societies: A Selective Review.' *Resources for Peace in Traditional Religions Acts of the Colloquium Rome, 12-15 January 2005 Pro Manusripto.* Vatican City: Pontifical Council for Interreligious Dialogue, 2005.

O'Connor, Edward. *From the Niger to the Sahara: The Story of the Archdiocese of Kaduna.* Ibadan, Nigeria: SMA Fathers, 2009.

O'Donnell, Desmond. *God Is Love: A Simplified and Abridged Version of Deus Caritas Est. An Encyclical Letter from Pope Benedict XVI.* Dublin, Ireland: Columba Press, 2005.

Ojo, Matthew A., and Folaranmi T. Lateju. 'Christian-Muslim Conflicts and Interfaith Bridge-Building Efforts in Nigeria.' *The Review of Faith & International Affairs* 1, no. 8 (2010): 31-38.

Ojo, Matthew A. 'Pentecostal Movements, Islam and the Contest for Public Space in Northern Nigeria.' *Islam and Christian-Muslim Relations* 18, no. 2 (2007): 175-88.

Okunlola, John Lola. 'Solidarity Step: Inter-Religious Unity in Nigeria.' *Journal of Stellar Peacemaking* 4, no. 1 (2009).

Omonokhua, Cornelius A. *Welcome to Interreligious Dialogue: A Call to Religious Tolerance and Peaceful Coexistence.* Benin: Hexagon Information Services, 2004.

Onaiyekan, John O. *Thy Kingdom Come Democracy and Politics in Nigeria Today: A Catholic Perspective.* Abuja, Nigeria: Gaudium Et Spes Institute, 2003.

Opeloye, Muhib O. 'The Socio-Political Factor in the Christian-Muslim Conflict in Nigeria.' *Islam and Christian-Muslim Relations* 9, no. 2 (1998): 223-37.

Opeloye, Muhib O. 'Religious Factor in Nigerian Politics: Implications for Christian-Muslim Relations in Nigeria.' *Journal of Muslim Minority affairs* 10, no. 2 (1989): 351-60.

Orji, Nwachukwu. 'Eat and Give to Your Brother: The Politics of Office Distribution in Nigeria.' *In-Spire Journal of Law, Politics and Societies* 3, no. 2 (2008): 125-39.

Orobator, Agbonkhianmeghe E. 'Catholic Social Teaching and Peacemaking in Africa: A Tale of Two Traditions.' Elias O. Opongo (ed.). *Peace Weavers Methodologies of Peace Building in Africa.* Nairobi, Kenya: Paulines Publications Africa, 2008.

Orsutu, Donna. 'On the Front Line: Christifideles Laici and Lay Involvement in Interreligious Dialogue.' Denic C. Izizoh (ed.). *Milestones in Interreligious Dialogue: A Reading of Selected Catholic Church Documents on Relations with People of Other Religions.* Rome: Ceedee Publications, 2002.

Osaghae, Eghosa E., and Rotimi T. Suberu. 'A History of Identities, Violence and Stability in Nigeria.' *CRISE: Centre for Research on Inequality, Human Security and Ethnicity*, no. 6 (2005): 1-27.

Paden, John N. *Faith and Politics in Nigeria: Nigeria as a Pivotal State in the Muslim World.* Washington, DC: United States Institute for Peace Press, 2008.

'Parable of the Good Samaritan,' Jose Maria Casciaro (ed.). *The Navarre Bible: Gospels & Acts: Text and Commentaries, Reader's Edition.* Dublin, Ireland: Scepter Publisher, 1999.

'Pastoral Constitution on the Church in the Modern World.' Walter M. Abbott (ed.). *The Documents of Vatican II.* Trans. Joseph Gallagher. London: Geoffrey Chapman, 1966.

Pelikan, Jaroslav. 'Christianity.' Mircea Eliade (ed.). *The Encyclopaedia of Religion.* Vol. 9. New York: Macmillan Publishing, 2005, p. 348.

Pontifical Council for Justice and Peace. *Compendium of the Social Doctrine of the Church.* Dublin, Ireland: Veritas Publications, 2005.

PROCMURA. 'Church Leaders in Nigeria North Re-Orientate Themselves on Growing Complexity of Christian-Muslim Relations.' *A Quarterly News Letter of the Programme for Christian-Muslim Relations in Africa,* no. 75 and 76 (January-June 2008).

Quattrucci, Alberto. 'Christianity.' *Peace: A Single Goal and a Shared Intention Forum of Religious Representatives (Vatican City, 23 January 2002), Day of Prayer for Peace (Assisi, 24 January 2002).* Vatican City: Pontifical Council for Interreligious Dialogue, 2002.

Ramadan, Tariq. *Western Muslims and the Future of Islam.* New York: Oxford University Press, 2004.

Ratzinger, Joseph Cardinal. *Truth and Tolerance: Christian Belief and World Religions.* San Francisco: Ignatius Press, 2004.

'Relations with Non-Muslims.' *Train the Trainers Course (TTC) in Islam and Dialogue for Peaceful Coexistence Basic Module 101.* Minna, Nigeria: Da'wah Institute of Nigeria, 2010.

'Revelation.' *The Catholic Encyclopaedia.* Vol. 13. New York: Encyclopaedia Press, 1913.

'Revelation.' *Harper's Bible Dictionary.* New York: Harpers & Row Publishers, 1985.

'Revelation.' *New Bible Dictionary.* Wheaton, IL: Tyndale House Publishers, 1982.

'Revenge in the Name of Religion: The Cycle of Violence in Plateau and Kano States.' *Human Rights Watch* 17, no. 8 (May 2005): 1-83.

Ridgeon, Lloyd and Perry Schmidt-Leukel. 'Introduction.' Lioyd Ridgeon and Perry Schmidt-Leukel (eds.). *Islam and Interfaith Relations: The Gerald Weisfeld Lectures 2006.* London: SMC Press, 2006.

Rosenberg, Marshall B. *Speak Peace in a World of Conflict: What You Say Next Will Change Your World.* Encinitas, CA: Puddle Dancer Press, 2005.

Rukyaa, Julian J. 'Muslim-Christian Relations in Tanzania with Particular Focus on the Relationship between Religious Instruction and Prejudice.' *Islam and Christian-Muslim Relations* 18, no. 2 (2007): 189-204.

Rynne, Xavier. *Vatican Council II.* New York: Orbis Books, 1999.

Sachedina, Abdulaziz. *The Islamic Roots of Democratic Pluralism.* New York: Oxford University Press, 2001.

Sacks, Jonathan. *The Dignity of Difference: How to Avoid the Clash of Civilization.* London: Continuum, 2002.

Salih, Sani Mustapha. *Muhammad Rasulullah and the People of the Book: His Benevolence, Kindness, Large-Heartedness and Quest for Peace.* Kaduna, Nigeria: Essam International, 2010.

Salihu, Joseph (ed.). *Interreligious Dialogue and the Sharia Question.* Kano: Jaleyemi Group Publications, 2005.

Salza, John. *The Biblical Basis for the Papacy.* Huntington, WV: Our Sunday Visitor, 2007.

Sammak, Muhammad. in *Peace: A Single Goal and a Shared Intention Forum of Religious Representatives (Vatican City, 23 January 2002), Day of Prayer for Peace (Assisi, 24 January 2002).* Vatican City: Pontifical Council for Interreligious Dialogue, 2002.

Sanneh, Lamin. *West African Christianity: The Religious Impact.* New York: Maryknoll, 1983.

Sartoprak, Zeki. 'How Commentators of the Qur'an Define "Common Word."' John Borelli (ed.). *A Common Word and the Future of Christian-Muslim Relations.* Washington, DC: Prince Alwaleed Bin Talal Centre for Muslim-Christian Understanding, 2009.

Schaff, Philip (ed.). *Nicene and Post-Nicene Father of the Christian Church, St. Augustine's City of God and Christian Doctrine.* Vol. 2. Edinburgh: T & T Clark, 1997.

Schindler, David. 'The Way of Love in the Church's Mission to the World.' Livio Melina and Carl A. Anderson (eds.). *The Way of Love Reflections on Pope Benedict XVI's Encyclical Deus Caritas Est.* San Francisco: Ignatius Press, 2006.

Schineller, Peter (ed.). *The Church Teaches: Stand of the Catholic Bishops of Nigeria on Issues of Faith and Life.* Abuja, Nigeria: Gaudium Et Spes Institute, 2002.

Schineller, Peter (ed.). *Pastoral Letters and Communiqués of the Catholic Bishops' Conference of Nigeria, 1960-2002: The Voice of the Voiceless.* Abuja, Nigeria: Gaudium Et Spes Institute, 2002.

Schirch, Lisa. *Ritual and Symbol in Peacebuilding.* Bloomfield, NJ: Kumarian Press, 2005.

Scott, Appleby R. 'Globalization, Religious Change and the Common Good.' *Journal of Religion, Conflict and Peace* 3, no. 1 (2009).

Scott, Appleby R. *The Ambivalence of the Sacred, Religion, Violence and Reconciliation.* New York: Rowman & Little Field Publishers, 2000.

'Sharing Islam Through Dialogue.' *Train the Trainers Course (TTC) in Islam and Dialogue for Peaceful Coexistence Basic Model 101.* Minna, Nigeria: Da'wah Institute of Nigeria, 2010.

Shihab, Alwi. 'Christian-Muslim Relations into the Twenty-first Century.' *Islam and Christian-Muslim Relations* 15, no. 1 (2004): 65-77.

Siddiqui, Ataulla. *Christian-Muslim Dialogue in the Twentieth Century.* London: Macmillan Press, 1997.

Siddiqui, Mona. *How to Read the Qur'an.* London: Granta Books, 2007.

Singh, Harbans, *Peace: A Single Goal and a Shared Intention Forum of Religious Representatives (Vatican City, 23 January 2002), Day of Prayer for Peace (Assisi, 24 January 2002).* Vatican City: Pontifical Council for Interreligious Dialogue, 2002.

Smock, David R. (ed.). *Religious Contributions to Peacemaking: When Religion Bring Peace, Not War.* Washington: United States Institute for Peace, 2006.

Speight, Marston. 'Christians in the Hadith Literature.' Lloyd Ridgeon (ed.). *Islamic Interpretations of Christianity.* London: Curzon Press, 2001.

'Spiritual Resources of the Religions for Peace 16-18 January 2003.' *Spiritual Resources of the Religions for Peace: Exploring the Sacred Texts in Promotion of Peace.* Vatican City: Pontifical Council for Interreligious Dialogue, 2003.

Svartvik, Jesper. 'Geschwisterlichkeit: Realizing that We are Siblings.' In *Kirche und Synagoge: Ein Lutherisches Votum.* Herausgegeben von Folker Siegert: Vandenhoeck & Ruprecht, 2012.

'Synod of Bishops XII Ordinary General Assembly.' *The Word of God in the Light and Mission of the Church: Lineamenta.* Abuja, Nigeria: Catholic Secretariat of Nigeria, 2007.

Talbi, Muhammad. 'Islam and Dialogue Some Reflections on a Current Topic.' Joseph Kenny (ed.). *Views on Christian-Muslim Relations.* Lagos, Nigeria: Dominican Publications, 1999.

Tanko, Bauna Peter. 'Sharia: Implications for Christians.' Joseph Salihu (ed.). *Interreligious Dialogue and the Sharia Question.* Kano: Jaleyemi Group Publications, 2005.

Tanko, Bauna Peter. *The Christian Association of Nigeria and the Challenge of the Ecumenical Imperative.* Jos, Nigeria: Fab Anieh Nig, 1991.

Teasdale, Wayne. 'Interreligious Dialogue since Vatican II.' *The Monastic Contemplative Dimension Spirituality Today* 43, no. 2 (1991): 119-33.

Thampu, Valson. 'Models of Interreligious Dialogue.' Hans Ucko, Charlotte Venema, and Ariane Hentsch (eds.). *Changing the Present, Dreaming the Future: A Critical Moment in Interreligious Dialogue.* Geneva: World Council of Churches, 2006.

'The Interfaith Encounter.' *Grosvenor Essay.* No. 3. Edinburgh: The Committee for Relations with People of Other Faiths and the Doctrine Committee of the Scottish Episcopal Church, 2006.

The Nigerian Constitution: 1963, 1979, 1999: A Compendium. Lagos, Nigeria: Olakanmi & Co LawLords Publications, 2008.

'The Church and Other Believers,' in Richard Viladesau and Mark Massa (eds.), *World Religions: A Sourcebook for Students of Christian Theology.* New York: Paulist Press, 1994.

Troll, Christian W. 'Catholic Teachings on Interreligious Dialogue. Analysis of Some Recent Official Documents, with Special Reference to Christian-Muslim Relations.' Jacques Waardenburg (ed.). *Muslim-Christian Perceptions of Dialogue Today.* Leuven: Peeters, 2000.

Ucho, Hans, Charlotte Venema, and Ariane Hentsch (eds.). *Changing the Present, Dreaming the Future: A Critical Moment in Interreligious Dialogue.* Geneva: World Council of Churches, 2006.

Ukiwo, Ukoha. 'Politics, Ethno-Religious Conflict and Democratic Consolidation in Nigeria.' *Journal of Modern African Studies* 41, no. 1 (2003): 116-20.

Volf, Miroslav. *Allah: A Christian Response.* New York: HarperOne, 2011.

Volf, Miroslav. 'A Common Word for a Common Future.' Volf Miroslav, Muhammad, bin Ghazi, and Melissa Yarrington (eds.). *A Common Word Muslims and Christians on Loving God and Neighbour.* Cambridge, UK: William B. Eerdmans Publishing, 2010.

Walsh, Michael and Brian Davies (eds.). 'Pacem in Terris,' in *Proclaiming Justice and Peace: Documents from John XXIII to John Paul II.* London: Collins Liturgical Publications, 1984.

Walter, Rodney. *How Europe Underdeveloped Africa.* London: Bogle-L'Ouventure Publications, 1973.

Watt, Montgomery W. *Islam and Christianity Today: A Contribution to Dialogue.* London: Routledge & Kegan Paul, 1983.

Waugh, Earle H. 'Peace.' Jane Dammen McAuliffe (ed.). *Encyclopaedia of the Qur'an.* Vol. 4. Boston: Martinus Nijhoff Publishers, 2004.

White, Andrew. *The Vicar of Baghdad Fighting for Peace in the Middle East.* Oxford: Monarch Books, 2009.

Yaran, Cafer S. *Understanding Islam.* Edinburgh: Dunedin Academic Press, 2007.

Yusuf, Bilkisu Hajiya. 'Managing Muslim-Christian Conflict in Northern Nigeria: A Case Study of Kaduna State.' *Islam and Christian-Muslim Relations* 18, no. 2 (2007): 242-45.

Yusuf, Bilkisu Hajiya. 'Sharia and Non-Muslims Fears and Expectations.' Joseph Salihu (ed.). *Interreligious Dialogue and the Sharia Question.* Kano: Jaleyemi Group Publications, 2005.

Zedalla, Debra. *Female Suicide Bombers.* Honolulu: University of Hawaii Press, 2004.

MAGAZINE ARTICLES

Bennett, Michael. 'Reconciliation.' *Africa—St Patrick's Missions*, July-August 2011, 14-15.

Jeanrond, Werner G. 'What Salvation Do We Await? Aquinas Lecture 2010, Part 1.' *Open House*, June-July 2010, 7.

'Turkey, November 28-1 December 2006, Pope Encourages Turkish Christians to Live in Harmony with Muslims.' In Pope Benedict XVI, The Life and Works of Joseph Ratzinger 'Opening the Doors to Christ', *A Special Publication from the Publishers of The Universe Catholic Weekly* (Washington), 2008, 52-53.

NEWSPAPER ARTICLES

Abbah, Abdallah. 'Towards Lasting Peace in the North.' *Leadership* (Nigeria), 27 December 2011.

Abdulmalik, Ibrahim. 'Re: Almajiri Education.' *The Nation* (Nigeria), 05 April 2010. http://www.thenationonlineng.net (Accessed April 05, 2010).

Abdulsalami, Isa. 'Jos Crisis: Government Gives Shoot-On Sight Order,' *Guardian News* (Nigeria), 30 November 2008. http://www.ngrguardiannews.com/news/ article02//indexn2_html?pdate=301108&ptitle=Jos%20Crisis:%20Govt%20 Gives%20Shoot-on-sight%20Order (Accessed November 30, 2008).

Abdulsalami, Isa and Nkechi Oyendike. 'Jonathan Blames Religious, Ethnic Crises in African Politicians.' *Guardian* (Nigeria), 16 June 2010.

Abubakar, Muhammad. 'Jonathan Bemoans Failure of Education Policies.' *Guardian* (Nigeria), 05 October 2010. http://www.ngrguardiannews.com (Accessed October 05, 2010).

Abuh, Adamu. 'Praying and Working for Peace in Kano.' *Guardian* (Nigeria), 24 June 2010. http://www.guardiannewsngr.com (Accessed June 24, 2010).

Adesina, Sulaimon. 'MUSWEN Scribe Advocates Religious Teaching in Tertiary Institutions.' *Tribune* (Nigeria), 25 June 2010. http://www.tribune.com.ng (Accessed June 25, 2010).

Adinoyi, Seriki. 'ECWA Laments Attacks on its Churches.' *This Day* (Nigeria), 12 June 2010. http://www.thisdaylive.com (Accessed June 21, 2010).

Adinoyi, Seriki. 'Jos: ECWA Calls for Sack of Army Chief.' *This Day* (Nigeria), 19 June 2010. http://www.thisdaylive.com (Accessed June 19, 2010).

Adinoyi, Seriki. 'Plateau Raises Alarm over Fresh Plot to Attack Jos: Speakers Want FG to Intervene in Recurring Crisis.' *This Day* (Nigeria), 14 June 2010. http:// www.thisdaylive.com (Accessed June 14, 2010).

Adinoyi, Seriki. 'NGO Donates Relief Material to Victims.' *This Day* (Nigeria), 17 February 2010. http://www.thisdaylive.com (Accessed February 17, 2010).

Agbambu, Chris. 'Lack of National Security Policy, Nigeria's Major Problem.' *Tribune* (Nigeria), 01 August 2011. http://www.tribune.com.ng (Accessed August 01, 2010).

Agbese, Andre. Lalo Mahmud, and Bashiru Misbahu, 'Many Killed in Jos Violence,' *Daily Trust* (Nigeria), 18 January 2010.

Ahmed, Attahiru. '1.2 Beggars Roaming Zamfara Streets-Gov Yari.' *The Sun* (Nigeria), 05 October 2011. http://www.sunnewsonline.com (Accessed October 05, **2010**).

Aimurie, Isaac, Chizoba Ogbeche, Achor Abimaje, and Palang Gonji. 'Fresh Attacks: 18 Killed in Jos Children, Women Feared Dead.' *Leadership* (Nigeria), 12 January 2011.

Ajani, Oluwakemi. 'Women Need to Take Their Future in Their Hands.' *Guardian* (Nigeria), 15 April 2012. http://www.ngrguardiannews.com (Accessed April 15, 2012).

Akasheh, Khaled. 'Nostra Aetate: 40 Years Later.' *L'Osservatore Romano* (Rome), 28 June 2006. http://www.ewtn.com/library/CHISTORY/chrstnsmslms.htm (Accessed, June 12, 2010).

Akogun, Kunle. 'Restore Peace in the North, Mark Tells ACF.' *This Day* (Nigeria), 18 November 2011. http://www.thisdaylive.com (Accessed November 18, 2011).

Akogun, Kunle and Michael Olugbode. 'Over 136 Dead in Yobe Boko Haram Attacks.' *This Day* (Nigeria), 06 November 2011. http://www.thisdaylive.com (Accessed November 06, 2011).

Alabi, Christiana T. 'Lemu Panel: Community Demands State for Southern Kaduna.' *Daily Trust* (Nigeria), 30 June 2011. http://www.dailytrust.com (Accessed June 30, 2011).

Alli, Yusuf. 'Why Federal Government Must Create Jobs, Expand Economy.' *The Nation* (Nigeria), 26 October 2011. http://www.thenationonlineng.net (Accessed October 26, 2011).

Aminu, Yusuf. 'Relief Comes for Violence Victims,' *The Nation* (Nigeria), 27 August 2011. http://www.thenationonlineng.net (Accessed August 27, 2011).

Aodu, Abdulraheem. 'ACF, CAN Congratulates Muslims on Eid-el-Kabir.' *Daily Trust* (Nigeria), 08 December 2008. http://www.dailytrust.com (Accessed December 08, 2008).

'Archbishop Onaiyekan Visits National Mosque, Seeks Peace, Mutual Respect.' *Leadership* (Nigeria), 19 January 2012. http://www.leadership.ng (Accessed April 30, 2012).

Arinze, Francis. 'Education for Dialogue: A Duty for Christians and Muslims.' *L'Osservatore Romano* (Rome), 20/27 December 2000. http://www.ewtn.com/library/CURIA/PCIDMUSL.HTM (Accessed August 18, 2010).

Aruwan, Samuel. 'Emir Task Religious Leaders on Peaceful Coexistence.' *Leadership* (Nigeria), 08 August 2010. http://www.leadership.ng (Accessed August 08, 2010).

Baba, Hamzat. 'Only Dialogue Can Return Peace to Nigeria.' *Leadership* (Nigeria), 16 July 2011. http://www.leadership.ng (Accessed July 16, 2011).

Bege, Joseph. 'CAN Condemn Attacks.' *The Sun* (Nigeria), 28 July 2009. http://www.sunnewsonline.com (Accessed July 28, 2009).

Bilkisu, Hajiya. 'Agenda for Interfaith Dialogue in Northern Nigeria.' *Daily Trust* (Nigeria), 09 June 2010. http://www.dailytrust.com (Accessed June 09, 2010).

'Boko Haram Scare in Abuja.' *Vanguard* (Nigeria), 02 October 2010. http://www.vanguardngr.com (Accessed October 02, 2010).

'Breaking News: Fresh Post-Election Violence Claims Lives in Northern Nigeria.' *Punch* (Nigeria), 18 April 2011. http://www.punchng.com (Accessed April 18, 2011).

'CAN, Okogie Greet Muslims at Ramadan.' *Vanguard* (Nigeria), 15 August 2010. http://www.vanguardngr.com (Accessed August 15, 2010).

Christians Association of Nigeria. 'Christians' Right Breached.' *Vanguard* (Nigeria), 05 September 2009. http://www.vanguardngr.com (Accessed September 05, 2009).

Dambatta, Salisu N. 'NIREC Calms Religious Frayed Nerves.' *Daily Trust* (Nigeria), 22 June 2008. http://www.dailytrust.com (Accessed June 22, 2008).

Dunn, Ian. 'Faith Leaders in Scotland Pray for Peace.' *Scottish Catholic Observer* (Scotland), 04 November 2011.

Ebije, Ayegba Israel. 'Gwada Easter Mayhem—Muslim, Christian Trade Blame.' *Daily Trust* (Nigeria), 18 April 2009. http://www.dailytrust.com (Accessed June 13, 2010).

Ebije, Noah, Muhammad Garba, Orji Nudubuisi, Shaibu Abullahi, and Emmanuel Adeyemi. 'Kaduna, Katsina, Kogi, Yobe, Niger, Sokoto Boil: VP, Emir of Zauzau, PDP Chieftains' Houses Torched, 20 Feared Killed in Kaduna, Curfew Imposed, Soldiers Take Over Sokoto Streets.' *The Sun* (Nigeria), 19 April 2011. http://www.sunnewsonline.com (Accessed April 19, 2011).

Ebiri, Kelvin. 'Why Conflict Persists in Nigeria, by Kukah, Mbillah.' *Guardian* (Nigeria), 01 October 2010. http://www.ngrguardinnews.com (Accessed October 01, 2010).

Edukugho, Emmanuel. 'Reviving an Ailing Education Sector.' *Vanguard* (Nigeria), 10 November 2010. http://www.vanguardngr.com (Accessed November 10, 2011).

'Empower Inter-Religious Councils on Tolerance—CAN.' *Leadership* (Nigeria), 10 July 2011. http://www.leadership.ng (Accessed July 10, 2011).

'Ex-Minister Decries Religious Politics.' *Punch* (Nigeria), 18 April 2011. http://www.punchng.com (Accessed April 18, 2011).

Eyoboka, Sam. 'Sultan, CAN Leaders Propose Pathway to Lasting Peace in Jos.' *Vanguard* (Nigeria), 07 December 2008. http:www.vanguardngr.com (Accessed December 07, 2008).

'Female Suicide Bomber Kills Somali Sport Chiefs.' *Vanguard* (Nigeria), 04 April 2012. http://www.vanguardngr.com (Accessed April 04, 2012).

Gbadamosi, Saliu. 'Don Laments Muslim's Lackadaisical Attitude to Education.' *Tribune* (Nigeria), 17 September 2010. http://www.tribune.com.ng (Accessed September 17, 2010).

Gbadamosi, Saliu. 'FOMWAN Advocates Equal Opportunity for Muslims.' *Tribune* (Nigeria), 01 May 2010. http://www.tribune.com.ng (Accessed May 01, 2010).

Gyam, Coffie Charlse. 'Sultan Appeals for Calm.' *Guardian* (Nigeria), 30 November 2008. http://www.ngrguardiannews.com (Accessed November 30, 2008).

Haruna, Muhammad. 'People and Politics, Genocide on the Plateau: The Way Out,' *Gamji* (Nigeria), 2010. http://www.gamji.com/haruna/haruna312.htm (Accessed August 5, 2011).

Ibrahim, Muhammad. 'Teachers Training Key to Attainment of Millennium Development Goals.' *New Nigeria* (Nigeria), 26 July 2011. http://www. newnigeriannews.com/national_2.htm (Accessed July 26, 2011).

Idegu, Yusufu A. 'Jos Boils Again, 10 Feared Dead.' *The Nation* (Nigeria), 09 January 2010. http://www.thenationonlineng.net (Accessed 09, 2010).

Idris, Hamza. 'Suicide Bomber Hits Yobe SSS HQ, 4 Killed.' *Daily Trust* (Nigeria), 26 December 2011.

Idris, Hamza. 'Boko Haram Claims Responsibility,' *Daily Trust* (Nigeria), 26 December 2011.

Ihyongo, Fanen. 'Peace Talks as Jukun Celebrate.' *The Nation* (Nigeria), 24 August 2011. http://www.thenationonlineng.net (Accessed August 24, 2011).

Imam, Imam. 'Nigeria: Kaduna's Jerusalem and Mecca.' *This Day* (Nigeria), 10 April 2010. http://www.allafrica.co/stories/201004130074.html (Accessed April 20, 2010).

'International Day for Tolerance.' *Tribune* (Nigeria), 17 November 2010. http:// tribune.com.ng (Accessed November 17, 2010).

Ishola, Michael. 'NIREC Scribe Advocate Interfaith, Inter-communal Dialogue.' *Tribune* (Nigeria), 20 June 2010. http://www.tribune.com.ng (Accessed June 20, 2010).

Iweala, Okonjo. 'Nigeria Needs Critical Infrastructure to Support Job Creation.' *Guardian* (Nigeria), 30 August 2011. http://www.ngrguardiannews.com (Accessed August 30, 2011).

James, Abraham. 'Fresh Violence Erupts in Jos.' *Sunday Mirror* (Nigeria), 09 January 2011. http://www.nationalmirroronline.net/news/3479.html (Accessed January 09, 2011).

Jimoh, Abbas. 'Suicide Bombers Spoil Christmas.' *Daily Trust* (Nigeria), 26 December 2011.

John Paul II, Pope. 'Muslims and Christians Adore the One God.' *L'Osservatore Romano* (Holy See Rome), 05 May 1999. http://www.ewtn.com/library/papaldoc/ jp2muslm.htm (Accessed May 27, 2010).

Jombo, Okechukwu. 'Catholic Bishops Back Call for New Constitution.' *Nigerian Pilot* (Nigerian), 07 March 2012. http://www.nigerianpilot.com (Accessed March 09, 2012).

'Jos Violence: Everyone Lives in Fare of His Neighbour.' *People's Daily* (Nigeria), 17 April 2011. http://www.peoplesdaily-online.com (Accessed April 17, 2011).

Kalu, Uduma. 'Al-Quaeda-Boko Haram Links in Kano since 2009.' *Vanguard* (Nigeria), 24 December 2012. http://www.vanguard.com (Accessed March 03, 2013).

Kenny, Joseph. 'The Bishop and Sultan in Sokoto.' *Guardian* (Nigeria), 23 October 2011. http://www.ngrgurdiannews.com (Accessed October 23, 2011).

Laide, Akinboade. 'Jos Crisis Unfortunate—FG.' *Vanguard* (Nigeria), 29 November 2008. http://www.vanguardngr.com/content/view/22933/42/ (Accessed November 29, 2008).

'Lemu Report on Election Violence.' *Guardian* (Nigeria), 25 October 2011. http://www.ngrguardiannews.com (Accessed October 25, 2011).

Lewis, Tayo. 'Poverty: UN's Timely Warning,' *Tribune* (Nigeria), 28 October 2011. http://www.tribune.com (Accessed October 28, 2011).

Makinde, Femi. 'Kukah Blames Nigeria's Problems on "Accidental" Leadership.' *Punch* (Nigerian), 14 October 2011. http://www.punchng.com (Accessed October 14, 2011).

Mamah, Emeka. 'Makarfi Lists Northern Region's Woes.' *Vanguard* (Nigeria), 01 August 2011. http://www.vangurdngr.com (Accessed August 01, 2011).

Mamah, Emeka and Eyoboka Sam. 'Boko Haram Threatens Jonathan.' *Vanguard* (Nigeria), 13 April 2012. http://www.vanguardngr.com (Accessed April 14, 2012).

Mark, Monica. 'Boko Haram Vows to Fight until Nigeria Establishes Sharia Law.' *Guardian* (United Kingdom), 27 January 2012. http://www.guardian.co.uk/world/2012/jan/27/boko-haram-nigeria-sharia-law (Accessed March 28, 2010).

Mark, Monica. 'Nigerian Islamist Group's Leader Claims to be at War with Christians.' *Guardian* (United Kingdom), 11 January 2012. http://www.guardian.co.uk/world/2012/jan/11/nigeria-Islamists-claims-war-Christians (Accessed March 28, 2012).

McGrath, Micheal. 'Religious Education and Having Faith in Our Schools.' *Scottish Catholic Observer* (Scotland), 19 August 2011.

Menk, Ibrahim Musa. 'Islam Demands Good Neighbourliness.' *Daily Trust* (Nigeria), 18 April 2011. http://www.dailytrust.com (Accessed April 18, 2011).

Muhammad, Bala. 'Still on Boko Haram.' *Daily Trust* (Nigeria), 07 January 2012.

Muhammad, Ibrahim. 'Religious, Traditional Rulers Urge Christians and Muslim Unity.' *Daily Trust* (Nigeria), 19 July 2010. http://www.dailytrust.com (Accessed July 19, 2010).

Muhammad, Sa'ad S. 'The Quest for Peace and Religious Harmony.' *Daily Trust* (Nigeria), 09 June 2010. http://www.dailytrust.com (Accessed June 09, 2010).

Muhmmad, Sa'ad S. 'How to Achieve Peace in Nigeria.' *Vanguard* (Nigeria), 19 November 2007. http://www.nigerianmuse.com (Accessed July 19, 2008).

'Muslim Leaders Condemn Mayhem.' *Daily Trust* (Nigeria), 05 August 2009. http://www.dailytrust.com (Accessed August 05, 2009).

Muyiwa, Adeyemi. 'Kukah Blames Nigeria's Woes on Conscription of Office Holders.' *Guardian* (Nigeria), 12 October 2011. http://www.ngrguardiannews.com (Accessed 12, 2011).

'Nigerian Death Toll from Boko Haram Attacks "Nears 1,000".' *Guardian* (United Kingdom), 24 January 2012. http://www.guardian.co.uk/world/2012/jan/24/boko-haram-killed-nearly-1000 (Accessed March 28, 2012).

Nkwocha, Stanley. 'Sultan Cautions Oritsejafor on Buhari.' *Leadership* (Nigeria), 27 April 2011. http://www.leadershipeditors.com (Accessed April 27, 2011).

Nzeshi, Onwuka. 'Sultan, Onaiyekan Condemn Killings.' *This Day* (Nigeria), 22 January 2010. http://www.thisdayonline.net (Accessed January 22, 2010).

Obateru, Taye and Daniel Idonor. 'Jos Xmas Eve Blast: 32 People Confirmed Dead, 74 Hospitalised.' *Vanguard* (Nigeria), 26 December 2010. http://allafrica.com/stories/201012260001.html (Accessed March 10, 2011).

Obogo, Chinelo. 'Politics, Religion, Deaths and Boko Haram.' *The Sun* (Nigeria), 18 January 2012. http://www.sunnewsonline.com (Accessed 18, 2011).

Okocha, Chuks.'PDP Insist on Zoning Presidency to North,' *This Day,* Nigeria, 03 May 2010. http://www. allafrica.com/stories/201005030062.html (Accessed July 10, 2010).

Oladele, Bisi. 'Why Dialogue with Boko Haram Is Tough, by Kukah.' *The Nation* (Nigeria), 04 October 2011. http://www.thenationonlineng.net (Accessed October 04, 2011).

Oladele, Bisi and Oseheye Okwuofu. '13 Injured in Ibadan Sectarian Clash.' *The Nation* (Nigeria), 23 August 2010. http://www.thenationonlineng.net (Accessed August 23, 2010).

Oladipo, Adelowo. 'Nigeria's Education Sector Needs Revolution.' *Tribune* (Nigeria), 14 September 2011. http://www.tribune.com.ng (Accessed September 14, 2011).

Olaniyi, Muideen. 'Nigerian Muslims Are Not at Loggerheads with Christians—NSCIA.' *This Day* (Nigeria), 04 February 2010. http://www.thisdayonline.com (Accessed February 04, 2010).

Oloja, Martins, Lawal Iyabo, and Musa Njadvara. 'Sultan, Onaiyekan, Sheriff Decry Boko Haram Crisis.' *Guardian* (Nigeria), 13 August 2009. http://www.ngrguardiannews.com (Accessed August 13, 2009).

Oluwalana, Sam. '2011: A Year Marred by Insecurity.' *National Mirror* (Nigeria), 26 December 2011.

Onah, Mathew. 'Taraba: 8 Die, 40 Injured in Wukari Religious Riot.' *This Day* (Nigeria), 14 July 2010. http://www.thisdayonline.com (Accessed July 14, 2014).

Orude, Paul. 'Presidential Poll Riots: 59 Killed, 84 Churches Burnt in Bauchi, Gombe, Kaduna.' *The Sun* (Nigeria), 21 April 2011. http://www.sunnewsonline.com (Accessed April 21, 2011).

Oweh, Innocent. 'Towards Effective Education System.' *Daily Independent* (Nigeria), 10 October 2010. http://www.independentngonline.com (Accessed October 10, 2010).

Owen, Richard. 'Saudi King Extends Hand of Friendship to Catholic Church.' *The Times* (Scotland), 18 March 2008.

Owuamanam, Jude. '20 Killed in Renewed Jos Violence.' *Punch* (Nigeria), 30 August 2011. http://www.punchng.com (Accessed August 30, 2011).

Owuamanam, Jude. 'Relief Materials Pour in for Victims.' *Punch* (Nigeria), 01 February 2010. http://www.punchng.com (Accessed February 01, 2010).

Owuamanam, Jude. 'Jos Crisis: CAN, AC Condemn Action . . . PDP Calls for Caution.' *Punch* (Nigeria), 30 November 2008. http://www.punchng.com (Accessed November 30, 2008.

Oyekanmi, Rotimi L. 'Borno's Education Sector Suffers Neglect.' *Guardian* (Nigeria), 28 October 2010. http://www.ngrguardiannews.com (Accessed October 28, 2010).

Oyendika, Nkechi and Laola Akande. 'African Religious Leaders Meet in Abuja to Work for Peace.' *Guardian* (Nigeria), 15 June 2010. http://www. ngrguardiannews.com (Accessed June 15, 2010).

Peter, Marie-Therese. 'Christian Women Donate to Muslims.' *The Nation* (Nigeria), 07 November 2011. http://www.thenationonlineng.net (Accessed November 07, 2011).

Qudirat, Hakeem-Apanpa. 'Muslim Clerics Condemn Jos Crisis.' *Tribune* (Nigeria), 05 December 2008. http://www.tribune.com.org (Accessed December 05, 2008).

Reilly, Stephen. 'Religious Leaders Promote Pathway to Peace.' *Scottish Catholic Observer* (Scotland), 04 November 2011.

'Religious Violence in Niger State.' *Punch* (Nigeria), 26 April 2009. http://www. punchng.com (Accessed April 26, 2009).

Rotimi, Ajayi. 'Carrot: New Violence Solving Mechanism in the North.' *Vanguard* (Nigerian), 06 November 2011. http://www.vanguardngr.com (Accessed November 06, 2011).

Sabiu, Muhammad and Dipo Laleye. 'Presidential Election Fallout.' *Tribune* (Nigeria), 20 April 2011. http://tribune.com.ng/index.php/front-page-news/20743 (Accessed April 20, 2011).

Shettima, Abba Gana. 'Religious Politics without Religion.' *Daily Trust* (Nigeria), 20 May 2010. http://www.dailytrust.com (Accessed May 20, 2010).

Shiklam, John. 'Kukah Blames Ethnic, Religious Clashes on Military Rule.' *This Day* (Nigeria), 26 June 2011. http://www.thisdayonline.com (Accessed June 26, 2011).

Shobayo, Isaac. 'Renewed Hostility: 20 Killed, 50 Vehicles Burnt in Jos.' *Tribune* (Nigeria), 30 August 2011. http://www.tribune.com (Accessed August 30, 2011).

Shobayo, Isaac and Chris Agbambu. 'Jos Crisis Spreads: 18 Killed in Riyom.' *Tribune* (Nigeria), 12 January 2011. http://www.tribune.com (Accessed January 12, 2011).

Shuaibu, Ibrahim. 'Shema: Don't Use Religion, Ethnicity to Create Disunity.' *This Day* (Nigeria), 13 May 2011. *http://www.thisdayonline.com* (Accessed May 13, 2011).

Smith, David. 'More than 700 Inmates Escape during Attacks on Nigerian Prison.' *Guardian* (United Kingdom), 08 September 2010. http://www.guardian.co.uk/world/2010/sep/08/Muslim-extremists-escape-nigeria-prison (Accessed March 28, 2012).

Smith, David. 'Nigerian "Taliban" Offensive Leaves 150 Dead: Islamic Group Opposed to Western Education, Boko Haram, Launches Attacks Across Four Northern Provinces.' *Guardian* (United Kingdom), 27 July 2009. http://www.guardian.co.uk/world/2009/jul/27/boko-haram-nigeria-attacks (Accessed March 13, 2012).

Solahudeen, Aduljeleel. 'Islam and Child's Right to Education.' *Tribune* (Nigeria), 03 June 2011. http://www.tribune.com.ng (Accessed June 03, 2011).

Soniyi, Tobi. 'Army Absolves Self from Killing of Boko Haram Leader.' *This Day* (Nigeria), 25 October 2011. http://www.thisdaylive.com (Accessed May 25, 2012).

Sultan, Abubakar. 'Islam and Peace Building in West Africa (1) Imperatives of Knowledge, Justice and Anti-Corruption.' *Vanguard* (Nigeria), 10 October 2011. http://www.vanguardngr.com (Accessed October 10, 2011).

Ugwoke, Francis. 'Boko Haram: Islamic Leaders to Vet Clerics.' *This Day* (Nigeria), 08 April 2009. http://www.thisdayonline.com/nview.php?=150620 (Accessed April 08, 2009).

Waheed, Adebayo. 'Religion: An Engine to Propel Society to Greater Heights—Deji.' *Tribune* (Nigeria), 29 October 2010. http://www.tribune.com.ng (Accessed October 29, 2010).

'We Fear That Nigeria Might Become Islamised, Says Primate Okoh of the Anglican Church of Nigeria.' *Sahara Reporters* (Nigeria), 21 August 2011. http://www.saharareporters.com (Accessed August 21, 2011).

'We Care for Both Needy Christina, Muslims Says Sheikh Muhammad.' *People's Daily* (Nigeria), 03 August 2011. http://www.peoplesdaily-online.com (Accessed August 03, 2011).

'Yar'Adua's Appointments Call for Concern, Says CAN Scribe.' *Guardian* (Nigeria), 31 July 2009. http://www.ngrguardiannews.com (Accessed July 31, 2009).

Yesufu, Adenike. 'And Peace for All.' *Vanguard* (Nigeria), 25 July 2010. http://www.vanguardngr.com/2010/07/25and-peace-forall/ (Accessed July 25, 2010).

Yushau, Ibrahim A. 'Sultan to Establish Almajiri Foundation,' *Daily Trust* (Nigeria), 21 February 2011. http://www.dailytrust.com (Accessed February 21, 2011).

Yusuf, Ibrahim A. 'Okogie Preaches Love among Nigerians.' *The Nation* (Nigeria), 26 June 2011. http://www.thenationonline.net (Accessed June 26, 2011).

Yusuf, Bilkisu Hajiya. 'Building an Interfaith Bridge of Peace.' *Leadership* (Nigeria), 05 June 2008. http://www.leadershipeditors.com (Accessed June 05, 2008).

INTERNET SOURCES

Abdullahi, Arazeem A., and L. Saka. 'Ethno-Religious and Political Conflict: Threat to Nigeria Nascent Democracy.' *Journal of Sustainable Development in Africa* 9, no. 3 (2007), 21. http://www.jsd-africa.com (Accessed March 16, 2010).

Abimboye, Demola. 'The Damages Religious Crises Have Done to the North.' *Newswatch Magazine,* 28 October 2009. http://www.newswatchngr.com (Accessed June 07, 2010).

'A Communiqué issued at the end of the seminar on Interreligious dialogue Organised by the Nigeria Conference of Women Religious (NCWR) in Kaduna,' 2008. http://www.sndden.wordpress.com/2008/12/12/interreligious-dialogue-organised-by-the-nigeria-conference-of-women-religious/ (Accessed November 10, 2011).

ACCORD/UNHCR, Nigeria. 'The Final Report of 8th European Country of Origin Seminar, June 28-29 2002, Vienna, 161.' http://www.unhcr.org/refworld/country, ACCORD, NGA,402d06554,0.html (Accessed June 26, 2008).

Adegbite, Lateef Abdul. 'Unity of the Nigerian Ummah: An Imperative for the 21st Century.' http://www.islamicforumng.org/FWI/Chapter%202 (Accessed November 13, 2011).

Akaeze, Anthony. 'From Maitatsine to Boko Haram.' *Newswatch Magazine,* 28 October 2009. http://www.newswatchngr.com (Accessed April 19, 2010).

Alao, Abiodun. 'Islamic Radicalisation and Violence in Nigeria.' 2012. http://www.securityanddevelopment.org/pdf/ESRC%20Nigeria%20Overview.pdf (Accessed February 25, 2013).

Allen, John J. 'Benedict XVI Sets New Papal Record for Mosque Visit.' 2009. http://ncronline.org/news/vatican/benedict-xvi-sets-new-papal-record-mosque-visits (Accessed April 30, 2012).

Aluaigba, Moses T. 'Circumventing or Superimposing Poverty on the African Child? The Almajiri Syndrome in Northern Nigeria.' *Childhood in Africa* 1, no. 1 (2009): 9-24. http://www.afrchild.ohio.edu/CAJ/articles/AluaigbaCAJ2009.pdf (Accssed March 14, 2011).

Annan, Kofi. 'The Vital Role of Women in Peace Building.' http://www.huntalternatives.org/pages/460_the_vital_role_of_women_in_peace_building.cfm (Accessed February 19, 2012).

'Archbishop's Visit to Dawoodi Bohra Mosque and Jain Temple.' 2010. http://www.archbishopofcanterbury.org/articles.php/989/archbishops-visit-to-dawoodi-bohra-mosque-and-jain-temple (Accessed April 30, 2012).

Arinze, Francis. 'Christian-Muslim Relations in the 21st Century, 5 June 1997, A Talk Given at the Centre for Christian-Muslim Understanding in Georgetown University, Washington.' http://www.sedos.org/english/arinze.htm (Accessed August 13, 2010).

Arinze, Francis. *Reflections by Cardinal Francis Arinze on the Day of Prayer at Assisi, 24 January 2002* (Vatican City: Pontifical Council of Interreligious Dialogue, 2002). http://www.vatican.va/roman_curia/pontifical_councils/interelg/documents/rc_pc_interelg_doc_20020116_arinze-assisi_en.html (Accessed August 13, 2010).

Barghouti, Marwan. 'Islam.' http://www.barghouti.com/Islam/meaning.html (Accessed July 22, 2011).

BBC News. 'Child Beggars of Nigeria's Koranic Schools.' 2008. http://www.news.bbc.co.uk/1/hi/world/africa/7796109.stm (Accessed September 24, 2011).

BBC News. 'Abuja Attack: Car Bomb Hits Nigeria UN Building.' 2011. http://www.bbc.co.uk/news/world-africa-14677957 (Accessed March 23, 2012).

BBC News Africa. 'Jos Bombing: Politicians Fuel Nigeria Unrest.' 2010. http://www.bbc.co.uk/news/world-africa-12086630?asid=6cd0fcc1 (Accessed June 25, 2011).

Benedict XVI, Pope. 'Address the Great Challenges that Mark the Post-Modern Age.' *Papal Message on Cultural and Religious Dialogue*, 2008. http://www.zenit.org (Accessed December 15, 2008).

Benedict XVI, Pope. 'Day of Reflection, Dialogue and Prayer for Peace and Justice in the World "Pilgrims of Truth, Pilgrims of Peace".' *Address of His Holiness Benedict XVI at the Meeting for Peace in Assisi* (Rome Vatican City: Libreria Editrice, 2011). http://www.vatican.va/holy_father/benedict_xvi/speeches/2011/october/documents/hf_ben-xvi_spe_20111027_assisi_en.html (Accessed November 12, 2011).

Benedict XVI, Pope. 'Africae Munus.' *Post-Synodal Apostolic Exhortation of His Holiness Pope Benedict XVI to the Bishops, Clergy, Consecrated Persons and the Lay Faithful on the Church in Africa in Service to Reconciliation, Justice and Peace* (Benin Republic: Libreria Editrice Vaticana, 2011), no. 21. http://www.vatican.va/holy_father/benedict_xvi/apost_exhortations/documents/hf_ben-xvi_exh_20111119_africae-munus_en.html (Accessed November 26, 2011).

Boulding, Elise. 'Peace Culture: The Problem of Managing Human Difference.' *Cross Currents* 48, no. 4 (1998). http://www.crosscurrents.org/boulding.htm (Accessed March 26, 2011).

Bouta, Tsejeard Kadayifci-Orellana Ayse S., and Abu-Nimer Muhammad. *Faith-Based Peace-Building: Mapping and Analysis of Christian, Muslim and Multi-Faith Actors* (Hague: Netherlands Institute of International Relations Clingendael, 2005), 36. http://www.salaminstitute.org/FaithBasedActors.pdf (Accessed March 13, 2011).

'Building Interreligious Trust in a Climate of Fear: An Abrahamic Trialogue.' *Special Report*, no. 99 (Washington: United State Institute of Peace, 2003), 8. http://www.usip.org (Accessed June 04, 2010).

CAFOD. 'Faith in Nigeria.' 2010. http://www.cafod.org.uk/about-us/what-we-do/conflict-and-peace/faith-in-africa/faith . . . (Accessed February 02, 2011).

Catholic Arch Diocese of Jos Nigeria. 'Kaigama Opens Interfaith Youth Vocational Centre.' 2011. http://www.archjosnigeria.org/archjosnews.php?id=1 (Accessed June 10, 2012).

'Communiqués (NIREC).' 2010. http://www.nirecng.org (Accessed June 25, 2011).

Connelly, John. 'Converts Who Changed the Church: Jewish-Born Clerics Helped Push Vatican II Reforms.' *The Jewish Daily Forward* (New York), 30 July 2012. http://www.forward.com (Accessed March 05, 2013).

Daniel, Patriarch H.B. 'Peace: A Divine Gift and Human Responsibility.' A Speech Addressing the IEPC Consultation on 'Peace Ethics in Orthodoxy', Bucharest, 30 June 2009. http://www.overcomingviolence.org/en/resources-dov/wcc-resources/documents/presentations-speeches-messages/peace-a-divine-gift-and-human-responsibility.html (Accessed May 20, 2011).

'Dialogue and Proclamation Reflection and Orientations on Interreligious Dialogue and the Proclamation of the Gospel of Jesus Christ (1).' *Pontifical Council for Interreligious Dialogue* (Rome Vatican City: Libreria Eitrice, 1991), no. 42. (Accessed July 23, 2010).

Didymus, Thomas John. 'Boko Haram Linking up with Al-Qaeda, Al-Shabaab Says US Commander.' *Digital Journal* (June 2012). http://www.digitaljournal.com/article/327424 (Accessed March 03, 2013).

'Documents Link Boko Haram to Bin Laden.' 2012. http://www.world.myjoyonline.com/pages/nigeria/201204/85757.php (Accessed March 03, 2013).

Dubois, Heather. 'Religion and Peacebuilding: An Ambivalent yet Vital Relationship.' *Journal for Conflict and Peace* 1, no. 2 (2008). http://www.plowsharesproject.org/journal/php/article.php?issu_list_id=10&article_list_id=32 (Accessed February 23, 2011).

Edevbaro, Daniel. 'Promoting Education within the Context of a Neo-Patrimonial State: The Case of Nigeria.' *The United Nations University World Institute for Development Economies Research*, vol. 123 (1997): 8-9. http://www.wider.unu.edu/publications/working-papers/previous/en_GB/wp-123/_files/82530852629257468/default/WP123.pdf (Accessed July 06, 2010).

Endah, Agustiana T. 'Women and Peace-Building Central Sulawesi and North Maluku.' 2004. http://www.internal-displacement.org/8025708F004CE90B/(httpDocuments)/63E2621B492E7276C12577F8003710EA/$file/Indonesia_-_Thematic_Assessement,_Women_and_Peace-Building.pdf (Accessed March 30, 2012).

Fakayo, Olusegun. 'The Gospel of Materialism—Nigerian Pentecostalism and Hypocrisy.' 2008. http://www.nigeriansinamerica.com (March 18, 2013).

Falayi, Kunle. 'Latin American Drug Cartels Fund Boko Haram, Ansaru-Report.' *Punch* (Nigeria), 09 March 2013. http://www.punch.com (Accessed March 09, 2013).

Fearon-Idowu, Josiah. 'Conflict and Cooperation Between Christians and Muslims in Nigeria.' 16 February 2005, Paper Presented at the Fourth Borderlands Lectures

St. Johns College Durham. http://www.dur.ac.uk/resources/johns/publications/ conflict.pdf (Accessed April 10, 2010).

Fearon-Idowu, Josiah. 'No Peace in Nigeria without Dialogue between the Muslims and the Christians.' *Leadership* (Nigeria), 28 May 2011. http://leadership.ng/ nga/columns/274/2011/05/28/no_peace_nigeria_without_dialogue_between_ muslims_and_christians.html?quicktabs_2=0 (Accessed June 25, 2011).

Fearon-Idowu, Josiah. 'Interfaith Relations and Community Development: How Feasible? What Are the Obstacles? How Do We Surmount Them?' 22-24 January 2009, A Paper Presented at BBA Workshop with FBOs and NGOs from Plateau State, Kaduna, Nigeria. http://www.anglicandiocesekaduna.com (Accessed February 15, 2012).

'Final Declaration of the Participants in the Symposium on Spiritual Resources of the Religions for Peace (Rome, 16-18 January 2003).' *http://www.vatican.va/roman_ curia/pontifical_councils/interelg/documents/rc_pc_interelg_doc_20030211_ religions-peace_en.html* (Accessed February 14, 2010).

Fitzgerald, Michael L. 'Christian Muslim Dialogue: A Survey of Recent Developments.' 2000. http://www.sedos.org/english/fitzgerald.htm (Accessed April 03, 2008).

Gaiya, Musa A.B. 'The Pentecostal Revolution in Nigeria.' *Occasional Paper* (2002), 3. http://www.teol.ku.dk/cas/research/publications/occ._papers/gaiya2002.pdf (Accessed March 19, 2013).

Gbowee, Leymah. 'Peace Protest in Liberia.' Telephone Interview by Adam Smith (Oslo: 07 October 2011). http://www.nobelprize.org/mediaplayer/index. php?id=1639&view=1 (Accessed November 10, 2011).

Helminski, Kabir (ed.). *A Collection of Hadith on Non-Violence, Peace and Mercy* (Turkey: Threshold Publications, 2001). http://www.sufism.org/society/articles/ PeaceHadith.htm (Accessed June 10, 2011).

Herrmann, Stefan. 'Open Mosque Day Welcomes Non-Muslims in Germany.' 2011. http://www.presstv.ir/detail/202584.html (Accessed April 19, 2012).

Hissan, Riffat. 'What Does It Mean to Be a Muslim Today?' *Cross Current* 40, no. 3 (February 1990). http://www.crosscurrents.org/Hassan.htm (Accessed December 12, 2010).

Imam Muhammad, Ashafa N., and James M. Wuye. *The Pastor and the Imam: Responding to Conflict* (Lagos, Nigeria: Ibrash Publications Centre, 1999). http://www.rfiaonline.org/archieve/issues/7-2/534-imam-pastor-make-peace (Accessed June 02, 2010).

Ibrahim, Jibrin. 'Democracy and Minority Rights in Nigeria: Religion, Sharia and the 1999 Constitution.' 2002. http://www.cgirs.ucsc.edu/conferences/carnegie/ papers/ibrahim.pdf (Accssed September 04, 2010).

Interfaith Mediation Centre. 2009. http://www.imcnigeria.org/history.ht (Accessed July 24, 2011).

Interfaith Mediation Centre. 'Committed to Building Peace, Building Interfaith Cooperation and Good Governance.' 2009. http://www.imcnigeria.org/history. htm (Accessed July 24, 2011).

Interfaith Mediation Centre of Muslim-Christian Dialogue Forum (IMC-MCDF). 2007. http://www.changemakers.com/comprtition/entrepreneuring-peace/entries/ interfaith-mediation-cntre-Muslim-Christian-dialogue-f (Accessed July 19, 2011).

International Crisis Group. *Northern Nigeria: Background to Conflict, Africa Report*, no. 168, December 2010, Dakar/Brussels, 4-5. http://www.crisisgroup.org (Accessed June 27, 2011).

Ioannes, Paulus PP. II. *Redemptoris Missio: On the Permanent Validity of the Church's Missionary Mandate* (Vaticana: Libreria Editrice, 1990). http:// www.vatican.va/holy_father/john_paul_ii/encyclicals/documents/hf_jp-ii_ enc_07121990_redemptoris-missio_en.html (Accessed September 08, 2010).

Ioannes, Paulus PP. II. *Centesimus Annus* (Rome Vatican City: Libreria Eitrice, 1991). http://www.vatican.va/holy_father/john_paul_ii/encyclicals/documents/ hf_jp-ii_enc_01051991_centesimus-annus_en.html (Accessed September 08, 2010).

Irobi, Godwin E. 'Ethnic Conflict Management in Africa: A Comparative Case Study of Nigeria and South Africa.' 2005. http://www.beyondintractability.org/ casestudy/irobi-ethnic (Accessed May 17, 2010).

Iwuanyanwu, Rosita. 'Interreligious Dialogue Organised by the Nigerian Conference of Women Religious, December 2008.' http://www.sndden.wordpress.com (Accessed November 10, 2011).

Iya, Abubakar. 'Citation on Sir Ahmadu Bello Sardauna of Sokoto.' 2006. http:// www.arewaonline-ng.com/sardauna/citation.html (Accessed March 25, 2010).

Jackson, Aj. 'African Women in Conflict: More Than Only Helpless Victims.' *The Academic Journal of New York University's Centre for Global Affairs* 5, no. 1 (2010) http://www.perspectivesonglobalissues.com/archives/fall-2010-conflict/ african-women-in-conflict/ (Accessed January 25, 2012).

John Paul II, Pope. 'Dialogue Between Cultures for a Civilization of Love and Peace.' *Message of His Holiness Pope John Paul II for the Celebration of the World Day of Peace, 1 January 2001* (Rome Vatican City: Libreria Editrice, 2001). http:// www.vatican.va/holy_father/john_paul_ii/messages/peace/documents/hf_jp-ii_ mes_20001208_xxxiv-world-day-for-peace_en.html (Accessed November 25, 2010).

John Paul II, Pope. 'Tertio Mellenio Adveniete.' *Apostolic Letter of His Holiness Pope John Paul II to the Bishops, Clergy and Lay Faithful on Preparation for the Jubilee of the Year 2000* (Rome Vatican City: Libreria Editrice, 1994). http:// www.vatican.va/holy_father/john_paul_ii/apost_letters/documents/hf_jp-ii_ apl_10111994_tertio-millennio-adveniente_en.html (Accessed November 25, (2010).

John Paul II, Pope. 'The Family Creates the Peace of the Human Family.' *Message of His Holiness John Paul II for the XXVII World Day of Peace, 1 January 1994* (Rome Vatican City: Libreria Editrice, 1993), no. 1 http://www.vatican.va/holy_father/john_paul_ii/messages/peace/documents/hf_jp-ii_mes_08121993_xxvii-world-day-for-peace_en.html (Accessed November 25, (2010).

John Paul II, Pope. *Congregation for the Doctrine of the Faith Declaration Dominus Iesus on the Unicity and Salvific Universality of Jesus Christ and the Church* (Rome Vatican City: Libreria Editrice, 2000). http://www.vatican.va/roman_curia/congregations/cfaith/documents/rc_con_cfaith_doc_20000806_dominus-iesus_en.html (Accessed September 08, 2010).

John Paul II, Pope. 'Pacem in Terris: A Permanent Commitment.' *Message of His Holiness Pope John Paul II for the Celebration of the World Day of Peace, 1 January 2003* (Rome Vatican City: Libreria Editrice, 2002), no. 9. http://www.vatican.va/holy_father/john_paul_ii/messages/peace/documents/hf_jp-ii_mes_20021217_xxxvi-world-day-for-peace_en.html (Accessed November 25, 2010).

John Paul II, Pope. 'To Reach Peace, Teach Peace.' *Message of His Holiness Pope John Paul II for the Celebration of the Day of Peace, 1 January 1979* (Rome Vatican City: Liberaria Editrice, 1978), no. 2. http://www.vatican.va/holy_father/john_paul_ii/message/peace/documents/hf_jp-ii_mes_19781221_xii-world-day-for-peace_en.html (Accessed November 25, 2010).

John Paul II, Pope. 'Believers United in Building Peace.' *Message of His Holiness Pope John Paul II for the XXV World Day of Prayer for Peace* (Rome Vatican City: Libreria Editrice, 1992). http://www.vatican.va/holy_father/john_paul_ii/messages/peace/documents/hf_jp-ii_mes_08121991_xxv-world-day-for-peace_en.html (Accessed November 25, 2010).

John Paul II, Pope. 'Christifideles Laici.' *Post-Synodal Apostolic Exhortation of His Holiness John Paul II on the Vocation and the Mission of the Lay Faithful in the Church and in the World* (Rome Vatican City: Libreria Editrice, 1998), no. 35. http://www.vatican.va/holy_father/john_paul_ii/apost_exhortations/documents/hf_jp-ii_exh_30121988_christifideles-laici_en.html (Accessed November 25, 2010).

John Paul II, Pope. 'Meeting with the Muslims Leaders Omayyad Great Mosque, Damascus.' *Address of the Holy Father*. http://www.vatican.va/holy_father/john_paul_ii/speeches/2001/documents/hf_jp-ii_spe_20010506_omayyadi_en.html (Accessed April 30, 2012).

Johnston, Douglas. 'The Words of the Johnston Family ICRD Founder's Address to Interfaith Audience, March 2009.' http://www.tparents.org/Library/Unification/Talks/Johnston/Johnston-090300.htm (Accessed June 27, 2010).

Kadayifci-Orellana, Ayse S. 'Among Muslims, Peace Building Takes on Its Own Distinct Forms.' *Harvard Divinity Bulletin* 35, no. 4 (2007). http://www.thecmcg.com (Accessed March 09, 2011).

'Kaduna Communiqué.' 2010. http://www.globalministries.org/news/news/ Kaduna-Communique.pdf (Accessed November 10, 2011).

Kenny, Joseph. 'The Spread of Islam in Nigeria: A Historical Survey.' 22-24 March 2001, A Paper Given at a Conference on Sharia in Nigeria, Enugu, Nigeria. http://www.josephkenny.joyeurs.com/Sist.htm (Accessed March 29, 2010).

Kenny, Joseph. 'Interreligious Dialogue in Nigeria: Personal Reminiscence of 40 years,' in Anthony A. Akinwale (ed.), *All that They Have to Live on. Essays in Honour of Archbishop Onaiyekan and Msgr. John Aniagwu.* Ibadan, Nigeria: Dominican Institute, 2004. http://www.josephkenny.joyeurs.com/onaiyekan.htm (Accessed July 03, 2011).

Kobia, Samuel. 'Overcoming Violence: An Ecumenical Task.' 27 October 2005, A Speech Given at an International Conference on *Violence and Christian Spirituality*, Boston. http://www.gewaltueberwinden.org/de/materialien/ oerk-materialien/dokumente/praesentationen-ansprachen/overcoming-violence-an-ecumenical-christian-task.html (Accessed October 10, 2011).

Komolafe, Jide. 'Politicization of Religion and the Origins of Fundamentalisms in Nigeria.' http://nigeriaworld.com/feature/publication/jide-komolafe/011912.html (Accessed February 19, 2012).

Krause, Jana. 'A Deadly Cycle: Ethno-Religious Conflict in Jos, Plateau State, Nigeria.' *Executive Summary Working Paper* (June 2011),. http://www. genevadeclartions/fileadmin/docs/regional-publications/GD-ES-deadly-cycle-jospdf *(Accessed April 23, 2012).*

Küng, Hans. 'Christianity and World Religions: Dialogue with Islam.' Leonard Swidler (ed.), *Muslims in Dialogue: The Evolution of a Dialogue* (Lewiston, NY: Edwin Mellen Press, 1992), pp. 161-62. http://www.global-dialogue.com/ swdlerbooks/musli.htm (Accessed March 02, 2008).

Landsted, Lea Anne. *Moving Beyond Stereotypes.* A Report about Stereotypes and Mutual Prejudices in Education and Media and the Middle East, May 2006, Copenhagen, 13-15. http://www.detarabiskeinitiativ.dk/dccd/cku.nsf/images/ forside1/$file/alreport.pdf

Lanfry, Jacques P. 'Islamic-Christian Dialogue: Approaches to the Obstacles.' 1992. http://www.interfaithdialog.org/reading-room-main2menu-27/122-Islamic-Christian-dialogue-approaches-to-the-obstacles (Accessed June 03, 2010).

Lefebure, Leo. 'Healing Interreligious Relationships.' 2009. http://www.dicid.org (Accessed September 24, 2011).

Lemu, Aisha. 'Religious Education in Nigeria: A Case Study.' In *Teaching for Tolerance and Freedom of Religion or Belief* (Oslo: The Oslo Coalition on Freedom of Religion or Belief, 2002). http://www.folk.uio.no/leirvik/ OsloCoalition/AishaLemu.htm (Accessed April 11, 2010).

Longhurst, John. 'Muslim Project Invites Christians Towards Peace.' 2009. http:// www.acommonword.com (Accessed June 27, 2010).

Map of Nigeria. 1992. http://www.google.co.uk/search?hl=en&tbo=d&q=nigeria+sta tes&tbm=isch&tbs=simg (Accessed July 10, 2008).

Marshall, Katherine, Susan Hayward, Claudia Zambra, Ester Breger, and Sarah Jackson. 'Women in Religious Peacebuilding.' *Peaceworks*, no. 71 (2011), 6. http://www.usip.org (Accessed February 20, 2012)

Metuh-Ikenga, Emefie. 'Dialogue with African Religions (ATR): The Teaching of the Special Synod on Africa.' (1994). http://www.afrikaworld.net/afrel/metuh.htm (Accessed April 13, 2008).

'Message for the End of Ramadan 'Id al-Fitr 1429H./2008a.d. Christian and Muslims: Together for the Dignity of the Family.' *Pontifical Council for Interreligious Dialogue.* http://www.vatican.va/roman_curia/pontifical_councils/interelg/ documents/rc_pc_interelg_doc_20080919_ramadan2008_en.html (Accessed May 27, 2010).

Mirza, Sayed Kamran. 'An Exegesis of Islamic Peace.' 2002. http://www. faithfreedom.org/Articles/SKM/Islamic_peace.htm (Accessed March 09, 2011).

Mische, Patricia M. 'The Significance of Religions for Social Justice and a Culture of Peace.' *Journal of Religion Conflict and Peace* 1, no. 1 (2007). http://www. plowsharesproject.org/journal/php/article.print.php?issu_list_id=8&article_list_ id=23 (Accessed March 26, 2011).

Mombo, Esther. 'Reflections on Peace in the Decade to Overcome Violence.' *The Ecumenical Review* 63, no. 1 (2011): 71-76. http://onlinelibrary.wiley.com (Accessed May 20, 2011).

Most, William G. 'The Magisteruim or Teaching Authority of the Church.' 1990. http://www.ewtn.com/faith/teachings/chura4.htm (Accessed December 04, 2011).

Nasran, Muhammad M. 'The Concept of an Islamic State.' 2009. http://www.arts. ualberta.ca (Accessed March 10, 2010).

National Youth Council of Ireland. *Stereotyping of Young People Resource Pack.* Dublin, Ireland: The Equality Authority and the National Council of Ireland, 2008. http://www.youth.ie/sites/youth.ie/files/STEREOTYPING%20of%20 Young%20People%20RESOURCE%20PACK.pdf (Accessed September 03, 2010).

New World Encyclopedia. 'Ahmadu Bello.' 2008. http://www.newworldencyclopedia. org/entry/Ahmadu_Bello (Accessed October 10, 2011).

Nigeria. 'Institute for Peace and Conflict Resolution.' 2002. http://www.ipcr.gov.ng/ publi.html (Accessed November 10, 2011).

Nigeria Inter-Religious Council (NIREC). 2009. http://www.nirecng.org/hisoty.html (Accessed November 10, 2011).

'NIREC Quarterly Communiqué November 2008.' http://www.nirecng.org/docs/ NIREC_COMMUNIQUE_AT_KANO_MEETING.pdf (Accessed November 10, 2011).

'NIREC Standing Committees.' 2008. http://www.nirecng.org/docs/NIREC_ STANDING_COMMITTEES.pdf (Accessed November 10, 2011).

'NIREC Quarterly Communiqué May 2009.' http://www.nirecng.org/docs/jos_ communique.pdf (Accessed November 10, 2011).

'NIREC Quarterly Communiqué February 2008.' http://www.nirecng.org/docs/ COMMUNIQUE_OF_NIREC_1st_QUARTER_2008.pdf (Accessed November 10, 2011).

'NIREC Quarterly Communiqué April 2010.' http://www.nirecng.org/docs/Q1-2010-Communique-Bauchi.pdf (Accessed November 10, 2011).

'NIREC Quarterly Communiqué July 2010.' http://www.nirecng.org/docs/Q2-2010-Communique-Owerri.pdf (Accessed November 10, 2011).

'NIREC Quarterly Communiqué October 2010.' http://nirecng.org/docs/ Q32010-Communique.pdf (Accessed November 10, 2011).

'NIREC Quarterly Communiqué January 2011.' http://www.nirecng.org/docs/ IBADAN-COMMUNIQUE-2011.pdf (Accessed November 10, 2011).

Nigeria Inter-Religious Council (NIREC), 'Our Achievements,' 2010. http://www. nirecng.org/achieve.html (Accessed November 15, 2011).

Oche, Ogaba. 'Religion and Politics: Nigeria's Kaduna State Ignited a Powder Keg When It Adopted Sharia Law.' *Conflict Trends* (March 2003): 28-31. http://www. accord.org.za (Accessed April 25, 2010).

Ohize, Jose Emmanuel and Muhammad Jebba Adamu. 'Case Study of Youth Empowerment Scheme of Niger State, Nigeria in Poverty Alleviation.' *AU Journal of Technology* 13, no. 1 (2009): 47-57. http://www.journal.au.edu/ au_techno/2009/jul09/journal131_article07.pdf (Accessed December 02, 2011).

'OIKOUMENE.' *An Introduction to the World Council of Churches* (Geneva: World Council of Churches, 2010). http://www.oikoumene.org/fileadmin/files/ wcc-main/2010pdfs/WCCintro_ENG.pdf (Accessed July 02, 2010).

Okpanachi, Eyene. 'Building Peace in a Divided Society: The Role of Civil Society in Muslim-Christian Relations in Nigeria.' 4-6 June 2008, A Paper Presented at SHUR International Conference on 'Human Rights in Conflict: The Role of Civil Society.' Rome. http://www.shur.luiss.it/files/2009/06/okpanachi.pdf (Accessed April 08, 2010).

Onaiyekan, John. 'Muslims and Christians in Nigeria: The Imperatives of Dialogue.' 2001. http://www.sedosmission.org (Accessed February 11, 2011).

Onigbinde, Dorcas. 'Arms Trafficking in West Africa: The Role of Civil Society in Security Sector Reform.' *ACCORD—Conflict Trends* (2008), 45-48. http://www.humansecuritygateway.com/documents/CONFLICTTRENDS_ ArmsTrafficking_WestAfrica.pdf (Accessed November 13, 2011).

Oriyomi, Rafiu. 'Nigerian Muslims in Focus: United We Stand, Divide We Fall.' 2010. http://www.onislam.net/english/politics/africa/432172.html (Accessed June 28, 2011).

Ostien, Philip. *A Survey of the Muslims of Nigeria's North Central Geo-Political Zone* (London: Nigeria Research Network University of Oxford, 2012). http://www3.qeh.ox.ac.uk/pdf/nrn/Wp1Ostien.pdf (Accessed February 25, 2013).

Owojaiye, Moses B. 'Factors Responsible for Muslim-Christian Unrest in Nigeria: A Socio-Political Analysis.' 2010. http://pentecostalmovement.wordpress.com (Accessed November 10, 2010).

Paulus VI, PP. *Message of His Holiness Pope Paul VI for the Observance of World Day of Peace, 1 January 1968* (Rome Vatican City: Libreria Editrice, 1967). http://www.vatican.va/holy_father/paul_vi/messages/peace/documents/hf_p-vi_mes_19671208_i-world-day-for-peace_en.html (Accessed November 25, 2010).

Peace Building Initiatives. 2007. *http://www.peacebuildinginitiative.org* (Accessed June 13, 2011).

Peace Building Initiative. 'Religion & Peacebuilding: Religion & Peacebuilding Processes.' 2007. http://www.peacebuildinginitiative.org/index.cfm?pageId=1827#_ftn42 (Accessed March 26, 2011).

'Political Sharia? Human Right and Islamic Law in Northern Nigeria.' *Human Right Watch* 16, no. 9 (September 2004), 1-111. *http://www.hrw.org/fr/node/11981/section/4* (Accesse May 11, 2010).

Pontifex, John. 'Nigeria: Bishop Blames Renegade Politicians, Corrupt Police for Attacks on Churches.' 2011. http://www.indcatholicnews.com (Accessed November 08, 2011).

Pontifex, John. 'Muslim Leaders Apologise for 2009 Attacks on Christians.' 2011. http://www.indcatholicnews.com (Accessed August 02, 2011).

Pontifical Council for Interreligious Dialogue. *Sixth Colloquium Joint Declaration of the Pontifical Council for Interreligious Dialogue (Vatican) and the Centre for Interreligious Dialogue of the Islamic Culture and Relations Organisation* (Tehran, Iran), 2008. http://www.vatican.va/roman_curia/pontifical_councils/interelg/documents/rc_pc_interelg_doc_20080430_rome-declaration_en.html (Accessed September 08, 2010).

Pontifical Council for Inter-Religious Dialogue. Dialogue and Proclamation Reflection and Orientation on Interreligious Dialogue and the Proclamation of the Gospel of Jesus Christ (1) (Rome, 1991). http://www.vatican.va/roman_curia/pontifical_councils/interelg/documents/rc_pc_interelg_doc_19051991_dialogue-and-proclamatio_en.html (1991) (Accessed September 08, 2010).

Pontifical Institute for Arabic and Islamic Studies. http://www.en.pisai.it/il-pisai/la-*storia.aspx* (Accessed April 24, 2010).

Ratzinger, Joseph. 'Are Non-Christians Saved?' 2007. http://www.beliefnet.com/Faiths/Chrisitanity/Catholic/2007/01/Are-Non-Christians-Saved.aspx (Accessed July 06, 2010).

Respecting One Another Religious Stereotyping Packet. New York: Office of Interfaith Relations Worldwide Ministries Division a Ministry of the General Assembly Council Presbyterian Church, 2003. http://www.presbyterianmission.

org/media/uploads/interfaithrelations/pdf/stereotyping.pdf (Accessed September 6, 2010).

Reychler, Luc. 'Religion and Conflict.' *The International Journal of Peace Studies* 2, no. 1 (1997). http://www.gmu.edu/programs/icar/ijps/vol2_1/Reyschler.htm (Accessed December 14, 2010).

Sampson, Cynthia. 'Religion and Peacebuilding.' I. William Zartman and J. Lewis Rasmussen (eds.). *Peacemaking in International Conflict: Methods and Techniques.* Washington, DC: United States Institute of Peace Press, 1997. http://www.beyondintractability.org/articlesummary/10513/ (Accessed June 15, 2008).

Shakir, Zaid Imam. 'The Concept of Peace and Justice in Islam.' 2011. http://www.irfi.org/articles2/articles_3051_3100/The%20Concept%20Of%20Peace%20and%20Justice%20in%20Islam.htm (Accessed March 20, 2011).

Siddiqui, Mona. 'The Spirit of Declaration.' *America, the National Catholic Weekly* 193, no. 12 (October 2005). http://www.americamagazine.org/content/article.cfm?article_id=4431 (Accessed July 14, 2010).

Soliman, Hisham. 'The Potential for Peace Building in Islam: Towards an Islamic Concept of Peace.' *Journal of Religion Conflict and Peace* 2, no. 2 (2009). http://www.plowsharesproject.org/journal/php/article.php?issu_list_id=12&article_list_id=39 (Accessed September 20, 2011).

Spencer, Richard. 'Pope Benedict XVI Visits Jordan Mosque in Effort to Heal Vatican's Rift with Islam.' 2009. http://www.telegraph.co.uk/news/worldnews/europe/vaticancityandholysee/5300283/Pope-Benedict-XVI-visits-Jordan-mosque-in-effort-to-heal-Vaticans-rift-with-Islam.html (Accessed April 30, 2012).

Stansky, Thomas. 'The Genesis of Nostra Aetate.' *America, the National Catholic Weekly* 193, no. 12 (October 2005). http://www.americamagazine.org/content/article (Accessed July 14, 2010).

'Summit on Inter-Religious Dialogue and Peaceful Coexistence by the Nigerian Inter-Religious Council (NIREC) Held on 21-25 January 2009 at Minna, Niger State.' http://www.nirecng.org/home/docs/youth_summit_report.pdf (Accessed June 10, 2011).

Swidler, Leonard. 'The Dialogue Decalogue Ground Rules for Interreligious, Interideological Dialogue.' *Journal of Ecumenical Studies* 20, no. 1 (1983). http://www.sacredheart.edu/pages/13027_the_dailogue_decalogue_by_leonard_swidler . . . (Accessed January 25, 2008).

Thavis, John. 'Vatican Official: Relations with Muslims Better, but Problem Remains.' 2009. http://www.catholicnews.com/data/stories.cns/0902850.htm (Accessed June 27, 2010).

'The Kaduna Peace Declaration of Religious Leaders 22 August 2002.' http://www.nifcon.anglicancommunion.org/work/declarations/kaduna.cfm (Accessed November 10, 2011).

'The Nobel Peace Prize 2011.' http://www.nobel_prizes/peace/laureates/2011/ (Accessed November 14, 2011).

The Pew Forum on Religious and Public Life. 'Historical Overview of Pentecostalism in Nigeria.' 2006. http://www.pewforum.org (Accessed March 19, 2013).

Ukpong, Pius Donatus. 'The Presence and Impact of Pentecostalism in Nigeria.' (2006), 7. http://www.glopen.net (Accessed March 18, 2013).

UNESCO. 'Declaration of Principles on Tolerance Proclaimed and Signed by the Member State of UNESCO on 16 November 1995.' *http://www.unesco.org* (Accessed October 10, 2011).

United Nations Universal Declaration on Human Rights, 1998. http://www.un.org (Accessed October 03, 2011).

Vendley, William F. 'The Power of Inter-Religious Cooperation to Transform Conflict.' *Cross Currents* 55, no. 1 (2005). http://www.thefreeelibrary.com (Accessed April 22, 2011).

Walker, Andrew. 'What is Boko Haram?' *Special Report.* Washington, DC: United State Institute of Peace, 2012. http://www.usip.org (Accessed January 03, 2013).

Walker, Ray. 'Jos Violence: Everyone Lives in Fear of His Neighbour.' *BBC News*, 07 April 2011. http://www.bbc.co.uk/news/world-africa-12985289 (Accessed April 23, 2012).

World Council of Churches. 'Guidelines on Dialogue with People of Living Faiths and Ideologies, 1979.' http://www.oikoumene.org/resources/documents/wcc-programmes/interreligious-dialogue-and-cooperation/interreligious-trust-and-respect/guidelines-on-dialogue-with-people-of-living-faiths-and-ideologies.html (Accessed April 23, 2010).

World Council of Churches. 'Overcoming Violence Churches Reconciliation and Peace: WCC Living Letters Team Calls on Religions to Work for Peace in Nigeria.' 2010. http://www.overcomingviolence.org/en/news-and-events/news/dov-news-english/article/7839/wcc-living-letters-team-c.html (Accessed July 23, 2010).

World Council of Churches. 'Christian Discipleship in a Broken World.' 11-16 May 2008, A Statement on Peace Building by Participants of the Seminar, "Religion: Instruments of Peace or Causes of Conflict?", Bossey. http://www.overcomingviolence.org/fileadmin/dov/files/iepc/expert_consultations/statement.pdf (Accessed July 04, 2011).

Wuye, James and Muhammad Ashafa. 'The Pastor and the Imam: The Muslim-Christian Dialogue Forum in Nigeria.' *People Building Peace II.* Hague, the Netherlands: European Centre for Conflict Prevention, 2009. http://www.peoplebuildingpeace.org (Accessed May 17, 2011).

'Yelwa-Shendam Peace Affirmation 19 February 2005.' http://www.online.usip.org/interfaith/3_3_2.php (Accessed November 10, 2011).

Yonah, Alexander. *Terrorism in North Africa & the Sahel in 2012: Global Reach & Implications.* Arlington, TX: International Centre for Terrorism Studies, 2013.

http://www.potomacinstitute.org/attachments/article/1358/Terrorism%20in%20 North%20Africa%20&%20the%20Sahel.pdf (Accessed March 09, 2013).

Yonnoulatos, Anastasios. 'Problems and Prospects of Inter-Religious Dialogue.' *The Ecumenical Review* 52, no. 3 (July 2000). http://www.findarticles/p/articles/ mi_m2065/is_3_52/ai_66279075 (Accessed June 20, 2010).

Yucel, Imam Salih. 'Qur'an and Tolerance.' *Islamic Movement for Non-Violence,* 2007. http://www.Islamnon-violence.org/en/Qur'an-and-tolerance/ (Accessed March 20, 2011).

INTERVIEW

Wuye, James M. Interview by author, Kaduna, Nigeria, 15 January 2011.
Film/Documentary:
The Imam and the Pastor: A Documentary Film from the Heart of Nigeria, produced and directed. Alan Channer, 60 minutes, FLT films, 2006, DVD.
Paper Presentation:
Conroy, James C., and Robert A. Davis. 'Citizenship, Education and the Claims of Religious Literacy.' Paper Presented at a Colloquium on Religion and Public Life, 8 March 2010, Theology and Religious Studies Department, University of Glasgow.

UNPUBLISHED DISSERTATIONS

Ngabirano, Maximiano. 'Conflict and Peace Building: Theological and Ethical Foundations for a Political Reconstruction of the Great Lakes Region in Africa.' (Ph.D. Dissertation, Katholieke Universiteit; Leuven, 2003).

Umaru, Thaddeus B. 'Interreligious Dialogue as a Way of Building Peaceful Co-Existence between Christians and Muslims: Northern Nigeria Case Study.' (M.A. Dissertation, University of Bradford, 2008).

Documentation 1

THE KADUNA PEACE DECLARATION OF RELIGIOUS LEADERS, 22ND AUGUST 2002[924]

In the name of God, who is Almighty, Merciful and Compassionate, we who have gathered as Muslim and Christian religious leaders from Kaduna State pray for peace in our state and declare our commitment to ending the violence and bloodshed, which has marred our recent history.

According to our faiths, killing innocent lives in the names of God is a desecration of His Holy Name, and defames religions in the World. The violence that has occurred in Kaduna State is an evil that must be opposed by all people of good faith. We seek to live together as neighbours, respecting the integrity of each other's historical and religious heritage. We call upon all to oppose incitement, hatred, and the misrepresentation of one another.

- Muslim and Christians of all tribes must respect the divinely ordained purposes of the Creator by whose grace we live together in Kaduna State; such ordained purposes include freedom of worship, access to and sanctity of places of worship and justice among others.
- As religious leaders, we seek to work with all sections of the community for a lasting and just peace according to the teachings of our religions.
- We condemn all forms of violence and seek to create an atmosphere where present and future generations will coexist with mutual respect and trust in one another. We call upon all to refrain from incitement and demonization, and pledge to educate our young people accordingly.

---

[924] 'The Kaduna Peace Declaration of Religious Leaders 22 August 2002.' http://www.nifcon. anglicancommunion.org/work/declarations/kaduna.cfm

- Through the creation of a peaceful state we seek to explore how together we can aid spiritual regeneration, economic development and inward investment.
- We acknowledge the efforts that have been made within this State for a judicial reform and pledge to do all in our power to promote greater understanding of the reform, so that it can provide a true and respected justice in each of our communities.
- We pledge to work with the security forces in peace keeping and implementation of this Declaration in the State:
- We announce the establishment of a permanent joint committee to implement the recommendations of this declaration and encourage dialogue between the two faiths for we believe that dialogue will result in the restoration of the image of each in the eyes of the other.

This declaration is binding on all people in the State from this day of 22nd August 2002 and agrees that any individual or group found breaching the peace must be punished in accordance to the due process of the law.

Documentation 2

YELWA-SHENDAM PEACE AFFIRMATION, FEBRUARY 2005[925]

In the name of God, the Almighty, Merciful and Compassionate, we the representatives of the Muslims and Christians of various ethnic nationalities in Shendam local government area of Plateau State who have gathered here pray for true peace in our community and declare our commitment to ending the violence and bloodshed that deny the right to life and dignity.

LEADERSHIP: We the representatives of this community hereby acknowledge the paramountcy and rulership of His Royal Highness the Long Goemai of Shendam. We condemn the use of derogatory names to the paramount ruler by anybody within the community. We hereby resolve that His Royal Highness the Long Goemai of Shendam be addressed by his title and be acknowledged and respected as such. We acknowledge that lack of central leadership in Yelwa had contributed to the disharmony in Yelwa community. We resolve that the issue of chieftaincy of Yelwa be referred to Shendam traditional council for urgent steps to be taken, without prejudice to the accepted and approved method of the government.

- **RELIGION:** We hereby affirm our belief and faith in the sanctity of all religious places of worship, whether it is a Mosque, a Church or a Shrine. We condemn in strong terms the desecration of all places of worship, killings in the name of God, and call on all to refrain from incitement and exhibition of religious sentiments and or the instigation of such sentiments for selfish ends. We resolve to create an atmosphere where present and

---

[925] 'Yelwa-Shendam Peace Affirmation 19 February 2005.' http://www.online.usip.org/interfaith/3_3_2.php

future generations will coexist with mutual respect and trust in one another. We pledge to educate our young ones to embrace the culture of respect for these values.

- **ETHNICITY:** We acknowledge our ethnic and tribal diversity. We condemn in strong terms their negative application in our day-to-day life. We resolve that our ethnic and tribal diversity should be a source of our unity, strength and also a source of our economic and social development.

- **PROVOCATION:** We acknowledge the existence of the use of derogatory names towards each other in the past. We condemn in strong terms the use of derogatory names toeachother. We resolve to collectively respect and trust each other, and call upon all to refrain from this. We resolve to collectively respect and trust each other, and call upon all to refrain from the use of such derogatory names like 'Arna', 'Falak Muut', 'Jaap nhaat Yelwa', 'Gampang', etc. as perceived to be derogatory by groups concerned or affected.We resolve to refrain from the use of the media to cast aspersions and give incorrect and misleading information about our community. We call on the media to always cross check and balance information they publish in relation to our community.

- **INTIMIDATION:** We acknowledge and condemn the unruly behavior of our youth due to high rate of illiteracy, unemployment and exploitation of the youth as thugs and hangers on by politicians. We call upon all stakeholders, i.e. religious, community and political leaders, to put hands on deck to reverse this trend.We also resolve that the use of parallel markets in Yelwa-Nshar and the conversion of houses into market square in Yamini be referred to the local government council.

- **INJUSTICE:** We acknowledge and condemn the conversion of residence and places of worship into markets and other uses. Having so observed we are appealing to the parties concerned to in the name of God vacate those places for their rightful owners.

- **INTERNALLY DISPLACED PERSONS (IDPs)/MISSING PERSONS:** We note with concern that some of our brothers and sisters are still at large having been displaced. We therefore appeal to the authorities to take adequate steps to ensure their return and necessary rehabilitation. We also resolve that a joint search committee be constituted between the local government council, the Shendam traditional council and the law enforcement agents for the search of the missing members of the community.

- **GOVERNMENT ROLE ON EVEN DEVELOPMENT:** In view of the prevailing circumstances existing in our community, i.e. the non-functioning government structures and organizations like NITEL, Ministry of Agriculture (M.O.A.), Plateau Agricultural Development Project (P.A.D.P.),

Water Board, Electricity, Schools and Primary Health Care (P.H.C.), we passionately call on the government to resuscitate these institutions as they were prior to the crises in the community.

- **CONCLUSION:** We resolve to work collectively with the security agencies to maintain law and order in our communities.

Documentation 3

Muslim-Christian Jos Joint Communiqué, 2002[926]

At the conclusion of the five-day interfaith workshop, the participants issued the following joint communiqué: We identified causes of Nigeria's religious conflicts as: lack of tolerance and respect for each other's faith and practices, ignorance, failure to forgive, lack of understanding, lack of dialogue, rumour mongering, godlessness, lack of patience and restraint.

- Resolve that in handling conflicts, both Christian and Muslims need to pray for one another, exercise patience and restraint, respect each other's faiths and holy books, be willing to forgive and pursue peace, be honest and sincere and transparent with each other.
- Recommend that a central interfaith body be established with branches in states, local government areas (LGAs) and wards to monitor and evaluate interfaith dialogue in Nigeria.
- Resolve to see and love each other, unconditionally as brothers and sisters, showing goodwill at all times.
- Resolve to educate and enlighten our respective adherents, especially at the grassroots, about the true tenets of the other's faith.
- Recommend that Muslims and Christians freely continue to preach and propagate their respective religions as enshrined in the Nigerian constitution.
- Recommend that we shun religious bigotry in politics.
- Resolve to cultivate a culture of nonaggression at all times.

---

[926]   Smock, *Religious Contributions to Peacemaking*, 23-24.

- Resolve to promote equity, fairness and justice even at the expense of our respective communities.
- Call on the media to avoid biased and inciting journalism and to be objective and truthful in their reporting particularly as it relates to matters of religion.
- Recommend that an interfaith media monitoring unit be established.
- Recommend that guidelines for interfaith dialogue be published and circulated.
- Resolve to avoid using aggressive and abusive language [as well as] avoid finding fault and being confrontational.
- Enforce basic human rights and redress of wrongs through compensation.
- Resolve to ensure a peaceful and successful civilian-to-civilian transition come April 2003, for the survival of our nascent democracy in Nigeria.
- Muslim and Christian youth resolved to cooperate with the government to checkmate and expose perpetrators of violence in the name of our faiths for punishment according to the due process of law.
- Express concern about the failure of security services to make prompt and decisive responses to early warning signals of violent religious eruptions.

Documentation 4 (a)

QUARTERLY MEETING OF THE NIGERIA INTERRELIGIOUS COUNCIL (NIREC), HELD AT MURTALA MUHAMMED LIBRARY KANO CITY, KANO STATE NOVEMBER 13TH 2008[927]

The Nigeria Inter Religious Council (NIREC) under the Co-Chairmanship of the Sultan of Sokoto, who is also the President-General of the Nigerian Supreme Council for Islamic Affairs (NSCIA) His Eminence, Alhaji Muhammadu Sa'ad Abubakar CFR; and the President of Christian Association of Nigeria (CAN), His Grace Archbishop John Onaiyekan, (CON) held its Quarterly General meeting at the Murtala Mohammed Library Complex, from November 10-13th 2008.The meeting was attended by the principal officers and members of NIREC from all the states of the Federation including the Federal Capital Territory, Abuja.

The formal opening ceremony of the meeting was attended by His Excellency, the Governor of Kano State, Malam Ibrahim Shekarau who declared the meeting open. Other dignitaries included the Deputy Governor of Kaduna State Mr. Patrick Yakowa; representatives of the Governors of Sokoto and Zamfara states, Emirs, Traditional/Religious Leaders and Elder Statesmen from the North West Zone. Resource persons also made presentations on peaceful co existence and religious harmony and an interactive session also took place.

The Council:

Expressed its immense gratitude and appreciation to His Excellency, the Governors of Kano, Kaduna, Sokoto and Zamfara States, Government and people of

---

[927] 'NIREC Quarterly Communiqué November 2008.' http://www.nirecng.org/docs/NIREC_COMMUNIQUE_AT_KANO_MEETING.pdf

Kano State for the support and hospitality extended to the members. Sympathise with the Governor, the Emir and the people of Kano State on the recent unfortunate fire incident at Abubakar Rimi Market Kano Congratulate Emir on 45 years on the throne and wish him long life and good health

The Nigeria Inter Religious Council (NIREC) observed that:

Peace and security are prerequisite for development of the country. Kano is a cosmopolitan centre with a history of welcoming various groups, respect and accommodation of diversity Peace is a process of ensuring and sustaining justice, fairness and equity in the society.

The two major religions in the country, Islam and Christianity, preach the message of peace and respect for other religions. Sources of conflicts are multi-dimensional and mostly socio-economic and political in nature.

The elites are often involved in inciting people and fomenting social unrest to promote political or personal agenda feelings of marginalisation, disregard for the rule of law, poverty, injustice and inequity fuel conflicts. Corruption in the country is being manifested in pervasive poverty, denial of basic amenities, insecurity and collapse of infrastructure. The media have through sensationalism, inaccurate reporting and fraudulent manipulation of facts fuelled religious and other community crises

The Council resolved to:

- Call on Governments at various levels to grant compensation to victims of religious disturbances to enable them mitigate the effects of human and material losses caused by unwholesome activities of a few misguided elements.
- Caution reckless religious preachers who conduct inciting sermons without regard to the feelings of others and therefore fan the embers of religious misunderstanding and disturbances.
- Urge adherents of the two religions to adopt dialogue as an effective means of promoting understanding and peaceful co existence among the people
- Affirm our commitment to the pursuance of practical actions towards the resolutions of conflicts arising from interactions of peoples in a multi ethnic and multi religious society so that the impact of the Council would be felt by all.
- Call on Governments, groups and all Nigerians, particularly the Faith-based Organisations to build a systematic platform for peace and religious harmony in Nigeria through the promotion of socioeconomic justice, transparency and good governance.
- Call on the media to abide by the ethics of their profession which promotes social responsibility and demands factual and accurate reporting of events

- Urge Nigerians living in various parts of the country to be sensitive to the culture and religion of the people of the host community as a step to ensuring peaceful co existence
- Call for moral conversion of Muslims and Christians and urge them to tackle the pervasive corruption in the country by taking their religious values seriously and living by them.
- Call on Faith-based Organisations to educate their members on the tenets and injunctions of their religion
- Commend the Co-Chairmen of the Council for their dynamic and purposeful leadership His Eminence and His Grace.

Documentation 4 (b)

THE COMMUNIQUÉ 1ST QUARTER MEETING OF THE NIGERIA INTERRELIGIOUS COUNCIL (NIREC), HELD IN JOS PLATEAU STATE 18TH-20TH MAY 2009[928]

The Nigeria Inter Religious Council (NIREC) under the Co-Chairmanship of the Sultan of Sokoto, who is also the President-General of the Nigerian Supreme Council for Islamic Affairs (NSCIA), His Eminence, Alhaji Muhammadu Sa'ad Abubakar CFR, mni; and the President of Christian Association of Nigeria (CAN), His Grace Archbishop, Dr., John Onaiyekan, (CON) ably represented by Arch. Bishop Daniel Okoh, held its 1stQuarter General meeting at the Conference Hall, Hill Station Hotel Jos, Plateau State between the 18th and 20th of May, 2009. The meeting was attended by the principal officers and members of NIREC from across the states of the Federation.

The formal Opening Ceremony of the meeting was attended by His Excellency, the Governor of Plateau State, Da Jonah David Jang who also declared the meeting open. Other dignitaries included the Speaker, Plateau State House of Assembly; Secretary to the State Government; members of the State Executive Council; Traditional/Religious Leaders and Elder Statesmen from the North Central Zone of Nigeria.

- Whereas NIREC has preached religious tolerance, promoted understanding and co-existence among adherents of different faiths and made dialogue the bed rock of religious harmony in the country; the Council (NIREC):

---

[928] 'NIREC Quarterly Communiqué May 2009.' http://www.nirecng.org/docs/jos_communique.pdf

- Expressed its immense gratitude and appreciation to His Excellency, the Governor of Plateau State Da Jonah David Jang; Government, people of Plateau State and Gbong Gwom Jos for the support and hospitality extended to the members.
- Sympathised with the Government of Plateau State on the passing on of the late Gbong Gwom, Da Victor Dung Pam.
- Rejoiced with and congratulated the new Gbong Gwom of Jos, Da Jacob Gyang Buba, OFR.

The Nigeria Inter Religious Council (NIREC) observed that:

- Peace and security are gradually returning to Plateau State.
- Several probe Panels had been set up by the Federal and State Governments as well as the National and State Assemblies and await the outcome of their Reports for further deliberations. We hope that their findings and recommendations will lead to permanent peace in the State.
- Peace is a process of ensuring and sustaining justice, fairness and equity to all in the society.
- The two major religions in the Country, Islam and Christianity, preach peace and respect for other religions.
- Adherents of both religions must uphold peace in all their undertakings.
- Sources of conflicts are multi-dimensional and are mostly socio-economic and political in nature.
- The elite are often involved in inciting people and fomenting social unrest to promote political or personal agenda.
- Corruption in the country is of great concern and efforts must be intensified to reduce and if possible, erase it from our polity.
- Some media houses have through sensationalism, inaccurate reporting and wrongful manipulation of facts and other details fuelled religious and other crises in the society.

The Council resolved to:

- Use religion as an instrument for societal harmony, growth and recipe for a stronger and united Nigeria.
- Be totally committed to the cause of promoting peace, justice and fair play without fear or favour.
- Call on Governments at all levels to carry out specific activities aimed at promoting peace in their domains.
- Caution some religious preachers who conduct inciting sermons and thereby fan the embers of religious disharmony, misunderstanding and strife.

- Urge adherents of the two religions to adopt discourse as an effective means of encouraging peoples' understanding of peaceful co—existence.
- Affirm our commitment to the pursuance of practical actions towards the resolutions of conflicts arising from interactions of peoples in a multi ethnic and multi religious society so that the impact of the Council would be felt by all.
- Urge Faith-based Organisations to build an effective and efficient platform for peace and religious harmony in Nigeria through the promotion of socio-economic justice, transparency and good governance.
- Call on the electronic and print media to abide by the ethics of their profession which promote social responsibility and demand factual and accurate reporting of events.
- Urge the media to use their strategic position to promote religious harmony in the society.
- Urge the Federal and State Governments of Nigeria to create and sustain the 3 requisite environments for the actualization of the fundamental rights of all Nigerians to live, work and practice their trade or profession in any part of Nigeria without the fear of any molestation or expulsion without the due process of law.
- Urge all Nigerians to cultivate the culture of peaceful coexistence and promotion religious understanding and harmony.
- Urge those States that have not established State chapters of NIREC, to do so without delay in order to further promote love, peace, interaction and cooperation between Christians and Muslims.
- Commend the Co-Chairmen of the Council for their dynamic and purposeful leadership.
- Thank the President of the Federal Republic of Nigeria, Alhaji Umaru Musa Yar'Adua GCFR, for his continual support for the activities and programmes of the Nigeria Inter Religious Council (NIREC).[929]

---

[929] Other NIREC Communiques are: 'NIREC Quarterly Communiqué February 2008.' http://www.nirecng.org/docs/COMMUNIQUE_OF_NIREC_1st_QUARTER_2008. pdf; 'NIREC Quarterly Communiqué May 2009.' http://www.nirecng.org/docs/ jos_communique.pdf; 'NIREC Quarterly Communiqué April 2010.' http://www. nirecng.org/docs/Q1-2010-Communique-Bauchi.pdf; 'NIREC Quarterly Communiqué July 2010.' http://www.nirecng.org/docs/Q2-2010-Communique-Owerri.pdf; 'NIREC Quarterly Communiqué October2010.' http://nirecng.org/docs/Q32010-Communique. pdf; and 'NIREC Quarterly Communiqué January 2011.' http://www.nirecng.org/docs/ IBADAN-COMMUNIQUE-2011.pdf

Documentation 5

Communiqué Issued at the End of a National Youth Summit on Interreligious Dialogue and Peaceful Coexistence held in Minna, Niger state, January 2009[930]

Concerned by the threats posed to peace and security in Nigeria by religious intolerance in recent times, the Nigeria Inter-Religious Council (NIREC) with the support of Niger State Government organised a 5-day National Youth summit on interreligious dialogue and peaceful coexistence in Minna, Niger State, January 21-26, 2009. The main objective of the Summit was to provide a clement environment for Christian and Muslims youth leaders to exchange information on how to ease religious tensions in the country.

OBSERVATIONS

The Summit blamed the incessant religious crises in Nigeria on the fact that many adherents of the two leading religions in the country are not too grounded in the knowledge of the tenets of their religions. The situation is compounded by unguarded statements by cleric and leaders which often incite adherents to take arms against each other. The elite seeking to manipulate religion to advance personal and political interests benefit from the problem of youth unemployment which enables

---

[930] 'Communiqué Issued at the End of a National Youth Summit on Inter-Religious Dialogue and Peaceful Coexistence held in Minna, Niger State, 21-29 January 2009.' http://www.nirecng.org/home/docs/youth_summit_report.pdf

them to recruit their 'foot soldiers' very easily. The media further compounds the problem by the way they report religious conflicts.

The Summit resolved as follows:

- That a youth wing of NIREC should be established with the participants at the Minna Summit constituting the nucleus of the new outfit;
- That NIREC should partner with SPSP and Interfaith Mediation Centre in furthering the goals and objectives of the Minna meeting;

NIREC is encouraged to expand the scope of this initiative and the support of donor agencies ar solicited in this respect;

- Adherents of the two religions should uphold the tenets of their respective faith by understanding each other.
- Nigeria is a multi-religious state and therefore, our various governments should ensure fairness, equity and justice in their dealings with the various religious groups in the country.

RECOMMENDATIONS

The Summit recommended as follows:

- Pursuance of knowledge by the youths is considered desirable in order to leave a purposeful and dignified life devoid of intolerance and discord, with a view to contributing their quota to nation building. This should be encouraged by all governments.
- Peaceful coexistence and religious harmony are fundamental to development and therefore, youths are urged to respect religious sensibilities of Nigerians with a view to engendering and promoting peace and harmony as catalyst for national growth and development. 3. Participants are urged to be 'Ambassadors of Peace and Interreligious dialogue' in their respective states in order to sustain the gains and benefits of the Summit.
- Religious rights of individuals must be protected and guaranteed based on genuine dictates and requirements of their respective faiths. Hence fairness and justice must be ensured by our Governments.
- Islam and Christianity are better preached and practiced by our conduct rather than words and therefore, adherents are charged to be exemplary in their private and public lives.
- Continuous enlightenment and education on the tenets of the two religions is advocated to wipe out ignorance and intolerance.
- Peace Education should be included in school curriculum from primary to tertiary levels and also administered on every citizen.

- Summit urges media organisations to be patriotic by being objective, fair and accurate in the reportage of conflicts and events.
- The three tiers of governments and the political class should institute a transparent and enduring electoral process as well as ensure good governance.
- Security Agencies in the country should discharge their responsibilities without fear or favour.
- Creation of job opportunities for the teaming youths is an antidote to violence and insecurity in the country.
- The Federal Government was urged to include 'peace education' in activities at NYSC camps and urged to ensure religious sensitivity in all NYSC activities. COMMENDATION In conclusion, participants specially commended the Chief Servant of Niger State, Dr Mu'azu Babangida Aliyu, OON for ensuring religious and ethnic harmony in Niger State through various peace initiatives of his administration, amongst which is this summit successfully hosted by the Government. Moreover, delegates appreciate the organisational ability of the Local Organizing Committee. The Summit also expresses appreciation to the leadership of both the NSCIA and CAN for initiating the Summit which will go a long way at enhancing religious harmony in the country.

Finally, the partnership of NIREC with the Society for Peace Studies and Practice (SPSP) and the Interfaith Mediation Centre, Kaduna is commended and considered necessary for advancing the course of peace in Nigeria.

Documentation 6

A COMMUNIQUÉ ISSUED BY THE ASSOCIATION OF EPISCOPAL CONFERENCE OF ANGLOPHONE WEST AFRICA (AECAWA) INTERRELIGIOUS DIALOGUE COMMISSION, NOVEMBER 2003[931]

At the end of the annual study session/workshop held at the Catholic Social Centre, Kaduna, Nigeria, between the 10th and 14th November 2003, we the members of the Association of Episcopal Conference of Anglophone West Africa Interreligious Dialogue Commission comprised of the West African countries, The Gambia, Ghana, Nigeria Sierra Leone and Liberia, with scholars of Islam Christianity, African Traditional Religion and NGO's (Non-governmental Organisations) met and prayerfully reflected on the theme: 'Offer Forgiveness and Receive Peace: A Challenge to Multi-religious society.'

The Commission's choice of this venue, Kaduna was deliberate for a number of reasons:

To pray with the people of the State who suffered the ravages of religious intolerance.

To express our solidarity with the many commendable efforts towards reconciliation and recognise the efforts of all who have contributed to peace building.

---

[931]   'A Communiqué Issued by the Association of Episcopal Conferences of Anglophone West Africa (AECAWA) Inter-Religious Dialogue Commission,' in *Proto Dialogo* (Vaticano: Pontificum Consilium Pro Dialogo Inter Religiones, 2004), 75-77.

In the wider West African sub-region, we recognise the ongoing efforts by governments, genuine non-governmental organisations and communities towards harmonious coexistence, mutual respect and cooperation.

The Commission is convinced that there can be no peace without justice and no justice without forgiveness.

We recognise that fact that religion must not be allowed to be the reason for hatred, violence and conflict in our sub-religion. Rather, the three major religions, a reemphasised by their representatives as this seminar/workshop, encourage forgiveness as against revenge and hatred. At the same time, the representatives recognise the duty of the government to curb violence and injustice to take steps to prevent violence, lawlessness when there are obvious warning signs. They also bound to demand accountability from public official.

Christians are called upon to emulate the command of their Lord and Master. For the Christian, while social accountability is maintained, forgiveness is nonetheless an imperative, limitless and unconditional; unless you forgive, you will not be forgiven. It is an act of faith, an act of will and a choice to what Christ has done and has asked us to do (Matt. 6: 14-15; 18: 23-35; Lk. 24: 47). The power to forgive is from the Holy Spirit. The Christian forgives because God in Christ has forgiven us.

For Muslims, although legal retaliation or exacting of compensation is sanctioned, utter forgiveness is extolled as the best path, according to the will of Allah and the example of the Prophet.

The African Traditional religious point of view on forgiveness is not very different from the Christian or the Muslim perspective. It sees sin as an offence against community. The offender is held accountable for his acts, and for him to be forgiven, a process of reconciliation involves the community.

We recognise that peace is a gift not a wish. Peace is a plenitude of fulfilment, well-being and wholeness. It comprises security, tranquillity and harmony. It embraces justice and forgiveness. It is everybody's responsibility therefore to contribute towards the realisation of that peace which is the universal hope of the human family and a religious value for all.

Recognising the difficulties in offering forgiveness in order to achieve peace and conscious of the polarity that has been growing between the different religions in the sub-region, we recommend the following:

Principle of interreligious coexistence and dialogue should be taught at the grassroots level; homes, school, communities, churches, mosques.

Information concerning other religions should be sought from the competent and legitimate custodians and authentic sources of these religions. On their part, these custodians should be eager and ready to ensure that correct information about their religion is readily available.

We appeal to the government in our sub-region to continue to create an enabling environment for peace, reconciliation, justice and interreligious activities.

While we commend the efforts of the Christian and Muslim youth towards interfaith activities, we appeal to them not to allow themselves to be manipulated under the guise of religion by whomever. Rather, through seminars, workshops and conferences, they should be empowered to play a more positive role in the pursuit of justice and peace

We strongly recommend the interchange of dialogue at all levels, namely, national, provincial, diocesan and parish levels.

We appeal to the local and foreign media to positively report interreligious dialogue initiatives, since negative reporting do not help to create peace, forgiveness and harmony.

We recognise that in almost all instance, interreligious conflicts are preceded by clear sings. We therefore call on government and communities to set up safeguards to address issues before they escalate.

We encourage collaboration with agencies committed to the promotion of peace, justice and development.

Recognising that peace is a gift from God, we call on all people of goodwill to pray to God to give and make us instruments of peace.

As the Holy Father, Pope John Paul II pointed out during his visit to Kaduna in 1982, 'I am convinced that if we (Christians and Muslims) join hands in the name of God, we can accomplish much good. We can work together for harmony and national unity in sincerity and greater mutual confidence. We can collaborate in the promotion of justice, peace and development . . . and add to good ordering of the world as a universal civilisation of love.'

Documentation 7

Communiqué of Kaduna Catholic
Provincial Interreligious Dialogue
Seminar, June 2005[932]

We, the participants at the seminar/workshop organised by the Interreligious
Dialogue Committee of the Catholic Secretariat of Nigeria in conjunction with the
Kaduna Provincial Interreligious Dialogue Committee of the Catholic Church on the
theme *The Implications of the Implementation of the sharia in Northern Nigeria for
Christian* held at the Catholic Social Centre, Kaduna from 8th to11th June 2005 and
attended also by the representatives Jama'atu Nasril Islam National Headquarters,
Kaduna discussed, deliberated and hereby resolve as follows:

- The importance of Dialogue in our multi religious society cannot be over
  emphasised. There should be continuous dialogue between both Christians
  and Muslims for a better understanding of sharia in Islam.
- Mutual respect and appreciation for each other's religion should be
  encouraged as all levels.
- Dialogue is an act of charity that should be carried out in a spirit of
  sincerity.
- Both Islam and Christianity preach peace and we believe that without peace,
  there can be no sustainable development.
- The manipulation of religion for selfish end is strongly condemned.
- Adherent of both religions should show solidarity in the fight against social
  vices that cut across religions. Such issues as the HIV/AIDS pandemic,

---

[932]   Salihu, *The Sharia Question*, 86-87.

poverty, unemployment, abortion, immorality, corruption etc and work towards the elimination of these social evils.

- Members of both religions be encouraged to know more about the teachings of the other religion.
- Justice should prevail in all spheres of life such as admissions and employment based on merits rather than on religious and/or ethnic affiliation.
- Without a process of feedbacks to the various constituencies of our religions, interreligiousdialogue will yield little or no dividends.

Documentation 8

A COMMUNIQUÉ ISSUED AT THE END OF THE
SEMINAR ON INTERRELIGIOUS DIALOGUE
ORGANISED BY THE NIGERIAN CONFERENCE
OF WOMEN RELIGIOUS (NCWR) IN KADUNA,
DECEMBER 2008[933]

We, the members of the Nigeria Conference of Women Religious, having reflected and discussed on the theme: 'Made in the image and likeness of God' issue the following communiqué.

- We recommit ourselves to uphold the sacredness and dignity of the human person, irrespective of the differences of creed and race
- We are aware that the main sources of conflict between Christians and Muslims are intolerance, prejudice, bigotry, extremism borne out of ignorance and indoctrination among some Christians and Muslims. We regret that these violent attitudes are passed on from adults to children through overt and covert behaviours and suggestions. We declare our determination to promote peaceful coexistence with people of other religions and to make adequate efforts to learn and study the teachings of other religions so as to better understand their views and points.

---

[933] 'A Communiqué issued at the end of the seminar on Interreligious dialogue Organised by the Nigeria Conference of Women Religious (NCWR) in Kaduna,' 2008. http://www.sndden.wordpress.com/2008/12/12/interreligious-dialogue-organised-by-the-nigeria-conference-of-women-religious/

- We affirm the urgent need to harness our common grounds of agreement in our religions as tools for development of the human family and to respect the areas of differences among religions.
- We are impelled to constantly seek reconciliation and to always initiate the process of reconciliation through dialogue, negotiation and mediation. By so doing, we understand that we are gifts to each other.
- We acknowledge the need for a greater sensitivity in the use of language in addressing issues bothering on religion. Therefore, we commit ourselves to promoting the use of constructive languages in our places of apostolate.
- In the spirit of communion, we send our warmest greetings to our Muslim brothers and sisters as they go through the holy season of the Ramadan fast. May this holy exercise fire each member a new impetus for their personal, family and social existence.

Though we firmly believe that Jesus is the Son of God and the mediator between God and Human, we also recognize that the human race is basically of a common orgin, each created in the image and likeness of God

Documentation 9

KADUNA COMMUNIQUÉ: CHRISTIAN AND MUSLIM RELIGIOUS LEADERS TOGETHER FOR PEACE BUILDING, CONFLICT MANAGEMENT/PREVENTION AND RECONCILIATION, OCTOBER 2010[934]

We, Christian and Muslim religious leaders from 5 Northern and Middle Belt States of Nigeria namely: Bauchi, Plateau, Kano, Kogi and Kaduna, assembled together by the Programme for Christian-Muslim Relations in

Africa (PROCMURA) Nigeria North Area Committee, at the Jacaranda Retreat and Conference Centre in Kaduna from 6ᵗʰ to 9ᵗʰ October 2010, under the theme *'Christian and Muslim Cooperation for Conflict Prevention/Management, Peace Building And Reconciliation'*

Concerned that these 5 states among others in the region, are experiencing intermittent violent conflicts that militate against the peace of the states and peaceful coexistence between Christians and Muslims.

Recognising that Islam and Christianity wield the largest following in our regions and constitute the 2 major religious faiths in Nigeria.

Certain about the multifaceted causes of violent conflicts that range from political, economic, social, ethnic, religious and various machinations bordering on land ownership and power struggles.

Wary that in spite of the multiple causes, violent conflicts are often portrayed in national and international media as Christian and Muslim conflicts to the exclusion of all other causes.

---

[934] 'Kaduna   Communiqué,'   2010.   http://www.globalministries.org/news/news/
Kaduna-Communique.pdf

Conscious of the need for justice, peace and reconciliation for the development of the region.

Aware that the solution to violent conflicts of any kind in our states and in Nigeria at large, cannot appropriately be resolved without the active involvement of the leadership of Church and Mosque.

Perturbed by polemical utterances from both Christians and Muslims emanating from prejudices, stereotypes, militancy and extremism, political incitement and misinterpretations of the Bible and Qur'an, as well as the traditions of the two religions.

Alarmed by the infiltration of internal and external forces outside the area of violent conflicts, exacerbated by ethno-religious negative solidarity and how ethnicism easily finds an ally in religion.

Determined to uphold the principles of justice, peace and reconciliation rooted in our respective scriptures and traditions.

Convinced that ethnic, religious, social, cultural and political diversities are part and parcel of our African heritage which if harnessed properly can be more enriching and not divisive as is currently the case.

Do hereby:

Commit ourselves to engage with one another to set in motion proactive measures to uphold justice, safeguard peace, foster reconciliation and promote development.

Resolve to team up with all stakeholders and all people of goodwill within our dear country and others who have Nigeria at heart, to ensure that collectively we work towards sustainable peace in our states.

To this end we call on The Government of the Federal Republic of Nigeria

- To take stern action against inciters and perpetrators of violence
- To work towards the entrenchment of equality and social justice
- To comprehensively address the issue of indigene and settler, as embodied in the Nigerian constitution and which is interpreted in a manner that militates against national unity.
- To uphold the principles of good governance 4
- To be in the front line in supporting peace initiatives providing necessary fora for arbitration, peace building and reconciliation.
- To strongly reprimand the perpetrators of violence without fear or favour.

Christian and Muslim Leaders

- To facilitate Christian-Muslim cooperation and collaboration for peace and peaceful coexistence.
- To translate the good precepts for peace in Christianity and Islam into everyday living.

- To look introspectively and address the issue of negative perceptions, prejudice and stereotypes that exists between Christians and Muslims.
- To avoid in all manner and forms polemical preaching and in considerate language used against one another.
- To condemn publicly perpetrators of violence in the name of Islam and o f Christianity.
- To facilitate knowledge-exchange forums to dispel notions of negative solidarity.
- To constantly engage with government, traditional rulers and all stakeholders to prevent violent conflicts and set up a mechanism for peacemaking.

Christian and Muslim Women as the primary caregivers in the homestead and society and the bulk brunt bearers of violent conflicts;

- To establish a women's network for support and advocacy, predisposed to further root the crucial role of family in the community.

Youth

- To refuse and avoid being used as tools for violence. Non-governmental Organisations
- To take initiatives and support proactive measures to forestall conflict in the region

Adherents of the two religions

- To embrace the principle of unity in diversity and to demonstrate love, sacrosanct value for life, good neighbourliness and respect for the other's religion.

Media

- To play a unifying role in the country through the dissemination of information that promotes nationhood, rather than promulgating conflict creating information.

We articulate our sincere gratitude to PROCMURA for organizing such an invaluable forum and implore her to continue to engage with Nigeria to foster capacity building at the grassroots and national level with regards to Christian-Muslim constructive engagement for peace and development. In addition, to accompany us as we commit ourselves to replicate the values of this conference in our various states.

Documentation 10

First International Conference on Christian-Muslim Mutual Relations Organised by the Lutheran Church of Christ in Nigeria held in Miango, Plateau state, 2nd-6th November 1993[935]

At an International Conference on Christian-Muslim Mutual Relations held in Miango, Plateau State, Nigeria 2nd-6th November 1993, initiated by the Lutheran Church of Christ in Nigeria (LCCN) and supported by other local and international organisations and Churches, eminent scholars and participants from both Christian and Muslim communities gathered for presentations and discussions on various topics related to the theme of the conference: Christian-Muslim Relations.

The aim and objective of the Conference among others are to create a forum for mutual interaction and exchange of ideas to enhance understanding and peaceful existence in Nigeria. The Conference noted that:

- The two religions are in many respects similar in their teachings;
- In recent years deterioration has taken place in the relatively peaceful relationship between Christians and Muslims in Nigeria evidenced by growing violence, extremism and militancy;
- Crises in Nigeria are due to multiple causes, including economic, political as well as religious;

---

[935] McGarvey, *Muslim and Christian Women in Dialogue*, 417-19.

- Some Christian and Muslims have not put into practice the teachings of the Bible and Qur'an, especially on use of force;
- Mutual respect is generally lacking in Christian-Muslim relations;
- The use of provocative language during preaching is a strong factor contributing to tension and bitterness;
- Discrimination in different forms has become a problem in social, educational and political aspects of the society;
- There is growing tendency towards commercialisation of religion.

Recommendations; in the light of these observations, the Conference recommends that:

- The common foundation be used to build a new understanding for the need of peaceful coexistence through education. Religious leaders should
- Provide leadership by example
- Encourage taking initiative in arranging conferences and developing curriculum etc. that enhance peaceful coexistence,
- Develop the spirit of respect;
- Provocative language be avoided in preaching and teaching as well as in the use of cassettes and publication
- Any form of discrimination in employment, promotion of employees and sharing of resources should be discouraged by reviving moral and ethical standards in the society;
- The commercialisation of religion should be discouraged as much as possible
- Governments should support efforts of reputable religious organisations to promote Christians-Muslim dialogue as all levels;
- The government should make moral and religious instruction compulsory at all levels and encourage the learning of each other's religion;
- An interfaith Dialogue Centre which will promote the realisation of these recommendations should be established.

In conclusion this Conference recommends that efforts should be made to co-ordinate its work with that of other organisations that have similar projects in the area of Christian-Muslim dialogue.[936]

---

[936] Others communiqués include: International Conference on Christian-Muslim Mutual Relations Organised by the Lutheran Church of Christ in Nigeria, September 1995, August 1997, and August 1999. See McGarvey, *Muslim and Christian Women in Dialogue,* 420-25.

Documentation 11

A Guide for Teaching African Traditional Religion, Islam, Interreligious Dialogue in Catholic Major Seminaries, Houses of Religious Formation and Institutes of Higher Learning in Sub-Saharan Africa

INTRODUCTION

In 2001, the Pontifical Council of Interreligious Dialogue (PCID) conducted a survey in Africa of the contents of what is taught in major Seminaries and Catholic Universities and Institutes of Higher Learning with reference to Islam and Interreligious Dialogue. *Sixty-one* major Seminaries and *six* Catholic universities/ institutes of higher learning were contacted.

The follow is a synthesis of existing programmes in use in the ecclesiastical institutions consulted.

ISLAM

The aims of this course are:

- To give students basic information on Islam in order to understand the religious background of Muslims,
- To expose them to understand the points of contact for good relations between Christians and Muslims in order to foster mutual respect and fraternal coexistence,

- To help them to become aware of the difficulties that may arise in Christian-Muslim relations and of ways to overcome these,
- To help them appreciate the importance of the Church's efforts in the promotion of dialogue between Christians and Muslims,
- To help them understand the uniqueness of the Christian faith.

Two levels of teaching are provided: a long programme (two semesters) and a short programme (one semester). The two programmes are offered to help students know Islam: its history, its sacred texts, its foundations, its religious life, its plan for society, and its attitude towards other religions, especially Christianity. The difference in the two lies in the additional topics provided in the long programme which is aimed at deepening the knowledge of Islam. The short programme has only the basic information which is considered sufficient for a 'taste' of Islam.

A true knowledge of Islam would be incomplete without members of that religion. Thus a theoretical knowledge of Islam should be a step towards discovering human beings whose life is illuminated and sustained by faith in the one God.

INTERRELIGIOUS DIALOGUE

The aims of this course are:

- To prepare students to relate to people of other religion with respect and sensitivity;
- To facilitate the development of the students' understanding of the Catholic teaching on the approach to interreligious dialogue;
- To provide a context in which students can gain practical experience in various types of interreligious dialogue and reflect critically on that experience.

Interreligious dialogue is one of the most pressing challenges facing the Church today, especially in Africa. Pastoral agents and leaders need to be prepared to enter into interreligious dialogue with firm commitment to their Catholic faith, a commitment founded on divine revelation and on a n accurate understanding of theological principles. They also need to develop skills which will enable them to be open to people of other religions and to participate in different forms of interreligious dialogue.[937]

---

[937] Cf. Denis Chidi Isizoh, 'Introduction,' in Michael L. Fitzgerald, *A Guide for Teaching African Traditional Religion, Islam, Interreligious Dialogue in Catholic Major Seminaries, Houses of Religious Formation and Institutes of Higher Learning in Sub-Saharan Africa* (Vatican City: Pontifical Council of Interreligious Dialogue, 2004), 9-13.

ISLAM

1. Introduction
   1.1 Some local examples of students' experience of Islam.
   1.2 Global presentation of Islam, statistics & geography.
   1.3 The image of Islam in popular media.
   1.4 Elements of Arabic script (recommended).

2. Early Islamic History
   2.1 Socio-political, economical and religious context in Arabia and surrounding areas.
   2.2 The origin of Islam through the life of Muhammad and the Four rightly guided Caliphs.
   2.3 The Umayyad and Abbasid periods.

3. The Ummah and its Composition
   3.1 The Ummah and Islamic Identity.
   3.2 Early Divisions
      3.2.1 Sunnites
      3.2.2 Kharijites (Ibadiyya).
      3.2.3 Shi'ites (Isma'iliyyah etc.).
   3.3 Later Movements and Sects
      3.3.1 Sufism
      3.3.2 Wahhabiyya
      3.3.3 Muslim Brotherhood
      3.3.4 Ahmadiyya, etc.
   3.4 International Originations
      3.4.1 World Islamic Congress
      3.4.2 World Muslim League
      3.4.3 Organisation of Islamic Conference
      3.4.4 World Islamic Call Society, etc.
   3.5 Local Islamic structures & associations (in each country).

4. The Qur'an
   4.1 The Islamic idea of inspiration.
   4.2 The reverence given to Qur'an as the uncreated Word of God
   4.3 Format of the book
   4.4 Chronology of the Suras.
   4.5 Theory of abrogation.
   4.6 Styles and content of the different periods.
   4.7 The question of i'jaz.
   4.8 Select suras for study.

4.9 Peculiar uses of the Qur'an in Africa (healing & exorcism).

5. Sunna and Hadith
   5.1 Early Sunna
   5.2 The formation of the great collections of Hadith.
   5.3 The question of Authenticity.
   5.4 The authority of Hadith.

6. The five pillars of Islam and the question of Jihad

7. Articles of Islamic faith

8. The Islamic idea of Christianity according to the Qur'an, Sunna and Tradition.
9. Islamic Ethics
   9.1 According to the Qur'an
   9.2 In the Hadith
   9.3 In the life of Muhammad

10. Islamic law and the juridical schools
    10.1 Hanafi, Maliki, Shaf'I, Hanbali and Ja'fari (Shi'ites).
    10.2 Dietary regulations
    10.3 Family law-status of women, marriage and family and education of children.
    10.4 Islamic vision of life from birth to death.

11. Overview of Islamic Religious Sciences

12. Islam and Society

13. Modern and Current Trends of Islam

14. Islam in Africa
    14.1 General, Regional and local history.
    14.2 Sufi orders (especially in West Africa).
    14.3 Interactional (mutual impact) between Islam and local African cultures and religions.
    14.4 The struggle between 'pure' and African Islam.
    14.5 Da'wa:
         14.5.1 Strategies and factors favouring the spread of Islam.
                14.5.1.1 Trade and economy, political and military power.
                14.5.1.2 Marrying Christian women.
                14.5.1.3 Foreign influence and funding.

14.5.1.4 Education, scholarship and arabisation.

14.5.1.5 High profile in mosque location, loud speakers and dress.

14.5.1.6 Major Islamic declarations relevant to Africa.

14.5.2 Obstacles and resistance to Da'wa.

14.5.2.1 Memory of slave trade in some places.

14.5.2.2 Fear of Muslim hegemony.

14.5.2.3 A beneficiary mentality.

14.6 Current Trends of Islam in Africa, on the Local and Regional levels.

15. Theological Comparative Evaluation of Islam from Christian point of view.

16. Islamic Polemics, Apologies and Dialogue.

17. The Teaching of the Church and Attitudes of Catholics regarding Islam.

INTERRELIGIOUS DIALOGUE

1. Introduction

    1.1 Sharing of Contextual experience of relating with persons of other faiths.

    1.2 Religious Plurality in a Pluralistic world.

    1.3 Interaction and mutual influence of Religion.

    1.4 Necessity and Urgency of Interreligious Dialogue

    1.5 Definition terms: Religion, Dialogue, Interreligious Dialogue.

2. The Essence and Forms of Interreligious Dialogue

    2.1 A Description of the Meaning of Interreligious Dialogue.

    2.2 What it is not (e.g.: proselytism, syncretism, relativism).

    2.3 Forms of Interreligious Dialogue

        2.3.1 Dialogue of life.

        2.3.2 Dialogue of Action

        2.3.3 Dialogue of Theological Exchange.

        2.3.4 Dialogue of Exchange of Religious Experience

        2.3.5 Other Forms of Interreligious Dialogue.

3. Foundations of Interreligious Dialogue

    3.1 Philosophical Foundations

        3.1.1 Unity of Human Nature.

        3.1.2 The Quest for Truth.

    3.2 Theological Foundations

        3.2.1 Same God, Creator and Father of all.

        3.2.2 Jesus Christ, the Saviour of all.

3.2.3 The Holy Spirit at work in all.

3.2.4 One Destiny.

3.2.5 Sharing One Earth.

3.2.6 Interreligious Dialogue as an Integral part of Mission of the Church.

3.3 Social and Cultural Foundations

3.3.1 Kinship Relationships in African Cultures.

3.3.2 Political and Economic Interactions.

4. Some Biblical Examples

4.1 Jesus and the Samaritan Woman.

4.2 Paul

4.3 Other Examples.

5. Major Magisterial Documents on Interreligious Dialogue

6. Some Approaches to Interreligious Dialogue in the History of the Church

6.1 Patristic Period.

6.2 Medieval Period.

6.3 Period of Modern Missionary Expansion.

6.4 The Church and Contemporary Interreligious Organisations.

6.4.1 World Conference on Religion and Peace (WCRP).

6.4.2 Office on Interreligious Relations of the World Council of Churches in Geneva

6.4.3 Conference of the Parliament of World Religions.

6.4.4 Project for Christian-Muslim Relations in Africa (PROCMURA).

6.5 Contemporary Catholic Initiatives.

6.5.1 Pontifical Council for Interreligious Dialogue.

6.5.2 Pontifical Council for Culture.

6.5.3 Pontifical Council for Justice and Peace.

6.5.4 Commission for Religious Relations with Jews of the Pontifical Council for the Promotion of Christian Unity.

6.5.5 The experience of the Assisi 1986 and 2002.

6.5.6 Other Initiatives.

6.5.7 Local Initiatives.

7. Survey and Critique of Christian Theologies of Religions

8. The Basic Teachings of the Major Religions in Africa

9. Requirements and Conditions for Fruitful Interreligious Dialogue

10. Challenges to Interreligious Dialogue

11. Spirituality of Interreligious Dialogue

12. Pastoral Implications of Interreligious Dialogue.[938]

---

[938] For teachers notes, comments and explanations, see Fitzgerald, *A Guide for Teaching African Traditional Religion, Islam and Interreligious Dialogue*, 26-48.

Documentation 12

Da'wah Institute of Nigeria (DIN), The 2008 Prospectus of Da'wah Institute of Nigeria[939]

The DIN Vision

To be a dynamic organisation that develops resources and methods for the effective realisation of the *Ummah's* potentials for the dissemination and application of the correct message of Islam for greater social justice and peaceful coexistence.

Train-the-Trainers Courses in Islam and Dialogue (TTC)
Specialised Courses on Islam

ISLM101	Introduction to Islam
102	Brotherhood and Team-Building
103	Gender Issues in Islam
ISLM104	Interfaith Relations in Islam
105	Jihad and Spreading Islam
106	Islamic Faith and Worship
107	shariah and Islamic Law
ISLM108	Comparative Religion: Islam and Christianity
201	Principles and Methodologies of Da'wah
ISLM202	Ethics of Disagreement and Conflict Management in Islam and Dialogue

---

[939] Cf. Da'wah Institute of Nigeria, *The 2008 Prospectus of Da'wah Institute of Nigeria*, 4-22.

IFB101   Interfaith Bridge-building for Peaceful Coexistence

ISLM104   Interfaith Relations in Islam

Introduction and aims: This course handles the various issues and misconceptions related to the Islamic teachings on the relationship between Muslims and non-Muslims under various circumstances of peace and conflict. It aims at clarifying the position of the Qu'ran and *Sunnah* on this very misunderstood subject for better interfaith understanding and peaceful coexistence.

ISLM108 Comparative Religion: Islam and Christianity

Introduction and aims: This course aims at presenting the similarities and differences between Islam and Christianity with a view to creating greater respect and understanding of the differences, while appreciating the tremendous similarities between the two great faiths. It also aims at equipping the Muslim with basic information in explaining the difficulties Muslims have with Christianity, and the basis of Muslim belief.

In addition, the course covers some miscellaneous questions that sometime arise in Muslim-Christian interfaith discussions, such as;

Questions related to Jesus (pbuh)

- If Jesus (p) was neither killed nor crucified according to the Qur'an (4: 157), what then happened to him? Does his reported ascension mean he was the divine in any way? And what is the relevance of the end of Jesus (p) to Muslims?
- Does the miraculous birth of Jesus (p) not make him more special and divine?
- Why is Jesus (P) mentioned by name more often in the Qur'an than Muhammad (p)?
- In reference to Jesus (pbuh), what does the Qur'an mean by God 'breathed' of His spirit into Jesus (pbuh), or Jesus (pbuh) as 'a word from God'?
- Is Jesus (pbuh) not spiritually greater than Muhammad (pbuh) in light of the fact that Jesus healed a blind man, while according to the Qur'an (80: 1-4) Muhammad 'frowned and turned away when a blind man came to him'?
- Why should anyone follow the teachings of Muhammad if he was not certain that he himself would be going to Paradise? In contrast, Jesus clearly stated that he was the light the truth and the way.

ISLM202 Ethics of Disagreement and Conflict Management in Islam and Dialogue

Introduction and aims: Communication and globalisation are bringing Muslims and non-Muslims with different backgrounds, customs (*'Urf*) perspectives and priorities into contact. Like any other people, Muslims change as they interact, learn more and grow. Change is a precursor to conflict, and thus the need to manage change, and make the best out of it. Hence the need to understand, tolerate and accept some differences becomes vital. Dealing with conflicts equips the *Ummah* and its leadership with the skill and ability to handle problems, so that the *Ummah* does not lose direction or degenerate, but rather becomes a stronger and more effective team. This course aims to equip participants with appropriate and effective steps and tools to help understand, appreciate, manage and make the best use of disagreement or conflict situations.

IFB101   Interfaith Bridge-building for Peaceful Coexistence

Introduction and aims: This highly interactive course tries to ensure better peaceful coexistence between religious (Muslim and Christian) communities. It emphasizes the implications of the significant similarities between Christianity and Islam, and the need to understand and respect the differences. It also tries to identify and address common misconceptions, stereotypes, causes of tension, and how to ensure better bridge-building. Where possible, this course is conducted by both Muslim and Christian tutors together.[940]

---

[940]   For Teachers Notes, comments and explanations, See Da'wah Institute of Nigeria, *The 2008 Prospectus of Da'wah Institute of Nigeria*, 4-22.

Index

Lightning Source UK Ltd.
Milton Keynes UK
UKOW05f1658280714

235916UK00002B/34/P